American Imperatives

American Imperatives
The Cold War and Other Matters

Anders Stephanson

V
VERSO
London • New York

First published by Verso 2025
© Anders Stephanson 2025

The manufacturer's authorized representative in the EU for product safety (GPSR) is LOGOS EUROPE, 9 rue Nicolas Poussin, 17000, La Rochelle, France
contact@logoseurope.eu

All rights reserved

The moral rights of the author have been asserted

1 3 5 7 9 10 8 6 4 2

Verso
UK: 6 Meard Street, London W1F 0EG
US: 207 East 32nd Street, New York, NY 10016
versobooks.com

Verso is the imprint of New Left Books

ISBN-13: 978-1-78478-056-2
ISBN-13: 978-1-78478-058-6 (UK EBK)
ISBN-13: 978-1-78478-057-9 (US EBK)

British Library Cataloguing in Publication Data
A catalogue record for this book is available from the British Library

Library of Congress Cataloging-in-Publication Data

Names: Stephanson, Anders author
Title: American imperatives : the Cold War and other matters / Anders Stephanson.
Description: London ; New York : Verso Books, 2025. | Includes bibliographical references and index.
Identifiers: LCCN 2025001928 | ISBN 9781784780562 paperback | ISBN 9781784780579 ebk
Subjects: LCSH: Cold War | United States—Foreign relations—1945–1989 | World politics—1945–1989
Classification: LCC D843 .S79 2025 | DDC 909.82/5—dc23/eng/20250402
LC record available at https://lccn.loc.gov/2025001928

Typeset in Minion Pro by Hewer Text UK Ltd, Edinburgh
Printed and bound by CPI Group (UK) Ltd, Croydon CR0 4YY

Contents

Preface   1

I
The Cold War as a US Project

1. Fourteen Notes on the Very Concept of the Cold War   19
2. Liberty or Death: The Cold War as US Ideology   51
3. The Cold War Considered as a US Project   75
4. Cold War Degree Zero   97

II
On Diplomatic History

5. Writing the Cold War Circa 1950–90: A Triptych Extended   137
6. Considerations on Culture and Theory   189
7. War and Diplomatic History   207

III
US Foreign Relations

8. An American Story? Second Thoughts on Manifest Destiny   223
9. A Most Interesting Empire   253
10. Kennan's *Abendland*: On Nationalism, Europe, and the West   277
11. Senator John F. Kennedy: Anti-imperialism and Utopian Deficit   307
12. Law and Messianic Counterwar from FDR to George W. Bush   335

Index   363

Preface

Written during the decades since the early 1990s, these essays are, to put it a bit formally, attempts to figure out how constitutive concepts are generated and deployed on the political terrain as well as in our subsequent periodizations. As my late friend Fredric Jameson's often quoted injunction tells us, "You cannot not periodize"; and periodization is indeed what historians do in the main. The questions, then, are what and how and why. My view here has two sources, one analytical and the other historical. Most immediately, the political conjuncture of any given moment requires a reading of its salient ideological features: I think of this as a kind of categorical imperative. That reading, in the best of cases, will then yield a chart of decisive concepts followed in turn by further considerations tracing their particular histories. The assumption is that such concepts form semantic fields in which certain policy objects can appear while others are excluded, similarly so certain narratives about continuities and breaks, openings and closures. This also entails, of course, a critique of obfuscations, demasking misleading histories and categories. My particular historical focus is the United States and its peculiarities, especially as these pertain to the political project of what is commonly referred to as "the cold war." Why the United States is the central subject matter can be explained in part by the commonsensical fact that it is the most powerful presence in world politics, and so it has been since World War II. Thus it is good to know more rather than less about it; and any periodizing effort in that regard has to confront the cold war. There is an autobiographical element to this as well, on which I will elaborate later.

Periodization involves naming, a practice that is far from neutral and sometimes takes on a heavily ideological complexion. (Consider "the Spanish-American War," "the War of 1898," "the Cuban-Spanish-American War," and so on.) The cold war is the weightiest problem in the present collection, subject of four partly overlapping and successive attempts to come to grips with its character and periodization. It is a name that, in my view, can also serve as a developed concept; that is, properly delineated and historicized, it can provide real knowledge. For me, at any rate, it has yielded what may seem an eccentric conception of continuities and breaks, more about which below. Another name and discursive field pursued here is Manifest Destiny, a looser concept and not in itself a periodizing one in any immediate way. Coined in the mid-1840s as a staple of post-Jacksonian expansionism, it was at once indicative and coarsely instrumental. Both functions revealed something about the historical moment and not only about ethnic cleansing along with blatant land grabbing. The destinarian frame returned to center stage during the imperialist moment around 1900—recast to fit the changing times when the exceptionalist model of the nineteenth century was momentarily abandoned in favor of standard European empire. Destiny, however, never disappeared from the political lexicon in the United States, whether literally deployed or in other guises such as indispensability or lamentations concerning the allegedly lost spirit of America. The United States and empire are in turn the subject of another essay. Early on, empire designated a concept of continental space, expansion and political constitution by means of a unique model of reproducing the original state formation of the late eighteenth century; but in my view, empire remains a descriptive category. As such, it is often useful. For one thing, political constellations appear and act under that self-description, and one must pursue what that entails; but the category does not work transhistorically as an explanation.

If problems of concepts are common one way or another to all these essays, a certain division of topic and argument has seemed fitting. I have mentioned the four pieces devoted to the cold war—written at various points from the mid-1990s to 2012. Inevitably, there is some repetition, but the focus of each is different and the process of working through the problematic useful enough (I hope) to warrant the inclusion of all four. I have added some minor considerations to the first chapter, "Fourteen Notes on the Very Concept of the Cold War," but otherwise they appear virtually as published. Section II, "On Diplomatic History," foregrounds a related historiographical survey of US writings (circa 1950–1990) about the cold war and its origins. The subject matter, a disciplinary one, may seem archaeological at this point, and indeed it is, but precisely for that reason I think it's worth having as background and reference, if nothing else as a reminder of controversies, political as well as methodological, that perhaps still speak to us. In its original form, chapter five was actually the first I wrote featuring the concept and periodization of the cold war; but the opening account of Walter Lippmann's critique in 1947 of the article George F. Kennan wrote under the pseudonym "X," a critique that I take to be the privileged, symptomatic site of cold-war discourse, the beginning of its career, would reappear at some length in the ensuing interventions, and so that part was axed. The other two texts, chapters six and seven, are shorter reflections on, respectively, the analytical place of war (especially World War II) in diplomatic history and similarly the onset of culture as an important object of inquiry within the discipline. Composed as commentaries in the 1990s, they are of a certain moment but, again, of use as markers for that very reason. Diplomatic history, symptomatically a subfield within US history and concerned, by tradition, with higher echelons of policymaking, had scarcely made a tentative move into social history (William Appleman Williams was an early exception here) when it faced the transition into the diverse domain of culture in which we still now find ourselves, often at some considerable distance from, say, the White House.

The third and final section, "US Foreign Relations," includes articles on a disparate set of epochs and problems. In the first, I revisit the notion of Manifest Destiny, subject of a short book of mine that appeared in 1995. The text here (2006) tries to sharpen the concept by distinguishing full-blown, messianic articulations from versions that tend to limit it to the idea (grand enough) that the United States is invested with world-historical significance and is called upon to act accordingly. Next there is an account, as mentioned above, of how empire has been conceived and deployed in the US, beginning with the unique process by which new, self-constituting member states were added to the Empire of and for Liberty (Jefferson), a process I call expansion by cellular replication.

This is followed by an unpublished essay from the late 1990s on George F. Kennan and what he understood as the West, related as it was early on to a certain discourse on the Abendland formulated primarily by Catholic thinkers in Germany in the 1920s and pertaining to a kind of conservative, organicist, European ideal beyond the nation, a communitarian space between the US and the USSR. I have left the account of Kennan's Abendland as is: there has been a large body of writings on the idea of Europe over the intervening years but revising it in light of that literature would require a new essay and my basic view of Kennan, Europe, religion, and the West. I then return to the thematic of empire by tracing John F. Kennedy's early critique of imperialism—inchoate but sincere and unusual in his setting. The section ends with a polemic that has only seen the light in Italian, about the so-called war on terror (originally and more specifically the "war on terrorism") in relation to the US approach, highly problematic, to international law.

I now want to return briefly to the cold war, on which I have a few additional thoughts. It is (or was), as indicated, a particularly fraught concept, subject to intense polemics among historians as well as in circles beyond the profession, controversies less about concept and structure than about origins and blame for causing it, which is not unusual when it comes to wars in history.

Those days of controversy, to be sure, are long since gone. "The cold war" is now a name for a deadeningly obvious period of what we still tend to think of as the postwar, dispute largely having faded from the proceedings except for some particular events (for example, Korea) within its temporal and spatial boundaries. The term "cold war," then, has become a reified designation for a period whose contours and essentials are really a done deal, rather on a par with, say, the Great Depression. No historical name is innocent of bias and one can argue about causes and precise dates and space; but about the label and reality of the cold war as a period there will be little dissension. The cold war, one might then go on to say, was an age when world politics was defined by the presence (and eventual absence) of the Soviet Union and its hostile relations with the United States, which, as the remaining and globally dominant side of the dissolved polarity, has now assumed the air of normality, if not peace. In more recent times, the oxymoronic unipolarity of the 1990s has yielded to an intermittent, tentative comeback of cold war as a, largely, journalistic way of naming deteriorating relations with Russia and the People's Republic of China—one or the other or both. Hence, too, the occasional search in political science for a transportable concept to be applied to the present and near future, a search that by necessity involves a more or less serious investigation of what the first and original cold war entailed. Perhaps we will even see the reinvention of some proto-cold-war polarity between freedom and authoritarianism.

There are departures from convention, chiefly by temporal extension. Two of the senior scholars on the Soviet Union, Stephen F. Cohen (biographer of Nikolai Bukharin) and Stephen Kotkin (biographer of Joseph Stalin), historians of different generations but partly overlapping at Princeton, both argue—unusually and on diametrically opposite grounds—that the cold war never ended. Cohen, who died in 2020, took the position that the United States, during and after the extraordinary events of 1989–91, continued in triumphalist fashion to encourage de facto the degradation of the Soviet Union (and then Russia) instead of offering, in the name of long-term stability and openness, aid and support. On Cohen's view, this was nothing but the continuation of the cold war by other means; and there we still find ourselves, courtesy of the myopic United States. Kotkin, for his part, thinks 1989–91 is overrated as a break because the Russian core of ancient lineage survived, namely, the ingrained, futile and fatal disposition to compete with the West and achieve Great Power status, an exercise that invariably ends with hyper-concentration of power and personalist rule. And so the cold war is not to be equated or confused with the existence of the Soviet Union. It was and is a nigh on perpetual Russian syndrome. We are back, in short, to the classical orthodox and revisionist perspectives of the 1950s and '60s: blaming, respectively, the Soviet Union/Russia (Kotkin) or the United States (Cohen).[1]

I look at it in a different way. My view, shared by very few, is that the cold war was distinctly a US project that began in 1946–47 and ended in 1963. Its original impetus was to make internationalism—a euphemism for a worldwide scope of potential intervention—an unshakeable

---

1 For a synthetic statement by Stephen F. Cohen, see "Why We must Return to the US-Russian Parity Principle," *Nation*, April 14, 2015. Stephen Kotkin's equally synthetic view may be found in his review of Richard Overy's *Blood and Ruins: The Last Imperial War, 1931–1941* (London, 2022). See Kotkin, "The Cold War Never Ended: Ukraine, the China Challenge, and the Revival of the West," *Foreign Affairs*, May–June 2022.

shibboleth of bipartisan foreign policy. Thus it denied the legitimacy of the Soviet regime and banished sustained diplomacy as appeasement and moral dissipation. It was a frame as well as a policy—though officialdom was notably reluctant to embrace the term itself. Dean Acheson, when he thought about it, preferred the term "cold peace" and, though it was axiomatic that the Soviet Union embodied war (as overdetermined by the more fundamental dedication to world conquest) and the United States, peace, there was a sense that the duality of a war somehow spilled over into mutuality, to oneself as well. At the same time, auxiliary, partly alternative notions such as the Free World and national security did not have the same suggestive power as "the cold war." In the former case, the phrase worked as a general appeal, as a collective name for the natural state of humankind, lamentably under constant threat from enslaving agents such as the Soviet Union. Thus it was easily invoked. Still, it was unclear who was properly included. "Free" indeed came to be everything that was not under totalitarian, communist control.[2] This, of course, was unsatisfactory in the last analysis as the foundational negation—anticommunist—embraced all manner of unpresentable regimes. Moreover, the inscribed need to lead and guarantee the Free World entailed an internal distinction between the controlling agent, the indispensable agent, and the rest. However much recipients appreciated the largesse on offer or even invited the United States to enter, members of the lodge were not completely free in the Free World to exercise their sovereign right to act autonomously. (The malleable invocation of indispensability has notably been extended of late to a new, more capacious periodization that regards the seventy years since the end of World War II as the Liberal World Order, the present challenges to which, domestically and internationally, are patently clear.)

National security, meanwhile, was certainly irreproachable as an expression of perpetual worry in the pursuit of a state of no worry, *sine cura*; however, by the same token it was also devoid of immediate content, a posture and an empty abstraction, an axiom or a desire. The cold war, by contrast, conjured up combat, battle and, in effect, danger. It also featured a contradictory and expansive metaphorical register: cooling hot tempers is good but so is warming a chilly body. The enemy was concrete, visible and eminently cold. What could be colder and more inhospitable than Stalin's Moscow, and not only in winter?

---

2   See Peter Slezkine's forthcoming work *Free World: The Logic of US Leadership*.

Moreover, the powerful totalitarian scenario of the 1930s served retrospectively to sustain the position: totalitarian regimes, intrinsically bent on world conquest and impervious to change, made any attempt to negotiate with them useless, indeed counterproductive. Witness Munich in 1938. Totalitarian fascism had been crushed in war but totalitarian communism, headquartered in Moscow, not only remained intact but had been invigorated by that war.

Yet, paradoxically, the conflation of fascism and communism immediately invited sharp differentiation between them: the same but actually, it turns out, very different. Fascism (Hitler and Nazi Germany, chiefly) was impetuous, reckless, brashly and unthinkingly violent; communism, by contrast, was cautious, stealthy, sly, liable strategically to avoid open war in favor of operating in the shadows, subverting the social order of the Free, in short a lot more clever and a lot more dangerous.

The line of division in that regard was rigid and closed one way, and permeable the other: the Iron Curtain on the one hand (Winston Churchill's line from Stettin to Trieste, soon, alas, to be revised when Tito went his own way), and containment on the other. One wonders about the strategic connotations of such a heavy metaphorical construction: defensively it may have made sense for Moscow, but what of moving the whole thing expansively west? Not an easy proposition, presumably. Meanwhile, the line of containment in Europe between outside and inside was never a line proper because the parasitical (or cancerous) enemy was able to maintain a considerable presence in the form of domestic communist parties and other agents—and even without these forces there would be an urgent problem of keeping Western society prophylactically healthy, to foster vigor so as to prevent internal disorder.

The step from differentiation to the notion of hot (Hitler) and cold (Stalin) war is not great, though Walter Lippmann, who put the term "cold war" into public circulation in the fall of 1947, actually placed a good deal of the blame for the war—which he thought of as frozen relations—on the lack of realistic US dealmaking. Nevertheless, as Lippmann came to see, the policy worked well in anchoring at home the unprecedented engagements abroad in ostensible peacetime, engagements that included extensive alliances, albeit in his view not always in appropriate regions. Geopolitically, the result was indeed remarkably successful from an internationalist standpoint, above all that of the decisive Atlantic community. The posited threat from totalitarianism had silenced virtually all mainstream isolationists.

A bipartisan commitment to fighting the cold war on a global scale emerged, political disagreement limited to the means and strategies of how to do it, formulaically expressed in containment versus rollback. The Faustian price here lay in the inevitable gap between the unlimited threat and the limited range of what one could actually do: every administration was open to criticism for not doing enough or doing the wrong things (witness JFK's famous missile gap).

Only after the Cuban Missile Crisis and the beginning of Sino-Soviet split, followed by the disastrous (in due course) intervention in Vietnam, did cold-war orthodoxy mutate into something else—détente, relaxation of tension, and above all, recognition of the Soviet regime as a legitimate Great Power and along with that the advent of sustained diplomacy. By no means was this peace and reconciliation. It was, however, recognition of rivalry and competition under managed forms of sorts—reversing in that sense the 1946–47 moment when there had been an odd case of anagnorisis, the recognition (discovery) that the Soviet Union was in fact world-conquering totalitarianism, in turn calling for a US posture of no recognition, as such a power could have no legitimate interests. After 1963, in short, the situation is qualitatively different.

This, then, is when I think the cold war proper came to an end. Support for such a notion is scarce for obvious reasons: the cold war makes sense as a sizeable chunk of world-historical time, postwar, a seemingly transparent period featuring the US and the USSR as leading antagonists. And when the latter dissolves, so does the polarity and so does the war. This is the standard view from left to right, incidentally, traversing the political spectrum. There is a spontaneous element of truth in it insofar as something truly world historical did actually happen in 1989–91 with the collapse (or more accurately destruction) of the Soviet Union. Why not call that moment, conveniently, the end of the cold war? Significant obstacles, anomalies if you will, must however then be surmounted. First and foremost there is the Sino-Soviet split. As noted but not often addressed specifically from the angle of the cold war, the two giants of the communist world began the 1960s as allies of a kind but ended the decade as deadly enemies, Moscow denounced in Beijing as imperialist dogs or worse while outright armed clashes flared up in some border regions. By the early 1970s, *unthinkably by cold-war standards*, the USSR and the PRC had better relations with the US than with each other. If there was a cold war at that point, it made more sense to apply it to the polarity between the Union of Soviet Socialist Republics and the People's Republic of China.

The geopolitical terrain, in short, had changed profoundly. Any garden variety of realism (let alone Nixon and Kissinger's) could readily account for this, a classical cold-war view not easily so. For in the axiom "totalitarianism > world conquest > cold war > saving grace of the indispensable Leader of the Free World and its defense," there was little conceptual space for a fundamental split of international communism, the totalitarian antithesis of freedom. Tito in 1948 was one thing, an important but minor revision of the order of things; China an altogether different challenge. In 1971, it should be remembered, Beijing was still a radical regime, though by then coming around to the view that the main contradiction in the world was with Moscow, accordingly also the main enemy. Thus the otherwise incomprehensible Chinese support for the Pinochets of that time as objectively on the right (that is, the Chinese) side of history, firmly against the New Tsars in Moscow and its local agents such as Allende. Thus, too, the Chinese agreement with US neoconservatives that détente was appeasement. Beijing, at any rate, was now no longer a pariah but a regime deemed proper for a US alliance, however tacit. So the founding polarity of the cold war seemed to have fallen by the wayside along with the policy, the grand policy. One might object that the frame did not require a single polarity, though it is hard then to see how the basic props of the US articulation could survive. One could maintain, with some difficulty, that cracks in the axiomatic monolith were natural and even products of successful US policy. Nonetheless, in that case the setup had changed in its foundations. By any measure, totalitarian world conquest and the phantom of international communism had suffered a severe blow, surely, when Moscow had to keep a million men facing the PRC while Nixon, suitably feted, toured the two communist capitals. Ipso facto, deriving the cold war directly from the systemic differences between capitalism and communism/socialism, or, alternatively, between freedom and totalitarianism, no longer made much sense.

Meanwhile, a certain mutuality was recognized. Accepting the existence of a cold war always carried the implication, evil imputations notwithstanding, that both sides as indicated were in some way responsible for its conduct. Nuclear weapons provide the primary case in point. They signified the horrific effects if the cold war should ever turn hot. Doubtless, even before one could think of the balance of terror as parity (the US far outweighed the USSR at least into the late 1960s), nuclear arsenals served as deterrence. In that sense they were fundamental in keeping the cold war cold. However, only with considerable contortions could nuclear weapons ever be made to fit the original frame. The Eisenhower administration, for instance, tried to pass them off as ordinary munitions, just bigger bang for the buck. It didn't work. As everyone sensed, nothing by way of outstanding conflicts between Washington and Moscow could justify nuclear conflagration. In due course, too, the logic of these weapons and their use, a rarefied and phantasmagorical space, became rather similar for both sides. A certain mutual identity emerged, as manifested in the Test Ban (1963) and the Non-Proliferation (1968) Treaties. While the balance of terror is probably the iconographic essence of the cold war, I actually think of nuclear weapons as ideology killers.

As a policy and a vision, then, the cold war could never totally cover the facts. It was becoming more difficult for Washington to convincingly parade its clients and interventions as freedom incarnate. Once the binarism had gone—not only because of the Sino-Soviet conflict and decolonization/the third world but also, in a minor key, de Gaulle's European eccentricities—much of the energizing power of the grand policy faded. Vietnam, begun as cold-war counterinsurgency, turned into an intensive hot war for, essentially, the sake of credibility. Nixon and Kissinger continued that ruthless policy, though their lasting interest was always de facto to reassert US power in the name of power. The cold war was passé.

Competing concepts also appeared. Consider a very different setting and scenario: Cuba and the problem of anti-imperialism. Deeply disappointed over Khrushchev's retreat in the Missile Crisis (the rest of us no doubt thankful and Fidel Castro himself eventually came round) and after failing to make a deal with the Kennedy administration, the Cuban regime came to support various struggles, insurgencies and counterinsurgencies, first rather unsuccessfully in Latin America in the 1960s, then to greater effect in Africa in the 1970s. Was this sequence part of the cold war, even its intensification? I think not. From the Cuban vantage point, the whole notion of a cold war will have seemed secondary or even a category mistake. It certainly didn't cover the Cuban facts. Closer to hand was the far more real matrix of imperialism/anti-imperialism, subject as the country was to massive sanctions and imposed isolation by successive administrations in Washington (the exceptions being Jimmy Carter and Barack Obama). There was also the specifically third-worldist aspect, the Cuban identification with national liberation struggles in the colonial and postcolonial world. Insurgency, the privileged form here, meant armed struggle, *real war*, partisan war for victory—not a cold war. In the case of Cuba in Angola, it was a case of counterinsurgency, assisting the regime against rival forces backed from the outside as well as against South African incursions—again, armed force in no uncertain terms. In the bilateral context of Washington's continued exclusion of Cuba, one can perhaps speak of a cold war of sorts: the United States could not invade (the price of the Missile Crisis deal in 1962, but any other skullduggery was permitted), while Cuba could obviously do nothing much to the United States except offer solidaric support elsewhere for the forces of anti-imperialism. That support was not, it should be underlined, any simple proxy effort for Moscow. Cuba often acted on its own initiative, and, given the facts of material dependence, often surprised the Soviets in the process.

Latin America, Cuba aside, nevertheless represents a problem here: What of the widespread advent of militarized, intensely repressive and murderous regimes from the 1960s onward, forces acting officially with standard reference to internal subversion and the need in the name of anti-communism to destroy it? One might well argue that the process marks an exacerbation of the cold war and certainly not the opposite. The United States, after all, gave tacit and often material support to these violent regimes, and on occasion it also conducted outright intervention (the Dominican Republic, 1965). No president until Jimmy Carter—Nicaragua to his credit—could withstand accusations of permitting another Cuba in the region. Such scenarios, largely imagined but effective, served however to inscribe unequivocally Latin America as a dependably and properly American space. More and better anti-communism per se did not amount to intensified cold war. I rather doubt that Kissinger was at all interested in the domestic policies of the Allende regime. All things being equal, he would perhaps even have gone along; but things were not in fact equal, and the vicious Pinochet was an altogether better alternative.

The Soviet view, meanwhile, read the cold war as a potential replay of the 1930s, the threat to be handled by the defensive strategy of antifascism: prevent fascism by mobilizing the widest possible coalition on the widest possible platform (for example, peace and national independence, policies aimed, in theory, at forces outside the reactionary circles within monopoly capital supposedly gearing up to destroy the Soviet Union). Whatever its errors, this was a dialectical conception, an interactive binary, two sides locked in a contradictory unity that defined both. It was also a realist view. Social forces represent material interests and states act accordingly in interested ways. The cold war was a name, an American name, signifying an offensive on all levels against the Soviet Union and the rising democratic camp. Détente, any relaxation of tension, was predictably credited as a success for the Soviet peace policy—say, hearing Richard Nixon in the Kremlin announcing the end of the cold war in 1972 with a very jolly Leonid Brezhnev. Continuity marked the Soviet frame because the logic allowed it. Bad moments such as the cold war were the result of ascendant reaction and anti-Sovietism in the United States; good moments, dominant over time, the obvious effect of Moscow's steady progression along the historical path to the splendid end. After Stalin, however, Moscow had also begun to look beyond the boundaries of the immediate security zone and discover the virtues of anti-imperialism and even neutralism, forces not necessarily pro-Soviet but objectively belonging to the side of progress. This generated by the 1960s a great deal of competition in the third world with the United States (and eventually with China). From the Soviet standpoint, this was a realm beyond the emerging bilateral détente. Insisting that everything was in fact linked, Kissinger disagreed but, notably, not on any cold-war grounds. And if the cold war entailed a freeze on diplomacy, Kissinger's approach and practice may be described as its antithesis, hyperdiplomacy.

I emphasize a specific conjuncture in which the classical cold war ceased to mean very much and indeed did not answer to existing realities—diverse, fluid and violent as they often were. It is to insist on the *stricto sensu* position that, seriously, the essence of the cold war was an American affair that was over in 1963, resurrected briefly though it was in the early Reagan years. To restrict the term in such a specific manner is not to minimize the depth and extension of contradictions elsewhere and afterward. On the contrary, it is to open for inquiry beyond the founding polarity but with a clear view of what it is to invoke something called the cold war. When I say "essence," I'm not being literal. My periodization does not posit any real, ready-made object out there in history such as the cold war, which we can find if we only work hard and widely enough. Instead, the wager is that to proceed historically in explanatory pursuit of the object here is to provide an analytical account of its genesis as a project, its conditions of emergence. My periodization on that score, then, is far from standard. It is also a losing proposition. I have thus come to acquiesce, provisionally, to the everyday, sweeping view while, in the last instance, sticking historically to my original thesis.

A tense, personal, pre-teen experience of the Cuban Missile Crisis in October 1962 and the subsequent improvement in the climate after its apparent resolution form the beginning of my concern with the cold war and, eventually, its periodization. Cuba was faraway but nuclear war had been a constant dread and the Bomb a reality, threateningly near in fact because of the gigantic atmospheric tests carried out by the Soviet Union in the Arctic, northeast of Scandinavia. No one needed telling of the problems with nuclear clouds and fallout. The Test Ban Treaty a year after the Missile Crisis thus marked the political confirmation that things were improving and one could put the nuclear clouds out of one's mind or at least not at the forefront. That the spirit of tension was changing was by then evident in the hotline agreement in June 1963, presumably eliminating war by mistake. Reading Le Carré's *The Spy Who Came in from the Cold*, meanwhile, made an indelible impression on me as a critique of received opinion on the cold war. In a different register, so did horrific images in *Life* magazine of a self-immolating Buddhist monk in Saigon. A few years later, I spent a year (1966–67) attending high school in Michigan in a small town with an overwhelmingly Republican electorate. The community was completely white but for a single black family. Race riots in Detroit at the end of my sojourn seemed very distant. Vietnam was on the agenda, of course, amidst escalation, but ultimately I was astonished by the lack of knowledge among the people who should have been most concerned, namely, graduating males facing the draft.

I mention these recollections with misgivings as my subsequent periodization of the cold war can easily—too easily—be reduced to that experiential baggage: the Cuban Missile Crisis plays an important part in that delineation as does Le Carré's *Spy* and my year in Michigan (ultimately not only educational in all manner of ways but also genuinely friendly and open despite my idiosyncratic views on Vietnam). Massive escalation and intensification of the US presence in Indochina struck me, at that stage in a liberal frame, as political folly and moral quicksand—though I may be exaggerating the coherence of that view. From this personal sequence emerged at any rate an interest in Americana and historical curiosity about the deeper reasons for the peculiarities of the Americans, above all the peculiarity of the nonexistent socialist labor movement. At university, accordingly, following a well-trodden path, I went through the exemplary failures of successive prods in this vein: early working-class labor organizations in the nineteenth century, subsequently the Socialist Party in the early twentieth century, the Communist Party in the 1920s, and of course the same political movement in the much more successful Depression decade, the 1930s. By the time I got to that point, the exercise had become theoreticist overkill, holding the CPUSA responsible in effect for not having a better Althusserian grasp of the Rooseveltian state. Graduate forays into the whole span of US history then led me back to an erstwhile interest in foreign relations, partly because it was evident that the system was strikingly asymmetrical, at once vigorously interventionist across the universe and remarkably ignorant in the domestic grasp of that universe, thus reflecting in another register that the United States, to state the obvious, is more important to the outside world than the outside world is to the United States.

My return to foreign relations as a historical field coincided with, and was reinforced by, the advent of what sometimes came to be dubbed the second cold war, Ronald Reagan's intense and anything but farcical rejuvenation of the hoariest cold-war rhetoric along with massive remilitarization (a break already visible, it should be said, toward the end of the Carter administration). Reagan's visceral anti-communism, notably, did not mark any fundamental shift in relations with Beijing, where he found congenial agreement that détente was appeasement. Kennan, now in his late seventies, reemerged as a public intellectual sharply critical of this turn to cold war, especially as it pertained to matters nuclear. I had by then read the first volume of his *Memoirs*—a classic in its genre and a powerful account of his move in 1948–49 from foundational cold warrior to advocate for a realistic diplomatic approach to the Soviet Union, above all on the problem of Germany. Preliminary surveys of State Department documents for this crucial period overall (1946–50) revealed otherwise a surprising—surprising, at least to me—lack of analytical depth in the articulation of what was after all the greatest shift in the whole history of US foreign relations, the turn in peacetime to global defender of the Free World (and so on). The historic Kennan stood out here. As head of the new (1947) Policy Planning Staff, he generated a discourse on an altogether different level, one that lent itself to critique, arguments about objects, openings and limits.

That critique may be seen, then, against the specific backdrop of a rekindled cold war in the early 1980s—however hollow in content and transient in duration. Yet beyond the conjuncture here, my attempts were really informed by the alarming fact, true then as it is true today, regrettable then as it is regrettable today, that everyone on this earth has an enormous stake in how the United States chooses to be and act in the world.

I.
The Cold War as a US Project

1
Fourteen Notes on the Very Concept of the Cold War

The well-known is such because it is well-known, not known.
—G. W. F. Hegel

Ideas are displayed, without intention, in the act of naming, and they have to be renewed in philosophical contemplation.
—Walter Benjamin

Introduction

It was exasperation with an omnipresent cliché that occasioned these notes: "Now that the cold war is over, and so on." Every article on international affairs in the 1990s seemed to begin with it, often followed by reference to that other well-known fact, globalization. The formula became reified punditry, something akin to advertising language. It is not hard, of course, to see why it assumed such a self-evident aura. Doubtless the postwar period was dominated geopolitically by the US-USSR relationship; doubtless, too, therefore, something did come to a resounding end with the Soviet collapse. But the effect of this seamless periodization is to conceal qualitative shifts in the nature of the relationship. We forget, for example, that Richard Nixon announced the end of the cold war in Moscow in the early 1970s. Typically, moreover, the end is retrospectively inscribed in the beginning and in the whole nature of the period so as to allow its history to be rewritten as an explanation of the obvious. Other possible periodizations are thus barred or simply subsumed, say, in terms of decolonization, the economic rise of Japan and Germany, or the universalization of the European model of the nation-state.

Historians, discomfited by this flattening out of the historical real, tend to modify the image, not by reexamining the nature of the concept itself, but by adding ancillary aspects designed to make the epoch fuller, more realistic, more accurate. One way of achieving this reality effect is to reintroduce on stage the supporting actors of olden times—Europeans, for example—as part of an extended main cast. Another is to widen the stage itself to include new actors (for example, in the third world) and aspects (culture). A third option, perhaps the preferred one, is to focus on the archival findings made possible by the end, sources located in the East and so ensuring by default that reinvestigation of the real will henceforth be framed in terms of Soviet (and Chinese) pathologies. All these efforts are of some intrinsic value. If nothing else, they often generate important empirical findings. They are nonetheless duplicitous, unwittingly, in attenuating the very historical specificity of the cold war that they were intended originally to attain. They fill in the blanks. Yet the picture to be completed always seems to expand and indeed always will. There is no final or pristine cold war in the archives, or anywhere else for that matter, waiting to be discovered or uncovered.

My wager, on the contrary, is that if the term "cold war" is to have any explanatory value, then its periodization can only be achieved through the exact opposite process—one of rigorous, relentless narrowing through conceptual inquiry. Periodization should always be explicitly theorized, and the question here is ultimately if the very concept of the cold war can be produced, if indeed it has a concept. Otherwise it is perhaps better left on the heap of everyday banalities. A reflection on the conceptual conditions for talking about something called the cold war must situate it distinctly within the very opposition that ultimately framed it: war and peace. One should consider, at the very least, what kind of surrender (or peace) the cold war presupposed and embodied; and that in turn requires a derivation of our notions of war and peace.

My procedure here is essayistic as opposed to definitional. Organized historically around a set of proper names, these are provisional notes, schematic and incomplete. After a sketchy (but not brief) history of the conceptual pair of war and peace, I make a few basic claims in the final notes. Chiefly I argue that (i) the cold war was a US project, and (ii) its nature or logic was laid out (unintentionally) by Franklin D. Roosevelt during the tense moment of 1939–1941 and epitomized later in the notion of "unconditional surrender." By 1963, the cold-war project had run its course as orthodoxy and the premise of surrender faded: the Cuban Missile Crisis in October 1962 had demonstrated with horrific clarity that the US and USSR would have to manage their relationship; international communism was no longer a viable notion with the Sino-Soviet split; and the perennial problem of Berlin had stabilized with the Wall, however reprehensible it was. This did not mean an end to enmity or indeed intervention in all manner of ways; but the premise of unconditional surrender had been replaced by geopolitical competition and rivalry. *Recognition* was now the order of things, an order not reducible to any reinvented realist matrix of the European yesteryear but clearly a different frame of representation. Escalating war in Vietnam, pitched by official Washington as a quintessential cold-war operation, seemed to say otherwise. In fact, the ensuing debacle was the most graphic demonstration imaginable that the moment for such ideological undertakings was over, leading as it did to something close to a legitimacy crisis.

In short, I view the cold war as an ideological dominant, a structure for the articulation of US hegemony after World War II, turning it into an unanswerable proposition that, in attenuated form, is still with us as indispensability in the maintenance of the liberal world order. Notably, however, the formation did not preclude diverging incidents. Consider the mutual agreement in 1955 to end the occupation of Austria and neutralize the country: that moment, certainly a deviation from orthodoxy, did not initiate any new order. It was contained. The project remained intact. That project, it should be added, is analytically distinct from the related questions of origins and justifiability, or, for that matter, causes. Once the polarity (a problematic metaphor itself) is put into question, it will be seen not as an essence but a kind of situation around which other processes, relations and antagonisms evolve and revolve, none of them homologous with it, much less the same.

1. Bond and Leamas

Let us begin, however, with James Bond in "Nigger Heaven." That, at any rate, was Ian Fleming's title of the chapter in *Live and Let Die* (1954) wherein Bond goes to Harlem. The term, historically, was a racist designation for the segregated balconies in churches and theaters to which African Americans used to be consigned; and, subsequently, the name of a bestseller in the 1920s about Harlem culture. Fleming's villain is a SMERSH (that is Soviet) agent known as Mr. Big. Mr. Big hails from Haiti but now presides over a gangster empire in the ghetto, whence he also serves his murderous Moscow controllers. By means of his Haitian voodoo art, the charismatic Mr. Big dupes naive black people into becoming an army of foot soldier spies, highly efficient because, as servants, they are everywhere throughout (white) society but also invisible. Bond is surprised when M tells him of this exotic master criminal, since black people, to 007, seem "pretty law-abiding chaps," unless of course "they've drunk too much." M, however, soon sets him right. For Mr. Big, it turns out, has "a good dose of French blood" mixed in with his Haitian, thus perhaps explaining his capabilities in the realm of sinister organization.

When, during the very height of détente in 1972–73, Fleming's book was turned into a film, Mr. Big appears in an altogether different frame. He is now the head of a Harlem-based drug operation, whose object is to flood the US market with enormous amounts of heroin, produced (improbably) on a Caribbean island that he happens to control in another capacity and identity. Bond is called in to crush this threat to Western civilization that now, of course, has nothing at all to do with the Soviets. By then, in fact, the Bond movies had been devoted for several years to combating supranational and non-Soviet threats. The spirit (in Hegel's sense) of the cold war seemed dead as a doornail.

This was marked brilliantly by Le Carré's great novel *The Spy Who Came in from the Cold* (1963). The novel unfolds as an astonishing chain of inversions of basic cold-war binaries. Suffused with gloomy grayness, it made a mockery of the technicolor allure of the contemporary James Bond fantasies. The aging spy Alec Leamas, existentially weary and manipulated by his British masters with the utmost cynicism, was an altogether more symptomatic figure of the spirit of 1963 than Fleming's cold warrior.

It seems Fleming had once conjured up for his literary admirer John F. Kennedy a way to kill Fidel Castro, whose beard was to be sprinkled with radioactive material. The joke was taken seriously. By 1963, nevertheless, JFK was wondering if the Test Ban Treaty might not mark the moment of a "pause" in the cold war and the beginning of "cooperation" of sorts, indeed "the end of one era and the beginning of another." Fleming, who died in 1964, had actually begun to ponder something similar already in the late 1950s, and in the first Bond film (*Dr. No*, 1962) the villainous SMERSH had been replaced judiciously by SPECTRE, a suprastate organization of pure evil. The cinematic Bond (or his producers) had taken political notice and increasingly turned to comic book adventure in the name of saving the world.

2. Lippmann (i), Baruch, Swope, and Beaufre

The cold war forms a whole semantic field of meaning, whose emergent boundaries may be traced initially to its entry into public usage. Who actually coined it is disputable. In the autumn of 1947, Walter Lippmann's book contra Mr. X (George F. Kennan) made "the cold war" a common expression, but others could and did claim authorship. Bernard Baruch, for example, deployed the term that April. Yet his speech was not about the cold war but about the danger of inflation and the obverse imperative, as this Wall Street financier would have it, for American workers to put in longer hours and commit to no-strike pledges. He borrowed the term (as he freely acknowledged) from his speech-writing friend Herbert Bayard Swope, who in turn said he had first thought of it in the context of Hitler and in the 1939–40 "phony war"—a phrase Swope didn't like. Lippmann countered that he had picked it up from French sources in the 1930s, *la guerre froide* and *la guerre blanche*, being synonymous expressions for a state of war without overt hostilities. French lexicographers question his account. For what it's worth, my own quick perusal of contemporary dictionaries and encyclopedias revealed no such usage—except literally, in reference to World War I in the snowy Dolomites. In mid-August 1939, however, a captain in the French army, André Beaufre, published a reflective article on what he called *paix-guerre*, indicating the proliferation of intermediate states between declared war and peace. He traced this strategically to the difficulties of conducting outright war now that defenses had become hard to break. The ensuing *drôle de guerre* appeared to corroborate his view, but it was of course shattered the following spring by the *Blitzkrieg* that brought about French defeat in a matter of six weeks. Still, Beaufre's considerations were symptomatic of an awareness in the late 1930s that traditional categories had become dubious.

More about the intermediate aspect later. It remains that Lippmann put "cold war" into general usage as a historical and political term. Two other preceding uses are of interest here, one by Lippmann's contemporary George Orwell, the other by Don Juan Manuel in early fourteenth-century Castile (though, on closer inspection, the latter case turns out not quite to be so).

3. Orwell and Burnham

Right after the war, in October 1945, George Orwell talked about a cold war in the British Labour journal *Tribune*. He had already used the term in a book review in 1943 but without elaboration. His article ("You and the Atom Bomb") argued that the Bomb would become the preserve of a few Great Powers and thus relatively weaken the already weak, opening up a dystopian "prospect of two or three monstrous super-states, each possessed of a weapon by which millions of people can be wiped out in a few seconds, dividing the world between them." Probably, these states would then "make a tacit agreement never to use the atomic bombs against one another." Hence, Orwell surmised, "we may be heading not for a general breakdown but for an epoch as horribly stable as the slave empires of antiquity." Three such states, predicted Orwell, would emerge: the US, the USSR, and China/East Asia, the last still being only potential. Each would be "at once *unconquerable* and in a permanent state of 'cold war' with its neighbors." The Bomb, then, would perhaps "put an end to large-scale wars at the cost of prolonging indefinitely a 'peace that is no peace.'"

A "peace that is no peace," "tacit agreement," geopolitical division of the world in an oppressive order of atomic Great Powers "as horribly stable" as the old slave empires: Orwell's scenario illustrates some salient characteristics of what was indeed to come (the question was exactly when). However, his use of "cold war" passed unnoticed. The ensuing debate in the *Tribune* concerned weapons technology and how it might relate to bigger and smaller powers. Orwell went on, nevertheless, to redeploy the image of three globally hegemonic superstates in his relentlessly bleak classic *1984* (appearing in 1948, hence the inverted title), wherein "Oceania," "Eastasia" and "Eurasia" fight meaningless peripheral wars in the name of meaningless propagandistic slogans, every piece of news being manipulated and liable to be momentarily changed into its direct opposite.

Orwell took the geopolitical contours of this dreadful scenario from James Burnham's famous work of 1941, *The Managerial Revolution*. Burnham, at that earlier moment, had seen another tripartite division: Japan, Germany, and the United States. None of them would be able ultimately to conquer any of the other two, even in combination. A standstill would follow. Burnham's main point, from our perspective, was that there would be more and diffuse conflicts, but "since war and peace are no longer declared, it may be hard to know when this struggle is over and the next one begins." Here again, then, we get an embryonic idea of the cold war as a condition outside the normal polarity of peace and war. In his next contemplation (1947) within the genre of "whither the world," Burnham argued that this war/no war, what he otherwise referred to as World War III, had actually begun in Greece in April 1944. In the best of cases, however, it "might end its life in its beginning, like a new bud late-frosted." Burnham, too, was evidently evoking wintry images in 1947.

By that time well on his way from Trotskyist renegade to arch cold-warrior, Burnham was now advocating an American world empire. What he had in mind was "a state, not necessarily world-wide in literal extent but world-dominating in political power, set up at least in part through coercion" and extending "to wherever the imperial power is decisive, not for everything or nearly everything, but for the crucial issues upon which political survival depends." He believed this empire, founded on the atomic monopoly and featuring strong interventionism, could be combined with democracy at home, at the core. If the United States, an adolescent world power, failed in this imperial endeavor—by necessity an offensive one—the Soviet Union would succeed in its stead. An American empire, nevertheless, was already in the making, even if it was not being called that. Burnham's suggestion for an alternative and more congenial name—"the policy of democratic world order"—has a certain contemporary resonance in more ways than one.

The door was thus open for Burnham's ferocious attack in 1953 on the containment policy for its apparent lack of properly offensive qualities. Kennan's position, Burnham argued, was "pale and abstract." In a situation where there was "no clear line between war and peace" but "only different forms and stages of the continuous struggle for survival and dominance in the developing world system of the future," the United States needed active warfare, political warfare. Containment was merely holding the line, a recipe for defeat.

4. Don Juan Manuel and the Muslims

A more ancient lineage goes back to Don Juan Manuel in early fourteenth-century Spain, or more accurately, Castile. Juan Manuel was the grandson of the powerful Castilian king Ferdinand III, a major figure in the Reconquest of the Iberian peninsula from the Muslims; and Juan Manuel himself, aside from being one of the first prose writers in Spanish, was part of this military, political, cultural, and ideological struggle. He (and Iberians in general) had ample reason to ponder the nature of warfare between Christians and Muslims. Some modern writers (notably Fred Halliday) have seen Juan Manuel's analysis of the inconclusive, irregular skirmishes and raids with fluctuating frontiers and the context of incommensurate religious worldviews as analogous to the cold war. Indeed, they claim that Don Juan Manuel was the first to use the term. Halliday cites no authority but my guess is that his source is Luis García-Arias, a noted geopolitical thinker in Franco's Spain during the 1950s and '60s.

Don Juan Manuel's authorship, alas, happens to be something less than that. It would be more accurate to say that a nineteenth-century editor in Madrid coined "the cold war" through a mistaken transcription of Juan Manuel's work. The passage in *Libro de Los Estados* that García-Arias was referring to in the 1950s actually speaks (in the Spanish of the 1320s) of "la guera tivia." "Tivia" (in modern Spanish, "tibia") means tepid or lukewarm, something metaphorically very different, of course, from what should have been "la guerra fria." García-Arias, however, was relying on the 1860 (Gayala) transcription and edition of Juan Manuel's book; and this version does indeed say "la guerra fria." In a footnote, Gayala says that the fourteenth-century original seems to be "avia" (a microfiche transcript I found renders it "la g<u>'rra (avia) [tivia]"); but, as this makes no sense to him, he goes on to exercise a certain editorial privilege by substituting the more sensible "fria" instead. Thus, then, the first known use of "the cold war."

The passage indicates the difficulties of the cold war as a metaphor. Its antonym is presumably hot war, real war, rising temperature. But rising temperature could also mean a thaw, an improvement, a lessening of the risk of real war. To the extent, however, that cold also connotes frigidity in the sense of someone unresponsive, it is indeed quite suggestive. From that angle, Juan Manuel's image of the lukewarm war is actually not without relevance. While real war ("*muy fuerte et muy caliente*," strong and hot) has real results—death or peace—"la guera tivia" confers upon its respective parties neither peace nor honor. In short, it is not recognizable as a full-fledged, proper war between equal enemies. Inconclusive, it seems not to have real peace as its object.

Don Juan Manuel had a good deal of military respect for the Islamic fighters he had to contend with but was in the end too much of a Christian feudal lord to be able to see them as the kind of enemies that were one's equals (he himself had more than a few enemies in Castile and Aragon). Christian attitudes toward Islam—and Islam was in every way a fundamental problem—actually underwent several changes during the Middle Ages. At no point, however, did this concern result in any real knowledge, for Islam could not be situated within the dominant intra-Christian division between orthodoxy (in the conventional sense of "the right opinion") and heresy. Islam was a strange bird, monotheistic and Abrahamic, yet also profoundly different. It represented, all else aside, a thorny problem of classification.

The prevailing Christian view held that Muslim Saracens of Spain stemmed from Ishmael, Abraham's son by his Egyptian wife, Hagar. Thus they were outside the original covenant. Christians, by contrast, descended from Isaac, Abraham's son by Sarah. Isaac prefigured Christ and so by extension also the medieval Church, while Ishmael had been expelled into the desert; and Saracens, of course, were men of the desert. Much analytical effort was thus expended trying to explain away the apparent phonetic paradox of "Saracens" and "Sarah." Such were the preoccupations of the Church intellectuals, organic policy theorists of the medieval world.

Two monotheistic and universalist religions cannot, if the respective communities understand themselves as vehicles for salvation, truly recognize one another as geopolitical equals. The third Abrahamic religion, Judaism, sees salvation in terms of exclusion of the outside, a war for the preservation of the inside (though space here is a complicated issue and the inside, Israel notwithstanding, is arguably constituted by the law). Christianity and Islam, then, are marked by expansionary notions. Space over time will become unitary, the outside therefore conceived of as a space eventually to be conquered. The question is really only what sort of relation of nonrecognition one will maintain with it. Unlike Christianity, however, Islam was territorialized from the very beginning and involved in military conflict. Nonrecognition between the world or abode of Islam ("submission") and the world of war would not necessarily take the form of open war. On the contrary, one could engage in temporary treaties—truces—because the world was by definition temporary anyway. Thus *dar al-sulh*, the abode of treaty where one might for reasons of stalemate conclude agreements.

Islam also differentiated between various kinds of nonrecognizable enemies: Jews and Christians could be accepted as second-class citizens, while no compromise was possible with atheists and polytheists. Jihad ("strife" or "struggle" in the path of God, "holy war" actually being a Greek term) could take different forms. Truces, as they tend to do when prolonged, became coexistence. Opinions differ on the matter, but real peace treaties were arguably concluded with Christian powers in the sixteenth or seventeenth century. Not until the end of the Crimean War in 1856, however, did Christian Europe, on its part, fully recognize the Ottomans as part of the family of nations proper. Which brings us to the roots of the Christian view of war and peace.

5. Augustine and Aquinas

Writing at the tail end of the Roman Empire and convinced that the End of Time was near, Augustine put forth a set of terms about peace and war that would travel authoritatively down through the centuries, as Time in fact did not come to an End. By Augustine's day, of course, Christianity had become state religion, territorialized and ready to persecute pagan and other dissent by violent means. Most of Augustine's view on the subject was taken from classical Roman authors, mainly Cicero, with some crucial Christian (indeed Augustinian) elements added. World order was, in principle, about peace and justice, *pax* and *iustitia*, connoting a tranquil condition of rest where everything would be in its proper, paradisical place. But life on earth after the Fall was inherently tainted by Sin and so, by definition, merely temporal. Eternal peace, real peace, *pax aeterna*, could only occur after the Second Coming. Actually existing peace on earth, meanwhile, was nothing but a *pax temporalis*, a sort of simulacrum of the real thing (Augustine's neo-Platonic leanings are at work here).

Within that shadowy context of imperfection, however, it remained that Christians desired just peace while the heathen wanted an iniquitous one, a perverse peace of domination and subservience, a peace that is "not worthy even of the name of peace." Nevertheless, good and bad alike seek *some sort of peace*. Even *pax falsa*, wicked peace, as opposed to *pax vera*, is peace of a kind. War, then, is derived and defined in terms of its goal, peace.

By the High Middle Ages, this Augustinian framework had been modified (along with his radical distinction between the earthly and godly domains) so that *pax temporalis* could quite well be imagined in the here and now as *pax vera*. Thus Aquinas, writing in the thirteenth century, distinguishes *pax vera* from *pax apparens*, the peace of power and injustice. Unreal peace had become, significantly, the province, not of humankind and earthly existence as such, but spatially of the heathen outside. Inside *res publica Christiana*, peace (following, notably, the arguments of that old teleological heathen Aristotle) was the very condition that made it possible for human beings to be human. Aquinas, however, did allow for agreements ("concord") with heathens outside the normative community of Christians, technically signifying an existence alongside without violence.

6. Hobbes and Grotius

Medieval peace, then, is understood as the natural condition, marked by *iustitia* (meaning both right order and justice), *caritas, tranquillitas, securitas*. War is disturbance, upsetting the right order of justice and hence unnatural. Private feud and public war are not clearly distinguished. The medieval order disintegrates in due course and individual states begin to emerge, themselves eventually falling into confessional civil wars in the early modern period. A situation of extreme insecurity ensues. These intra-Christian conflicts actually included absolute negations along the lines of a cold war. Consider Oliver Cromwell's position on Spain in the seventeenth century: peace with France was possible but not with "papist" Spain, for "The pope," as he put it, "maintains peace only as long as he wishes." (This, en passant, corresponds precisely to George F. Kennan's cold-war argument about the Soviet Union.)

Hobbes, Cromwell's contemporary, is the theorist who breaks most decisively with the medieval conception by making war and insecurity the natural state, thus requiring all reasonable human beings to create an unlimited, absolute sovereignty, an artificial man, so as to prevent nature from having its way. Only thus could one make possible commodious living for everyone. Legitimacy, then, is for him solely a matter of *securitas pacis*. Justice has disappeared, or, rather, it is transformed into law and order. Authority makes peace, says Hobbes; Truth does not. Truth, on the contrary, is associated with religious claims and so, in his view, with the very fanaticism that had initiated the devastating civil wars.

Yet in the seventeenth century the imposing word of Hobbes was not everywhere the word of polite society. Theorists of natural rights offered less radical alternatives, the most noteworthy here being that of Grotius. Hobbes, interestingly, had expanded the notion of war beyond "actual fighting" to mean "the known disposition thereto during all the time there is no assurance to the contrary." The room for real peace in the sense of full security in external relations seemed correspondingly narrow. Grotius, by contrast, maintains the conventional distinction based on the presence or absence of open fighting. He also insists (following Roman models) that war must properly be declared; but he takes one step further and, crucially, turns it into a distinct condition, a state of affairs. War making as such is, moreover, conceived of as taking place in a theater, an external space of confrontation.

In the course of his argument, Grotius invokes the authority of Cicero to the effect that between war and peace there can be no intermediate. But the Ciceronian passage he refers to (*Inter pacem et bellum nihil medium* appears in *Philippic Eight*) is actually talking about civil war. Cicero is concerned to classify it as a real war as opposed to a mere *tumultus*. Grotius transfers this to the whole range of emergent rules and regulations designed to control war in postconfessional Europe, the process whereby war was banished to the outside of the state and, conversely, the inside became an inviolable, absolute sovereignty. War, from then on, is seen as a legitimate property and defining aspect of that sovereignty. It becomes a political means, governed by certain explicit conventions that Grotius does more than anyone to codify as *ius gentium*, international law.

All in all, it is a dehistoricized, seemingly timeless order he construes. One of its founding pillars is the razor-sharp distinction between war and peace. War, moreover, is conducted for limited aims and does not, in principle, entail the liquidation of the enemy. On the contrary, the enemy is an equal—a just enemy—a conception that becomes the premise for the Grotian juridico-political edifice. Correct forms of hostility cannot be based on confessional or ideological difference, provided one is a member of the reigning European family of nations. This, in turn, permits theorization of land appropriations from indigenous peoples in the newly "discovered" territories across the ocean, appropriations that were a precondition for the emergence of the European state system of limited war in the first place.

The medieval *res publica Christiana* is thus recast into Europe precisely through the emergence of this new system of regulated war, condensed at the Peace of Utrecht of 1713 in the principle of Balance of Power. Diversity and proper balance, the absence of a single dominant or universal monarchy, is henceforth a central part of the very definition of Europe.

7. Rousseau, Paine, Kant

Europe, in Rousseau's words, is thus "no mere fanciful collection of peoples with only a name in common as in Asia and Africa": it is a "real society" with common "religion, manners, customs and even laws." As was his wont, however, Rousseau sets up this idyllic extreme only to demolish it with a paradox or discrepancy. For this "resplendent sanctuary of science and art" is congenitally given to all manner of bloody carnage. "So much humanity, in principle," he says, "so much cruelty in deed." Europe is in fact nothing more in the end than a "pretended brotherhood" where nations are "in a state of war" with one another and treaties "represent passing truces rather than true peace." Hence the need for a system, rationally imposed, of collective security.

Though he is not very original on the topic, Rousseau represents an important shift by the eighteenth-century Enlightenment toward a critique of war. Morality aside, for these thinkers the worst thing about war is that it is stupid. Balance and natural diversity are good, but war in the name of balance is bad and silly. Yet the condemnation of intra-European war as irrational entailed an interesting corollary. For the Enlightenment also reinvents the principle of just war as civil war against the ruling order. What is reasonable is just, and human beings can determine what is reasonable and therefore just. If the ruler/state fails to conform to this reasonable Truth or suppresses the right to express it, he/it is illegitimate, whereupon one has the right to inflict violence in response. The inside (sovereignty itself) is thus no longer beyond dispute. It is subject to moral reasoning, questions of good and evil, good and bad, absolute notions of right and wrong, now in the name of reason, which is to say, a secularized version of God.

This could then be translated into a notion of international peace as intrinsically linked to the nature of domestic society and its political regime. Thomas Paine, for example, typically assumed that monarchy meant war and republics peace. Europe he considered "too thickly planted with Kingdoms to be long at peace," though the republics that did exist there were "all (and we may say always) in peace." Republican regimes, being natural, would reasonably negotiate any conflict; monarchies, by contrast, would go to war. Kant developed a concept along the same lines but less radical. Perpetual (real) peace would only come with generalized republican government, a system he conceived of as the opposite of despotism. Not to be equated with any democracy, a republican regime is an aggregation of free and equal citizens under a single law coupled with representative government. As a collectivity, these free citizens would naturally not consent to war because of all the "calamities" it would impose upon themselves. A "subject" (despotic) form of state could, by contrast, engage in war arbitrarily at any time, "as if it were a kind of pleasure party."

Kant, as befitted a pious follower of the Augustinian monk Martin Luther, had some similarities here with Augustine; but his position was ultimately weaker. Everlasting peace does not imply "tranquility of order" modeled on heavenly repose, merely rational resolution of extant conflicts. This quintessentially bourgeois outlook found a contemporary counterpoint in Adam Smith's (and Paine's) British understanding of open commerce as a symbol of, and means to, peace. Maximum trade, henceforth, could be contrasted with the mercantilism of rigidly demarcated states, whose very existence was conducive to war. War, in short, was inherently irrational. Bentham, utilitarian *par excellence*, called it "mischief upon the largest scale." Kant, writing in a different idiom, put it more pompously: "From the throne of its moral legislative power, reason absolutely condemns war as a means of determining the right and makes seeking the state of peace a matter of unmitigated duty" (for which practical purpose, Kant opined, one would then need a federation or league of nations). Accordingly, unlike Paine and the French Revolutionaries, Kant did not envisage any war to implement this new rationality, any war to end all wars. But this was always a possible alternative understanding of the project.

The shift to domestic derivation was an epochal one. In various ways it would later influence both US and Soviet self-conceptions of what it is to lead the upward progression of objective history.

8. Hegel and Clausewitz

The American and French Revolutions implemented, in differing ways, this new philosophy of enlightened right. The radical thrust of the French failed however and the European system managed to regroup in the nineteenth century into a semblance of its old balance. Parallel, therefore, to British models of rationality and commercial peace (under British commercial hegemony of course), the geopolitical notion of war as rational means of policy survived. In some quarters, it even transmogrified into a sort of bellicism—war as a good thing for the fiber of society, seemingly inscribed in the very struggle for survival that defined Life as such. Since the body politic was now understood as a people rather than merely a dynastic possession, war could serve to fuse the multitude as a collectivity. Hegel, against his eighteenth-century predecessors, was thereby able to deny that war was an "absolute evil," though the traditional proviso still obtained that states would "reciprocally recognize each other as states" even during war. Legitimate war, then, would issue in a settlement, peace. The object was victory, but victory did not mean liquidation. War was ultimately not the "total" one of the French revolutionary period but the limited version of yesteryear, professional and regulated according to "civilized" rules, modeled on the old personal duel.

Hegel's thinking on identity and difference pertained to the European-centered family of nation-states. Thus he argued conventionally (as did most Americans) that international law pertained to peoples recognized as equals but not to nomads or Amerindians. In a different key, he also maintained that "religious views may entail an opposition at a higher level between one people and its neighbors and so preclude the general identity which is requisite for recognition." The reference was to Jews and Muslims, but it has clear implications in our context.

Perhaps Hegel's original contribution was indeed his phenomenological problematic of recognition and acknowledgement (*anerkennen* means both). A much-simplified version would run something like this: The self-conscious Subject confronts the other as object, demanding recognition without according recognition in return. The other acts similarly and a struggle for death ensues. But such unilateral premises render the situation contradictory. To gain acknowledgement as the universal Subject necessitates someone who acknowledges this. Killing the other obviously destroys that possibility; but even if he (Hegel sees it as a he) relents and submits, my victory is hollow and trivial precisely because his recognition will not, insofar as he is subjugated, be a full or proper one in which I can see my value as Self affirmed and mirrored. To accord reciprocity, by contrast, would mean relinquishing my claim to universality.

We will want to revisit this contradiction later. Let us now turn instead to Clausewitz, Hegel's contemporary. These two extraordinary thinkers traveled in the same circles in the late 1820s, but their relation, if any, is undocumented and the question of intellectual influence an open one. Both, at any rate, died prematurely two days apart in November 1831 in Europe's first cholera epidemic (though Hegel's actual cause of death is not entirely clear).

What is of central interest here in the military theorist is his key concept of polarity (*Polarität*). Clausewitz railed, rightly, against the empty technicism and metaphorical language of authoritative writings on war in his day. He himself, nevertheless, deployed a whole range of metaphors taken from seventeenth- and eighteenth-century science, chiefly but not exclusively physics: friction, mass, force, gravity, evaporation, vacuum, refraction, equilibrium, electrical charge, and so on. Polarity appears to have been borrowed from electromagnetics. By the early nineteenth century, however, it had also become an ontological commonplace in German thought: the idea, in other words, that life and things really consist of an interlocking unity of attraction and repulsion. Kant had systematized this notion (on dubious grounds, he thought it Newtonian). Through Herder and others it reached Hegel, for whom, famously, it became not only an interactive principle but a negational one: the identity of the opposition is based on negation of the Other and is thus negational in itself.

Later in the nineteenth century, the metaphorical use of polarity turned nebulous, signifying entities or forces moving in opposite directions. How the term eventually entered international relations theory, I do not know; but there it seems to mean mere opposition, systematic opposition in a spatial configuration of power centers. Hence the beloved "bipolarity" and "multipolarity," both of which, electromagnetically speaking, would seem absurd: redundant in the first case, oxymoronic in the second. Polarity is presumably by definition a duality. This, in any event, is how Clausewitz uses it. Thus for him (and Hegel) it means a situation where the negative and the positive "exactly cancel one another out," more concretely, a confrontation of two sides engaged symmetrically in a battle for victory. You win or you lose. But the point (metaphorical or not) is also that there is continuous *interaction* (*Wechselwirkung*). In a way, then, it is a dialectical opposition. Identity ceases to exist when one pole disappears along with the opposition.

Hence Clausewitz sees struggle for victory through decisive battle as the very nature or essence (*Wesen*) of war. Bloodletting is to war what cash payment is to commercial transactions. "Like two incompatible elements, armies must continually destroy one another. Like fire and water they never find themselves in a state of equilibrium, but must keep on interacting until one of them has completely disappeared. Imagine a pair of wrestlers deadlocked and inert for hours on end!" War, then, is about throwing the enemy down, eliminating his will to fight. But this ontological proposition is then, in typical Clausewitzian manner, modified in reality. Because, among other things, defense is inherently stronger than offense, war can lapse into a desultory state and lose much of its basic polarity. Intensity is however also a function of politics, political purpose. The less maximalistic one's political aims, the less intense therefore the polarity.

9. Marx, Engels and Lenin

Clausewitz pondered war in a European frame, war as epitomized in a battle performed in a baroque theater. Yet his own experience of war (beginning at the age of thirteen) was in the devastating confrontations with the French; and Clausewitz remained uncertain about the relation of total war to political liquidation. Hegel, on the other hand, stuck to the traditional view that the enemy's internal order was beyond attack. International (that is European) law protected domestic institutions in wartime.

Hegel's lineal descendants Marx and Engels thought otherwise. To them, nation-states were unreasonable and bound to be undermined by the globalization of capital. More originally, they also claimed that the whole apparatus of inside and outside, sovereignty in short, served to hide the real nature of the state, namely, class rule. In a way, then, one was always already in a sort of war, a class war, whether openly declared or merely smoldering. Class conflict was a state of affairs resulting from a certain mode of production; and as long as it remained, there could be no *pax vera*, only *pax apparens*.

Traditional war between states, meanwhile, was ultimately irrational and bad, but one had to contend with it as intrinsic to an unjust order that was to be abolished. What they meant by "contending" actually changed several times, from the view that capitalist war would provide openings for revolution to the opposite that it would prevent it. Engels, who wrote professionally on the subject, ultimately came to think that war would mean world war and culminate in disaster.

Lenin carried this Marxist Enlightenment critique to its fullest expression. For him, too, the state was an instrument of class rule and so, therefore, was the international state system of capitalist rapacity. Against this, he set the legitimacy of class war, his Marxist reformulation of the just civil war so abhorred by Hobbes and every conservative statesman ever since. Capitalism, then, was war, struggle to the death.

No Augustinian peace could be envisaged until the world had become socialist and rational.

This was merely reworking Marx's concept of legitimate class war as an always existing structural condition of antagonism. Going beyond Marx, however, Lenin also militarized party politics, eventually rendering it positively Clausewitzian. Class war is class politics by other means. The Party thereby becomes the equivalent of the State and politics a matter of battles, alliances, strategy, and tactics, all organized around the pivotal notion of a single main enemy. This construes an absolute enemy precisely in the sense of the Clausewitzian battle; but, crucially, it is an enemy bereft of legitimacy.

Had that concept prevailed in the ensuing century in the form of global class warfare, the question of the cold war would have corresponded much better to the picture of historiographical traditionalism in the United States. But the Revolution was territorialized in a single, if huge, land mass. By 1923 the international civil war had failed everywhere except in Lenin's native land (and perhaps he was right in thinking that it would then fail there as well). His vision was followed not by Trotsky's internationalism but Stalin's Fortress USSR. At no time was Trotsky's notorious formula at Brest Litovsk—"neither war nor peace"— in the basic interest of Stalin's Fortress. Lenin's view did survive, however, in different and reinvigorated form in the figure of Mao, theorist of protracted civil war and invasion of the enemy's social order; but that is another story.

10. Stalin

The anomaly of a revolutionary socialist state amid capitalist ones was worked out by Stalin from the mid-1920s onward. He did this first by territorializing Marx and Lenin's always existing contradiction between capital and labor into one between the Soviet Union and the outside. The historic interests of progress henceforth were lodged in Soviet territory—or, more precisely, in the Kremlin and the class interests it represented. (A corresponding notion of historical chosenness and progress toward true humanity had of course long reigned in the United States.) Yet the contradiction of capital and labor, conceived of in Marx as a single structure of continuing interaction between two antagonists, could be defused, at least potentially, in the Stalinist reworking because of the physical separation from the outside, the severing of real interaction. And separation was indeed Stalin's instinctive strategic aim. Once situated at the geopolitical level, the fundamental contradiction could thus take any number of forms since interaction (or the dialectic) was no longer *a priori* present in the structure itself, much less its defining feature. The Other was externalized, symbolically present on the inside only as a constituent hostile outside or as foreign agents, usually in the guise of deviationists serving evil forces.

Stalin's second move (which he did not originate but sanctioned) had to do with alliance politics. Put simply, if monopoly capitalism, grounded in an ever-slimmer class basis, was inherently stagnating and so tended to resort to war at home and abroad, then it made no sense at all for the USSR, once the massive power of fascism had been understood, to engage in any drastically offensive maneuvers—or for that matter, after 1945, in any cold war. On the contrary, building coalitions of the widest possible kind against the narrowly based monopoly factions would be the marching order. Thus, beyond the tendency to separation and distance, there was nothing *as such* in the Soviet position after 1935 that made stable, nonrevolutionary relations with capitalist powers impossible: the main enemy was not intrinsically linked to bourgeois states or their nature. Contradiction had to do with a transnational class, or more accurately, a small fraction of that class. Whereas the political embodiment of Progress was always to be found in the Kremlin, the embodiment of Reaction could be found in a variety of places. Its precise location was contingent, subject to decision in typically voluntarist Stalinist manner. Hence the constant postwar reference to the mysterious influence of reactionary circles on Western state policy, when the latter turned hostile to Moscow's position.

It is wrongheaded, therefore, to pose the historical question in terms of putative contrast between a realist Stalin and a communist Stalin (or between *Realpolitik* and ideology). There was every reason for Stalin to maintain stable, if distant, relations with the major capitalist powers in the name of a common antifascist legacy. This, in his view, was prudent Marxist-Leninist geopolitics, though it did not turn out that way.

Stalin lost the political contest over antifascist legitimacy after the war, partly because of massive Western superiority, partly because, as a crude reductionist, he had a very limited understanding of how the

West in general, and the United States in particular, actually operated. Thus he found himself faced in 1949 precisely with the kind of scenario he most devoutly must have wished to avoid, a huge and powerful US-led coalition directed against his regime in a cold war. From his standpoint, it is in fact difficult to imagine a more disastrous turn of events short of all-out war.

11. Wilson and Roosevelt

It is time, then, to turn west again. The American experiment in Enlightenment politics was allowed to expand, largely undisturbed, in the name of Reason and Light across the continental expanse. The US, embodying right, could by definition not wage unjust war. Dispute arose in domestic politics about the perversion of this original and universal right, about its concrete meaning. Could it, for example, include slavery? That question had to be settled by a massive civil war. Yet the self-conception of universal right certainly survived.

Fast-forward now to the end of World War I and Woodrow Wilson. Wilson spoke famously in the name of humanity and rendered all enemies by nature therefore inhumane and/or criminal. In doing this he was, as he himself said, merely expressing American traditions, which were also those of humanity at large. War to end all wars (once it had been decided upon) was perfectly legitimate, just as the radical Enlightenment had said all along; and the opposition to such an obviously legitimate aim had to be eliminated forthwith, or at least not allowed participation in the new normative community of the world.

The resort to war as an analogue is a common one in American history: war on depression, war on drugs, war on poverty, war against a whole range of ills, amounting to a homespun sort of metaphorical bellicism. Wilson fused, in traditional American ways, this secular concept of reasonable conduct with a thoroughly Protestant notion of election and mission into a full-fledged ideology of US exceptionalism (though, paradoxically, one whose success would have eliminated that very status by making the world outside identical). His project of a new international order of law, discussion, and economic openness met with not much more success than Lenin's alternative. Both projects were ultimately undermined by fascism, the future specter of which the two originators, in a weird way, had each sensed, if in radically different frames.

As alluded to at the outset, the background here was, *pace* Cicero and Grotius, the proliferating intermediate states of war in the 1930s. In part this had to do, arguably, with the intense legalism of the 1920s, legal procedure as international norm and the criminalization of war itself. The paradoxical effect was actually that the space for war as nonwar increased. The Japanese war against China, causing massive casualties, was thus allegedly an "incident"; the Italian Fascists invented the term "not-warmaking" to describe their intervention in the Spanish Civil War; and Hitler expanded his territory successfully by means of threats and bullying that never had to become open war (until they did). The whole set of conventional distinctions and institutions pertaining to war and peace (declaration, rules of conduct, rights of noncombatants, neutrality, in short, international law) that had emerged from Hobbes and Grotius onward and had been most extensively codified in the Hague Convention of 1907 seemed increasingly meaningless. Though the actual incidence of nondeclared "states of hostilities" was not new, the 1930s mark the apparent end of the traditional notion of there being no intermediate space between war and peace. Consequently, thinking ahead, it is tempting to understand the cold war as just, say, a version of neither war, nor peace, and be done with it. This is too hasty, however, for the many complicating manifestations of war as not-war or peace as not-peace or "peace-war" in the decade did not amount to any cold war as I will delineate it, though the story of the 1930s becomes, conceptually and politically, an indispensable element in its emergence. That is, the cold war would have made little sense without the diplomatic lessons of the Depression decade, lessons condensed above all in the postwar parable about dictatorship and appeasement. To that frame must be added, too, the more precise and far-reaching articulation represented by Franklin D. Roosevelt during 1939–41. For the matrix or logic of the American cold war project after the war was established by Roosevelt in his attempt, in my view generally justified, to prepare the United States for (and, by less justifiable means, steer it toward) the "inevitable" open war.

Roosevelt had taken note in the 1930s of the ominous changes in established norms of war and peace. He was, however, also well aware of earlier anomalies, not all negative ones. In what otherwise may have seemed an obscure historical reference, he and his administration began to highlight the naval war of 1798 against France as a "Quasi-War." FDR used the suggestive term in 1939 precisely with regard to the difficulties of the old distinctions of peace and war. Already in the Quarantine Speech (quarantine "against the epidemic of world lawlessness") in October 1937, he was referring to "times of so-called peace." A good deal of ambivalence was, however, attached to this discourse, for these "times" and indeed the retrospective example of the Quasi-War itself formed an opening for Roosevelt. *On the one hand*, by spring 1939 (as Hitler gobbled up the rest of Czechoslovakia) it was clear that dictators could not be dealt with in ordinary ways because they didn't act in ordinary ways. Hitler's unabashed lawlessness rendered agreement useless (until Pearl Harbor, Roosevelt's Exhibit A was almost always Hitler): "Live at peace with Hitler? The only peace possible with Hitler is the peace that comes from complete surrender. How can one speak of a negotiated peace in this war when a peace treaty would be as binding upon the Nazis as the bond of gangsters and outlaws?" It would be hard to guess that the United States was technically at peace with Germany in July 1941 when he made that statement. Any peace with lawless aggressors, then, was a *pax falsa*, merely "another armistice," as FDR said. In short, gangsterism, operating in the intermediate zone between war and peace, had to be eliminated in no uncertain terms. *On the other hand* (this was less obvious), if war and peace had lost their distinction because of international gangsterism, it was also the case, *ipso facto*, that decent powers such as the United States must have a certain license to act in the intermediate zone as well. To be more precise, the unconventional Quasi-War had been a success: John Adams and Congress created a navy, which established order on the vital trade routes of the Caribbean, but no general war with France was ever declared. It worked. And so Roosevelt came to generate his own Quasi-War, a whole series of manifestly unneutral acts that, in his effective formulation, made the United States "the arsenal of democracy" (and more).

The intermediate zone, then, harbored lawlessness as well as necessary action to combat it, action that did not under any circumstances include negotiation and agreements. From the posited lawlessness came indeed the notion of "unconditional surrender," enunciated with Churchill at Casablanca in 1943 but actually present from the beginning in Roosevelt's outlook. Unconditional surrender was coupled with a new, globalist notion of US security as the postwar implementation of basic features of freedom as outlined in the Atlantic Charter and Roosevelt's Four Freedoms speech. This position can be condensed into three propositions: (i) everything that is not *pax vera*, a true peace, is by definition war, whatever the actual current relations; (ii) there can be no true peace with power X because of certain qualities Y in the domestic makeup of that power; and (iii) whoever is not my explicit friend (friendship being a question of identity with a set of universals) is my explicit enemy. We have here, in its essentials, what would become the matrix of the cold war as a US project.

12. Roosevelt and Truman

Roosevelt, being Roosevelt, adjusted his frame politically after June 22, 1941, and began to differentiate de facto between dictators. He had always thought that Mussolini's fascist regime could have been bought off, and now, after the Nazi invasion of the Soviet Union, he saw that the actual dynamics of the situation might well require him to treat Stalin's USSR pragmatically as the kind of dictatorship that had the potential, if treated as a would-be member of the world of peace, eventually to become a real one. So while the matrix remained in place, the juggling began. Roosevelt had to engage in a game of simulation, hoping that the world of events and realities would come to approximate the world of shadows. Hence the playing for time, hence the exclusive focus on things military, hence the avoidance of fundamental political problems and contradictions.

Regrettably, this did not work. One of the reasons was the deeper differences in the Soviet and US conception of the wartime coalition. The former was negative and defensive, logically so in accordance with the theory of antifascist class and state alliances: common interests from bourgeoisie to working class dictated that fascism, monopoly capitalism in its most reactionary and warmongering form, be prevented. Winning would not completely remove these avatars of stagnant monopoly capitalism, but the postwar coalition of antifascist forces could, if properly managed and maintained, keep them under wraps. The preconditions for a *pax vera* would then doubtless come at some undefinable future date, once the historic example of rationally planned production would have been demonstrated near and afar. This perspective is why, even after 1947, Moscow's official line of opposition to the United States took place defensively under the name of national independence, not socialist revolution. The American stance, by contrast, was positive and offensive. It was not only a matter of preventing something from reoccurring but of achieving, in principle, *pax vera* in the here and now. Once, on closer inspection, it turned out that the Soviet Union did not fit positively the bill of a true friend, it could logically only be a true enemy, not an equal enemy of the duelist kind but an absolute enemy with whom there could be no real peace, only a peace, in Augustinian terms, "not worthy even of the name of peace."

By that time, the New Deal elements in the original Rooseveltian peace ("freedom from want") had been compressed by Truman into an entirely abstract notion of Freedom, defined positively as that which resides in the United States with spiritual environs and negatively as that which is not Totalitarianism. Deciding who was a true friend from then on was comparatively easy. One should add here that freedom was not yet directly equated with capitalism, at least not unblushingly. The collective memory of the Depression and war was still fresh enough to make one liable to think that behind free enterprise lay enterprise but nothing automatically free.

The totalitarian Other, then, was constitutively present in symbolic form as a constant threat to universal freedom and concretely as evil foreign bodies. Given concrete historical sanction through the lessons of Munich, Roosevelt's original matrix was thus recast and redeployed in a project of unprecedented global scope, military, political, ideological and economic. NSC 68 (the foundational policy document of 1950) epitomized this new and transformed negation. All the basic Rooseveltian themes of the implacable enemy, infiltration and subversion, civilizational negation, worldwide struggle, and infinite strategic needs are present. "The cold war," says NSC 68, "is in fact a real war." Negotiation must therefore always be deferred until a proper relation of strength has been achieved and the Soviet Union can be "forced" into the realm of the "acceptable." Success on that score, given the essential nature of Soviet expansionism, would eventually spell the end of the Soviet Union itself: unconditional surrender. To ensure this scenario, then, only one policy was rational for the United States: massive expansion of the war machine.

13. Lippmann (ii), Kennan, Fanon

All of which brings us full circle back to that famous nondebate between Lippmann and Kennan in 1947–48. For in the end I want to argue that Kennan's early postwar position did express (let us leave aside his intentions) the logic of the US-induced cold war perfectly and that Lippmann saw this instantly and it quite rightly hit him hard. Built into Kennan's notion of containment was a deliberate moment of diplomatic refusal, a period of recharging the Western batteries and rearranging the power configuration. To Kennan's dismay, that temporary recharge became a perpetual and indeed accelerating recharge, coupled with endless deferment of diplomacy. Kennan actually imagined the future along the lines of a metaphor he took from Molotov at the time, the image of a long-term fencing match, a game of thrusts and parrying, back-and-forth, not a lethal exercise but within the range of measures short of war, eventually resulting in some new and perhaps more favorable situation. In that sense there would be real dialogical interaction, though conflictual.

What ensued instead was something like the frozen dialectic of Frantz Fanon's colonial world, the absolute spatial separation between settler and native in which there is no real *Wechselwirkung*, no interaction in Hegel's and Clausewitz's sense and therefore no mediation either, only potential annihilation. "The zone where the natives live is not complementary to the zone inhabited by the settlers. The two zones are opposed, but not in the name of any higher unity. Obedient to the rules of pure Aristotelian logic, they both follow the principle of reciprocal exclusivity. No conciliation is possible, for of the two terms, one is superfluous." Kennan's original formulation, however, was duplicitous in the actual movement to freeze things. His vacillation between the idea of Moscow as nefarious power professionals and Moscow as nefarious fanatics locked in the shadow world of Plato's cave meant that he could never offer a real rationale why Washington should risk dealing with them. And Washington never really did, much to Moscow's surprise. Kennan himself was surprised. At one point he was even baffled to discover that it was the Soviet Union that was behaving like a traditional great power while the United States was being unorthodox. So, in that perspective, one should take seriously the ensuing Soviet conception, *however self-serving*, of the cold war as the Western policy of strength and non-negotiation as opposed to Moscow's line of peace and reduction in tension. One need not embrace the Soviet position to see that the cold war as embodied in the American stance was utterly against Stalin's interests, that he would have liked precisely what he said he wanted: negotiations, deals and reduction in tension, coupled with relative isolation, and above all, recognition as an equal. Instead the USSR became a pariah.

One can object that this was exactly what the Soviet regime deserved because it had impinged unduly on the security interests of others and/or because it remained wedded to long-term revolutionary goals. Here I side with Lippmann. Lippmann saw in containment the danger that diplomatic dialogue, normal relations, probing negotiation, and resolution of issues of mutual interest would pretty much cease. We don't have to like them, he intimated, just negotiate their and our own withdrawal from Central Europe and very likely a certain normalcy and independence would return.

In the end, it would take half a century, an arms race of unimaginable waste, and a collapse to achieve that normalcy, and it was a fleeting one.

14. Politics, Polarity and Space

For the United States, communism was the equivalent of war, and the communist HQ lay in Moscow. There could be no real peace, consequently, with the Soviet Union, indeed no real peace in the world as such, unless the Soviet Union ceased being the Soviet Union and communism ended. For the Soviet Union, by contrast, there could be peace with the United States but not until the influence of "reactionary, warmongering monopoly capitalism" had been neutralized and the regime assumed a more normal bourgeois character. The index of such normalcy and decrease in reaction was of course the precise extent to which the United States responded to the Soviet-led overtures for interstate peace in the world. Such a theoretical procedure would have been unthinkable to Marx, but it was one plausible codification of the unexpected necessity of a post-Leninist geopolitics. This, then, was the structural difference or discrepancy that gave rise to the cold war as a situation and provided its laws of motion.

The master signifier around which the struggle initially came to be articulated was World War II, or more precisely, what it had meant to negate fascism in that war. No one could question that act in itself; it was a case of universal right. But to claim the same role now and, conversely, to cast the former ally and present enemy in the role of fascism, was not mere repetition. It was a new constitution of the Other and a new affirmation of the Self as the negation of that that was thus being excluded.

What remains is a brief elucidation of the ensuing epoch itself. I need to raise, in particular, the question of Clausewitzian polarity and Hegelian recognition. If all politics is in some sense about polarization, the problem is still whether this particular polarity is a battle to the death, a clash of two wills to complete victory, or another kind of antagonism. A battle to the death the cold war certainly was, but to a kind of *abstract death*. Elimination of the enemy's will to fight—victory—meant more than military victory on the battlefield. It meant, in principle, the liquidation of an enemy whose right to exist, let alone equality, one did not recognize. Liquidation alone could bring real peace. Liquidation is thus the truth of the cold war. In that sense, civil war is the real analogue. Yet all of this is in principle. For the more important fact is of course that the cold war was never a real war. The authors of NSC 68 got it wrong. As Raymond Aron says somewhere, the leaders of the US and the USSR always made every effort to avoid real war. Only for very brief moments (Berlin, Korea) did it even approximate Roosevelt's concept of Quasi-War. NATO and Warsaw Pact powers never once went to war with one another. Soon, indeed, the cold war took the impossible Clausewitzian form of deadlocked wrestlers rather than armies continually destroying another. Anything but lukewarm, it nevertheless brought "neither peace nor honor" to its antagonists. Had the struggle escalated into open war or one side capitulated early on, there would have been nothing much to ponder. So it is the deadlock that warrants exploration: a struggle to the death that is at the same time Orwell's "tacit agreement."

The terminological problem here has already been noted. "The cold war" is tricky because it is both metaphor and not metaphor. Its meaning hovers uncertainly between war and warlike. Absolute hostility, the antithesis of peace, is coupled with the absence of real war. Interaction freezes, or is reduced to ideological and political monologues, the polarity marked by immobility and frigidity. In a way, then, it is the very reverse of a Clausewitzian understanding of war: the political purposes are total, maximalistic and intensely polar, but unlimited enmity is not reflected in real fighting. The defining, decisive battle never comes. Unlike the escalating intermediate forms of war leading up to World

War II, this one freezes at the center. Spatial demarcation and immobility mark the polar axis. The cold war both produces a space and is produced by it. Perhaps, then, the original magnetic metaphor is better than Clausewitz's appropriation would have it: in the very middle, a neutralized nullity between poles is locked in the equilibrium of attracting opposites.

One might thus reformulate the matter as a paradox: the cold war is warlike in every sense except the military one. Its truth is war for unconditional surrender, but the reality is the kind of war one has when war itself is impossible. It is war as an ideological, political and economic claim to universality, taking place not in the two-dimensional space of traditional battles but mediated through other realms when not, as universality, actually eliminating space altogether. The militarization of the respective inside and the attendant strategic games are an interaction of continuing mutual destruction endlessly deferred. Real war, meanwhile, is displaced beyond the militarized heartlands onto the periphery, articulated in regional and local conflict that often have little to do with the polarity as such. Thus the cold war appears in spaces of the third kind as militarization and death, as crushing effects, but these are not exactly the same thing. If the term designates a certain antagonism between the US and the USSR, the specificity of these other conflicts and processes can be preserved and grasped. The cold war was not everything that happened between 1947 (or any other year) and 1990.

If one sees the relationship accordingly as a conflictual mixture where both sides are utterly opposed but also always realize the impossibility of open war, then the real driving force of the cold war is the contradictory unity of nonwar and nonrecognition, where the latter is not only warlike but the higher kind of lack of equality that Hegel is referring to in situations of normative incommensurability. The end of the cold war, in my analysis, will then come when both sides recognize each other explicitly as legitimate antagonists, when "they recognize themselves as mutually recognizing one another," when they recognize that conflict can never be resolved by means of war, when China goes its own way, when the Cuban Missile Crisis is over and the Test Ban Treaty is signed, when deterrence replaces liquidation as the master signifier and new dominant, when Leamas dies his defiant death in Berlin because both sides have essentially become the same, and when Bond goes on to fight villains of a new kind.

Bibliographical Note

Aside from obvious classical texts (for example Augustine's *City of God*, Hegel's *Phenomenology of Spirit, Science of Logic, Philosophy of Right*, and so on), I have necessarily borrowed from many secondary sources. First among them are Wilhelm Janssen's two extensive entries "Krieg" and "Friede" in *Geschichtliche Grundbegriffe* (ed. O. Brunner, W. Conze, R. Koselleck). The work of Reinhart Koselleck hovers over the entire exercise, and through him, a bit more distantly, so does that of Carl Schmitt (especially the latter's "Die Geschichtliche Struktur des heutigen Welt-Gegensatzes von Ost und West," in *Freundschaftliche Begegnungen. Festschrift für Ernst Jünger zum 60. Geburtstag* (Frankfurt, 1955) and "Die Ordnung Der Welt nach dem zweiten Weltkrieg," in *Schmittiana-II* (Brussels, 1990). André Beaufre's article on "Peace-War" may be found in *Revue des Deux Mondes* 52:4 (August 15, 1939). (Eventually Beaufre became an expert on deterrence.) Don Juan Manuel's *Libro de Los Estados* is available in an excellent Oxford edition in Spanish (1974). On Christians in the Iberian frame, see Elena Lourie, "A Society Organized for War: Medieval Spain," in *Past and Present*, 1966, 54-76. For Luis García Arias, see his "El Conceptio de Guerra y la Denominada 'Guerra Fria'" in Arias, *La Guerra Moderna y la Organizacion Internacional* (Madrid, 1962). (I do not pretend, by the way, to any expertise in Spanish; my delineation was done with the help of dictionaries, French, an Italian-restaurant owner in New York, a waiter from El Salvador and my late colleague Edward Malefakis.) My own periodization (in which the cold war ends in 1963) was originally presented in a historiographical essay, "The United States," in David Reynolds, ed. *The Origins of the Cold War in Europe: International Perspectives* (New Haven, CT, 1994). On the historico-juridical question of war, see Frederick H. Russell's excellent *The Just War in the Middle Ages* (Cambridge, 1975); Fritz Grob, *The Relativity of War and Peace: a Study in Law, History, and Politics* (New Haven, CT, 1949); Josef L. Kunz, "Bellum Justum and Bellum Legale" [1951] in *The Changing Law of Nations* (Columbus, OH, 1968); John Kelsay, James Turner Johnson, eds., *Just War and Jihad: Historical and Theoretical Perspectives on War and Peace in Western and Islamic Traditions* (New York, 1991); Majid Khadduri, *War and Peace in the Law of Islam* (Baltimore, 1955); R. W. Southern, *Western Views of Islam in the Middle Ages* (Cambridge, MA,

1962). Barry Gowan's "Gravity, Polarity and Dialectical Method" in *Hegel and Newtonianism*, ed. M. J. Perry (Dordrecht, 1993) was very helpful. See also Michael Inwood, *A Hegel Dictionary* (Oxford, 1992). George Orwell's article "You and the Atom Bomb" in the *Tribune* appeared on October 19, 1945. One earlier case, a book review, "Freud or Marx?" in the *Manchester Evening News*, December 9, 1943, speaks of "cold war" as the period before the war in which totalitarian dictators elsewhere bewildered the English public by all manner of incomprehensible street politics. On Swope, see Alfred Allan Lewis's chatty *Man of the World, Herbert Bayard Swope: A Charmed Life of Pulitzer Prizes, Poker and Politics* (Indianapolis, 1978) and William Safire, *Safire's Political Dictionary* (New York, 1978) (though he gets only part of the story and some of it wrong). On FDR, see Raymond G. O'Connor, *Diplomacy for Victory: FDR and Unconditional Surrender* (New York, 1971) and Anne Armstrong, *Unconditional Surrender: The Impact of the Casablanca Policy on World War II* (New Brunswick, NJ, 1961); and of course Warren Kimball, *The Juggler: Franklin Roosevelt as Wartime Statesman* (Princeton, 1994). On Marx, see Amanda Peralta . . . *med andra medel: Från Clausewitz till Guevara—krig, revolution och politik i en marxistisk idetradition* (Gothenburg, 1990). Raymond Aron's *Clausewitz* is a bit disappointing, considering Aron's philosophical credentials, but it says some useful things about polarity. Fanon's remarks are to be found in *The Wretched of the Earth* (New York, 1968), 38–9; having read the passage many times before without noting anything much, I was brought back to it through Ato Sekyi-Otu's *Fanon's Dialectic of Experience* (Cambridge, MA, 1996). Timo Pankakoski's "Carl Schmitt Versus the 'Intermediate State': International and Domestic Variants," in *History of European Ideas* 39:2 (2013), 241–66 has much of interest on both Schmitt and the intermediate state. Schmitt is not given a specific entry in my essay though he hovers in the background.

The lexical genealogy of the term in pristine form can only yield so much. One finds mention here and there but rarely relevant enough to affect the operative idea, if one can call it that. One serious addition: Eduard Bernstein, the German Social Democrat, speaks in 1893 of competitive armament as *"kalte Kriegsführung"* and indeed an "art of war"; and again in 1914 before war has broken out as *"diesen stillen Krieg, diesen Kalten Krieg, wie man ihn genannt hat, den Krieg der Rüstungen"*—he doesn't tell us who is calling it a cold war but the point is clearly that frantic armament itself becomes a kind of silent warfare, standing in reserve but expressive of hostility of warlike proportions. The idea could then be applied to our postwar context after 1945 or at least 1950. My view is that by the 1960s armaments in the most lethal domain, that is, the nuclear one, are deterrence, not war itself. The secondary reference here is Joseph M. Siracusa, "Will the Real Author of the Cold War Stand Up?," *SHAFR Newsletter* September 1982, 9–11. Siracusa in turn got it—I think—from fellow Australian Roger M. Fletcher's dissertation on Bernstein et al., published under the title *Revisionism and Empire: Socialist Imperialism in Germany 1897–1914* (London, 1984). For a more recent survey and argument, see Gilbert Achar, *The New Cold War: The United States, Russia, and China from Kosovo to Ukraine* (Chicago, 2023).

2
Liberty or Death: The Cold War as US Ideology

A few weeks after Harry Truman announced his Doctrine in March 1947, Dean Acheson went to Mississippi to give an address about the need for economic assistance to Europe. Joseph M. Jones, who had drafted much of the speech on Acheson's instructions, would later call the event "historymaking," a crucial part of that heroic moment in the spring of 1947 when US policy changed emphatically for the better and grand deeds were accomplished. The point of Acheson's speech was that without restored prosperity in important but now devastated economies abroad there would be no stability in the world and ultimately no security for the United States. It was an argument about political economy combined with a predictable exhortation to action. Attached to it was also a set of allusions, already obligatory, to the new cold-war frame of the Truman Doctrine. Thus Acheson spoke of the imperative to aid "free peoples" who were struggling to maintain their independence, democracy and freedom "against totalitarian pressures."[1]

Acheson was addressing the Delta Council, which is described in *Fifteen Weeks,* Jones's well-known book of the mid-1950s, as "a

---

1   Joseph Mario Jones, *The Fifteen Weeks* (New York, 1964 [1955]), 30, chap. 2, *passim*; Dean Acheson, "The Conduct of Foreign Relations: Requirements of Reconstruction," *Vital Speeches,* May 15, 1947, 485–7. Eric Foner originally alerted me to the Mississippi event. See his *Freedom: An American Story* (New York, 1998), 259.

remarkable organization of farmers and small businessmen." The Council, in Jones's view, had been a driving force behind much of the economic diversification that had turned the Mississippi Delta into "one of the most progressive and prosperous regions in the South." Acheson himself writes in his memoirs of "picturesque but ramshackle shanties giving way to neat, well-fenced farms and painted houses" and remembers the occasion as "an easy-going, good-natured, shirt-sleeved, thoroughly American one."[2]

An American occasion it may well have been but perhaps not in the sense Acheson had in mind. The Delta Council was in fact, as the most recent historian of the region puts it, "an advocacy organization for the largescale planting and business interests." One is not surprised to learn that it was lily-white in composition and segregationist in spirit. A leading member typically called it "a striking example of democracy at work," it being open to "any white person." In the elections a year later, 95 percent of this progressive region voted for Dixiecrats, extreme white supremacists in a US culture mired in white supremacy.[3]

Several things interest me about this episode. There is, as is already implied, the obvious hypocrisy of Acheson's language, the appeal to global principles of democracy and freedom amid a Southern regime dedicated to apartheid and racial oppression. More intriguing is the question of whether he failed to see the contradiction in 1947 or chose to ignore it. When he composed his memoirs in the late 1960s, a decade of bitter, sometimes lethal struggles over civil rights, he must surely have seen the problem; but he may just have found it impolitic to bring it up. For his memoirs were meant to counteract the "mood of depression, disillusion and withdrawal" among youth in the 1960s, so Acheson

---

2   Jones, *Fifteen Weeks*, 26; Dean Acheson, *Present at the Creation: My Years in the State Department* (New York, 1969), 228.

3   James C. Cobb, *The Most Southern Place on Earth: The Mississippi Delta and the Roots of Regional Identity* (New York, 1992), 207, 226; Nan Elizabeth Woodruff, "Mississippi Delta Planters and Debates over Mechanization, Labor, and Civil Rights in the 1940s," *Journal of Southern History* 60, no. 2 (May 1994): 263–84 (quotation on p. 269). William Wynn, who had invited Acheson (a stand-in for Truman) to the Council, was the "most prominent lawyer in the Delta" and the owner of a 10,000-acre plantation. See Ann Waldron, *Hodding Carter: The Reconstruction of a Racist* (Chapel Hill, NC, 1993), 68. Wynn's name is misspelled in Jones's and Acheson's accounts alike, the latter following the former.

wanted to tell a contrasting "tale of large conceptions, great achievements, and some failures."[4]

Such an intentional silence would have been quite in character, for Acheson did not much care about his rhetorical means as long as his strategic ends were accomplished. His most immediate object in Mississippi was to generate support for what would eventually become the Marshall Plan. There was also the long-term aim of putting the United States systematically into the world in a properly leading position once and for all. Such circumstances demanded hyperbole. One might thus read his binary language in an entirely tactical way, as necessary ideological ornamentation or the kind of complexity reduction required by any new system in need of distinguishing itself. Even the more ardent Harry S. Truman, in casting the cold war as a struggle of freedom against totalitarianism, had acknowledged in an underhanded way that his grand abstraction had asterisks, hinting that the democratic credentials of Greece were not perhaps altogether in order and contenting himself with referring to Turkey, the other designated target of military aid, merely as an "independent and economically sound state" in need of "modernization." It did not take a cynical observer, moreover, to see that, beyond Truman's division of the world into two antagonistic forms of life, what was really at stake at that moment was the strategic importance of the Eastern Mediterranean: geopolitics, in other words.[5]

Thus a strategic analysis, however reductionist, seems to have a certain local validity here. The central difficulty, after all, for US policymakers who think of themselves as internationalist has always been that the outside world matters a great deal less to the United States than the other way around. Thus the unending quest to justify actions abroad in a way that makes sense to the public, or more precisely, to sufficiently large segments of the dispersed ruling class as represented in the dispersed political system. It so happened here, as Acheson was keenly

---

4 Acheson, *Present at the Creation*, preface, n.p. Then again the "oversight" might also have been sheer Achesonian defiance. Notably, James Chace, Acheson's most recent biographer, retells the Delta story without seeing any irony either: *Acheson: The Secretary of State Who Created the American World* (New York, 1998), 171. Chace is an exemplar of a tendency now to turn Acheson into a symbolic representation of the heroic age, sadly passed, when there was a world policy stage for dramatic action to take place in the name of American internationalism.

5 Truman's speech can be found in Jones, *Fifteen Weeks*, 269–74. "Complexity reduction" is Niklas Luhmann's concept. See his *Social Systems* (Stanford, CA, 1995).

aware, that the local ruling class of the cotton kingdom was atypically connected to the world and hence receptive in principle to his economic logic. Yet he felt compelled ultimately to put the matter in Truman's dichotomous terms. A purely instrumental view of ideology as rhetorical means to strategic ends misses the question, then, of why internationalists deployed the particular political language they did and how they came to inhabit it.

From Slavery to Totalitarianism

The historical peculiarities involved were brought home to me forcefully when I reread NSC 68 recently. Three years after Truman's original binary, "slavery" had replaced "totalitarianism," a modern neologism, as the central antithesis of freedom. NSC 68, shortly to be given foundational status by the Korean War, revolves indeed almost obsessively around the epic struggle between freedom and slavery—a charged thematic in US history. Would it perhaps have affected Acheson's address to the Delta Council? To speak sternly of the need for a universal struggle against slavery in Mississippi would (one imagines) have triggered mixed feelings among the audience. Yet I was also reminded that numerous propagandists of the revolutionary era, in attacking the putatively despotic attempts of George III to enslave the colonies, did not stop to consider very long, if at all, the central, indeed decisive, role of actually existing slavery in colonial economy and society. Not everyone, it turned out, was born free in the land of the free or was invested with any inalienable rights; but this did not prevent the most uninhibited appeals to such universal principles or induce much sense of contradiction, paradox, and irony.[6]

These initial observations and questions occasioned second thoughts on an earlier attempt that addressed, in part and from another angle, freedom and slavery in the context of the cold war. That analysis had been prompted by the odd absence within cold-war historiography of

---

6 The full text of NSC 68 can be found in United States Department of State, *Foreign Relations of the United States* [*FRUS*], 1950, 1:237–92. All page references henceforth are to this volume. On views of slavery in the Revolution, see David Brion Davis, *The Problem of Slavery in the Age of Revolution, 1770–1823* (Ithaca, NY, 1975).

any extensive thought on what precisely it was that made the cold war a cold war. The focus, however, was on the polarity between war and peace: it seemed that one might begin to disentangle the concept by asking what sort of surrender it presupposed. Following the acute Walter Lippmann, who made the term a concept, I took the US refusal after mid-1947 to engage in normal diplomacy as the defining element in the cold war; and I saw this in turn as a development of the concept of unconditional surrender, taken directly from the Civil War, that Franklin D. Roosevelt had set forth on the eve of the American entry into World War II. He proposed, simply put, that because peace for dictators was really just a covert war, one could never achieve peace with them through negotiation, only by liquidation. This is the thinking that, when translated to the post-1947 period, made it possible for the authors of NSC 68 to intimate that the Soviet Union had initiated the cold war just by being the Soviet Union and to argue that any negotiations would have to be postponed until the moment (endlessly deferred) when the West had achieved such a position of strength that it could dictate terms. I then argued that the cold war ended in 1963, when the Kennedy regime recognized the Soviet Union as a legitimate great power and thus laid the foundation for détente (the preconditions being the Sino-Soviet split, the apparently final division of Germany, and, above all, the experience of the Cuban Missile Crisis).[7]

Taking that analysis as a given, then, I want to push the matter further by asking not so much what made the cold war a cold war but what made it into a specifically American one. My wager is that just as Roosevelt's reference to the Civil War was not merely one of his typical whims, the related appearance of freedom and slavery in NSC 68 signifies something more than empty rhetoric. The latter trope has a long genealogy in the United States, going back beyond the Civil War through the Revolution

---

7 The original argument was put forth in Anders Stephanson, "The United States," in D. Reynolds, ed., *The Origins of the Cold War in Europe: International Perspectives* (New Haven, CT, 1994), an amended version of which is reproduced in chapter five of the present volume. The corollary, "Fourteen Notes on the Very Idea of a Cold War," was first published on *H-DIPLO* and now appears in slightly revised form as chapter 1. John F. Kennedy, though not figuring here, thought about foreign relations more systematically than any President since Wilson. Only Richard Nixon compares. See chapter 11. Kennedy is also the only one to my knowledge to quote both Patrick Henry's "liberty or death" and Abraham Lincoln's "half slave/half free"—neither instance being his finest hour.

into the seventeenth century. It represents, in fact, a deep and extended tradition. Far more intricate than any simple Manicheanism, that tradition fuses (in the main) radical Protestantism with classical republican and liberal thought, generating a specifically American language of politics, unthinkable anywhere else. It is a language of evil plots, sins and sinners, demons and saviors, corruption and redemption, dramatic choices in the name of humanity by anointed leaders on the edge of the abyss. And it is, also, a language about freedom and slavery and unconditional surrender. Since this peculiar vocabulary is also what, in my view, came to define the cold war, it seems worthwhile to attempt to chart it, perhaps as part of a more general quest for the sources of the US conduct. Is there, I ask, more than a superficial connection between Patrick Henry's "Give me liberty or give me death" and "Better dead than red"?[8]

My central reference point for this necessarily sketchy essay will remain NSC 68, the always useful Kennan intermittently providing auxiliary materials for contrast. It should be underlined that I do not intend to give a full analysis of NSC 68 and its many tensions and contradictions. Rather, I read it exclusively in terms of how its organizing thematic of freedom and slavery relates to a wider historical tradition that perhaps can best be described as freedom under siege. Such an exploration, it should be added, goes against the grain of much recent speculation on the cold war, which tends to focus on the Eastern side of the equation—as though the only controversial aspect regarding the Western side is the adequacy of its response.

---

8   William Wirt Henry, *Patrick Henry: Life, Correspondence and Speeches*, vol. I (New York, 1969 [1891]), 266. It is not certain that Henry ever uttered his immortal words, for the speech was reconstructed much after the fact. He is alleged to have put it thus: "'Is life so dear, or peace so sweet, as to be purchased at the price of chains and slavery?' No, 'Give me liberty, or give me death.'" Whatever the exact wording, it was not an unusual piece of rhetoric. The Second Continental Congress declared itself resolved in 1775 "to die freemen rather than to live slaves." Henry had perhaps a deeper personal sense for the contradictions involved than his slave-owning colleague Thomas Jefferson. As David Brion Davis says of Jefferson, he had a remarkable "capacity to sound like an enlightened reformer while upholding the interests of the planter class." See *The Problem of Slavery*, 182; see also Garry Wills, *Inventing America: Jefferson's Declaration of Independence* (New York, 1978), chap. 10.

Freedom and Slavery in the American Image

Freedom and slavery form a conceptual field in which the agents of the negative pole take on more than one guise: tyranny, despotism, and totalitarianism, to name the most prominent that were used interchangeably in the 1940s and '50s. Yet the first principle, the overdetermining *a priori,* so to speak, is not the negation, or the specific threat emanating from it, or even freedom as such—a master signifier that has taken on quite different concrete meanings and forms in US history.[9] The first principle, rather, is the dynamic notion that freedom is always already under threat, internally as well as externally, and that it must be defended by those so called upon. Freedom (or liberty) is understood as independence, as not being dependent on the will of any outside power. This state is natural, something innately given. Any loss of freedom, any movement in the direction of dependence, is defined as slavery. Such dependence/slavery does not have to be actual: the very threat of arbitrary imposition on the still independent self is a form of slavery because it is a constriction, a diminution, of autonomy.[10] The NSC 68 version of this posits that slavery cannot tolerate the very existence of freedom as an idea and must systemically attempt its liquidation. Freedom and its vanguard defender are thus "mortally challenged by the Soviet system" precisely because diversity and openness are inherently unacceptable to that system in turn.[11]

There are at least four partly overlapping sources for this notion, in one way or another traceable to England in the seventeenth century. First and foremost, there is the Judeo-Christian component, which takes two forms. "Man" is free and has rights to liberty because he is made in the image of God, who is the very definition of independence. This is then coupled with the powerful narrative, much intensified by the radical Reformation, about the persecuted remnant struggling to represent God's righteousness on earth until redemption and the final judgment take place. The outside is evil, and evil is by definition hostile and expansive. To confront and struggle against it, however, is not to mix with it

---

9   See Foner, *Freedom.*
10 I am following Quentin Skinner, *Liberty Before Liberalism* (Cambridge, 1998), chap. 1. See also Blair Worden's review in the *London Review of Books,* February 5, 1998.
11 NSC 68, 389.

but to suppress and extinguish it. As Calvin declared: "It is the godly man's duty to abstain from all familiarity with the wicked, and not to enmesh himself with them in any voluntary relationship." Crucially, however, the evil outside is potentially also present on the inside, if for no other reason than because we are sinners.

The history of the given community can then be written in terms of a series of apostasies, regenerations, and subsequent returns to first principles. To lead a Christian life, meanwhile, is always to resist the ever-present threat of the Devil or Antichrist. The latter impostor becomes an archetype in Protestant thought. The Pope is his first incarnation. For the English, more particularly, it is the Pope's successive agents, the great powers Spain and France, that come to fill the role. For the wayward descendants of this view in New England, however, the Antichrist would eventually appear in the guise of London; but by then antipopery had already blended with the general attack on tyranny and superstition. Various anti-Catholic movements, however, will recur in the United States until the cold war finally makes Catholicism truly American (and thus makes possible, if only barely, the election of the first Catholic president).[12]

The classical republican tradition, a strong and surviving one in the political language of the United States, is cyclical and more internalist in that freedom, indissolubly linked to community virtue, is always under threat from the inherent tendency to corruption and degeneration. It is a story about decline and fall, the central analytical reference being the

---

12 I have relied, chiefly, on Christopher Hill, *Antichrist in Seventeenth-Century England* (London, 1970); J. G. A. Pocock, *The Machiavellian Moment: Florentine Political Thought and the Atlantic Republican Tradition* (Princeton, NJ, 1975), chap. 15; Skinner, *Liberty Before Liberalism;* Kathleen Wilson, *The Sense of the People: Politics, Culture and Imperialism in England, 1715–1785* (Cambridge, 1995); Charles Taylor, *Sources of the Self: The Making of Modern Identity* (Cambridge, MA, 1989), 230; Robert M. Kingdon, "Calvinism and Resistance Theory, 1550–1580," in *The Cambridge History of Political Thought 1450–1700*, ed. J. H. Burns (Cambridge, 1991), 193–218; Dan Jacobson, *The Story of the Stories: The Chosen People and Its God* (New York, 1982); Ernest W. Nicholson, *God and His People: Covenant and Theology in the Old Testament* (Oxford, 1986); Sacvan Bercovitch, *The Rites of Assent: Transformations in the Symbolic Construction of America* (New York, 1993); J. C. D. Clark, *The Language of Liberty 1660–1832: Political Discourse and Social Dynamics in the Anglo-American World* (Cambridge, 1994). Calvin is quoted in Adam Seligman, "The Eucharist Sacrifice and the Changing Utopian Moment in Post-Reformation Christianity," in *Order and Transcendence: The Role of Utopias and the Dynamics of Civilizations*, ed. A. Seligman (Leiden, 1989).

fate of Rome. In the best of cases the story continues with regeneration and a return to virtue. Americans of the eighteenth and nineteenth century often imagined that they had escaped from this infernal historical trap, the continental expanse offering the stage for the final victory of liberty: instead of being a source of corruption, expansion becomes a safeguard against it.[13]

Such self-confident visions became rarer or at least more ambivalent in the twentieth century. As NSC 68 laments, a free society is vulnerable

> in that it is easy for people to lapse into excesses—the excesses of a permanently open mind wishfully waiting for evidence that evil design may become noble purpose, the excess of faith becoming prejudice, the excess of tolerance degenerating into indulgence of conspiracy and the excess of resorting to suppression when more moderate measures are not only more appropriate but more effective.

However, with a huge military buildup in mind, Paul Nitze and his coauthors are in this regard far more optimistic than George Kennan, Nitze's predecessor, for whom domestic ignorance, the corruptions of mass consumption and the evils of laxity offered the materials for a veritable jeremiad on domestic decline, a threat ultimately far more important to him than the actual Soviet one.[14]

The modern liberal discourse on individual freedom, emerging in the American Revolution and becoming fully articulated in the nineteenth century, is significant here chiefly because of its view of government and the role this view plays in the proliferating talk about freedom in the 1930s and onward. Liberty is individual liberty unconstrained by government except under the rule of (minimal) law. Power is assumed intrinsically to expand, encroach, and corrupt, never more so than in the case of centralized state power. Government as a phenomenon is therefore not only to be rigorously restricted in scope; it is by definition always too big, whence it follows that it is also

---

13 See Bernard Bailyn, *The Ideological Origins of the American Revolution* (Cambridge, MA, 1967); Pocock, *The Machiavellian Moment*, chap. 15.

14 NSC 68, 254–5. An outline of Kennan's jeremiad can be found in my *Kennan and the Art of Foreign Policy* (Cambridge, MA, 1989), part III.

always suspect. Interventionist liberals from the Progressive Era contest this view in the name of sound management, republican community, countervailing forces to new and gigantic forms of private power, and so forth.

The massive expansion of state authority in the New Deal then turns this conflict into a remarkably polemical one: the conservative or, more accurately, classical liberal reaction to Roosevelt centers on endangered individual and entrepreneurial liberty, after which much of the politics of the Depression comes to revolve discursively around that problem. Roosevelt appropriates this language with great skill and turns it against his accusers, expanding the notion of what it is to be free to include the right to minimal social and economic security and, famously, railing against the despotism of economic royalists. This conception is then readily available to him when he wants to explain to the US public in 1939–41 what is taking place abroad. By connecting lawless aggression with the narrative of the Civil War and the eternal struggle everywhere against creeping tyranny, Roosevelt was able to articulate his long-term goals in terms of the "four freedoms." Not until these had been everywhere secured would the struggle end (as would indeed history).[15]

A final aspect of freedom under siege is less pronounced in our context but worth mentioning because it lurks somewhere beneath the surface throughout. It is the idea of ancient Anglo-Saxon liberties. The eighteenth-century argument (of which Thomas Jefferson was a strong proponent) locates the origin of the celebrated ancient English liberties, which the American colonists were presumably fatally about to lose, in the tribal origins of the Teutons. History since the early Middle Ages can then be told as a series of usurpations by alien forces such as the Normans, or, alternatively, by power-hungry domestic tyrants and other corrupting interests, ever-present threats against which the defenders of ancient freedoms must ceaselessly struggle. In the nineteenth century this narrative becomes deeply enmeshed with quasi-scientific racism

---

15 On government and liberalism, see Michel Foucault, *Discipline and Punish* (New York, 1979), 89–90; Graham Burchell, C. Gordon, and Peter Miller, *The Foucault Effect: Studies in Governmentality* (Chicago, 1991); and Carl Schmitt, *The Concept of the Political* (New Brunswick, NJ, 1976). On FDR, see Daniel T. Rodgers, *Contested Truths: Keywords in American Politics Since Independence* (New York, 1987), 214–15; Foner, *Freedom*, chap. 9.

and eventually it is submerged in a more general, sometimes overtly imperialist, discourse on "civilization."[16]

What is common to these four dispositions is the imperative of vigilance for the sake of preserving freedom (in every sense), as well as the concomitant idea that any loss of freedom is slavery. As the United States is defined as the repository of freedom, any threat to it is a threat of enslavement and is against the basic principles of humankind. Any conflict, consequently, tends to become a question of antagonistic "ways of life" (to paraphrase the Truman Doctrine). Hence, too, the otherwise peculiar presumption of something called the American way and the auxiliary, more sinister, thesis that something or someone can be un-American.

The Negative Agent

I now want to explore the character of the negative agent, which is more of a structural position than anything real. Not that it is devoid of reality, but its function is largely derived from the assumption that freedom is under perpetual threat. While the structural space of enmity remains a constant, various concrete targets can fill it. Thus the enslaving tyrant has shifted from (to name but a few) King George III, whose "long train of abuses and usurpations" aimed to subjugate the colonies "under absolute Despotism," to the scheming slave power in the 1850s, to autocracy

---

16   Reginald Horsman, *Race and Manifest Destiny: The Origins of Racial Anglo-Saxonism* (Cambridge, MA, 1981); Garret Ward Sheldon, *The Political Philosophy of Thomas Jefferson* (Baltimore, MD, 1991), 25–7. Jefferson, as Horsman says (*Race and Manifest Destiny*, 21), believed in an "ideal Anglo-Saxon England" featuring "small political units" and "an elective king, annual parliaments, a system of trial by jury, and land held in fee simple." Where this vision eventually terminates can be gauged by the following view on Hawaii, expressed in the House of Representatives in 1898: "Sir, the fittest will survive. Under the providence of God, Anglo-Celtic civilization is accomplishing the regeneration of the planet. Its progress dispels barbarism and establishes order, dethrones despotism and ushers in liberty. Nothing can stay the onward march of the indomitable race that founded this Republic—the race which sooner or later will place the imprint of its genius and the stamp of its conscience upon civilizations everywhere." The "Anglo-Celtic" here was connected explicitly to the overall "conquest of the world by the Aryan races," January 20, 1898, Appendix to *Congressional Record, 55th Congress, 2nd Sess.* (Washington, DC, 1898).

in general and Germany in particular during World War I, to Kremlin-directed world communism after 1947.[17]

As NSC 68 would have it, the enslaving agent is bound by its very nature to destroy freedom and to that extent it is defined by the latter rather than by its own terms. Freedom is always about independence and what drives tyranny to enslave is the functional need to rid the world of any such autonomous sources of potential opposition, inside as well as outside. Consequently, the system is relentlessly searching to destroy what is not identical to itself. Tyranny is, however, also inherently unstable, for it is based in the end on the arbitrary will of the one rather than on the impersonal, constraining rule of law, the precondition of any free system. We recognize much of this analysis from Kennan's early cold-war writings; NSC 68 repeats it in cruder form.

Kennan, incidentally, also articulates an older Christian theme in this context. One ought not to complain too much about the evil deeds of the Kremlin, he says at the end of the X article, but be grateful instead

> to a Providence which, by providing the American people with this implacable challenge, has made their entire security as a nation dependent on their pulling themselves together and accepting the responsibilities of moral and political leadership that history plainly intended them to bear.[18]

Evil is a challenge, in short, sent by God to punish his people for their sundry misdeeds and to provide them, ingeniously, with a threat that will serve to regenerate them—if they choose to do the right thing. The same providentialist argument—a standard Christian explanation (against Manichaean heresies) for the existence of evil in a world supposedly governed by an omnipotent God—tends to appear throughout colonial and US history whenever a threat or crisis of difference occurs. Kennan's point, interestingly, follows his critique of the Soviet regime for its structural need of enemies and messianic belief in its own special place in history.[19]

---

17   The quotations are from the Declaration of Independence.
18   From Kennan's "The Sources of Soviet Conduct," written under the pseudonym X
19   George F. Kennan, writing as X, "The Sources of Soviet Conduct," *Foreign Affairs* 25, no. 4 (July 1947): 566–82 (quotation on p. 582).

The diagnosis of arbitrariness, lawlessness and usurpation of liberties is to no little degree derived from classical antiquity and especially the kind of aristocratic critique of individual power grabbing one finds in Cicero—though it is mediated through neo-Roman thinkers such as Machiavelli. There is, however, a related but more immediate source of particular relevance here, namely Montesquieu. In the mid-seventeenth century, he originated the concept of the "oriental despot," mostly as a coded warning (in the name of moderate aristocracy) that the French monarchy was deviating into a form of "Asiatic despotism." Voltaire, more favorably disposed toward both the East and absolute monarchy, said of Montesquieu's concept that he had "made for himself a hideous phantom in order to fight against it."[20]

This hideous phantom (for it had very little to do with the actually existing Ottoman Empire, its chief referent) is sharply dualistic. On the one hand, there is the all-powerful despot, on the other, his totally anonymous subjects, counting for nothing. They prostrate themselves before his every whim, before a despotic will that is wholly arbitrary, lawless and unpredictable. The result is random executions and torture. The system is devoid of legitimacy and works in the exclusive interest of its secretive ruler. Montesquieu also claims (following Aristotle) that despotic power is irreversible: it can be crushed from outside or collapse under its own internal contradictions but, crucially, it will not evolve into nondespotism. To this image he adds the Oriental lust for goods and sex.[21] That last luridness aside, however,

---

20 On Montesquieu, see Alain Grosrichard, *The Sultan's Court: European Fantasies of the East* (London, 1998); Voltaire is quoted on p. 31; and see also Springborg, *Western Republicanism and the Oriental Prince* (Cambridge, 1992). On the classical aristocratic critique of tyranny, see Hanna Fenichel Pitkin, "Are Freedom and Liberty Twins?," *Political Theory* 16, no. 4 (1988): 523–52. Indeed, the aristocratic components (equality before the law, equal right to speak) in subsequent theories of equality are not appreciated enough. The key question in liberalism (as opposed to democracy) is then always who qualifies for such equality, who counts. On Rome, see Chaim Wirszubski, *Libertas as a Political Idea at Rome During the Late Republic and Early Principate* (Cambridge, 1950) and Timothy J. Cornell, "Rome: The History of an Anachronism," in *City States in Classical Antiquity and Medieval Italy*, eds. Anthony Mahlo, Kurt Raaflaub, and Julia Emlen (Ann Arbor, MI, 1991). On Greece, see Kurt A. Raaflaub, "Democracy, Oligarchy, and the Concept of the 'Free Citizen' in Late Fifth-Century Athens," *Political Theory* 11, no. 4 (1983): 517–44.

21 See Mladen Dolar's introduction to Grosrichard, *The Sultan's Court*. Fear is the central principle of despotism and it envelops even the ruler himself, as Montesquieu argues in *The Spirit of the Laws* (Cambridge, 1989); see especially part I. Corruption is not only inescapable but turns in on and feeds on itself.

his account could stand as a fairly accurate summary of the US analysis of Stalin's regime.

Montesquieu's contrast between East and West eventually becomes an integral part of the emerging liberal argument about legitimacy, law and contracts. A legitimate as opposed to arbitrary social order is defined by the degree to which members of civil society are understood to have had a say in its construction, consented to it, and thus sanctioned its laws. Hence the colonial idea in the 1770s that George III was really only a representative, the "Chief Magistrate" of the empire, and that any monarchical imposition was therefore despotism, usurpation, and slavery, illegitimate acts against which one had the natural right, conceptually speaking, to commit regicide. Members of a properly legitimate order, by contrast, are obliged by their theoretical participation through representation to follow the given rules, which is why, presumably, this is a stable system as opposed to the artificial and essentially fragile structure of despotism. To break the rules is thus criminal to the point of treason, constituting in principle nothing less than an exit from society altogether and the forfeit of all rights to equal status. Extralegal opposition, consequently, can be treated and punished harshly as criminality. "No liberty for the enemies of liberty," as the old Jacobin apothegm of Saint-Just would have it.[22]

A similar notion of obligation can then be extended by later liberals to something imagined as the international community. The coalition of World War II, I think, was grasped in the United States as an embryonic form of international community in that contractual sense. When the Soviet Union was then seen lawlessly to break the given agreements—not living up to Yalta—one could reclassify it as just

---

22 See Foucault, *Discipline and Punish*, 89–90. I owe Saint-Just's apothegm to Michael Christofferson's dissertation, "The Anti-Totalitarian Moment in French Intellectual Politics, 1975–1984" (Columbia University, 1997). The peculiar effect of invoking such ethical principles tends to be the exit of ethics: "Our free society, confronted by a threat to its basic values, naturally will take such action, including the use of military force, as may be required to protect those values. The integrity of our system will not be jeopardized by any measures, covert or overt, violent or nonviolent, which serve the purposes of frustrating the Kremlin design, nor does the necessity for conducting ourselves so as to affirm our values in actions as well as words forbid such measures, provided only they are appropriately calculated to that end and are not so excessive or misdirected as to make us enemies of the people instead of the evil men who have enslaved them" (NSC 68, 244). This notorious formulation, ironically, was composed by John Paton Davies, soon to be exiled from the State Department and the country by McCarthyism.

another treacherous gangster regime that had to be liquidated, or, barring that, kept rigidly within its bounds, whilst the United States would reorganize and order the vast part of the now truncated one world that remained free or at least potentially so. The contractual theory of liberal society served in that sense to exacerbate the negative view of the Soviet adversary.

Kennan, in his more historical moods, possibly under Gibbon's influence, sometimes fell into Orientalist themes;[23] but the despotic matrix otherwise became part and parcel of a more general image of a particular form of antithetical, non-Western power. A striking contradictory division marks this image, especially in NSC 68. On the one hand, despotism is essentially brittle and unstable because (as already conceived of by Montesquieu) it lacks the organic ties and moderation of legitimate Western society; on the other, unlike the visibly regressive Ottoman Empire, contemporary Soviet despotism is developmentally dynamic, technologically on the advance, and organizationally powerful, capable, in short, of mobilizing immense hostile force. This contrast between weakness and strength is never resolved (or combined) into a single analytical frame.

In NSC 68 it thus appears as a constant oscillation. Yet the conceptual problem need not be resolved because the authors are not really interested in analyzing Soviet realities. Their strategic object is the massive mobilization and assertion of US power, but the point is not to launch any fundamental offensive against the bastions of Soviet despotism (the militant rhetorical gestures along these lines are typically short on substance). The aim instead is to create an irrevocable superpower and to order the non-Soviet world, for which purpose it is sometimes useful to posit Soviet strength, sometimes Soviet weakness. The theme of irreversibility, the structural inability of the Soviet system to reform and evolve, is assumed; qualitative change, meaning essentially destruction, can only come through the confrontation (as opposed to cooperation) with outside power dialectically combined with inside breakdown. On this basis, and on the other premise that Soviet despotism is a deadly,

---

23 William Pietz exaggerates this theme in arguing that the Western concept of totalitarianism in the postwar era essentially amounted to Orientalism plus technology. Pietz, "The 'Post-Colonialism' of Cold War Discourse," *Social Text* 19/20 (Fall 1988), 55–75. He had much more of a point, however, than my acid criticism of it in the same issue would indicate.

expansive threat, one can then proceed to more important things. Hence the curiously formulaic nature of the many passages about Kremlin evils, and hence the absence of any concrete analysis of the Soviet Union. Hence, too, the otherwise astonishing fact that no Soviet experts were consulted during the composition of the policy paper.[24]

Charles Bohlen, one such expert, was thus to complain to Nitze, quite rightly, that there had been no effort to assess "the great body of Soviet thought in regard to war between states or the even more elementary fact that any war . . . carries with it major risks to the Soviet system in Russia"; the apparent aim of NSC 68 being, as he added, "merely to justify the need for military buildup."[25]

Designs

Bohlen, sensing the abstract form of argument in NSC 68, also criticized its obsession with the "Kremlin design," the vision, as he put it, of some "mechanical chess player" with a fully worked out plan for "world domination."[26] Here Bohlen had hit upon something with deeper implications than perhaps he realized. The Kremlin design (often referred to as "fundamental") is contrasted asymmetrically in NSC 68 with "the purpose of the United States." The Soviet regime, then, is a clique in the Kremlin and not comparable to a properly legitimate country such as the United States. That the former has "designs" while the latter has a "purpose" is intrinsic to the distinction. For "design," meaning a secret plot, is a word with a long lineage in the always abundant language of conspiracy in the United States, a language that tends to find such schemes at the center of most alien threats. Designs are the very *modus operandi* of the illicit, enslaving power. Thus Jefferson, for example,

---

24 On the struggles of producing NSC 68, see David Callaghan, *Dangerous Capabilities: Paul Nitze and the Cold War* (New York, 1990), chap. 4. The "irreversibility" theme would of course reappear to good effect in Jeane Kirkpatrick's celebrated distinction in the 1970s between authoritarian and totalitarian governments.

25 Bohlen to Secretary of State, October 9, 1951, *FRUS*, 1951, 1:181.

26 Bohlen to Nitze, July 28, 1951, ibid., 107. Bohlen lost out here because he accepted (he thought) the basic premises of NSC 68. He was always a better political operator than Kennan, by then departed. However, while aware that something was profoundly wrong, Bohlen did not possess the intellectual depth and stamina to challenge Nitze's onslaught.

writes darkly of "a deliberate, systematic plan of reducing us to slavery"; and the subsequent Declaration of Independence speaks of the usurping "design" of the London tyrant. FDR refers to "the Nazi design to abolish the freedom of the seas" and achieve a "new world order." NSC 68 mentions the term no less than twenty-seven times.[27]

The arch-design here is probably to be found in English fears of the Catholic Counter-Reformation, with its College of Propaganda and sinister, secret vanguard of Jesuits; but there are numerous similar plots in its wake, all aiming to undermine liberty and righteousness. The devious design is typically stealthy in its effectuation, a creeping, slow movement to take over, cunningly orchestrated by secret cabals. Curiously, the advent of secularized rationalism in the eighteenth century reinforces this way of thinking: what appears on the surface must have some hidden but detectable cause of an instrumental nature.[28]

Catholics became a favored target in the antebellum period, as their religion was not only alien but lethally opposed to true America. "The systems," as one fervent critic argued, "are diametrically opposed: one must and will exterminate the other." Masons and Mormons, on a lesser scale, found themselves denounced in similar ways. But it is in the 1850s and during the Civil War that these political visions reach a crescendo in the attacks on the evil "slave Power."[29]

---

27 Jefferson, quoted in Gordon S. Wood, *The Creation of the American Republic, 1776–1787* (Chapel Hill, NC, 1998 [1969]), 39; Roosevelt, fireside chat, September 11, 1941, *The Public Papers and Addresses of Franklin D. Roosevelt* (New York, 1942), 10:386. A month later, FDR indicated another Nazi design, referring to a secret map of five future vassal states in the Western hemisphere.

28 On designs and plots, see Wood, *The Creation*, 39–42; David Brion Davis, *The Slave Power Conspiracy and the Paranoid Style* (Baton Rouge, 1969); Thomas M. Brown, "The Image of the Beast: Anti-Papal Rhetoric in Colonial America," in *Conspiracy: The Fear of Subversion in American History*, Richard O. Curry and Thomas M. Brown, eds. (New York: Holt, 1972); David Brion Davis, "Some Themes of Countersubversion: An Analysis of AntiMasonic, Anti-Catholic, and Anti-Mormon Literature," in ibid.; Clark, *Language of Liberty*, 39; Michael Lienesch, *New Order of the Ages: Time, the Constitution, and the Making of Modern American Political Thought* (Princeton, NJ, 1988), 208.

29 Davis, *The Slave Power Conspiracy*; quotation in Davis, "Some Themes of Countersubversion," 67.

The American Way of Conflict

Indeed, abolitionist writings offer a veritable inventory of the kinds of arguments one finds a century later in cold-war thinking. Consider, for example, the bizarre notion of "Captive Nations," coupling black slaves in the 1850s with Soviet "satellites" in the 1950s. Thus when William Henry Channing refers to Southern politicians as "a disciplined corps, schooled in the art of managing a small, embodied force, so as to subjugate vast multitudes," one recognizes the formula. Similarly so when Carl Schurz holds that "the slave power" cannot tolerate free labor, that it "is impelled by the irresistible power of necessity" to oppress its opponents and that it is systemically forced to seek "extension by an aggressive foreign policy." "The two principles," maintained the powerful preacher Theodore Parker, were "mutually invasive and destructive," and one must "overcome the other." The two could not coexist. The conflict, then, in Seward's famous word, was truly "irrepressible."[30]

Against that backdrop, it is intriguing to read Arthur Schlesinger Jr.'s attack in 1949 on the revisionist historians who had criticized abolitionist fanaticism for its role in bringing about the Civil War. Schlesinger connects abolitionism with anti-Nazism in the 1930s and anti-communism in his own times. Slavery, being a "betrayal of the basic values of our Christian and democratic tradition," opened up a conflict "far too profound to be solved by compromise." Just as one must not fall into any "sentimental theories about the needlessness of the Civil War," one must not now regard "our own struggles against evil as equally needless." For, he concludes, "the unhappy fact is that man occasionally works himself into a log-jam; and that the log-jam must be burst by violence."[31]

What manner of suitable violence Schlesinger was prescribing for unsentimental anticommunists of the moment is not clear. The model, however, is clearly Roosevelt's internationalist turn in 1939–40, seen as the reenactment of the activist Civil War period. Roosevelt's own appropriation of Civil War tropes occurred, of course, after the fact so to speak. It was a conscious play on what is today thought of as historical

---

30   Davis, *The Slave Power Conspiracy*, 11, 56, and *passim*; Carl Schurz, *The Speeches, Correspondence and Political Papers of Carl Schurz*, ed. Frederic Bancroft (New York, 1913), 1:130–33; Theodore Parker, *The Rights of Man in America* (Boston, n.d.), 367.

31   Arthur M. Schlesinger, Jr, "The Causes of the Civil War," *Partisan Review*, 10, October 1949, 969–81, quotations on pp. 979, 980.

memory. His actions were generated by his immediate experience of the 1930s, which persuaded him that the traditional distinction between war and peace had been blurred by the escalating aggressions of the dictators, by the piecemeal aggression promulgated in the name of "pacification," as he put it. The only real peace possible with these criminals was thus, in his words, "the peace that comes from complete surrender." It was in that context that, later, he invoked Unionist memories of the Civil War and referred to his policy as "unconditional surrender"—the policy of crushing the Confederacy because it was treason and because it embodied, presumably, the deeply un-American principle of slavery. It was a policy conveniently represented in the person of U. S. Grant, whose initials combined in a single sign the Unionist nation with the total war it implied and required.[32]

In June 1940, along the same lines, Roosevelt's new secretary of war, Henry Stimson, declared, on the authority of Lincoln, that the world could no longer survive "half slave and half free." Lincoln had used the formulation in his militant House Divided speech; and the biblical quotation about the house/nation he had borrowed from Theodore Parker. Stimson turned the house/nation into the whole world, wherein one principle or the other would have to emerge victorious. Between two incompatible principles, between self-government and despotism, between the everlasting norm of right and wrong, there could, again, be no compromise. This was very much Roosevelt's stated position as well: there could be no adjudication between "good and evil," as he said, "only total victory."[33]

---

32 Franklin D. Roosevelt, *The Public Papers and Addresses of Franklin D. Roosevelt. 1940 Volume: War—and Aid to Democracies* (New York, 1941), 9:xxx. On the genesis and various aspects of "unconditional surrender," see Anne Armstrong, *Unconditional Surrender: The Impact of the Casablanca Policy on World War II* (New Brunswick, NJ, 1961); Raymond G. O'Connor, *Diplomacy for Victory: FDR and Unconditional Surrender* (New York, 1971); Michael Balfour, "The Origin of the Formula: 'Unconditional Surrender' in World War II," *Armed Forces and Society*, 5:2 (1979): 281–301; Charles B. Strozier, "Unconditional Surrender and the Rhetoric of Total War: From Truman to Lincoln," Occasional paper 2 (New York, 1987).

33 Stimson quoted in the *New York Times*, June 15, 1940; Franklin D. Roosevelt, State of the Union Address, January 6, 1942, *The Public Papers and Addresses of Franklin D. Roosevelt* (New York, 1943), 11:42. The evidence for Lincoln's borrowing is circumstantial. In 1854, Parker gave a speech that highlighted the metaphor, and Lincoln read his assembled speeches, which were passed on by his law partner, one of Parker's correspondents. It was a deeply pessimistic speech: "See the steady triumph of

The no-compromise formula (which Roosevelt had adopted before the United States was actually at war) was a logical stance. If one posits an absolute conflict between eternal principles of moral right and moral wrong, then it makes sense that anything outside the former is by definition wholly unacceptable. An effect of this image of absolute antagonism was that domestic opponents of mobilization tended to be removed from the acceptable political map, classed, as Roosevelt once classed them, as "appeaser fifth columnists." Most opponents were crushed politically by Pearl Harbor anyway. Forthwith, they had to accept strong government, though significantly only when the new concept of national security was linked to US freedom, and the threat of tyrannical aggression. Acheson learned that lesson well. Eisenhower would of course raise some warning flags here; but these were largely gestures. For, as of 1941, it would always be possible in principle to argue the case for enormous military spending on the grounds that security and freedom were in danger. The meaning of freedom was also transformed early in the cold war: Roosevelt's "freedom from want" was symbolically replaced by "free enterprise" and given a much more patriotic and nationalist coloration.[34]

What is established, then, by the manner in which Roosevelt chose to situate the antifascist struggle in part as a reenactment of the Civil War (and by extension the American Revolution) is a certain notion of

---

despotism! Ten years more, like ten years past, and it will be all over with the liberties of America. Everything must go down, and the heel of the tyrant will be on our neck." Parker, *The Rights of Man in America*, 390–91; "House Divided" appears on p. 362. The biblical allusion is to Matthew 12:25: "Every kingdom divided against itself is brought to desolation; and every city or house divided against itself shall not stand." A little further on, Jesus says: "He who is not with me is against me; and he that gathereth not with me scattereth abroad" (King James Bible, the one Lincoln and Parker would have read; see also Luke 11). On Parker, see Perry Miller, "Theodore Parker: Apostasy within Liberalism," in Perry Miller, *Nature's Nation* (Cambridge, MA, 1967). On Lincoln, see Michael Burlingame, *The Inner World of Abraham Lincoln* (Urbana, IL, 1994), chap. 2.

34 David Green, *Shaping Political Consciousness: The Language of Politics in America from McKinley to Reagan* (Ithaca, NY, 1987), chap. 5; Roosevelt quotation on p. 155; Rodgers, *Contested Truths*, 214; Foner, *Freedom*, chap. 11. Propagating an image of the United States as the epitome of the free world reached formidable expression in the Freedom Train that toured the United States and achieved a massive audience in fall 1947, carrying on display, among other things, the Declaration of Independence and the Gettysburg Address. The proposal to include the Four Freedoms speech was declined.

absolute antagonism and enmity.[35] "Freedom under siege," accordingly, would act to defend itself with all the means at its disposal. The ensuing war did indeed become in every sense a total one, reaching its most unflinching expression on the Western side in vast firebombings and atomic blasts against civilian populations. The only truly peaceful and secure world would henceforth be one in which outlaws and dictators were extinct and everyone adhered to the fundamental principles of humanity, which, as Wilson had already said, were those embodied in the United States. In essence, this was to argue that everything that is not a true peace is by definition war and that there can be no such peace with certain powers because of qualities in their domestic makeup.)[36] Since it turned out that by 1947 the Soviet Union was not only failing to agree to these propositions but actively counteracting them, it had to be an absolute enemy in the manner that Roosevelt had outlined, whether formal conditions of peace obtained or not. In short, there could be no fundamental peace with Moscow and in the world as a whole until the Soviet Union was no longer the Soviet Union.

This, one should add, was not quite what Roosevelt had had in mind when he formulated his position in 1940–41. He was aware, in the end, that not all dictators are alike. The Hitler-Stalin Pact and the Winter War against the Finns could thus be put aside in 1941 and earlier sentiments of geopolitical affinity brought to the fore, narrativized with remarkable success as "United Nations alliance for eternal peace." When this story turned out to be untrue, it was replaced with equal celerity and power by the idea that totalitarian dictators are, after all, all alike.[37] This view became orthodoxy in the Truman administration.

Yet if NSC 68 thus chooses to define the Soviet Union as a total war against freedom and thinks that only the US counter-threat of "a global war of annihilation" is preventing more actual aggression, the authors

---

35 Talking increasingly about fascism in the late 1930s, Roosevelt studiously avoided negative labels such as "anti-fascist." But he used the derogatory term with some historical license, dubbing, for instance, the regime of George III "a fascist yoke." Green, *Shaping Political Consciousness*, 146.

36 Schmitt, *The Concept of the Political*. Here, in part, lies the origin of Wilson's repressive side.

37 A similarly startling shift takes place with regard to "Red China," a hideous phantom indeed throughout the 1960s but transformed in a few years to a land of idealistic barefoot doctors (and a quasi-ally). Such images have very little anchoring in any real social practices and are thus remarkably changeable.

know too that a full-scale war is not about to happen within the immediate future and that it would be a catastrophe. A certain equivocation thus pervades the document. For having offered the first fully codified image of the limitlessly evil empire, NSC 68 finds itself a little short on countermoves commensurate with the monstrous nature of the adversary. This particular logjam, alas, is not resolvable by violence, as morality would dictate, at least not frontal violence. The end result is something very much like the now suspect containment—deemed, symbolically speaking, altogether too passive—coupled with a huge military security state of global reach. Kennan's original formulation was never subject to such conceptual shortcomings, since his refusal of diplomacy was not grounded in any moral notion of an evil empire. For him the Soviet Union was always a historically distinct creation, to be assessed and dealt with as it was, in its particularity. From that angle, Moscow did not constitute a devastating threat, provided the West assembled itself in appropriate ways.[38] Soon indeed, Kennan came to realize that it might be in the Western interest to engage Moscow in a diplomatic manner with realistic proposals. A year after the X article he had in effect abandoned containment. But by 1948 it was already too late. Containment in the name of moral universals, containment as cold war if you will, became the order of the day.[39]

It might now be objected that a good deal of what I have said about the United States, historical particularities and religious references aside, would pertain to the Soviet Union as well. After all, a certain Enlightenment heritage marks both. Representing universal interests, the Soviet Union too assumed itself always to be under threat by the (class) enemies of humankind. The difference as regards the cold war and the reason it is not even in theory a Soviet project can be found in the diverging conception of fascism and alliances. Stalinism came to define the class foundation of fascism in a remarkably narrow manner as the most extreme parts of monopoly capitalism. A rigid stage theory

---

38 A major difference, it should be said, between the moment of Kennan's erstwhile attempt to break the Cold War impasse in 1948 and Nitze's call to arms in the spring of 1950 is the alarming advent of Soviet nuclear capability in 1949, the chief reason NSC 68 was generated in the first place.

39 Once the negativity inscribed in the posture (it was never conceived of as "doctrine") of containment was abandoned, so was the concept. Or, alternatively, one might say that it was reduced to a platitude, strategic considerations aside.

of history combined with the further thesis that capitalism had reached its developmental limits thus made it possible for Stalinist strategy to imagine eventual victory as the mere prevention of future manifestations of fascism and its likes. Consequently, its antifascist matrix, unlike that of the United States, was based on a negative rather than positive criterion: a political force that is not explicitly an enemy is, at least potentially, an ally. Anything outside of those extremists, even good sections of monopoly capital, could in theory be mobilized within the antifascist alliance. Hence the otherwise curious fact that the opposition to the Marshall Plan and communist politics generally after the break in 1947 were situated in a framework of national independence and peace rather than socialism and revolution.

And on that score it is necessary to state the obvious. There was no conceivable reason for Moscow, in its own terms, to act in such a way as to facilitate the emergence of a massively powerful Western anti-Soviet coalition under US leadership. Stalin, contrary to his own interests and with a very limited understanding of how the West operated, may have acted precisely in this manner and thus "caused" the cold war. This is certainly arguable. But it remains that the cold war was not a Soviet project. Amid the present triumphalism,[40] one might then ask more seriously what it was about the United States and its self-conception that made the cold war a natural way of being toward the world, and why indeed the cold war turned out to be the American way.

---

40 The identification of "democracy" with "free enterprise" and "the market" is perhaps the most invidious index of this political atmosphere. The emergent debate about "illiberal democracy" initiated by Fareed Zakaria has, if nothing else, the virtue of again rendering clear that there is no necessary connection between the one and the other. Eventually, perhaps, one will again be able to distinguish "free enterprise" from "freedom" and "democracy."

3
The Cold War Considered as a US Project

In July 1963, on the occasion of the Test Ban Treaty, John F. Kennedy remarked that the treaty might come to "symbolize the end of one era and the beginning of another." A few months later he referred to "a pause in the Cold War," a moment that, while not "a lasting peace," might be extended "into a period of cooperation."[1] Such a period did in fact ensue. We remember it—in so far as we do remember it—as détente. One historical casualty of the current conviction that the cold war subsumes the entire postwar period up to the collapse of the Soviet regime is the inconvenient advent of détente, explicitly understood as it was by both the United States and the USSR as the end of the undeclared war and the beginning of some form of conflictual cooperation along the lines of more traditional Great Power relations. I myself have always thought that the pause did turn into a new era. In making that argument, I have also tried to develop (or produce, if you will) the cold war as a genuine concept, as a historical category of explanatory power rather than the simple metaphorical term of description it now usually is. In a different register, finally, I have taken the view that the cold war was instigated by the United States, that it was, in fact, a US project. Persevering in this position may now seem a quixotic pastime. Perhaps one ought to accept the conventional wisdom and get on with it, on the

---

1 John F. Kennedy, *Let the Word Go Forth: The Speeches, Statements, and Writings of John F. Kennedy*, ed. Theodore Sorensen (New York, 1988), 293, 300.

assumption that what counts as the real is probably rational at some level. However, regardless of how passé one may consider it, this problematic reveals a curious capacity, for me at least, to generate new and irksome questions. Over time, my explorations of this issue have had less to do with the particulars of the epoch as an epoch and more with the historical conditions that made it possible for something like the cold war to appear as a project in the first place.

The view based on common sense seeks to uncover the essence of the cold war either in the systemic differences between the United States and the USSR, or, more commonly, in the (revolutionary and/or totalitarian) nature of the USSR. According to the latter perspective, which coincides perfectly with the official view of the United States in the 1940s and '50s, the USSR essentially continued the kind of relentless aggression short of war that marked the fascist powers in the 1930s. The cold war, then, is a new name for the all-too-familiar mode of totalitarian expansion by means of compulsive aggression, an inherent quality then graphically manifest in the surviving form of totalitarianism, namely, the Soviet dictatorship. The historical question then turns out to be whether or not Washington's response was adequate to this challenge.

Whether one focuses on systemic differences or on Soviet characteristics, however, the end of the Soviet Union consequently becomes, by definition, the end of the whole matter. Often, in fact, that blindingly obvious conclusion generates the putative premise of the argument, and not the other way around. I have polemicized against this way of looking at the problem elsewhere and will only point out now that a simple, epochal conception, all-encompassing as it tends to be, occasions serious problems of demarcation. What exactly is the cold war and where did it take place? After a metaphorical while, it turns out to be everything and nothing: suburban life in Los Angeles (why not?), educational reform in rural Australia, and decisional intrigue in the Pentagon. For better or worse, my argument goes in the opposite direction, toward, in the spirit of a delimiting critique, ever greater specificity. The cold war as a concept, for one thing, should be kept analytically distinct from origins and effects. As initially a peculiar projection of US power, it was never everything that happened between the United States and the USSR in the postwar period up to 1963 (or 1989); it was a dominant, an overdetermining structure whose effects cut synchronically across a range of other levels and terrains. Similarly, from a diachronic perspective, its effects do not all come to an end in 1963. Thus, for example, the US escalation in Vietnam in 1965 was a residual (and catastrophically misconceived) cold-war policy; the massive intervention on behalf of the forces of violent reaction in the Dominican Republic that same year was, by contrast, Great Power management of a line already drawn.

This chapter begins with a summary of the first (taxonomic) moment in the evolution of my view of the cold war, followed by a reconsideration of the second moment, wherein I trace anew the genealogy of the cold war through the decisive succession of nondialectical outlooks, strategies and policies that came to characterize the US way of being toward the world during and after World War II. In a brief coda, I adumbrate a possible third moment by asking how this particular way fits other historical forms in which the United States has projected itself as a world empire (understood to mean a great power that assumes it can never have any legitimate equal). As the reader will already have sensed, I offer these remarks in the spirit of classical revisionism: that of William Appleman Williams, of course, but also the revisionism of Gabriel Kolko, who initially advanced the argument that the cold war was really nothing other than massive expansion and violence on the part of the United States.[2] In addition to ignoring the explanatory potential of the concept, Kolko was also guilty of an egregious example of reductionism, as well as economic determinism, essentialism, historical simplification, crude anti-Americanism and assorted other ills; but he had a point.

Walter Lippmann's lucid critique of George F. Kennan's X article that popularized the "cold war" as a term, together with Kennan's own subsequent though unannounced shift in recognition of that forceful broadside, inspired my original argument. The columnist made (in our context) two simple but crushing points: (1) that Kennan's piece, along with the Truman Doctrine, expressed "a disbelief in the possibility of a settlement of the issues raised by this war"; and (2) that diplomacy, contrary to Kennan's conception, is not about intimacy but about the political resolution of issues of mutual concern. Containment, therefore, implied a refusal to engage in what states in conditions of peace normally

---

2 Gabriel Kolko, *The Politics of War* (London, 1969); Gabriel and Joyce Kolko, *The Limits of Power* (New York, 1972).

do. Consequently, Kennan's rejectionism seemed to Lippmann to be identical with that of the Truman Doctrine. Both gave expression, to gloss Lippmann's argument, to the conviction that the US-USSR relationship was marked by an incommensurability originating in the nature of the Soviet regime, which thus made agreements of a lasting kind impossible.

For Lippmann, by contrast, the systemic or traditional differences between the Soviet Union and the West appeared less important than the imperatives of state interest; and agreements on concrete issues such as the withdrawal of troops from central Europe should have been eminently workable or at least easy to verify—troops were troops, and troops could be counted. The actual term "cold war," Lippmann's umbrella term for the continuing impasse, was probably based on the experience of the so-called Phony War in 1939–40, when nothing much seemed to happen in the European theater, as well as on the various undeclared wars of fascist aggression in the 1930s. Kennan himself would soon go on, famously, to a very long lifetime of brilliant critiques of cold-war thinking, critiques that were also de facto auto-critiques. Diplomatic rejectionism, meanwhile, became official US policy. I used Lippmann's critique in order to set forth a typology (or definition) of the cold war as a series of features having to do with warlike conditions in a situation short of actual war, a war that might have been cold but was also essentially and maximalistically about the political liquidation of the other side. On this foundation, I offered a fairly precise periodization: the cold war ended in 1963, after the apparently final division of Berlin, after the advent of full-scale Sino-Soviet conflict and, perhaps most importantly, after the horrendous implications the Cuban Missile Crisis had induced, among other things, the Test Ban Treaty. The United States and the USSR ceased to operate on the assumption that the object of the exercise was to destroy the other. The one exception here, Ronald Reagan's fantasies of the early 1980s that are sometimes referred to, not unnaturally, as the second cold war, may indicate otherwise; but the comparative brevity of this episode only emphasized the shallowness of its structural underpinnings.

Even though this first moment rested on a taxonomy of the cold war as a system and structure, the originating, defining abnormality was located principally on the side of the United States. Kennan himself had eventually gone looking for the historical causes of the misreadings (as he perceived them) of his containment policy in the idealist peculiarities, if not perversions, of the United States. A historical inquiry, one coupled with a much stronger logical and conceptual aspect, seemed to me to be the next sensible step in my critique. This program was pursued along two avenues. First, there was a history of the whole concept of a cold war, its conditions of emergence, and its place within the general semantic field of peace and war. One basic feature of the cold war as it had been delineated was, as mentioned, a presupposition that no settlement or peace in the traditional sense—traditional in the European context since the seventeenth century—was possible. Indeed, from that perspective, the cold war constituted a return to the confessional, intramural wars of the preceding European era and to the extramural relationship between Europe and Islam. Second, it became apparent that what more immediately enabled (and I emphasize the term "enabled" as opposed to "caused") this return to centuries-old early modern forms of war in the late 1940s was Franklin D. Roosevelt's specific conceptualization of World War II—a topic upon which I now wish to elaborate.

Roosevelt understood World War II to be not a traditional war, but a police operation, albeit a massive one, against gangsterism. Hence his insistence on unconditional surrender. The fascist regimes had shown from the beginning, so far as he was concerned, that the distinction between war and peace meant nothing to them. Unleashing the big war was thus merely an exponential intensification of what had always been lawless aggression. To recognize the legitimacy of such regimes or to negotiate with them was preposterous: one does not negotiate with gangsters and outlaws. Roosevelt's polarity of gangsterism/order, in short, made retrospective sense of the international events of the 1930s. It also crucially allowed for the inclusion of the defensive Kremlin dictatorship among the forces of good. After the stunning events of June 1941, Roosevelt grasped (at least I think he did—interpreting Roosevelt always involves an element of guesswork) that dictatorship was not an accurate indicator of what states will do in international relations. Some dictatorships might well be much in favor of order, if not exactly law. Furthermore, by inserting a temporal dimension into the overall phenomenon, one could begin to see that cautious dictatorships contained the potential for favorable historical development if one dealt with them in an appropriate manner. Roosevelt's tactical and strategic vision, in other words, presumed two fundamentally diverging historical trajectories: fascism/gangsterism could intrinsically result only in disaster, death and destruction—the end of civilization; and the forces of order, on the other hand, while not entirely made up of Wilsonian democrats, could intrinsically evolve, if given time and resources, into a civilized system. This explains Roosevelt's attempt to deal with Stalin as a proper member of the civilized club. With international order restored, the Soviet regime might develop into something recognizably closer to home.[3] Though Roosevelt's tactical execution of this strategy was in many ways naive, clumsy and counterproductive, the strategy itself, given the nasty circumstances, was certainly defensible and perhaps even laudable.

It is important to note here that, contrary to Kennan's misconceived disgust at the time, FDR was not a typical US legalist. A little less forthrightly perhaps than his kin Theodore, Franklin Roosevelt was nevertheless always more interested in civilizational order than in the institutional sanctity of law as such. The court-packing scheme of 1937 alone should give skeptics cause to ponder. It is often forgotten today, moreover, that the "United Nations" was originally the name of the victorious wartime alliance, run in no uncertain terms by its three Great Powers, rather than some legalistically conceived universal organization of formally equal members. And this was indeed how, with suitable modifications, Roosevelt wanted it to continue. Law as formality and procedure, then, was less important than law as an expression of a certain orderly content, the minimal precondition of which was pacification and policing. All of this will immediately be seen for what it was, namely, an updated version of the old Progressive understanding of progress circa 1910, replete with paternalistic and indeed repressive aspects but not entirely without merit. In a wider perspective, however, (lawlike) order has no positive value beyond itself. Roosevelt, hypersensitive to US opinion, or to what he imagined it to be, and probably feeling the need for something explicitly positive, also chose to introduce the thematic of freedom into the picture by way of the Atlantic Charter and the Four Freedoms. Given what we know about ideology and the

---

3 This argument is inspired by Warren Kimball's voluminous and authoritative work on Roosevelt, especially his *The Juggler: Franklin Roosevelt as Wartime Statesman* (Princeton, NJ, 1994).

postwar epoch, this may now seem natural. In fact, it was mostly a contingent product of the immediately preceding, quite furious domestic struggles over the meaning of the New Deal, which had, of course, been attacked from the right precisely as a form of creeping subversion of the eternal verities of US freedom, a view most illustriously embodied in the Liberty League, political residence, for a moment, of the right-wing Democrat Dean Acheson. A semantic field centering on freedom, thus emerged that, though of very old lineage in the political language of the United States, had scarcely been a constant. The Progressive period, for example, the source of Roosevelt's own formative impulses, featured quite a different set of references. Political controversies over the New Deal, in any case, occasioned a left-liberal countermove whereby the concept of freedom was hurled back at the right after it had been reworked to include the novel notion of security, grasped as substantial rights to economic and social security for everyone. It took no great leap of the imagination to experience this combination of freedom/security as deeply persuasive, for these were times, after all, of extreme and continuous domestic insecurity. The idea that freedom was essentially about entrepreneurial rights to risk and roam without government restriction suffered a corresponding loss of resonance. Subsequently, once the place of the United States in the outside world had indisputably become insecure as well, Roosevelt was able to internationalize the domestic argument about the New Deal into a vision of a future world of peace and tranquility, a secure world of orderly government, individual rights and freedom of thought. Because the whole field of meaning was predicated on some notion of inherent rights—rights of individuals and nation-states alike in their capacity as autonomous, self-determining subjects—their international translation was not without embarrassments: for example, British colonialism, massive domestic repression in the Soviet Union, race relations, quasi-colonialism, and internment of Japanese American citizens in the United States. These problems were politically manageable, however, precisely because the gangsterism/order couplet was logically (and temporally) prior to freedom in its achieved form. This explains, for example, Roosevelt's resurrection of trusteeship as a benevolent instrument of (temporary) rule over and for immature colonial peoples.

For domestic reasons, too, the appropriation of "freedom" came to carry direct historical references to the US Civil War. Roosevelt himself, for example, liked to think that he took the formula of "unconditional surrender" from U. S. Grant. More important, some of his chief cabinet figures began to depict the struggle in the rhetoric of abolitionism. Thus, Henry Stimson, Roosevelt's future (Republican) secretary of war, recycled and globalized Lincoln's famous biblical reference to a House Divided that cannot stand, but has to become either slave or free. Henry Wallace, on the left, spoke in the same spirit of a "fight to the death between the free world and the slave world," again, along the lines of the United States in the 1860s. The "house" (grasped as the whole world) might now be bigger, but there could still be "no compromise with Satan."[4] For Roosevelt, this language was far less resonant, I think, than that of gangsterism, policing and order. The trope, however, of a global civil war to the death, taking place in quasi-biblical terms and concerning the abolition of slavery, was a potent one and had now been irrevocably introduced into public discourse.

In another crucial move, Roosevelt went on to connect order and freedom through a truly maximalistic claim concerning security, a claim that opened up unforeseeable and unfortunate consequences: there would and could be no final security for the United States (or for everyone else anywhere in the world) until the globe as a whole recognized and encompassed the freedoms that had been so unmistakably announced to be basic. The argument was no doubt directed at what is usually referred to pejoratively as "isolationism," but which was (and still is) a view that favors unilateralism abroad, along with interventionism in the Western hemisphere and sometimes in the Asian Pacific. Whatever its polemical target, however, Roosevelt's fusion of order, freedom and security had the effect of making every event everywhere in the world a priori subject to an initial negative calculation. Rather than just having to demonstrate, positively, that a specific international occurrence might at times be a vital security concern, the policymaker now had to show, in principle, that any given event or development anywhere could not possibly be a security problem. This was very hard to do if the ultimate content of security was a positive recognition of freedom. If, moreover, the world was divided by a line defined by such a concept, then any gain anywhere by the forces of unfreedom would be

---

4 Henry A. Wallace, *The Price of Free World Victory* (New York: 1943), 375. Stimson's use can be found in the *New York Times*, June 15, 1940.

an infringement on the security of the United States; and the size and significance of the gain would arguably be irrelevant since freedom itself was supposedly indivisible. The complications here were not apparent in Roosevelt's period, for a dividing line in times of actual war was clearly drawn (as a front). What's more, that particular war not only affected the world as a whole but was decidedly about that world as well. The free world during World War II was thus easily and minimally defined as all areas not under the control of fascism. Liberated areas, more specifically, were those that had been cleared of fascist military power by means of violence. The free world, then, was in effect an antifascist concept and a clearly demarcated one.

This logic became considerably more difficult to handle once it was connected to anti-communism and Roosevelt's matrix had been projected onto a world technically at peace—once, in short, it had been explained to everyone's satisfaction after the war that the house/world was indeed still divided, and that an evil empire occupied a huge and expanding part of it. The difficulties of the Truman administration in trying to write off such a catastrophic backward movement of the line as the loss of China are readily understood: the line there was indeed still drawn as a military front, and it moved visibly in one direction. Elsewhere, the graphics of the dividing line were far more diffuse and yet it had to be drawn. For once the game had been conceptualized in the manner of a real (if cold) war for security defined as the final victory of indivisible freedom, there had to be a line drawn everywhere because, in principle, a line was there to begin with. One could not make it visible.

Hence, the idea of a civil war and unconditional surrender, together with the maximalistic notion of security as freedom, produced a solid theoretical foundation for US globalism. The completion of this ideological operation was greatly facilitated by the introduction of another concept—namely, totalitarianism. It became available to Truman after the war as a way of making sense of what was read as Soviet intransigence and impositions: crude power moves, subversion and conspiracy, and unilateral takeovers, all in flagrant contravention of agreements honestly concluded. Tyrants, in the end, were tyrants, and tyrants recognized only the language of force, and so on, and so on. Totalitarianism thus served to collapse the differences between fascism and communism and, in the larger scheme of things, to render morally and politically suspect any argument in favor of defined limitations on US commitments. The only feasible American counterargument, that of the Republican right, was to say that such commitments threatened to create an un-American Leviathan, a massive continuation not only of the wartime state but also, perhaps more frighteningly, of the hated New Deal apparatus. The globalist, however, could usually trump this. Had not the experience condensed in the names of Munich and Pearl Harbor conclusively shown what would happen when one played along with totalitarianism? Moreover, were these events themselves not, indeed, in large measure, the product of the Republican stab in the Wilsonian back after World War I? At any rate, the effects of merging two very different adversaries through the concept of totalitarianism are familiar: a simple historical projection of fascist modes of aggression onto the Kremlin. What is less familiar is that the cold war (though it never attained the terminological ubiquity in the late 1940s and early '50s it would later enjoy) became a useful category for the Truman administration by which to differentiate implicitly between fascism and communism. Both phenomena were inherently lawless and aggressive expressions of totalitarianism with which no lasting agreements could be made. The former, however, was adventuristic and prone to open (hot) war, while the latter preferred conspiracy, intimidation, secrecy, agents, proxies and creeping takeovers—in short, the tactics of a cold war. An interesting shift from Roosevelt's original matrix was thus taking place. His dominant sequence, "gangsterism—liquidation—policing—order—progress," was giving way to a different one, "totalitarianism—piecemeal aggression/cold war—counteraction (containment)—order in the free world—rollback." To put it another way, the reckless, hotheaded gangland figure of Al Capone was being replaced by a subversive, ruthless party/state, a disciplined, protean and patient machine of remarkable power and ingenuity, replete with agents and silent sympathizers, "a far-flung apparatus," in Kennan's celebrated phrase. What also made this form of totalitarianism such a formidable foe was that, unlike fascism, it evinced norms that seemed to overlap with one's own: no blasts against degenerate democracy but appeals to a presumably fuller version of it; no declarations and policies of racial superiority but critiques of it (not in the least as it was manifested in the United States); no rhetoric of geopolitical expansion but mobilization against American imperialism in the name of national independence; no superman ideology but a politics of supporting the people, the underprivileged and the colonized; no sneers against legality and agreements as such but apparent insistence on them; no glorification of war but, quite explicitly, a political platform based on forceful adherence to and promotion of peace. Condemning this communist worldview as hollow propaganda was easy, but the fact remained that, politically speaking, totalitarian communism was not the same as totalitarian fascism. The cold war, then, was one way of coming to terms with that difference and to provide space for a vast range of possible countermoves.

The person who provided the administration with much of the source material for this picture of the Soviet Union was, of course, George F. Kennan. Ironically, the returning Soviet expert operated within a radically different framework. Kennan was only marginally interested in totalitarianism. Moreover, he was not at all enamored with the shibboleths of what might be called the American tradition. Neither the Long Telegram nor the X article feature any accolades to freedom. The author himself was, indeed, a forthright admirer of Salazar's right-wing authoritarianism in Portugal, not as a model but as a particular implementation of the organic values of hierarchical rule in a particular place and culture. With such sensitivity to specificity, as it were, how and why did Kennan's Soviet investigations lead to a cold-war posture?

I will add here to the vast quantities of ink that have been devoted to these questions by comparing the crucial rejectionist (or nondialectical) component common to Roosevelt, Truman and Kennan—using the presidential names as convenient shorthand for something wider. For Roosevelt, there could be no proper relations with gangsters, only a struggle to the death by means of a (real) war. For Truman there could be no proper relations with totalitarians, only struggle to the death by means of a (cold) war. For Kennan, there could be no proper relations with regimes that operated outside, and fanatically against, the West, understood vaguely along Spenglerian lines as a decentered, varied world of many political traditions but anchored in the European West, a world of determinate limits, spiritually wracked, in fact, by a ruthless process of modernization and exhibiting signs of cultural disintegration that were evidenced nowhere more clearly than in the United States itself. Kennan's pessimism about the historical trends in the West, however, was muted in the immediate postwar years as he was called upon to articulate policy at the highest level. And the best policy toward antithetical, distasteful regimes was actually, all things being equal, a nonpolicy: dignified reserve, minimal interaction, pure distance. This was, in fact, his recipe for dealing with the Third World, as it was later to be known. The case of the Stalinist regime called for something more active, for it was at once the most fanatical and powerful foe, one that historical accident and Western betrayal in the shape of Hitler's criminal folly had managed to position in the middle of the civilizational heartland. Hence, Moscow could not be ignored in the manner that one could ignore unpleasant nationalist regimes in the decolonizing world. But it could perhaps be isolated. The United States, Kennan argued, should consequently act resolutely and vigorously to rejuvenate the Western remains while also preventing, by every means possible, any advances of the adversary into such parts of the world as may be deemed strategically vital to that West. Once the inherent need to expand by opportunistic consumption of putrid Western body parts had thus been thwarted, the Stalinist regime would eventually either collapse, change into something qualitatively different or at least mellow into manageable form.

All three strategic horizons begin, then, with the identification of a mortal threat whose nature and subsequent manifestations are given because of that threat's internal structure: a struggle to the death instigated by an opponent who denies one's right to exist and who has to do so because of their genetic composition. For Roosevelt and Truman, to engage that threat means to impose upon, to act upon, to eliminate; for Kennan (chiefly) it means to isolate or to ignore. All three insist that there can be no recognition of the opponent's political legitimacy. One can understand why Roosevelt thought this was obvious. Fascist war was obvious, the nature of fascism was obvious and the answer was obvious: all-out struggle to eradicate fascism once and for all. Things were, or should have been, far less obvious for Kennan and Truman. Soviet policy, as Lippmann realized, was in no little way a dialectical response to Western policy and not a product of any inner logic dictated by communist DNA; ample historical evidence demonstrated this. Stalin's policy, in particular, was ruthlessly traditional in its realism, a posture in turn eminently compatible with his coarse version of Leninism was also (as Kennan noted without deeper analytical consideration) a policy inclined to view the sphere of security as an autarky.[5]

---

5 Limited space does not permit any elaboration, but for a catastrophic example of what Stalin's political realism—or hyperrealism as I prefer to think of it—could produce,

More vital at the moment, however, are the differences between Kennan and Truman, which tend to disappear behind their rejectionist similarities (hence Lippmann's understandable amalgamation of the Truman Doctrine and the X article). Among his numerous impulses and sensibilities, Kennan combined two political strands: realism and, to put it infelicitously, a vaguely Spenglerian culturalism vis-à-vis the West.[6] The relation between the two was indeterminate, having affinities and overlaps, but also contradictions. The nondialectical element at stake in the present context was a product of his overarching, Western thinking. Real diplomacy could exist only within a certain realm of intimacy, civilization as proximity as opposed to distance. On grounds of cultural and normative difference, therefore, the West should maintain its natural Spenglerian distance except where absolutely necessary. To the straightforward realist (such as Lippmann) this made no sense at all. Political forces, according to that view, are about power, interests and security, whatever the ideological or cultural complexion of the regime in question. The central question is, thus, what sort of interested action any given configuration of power might generate or allow. Paradoxically, Kennan swung around in 1948 to seeking the solution to his central culturalist problem—namely, that of Europe itself—in just such realist terms. Domestic experience in the United States had reawakened his misgivings about the capacity of his government—a hopelessly fractured machinery working against the universalist idealism of public opinion—to conduct a suitably agile foreign policy. Meanwhile, Lippmann's critique, the successful prevention of a communist election victory in Italy, Tito's break with Stalin, Kennan's own internal defeat over the issue of NATO, and the militarization of the division of Europe propelled Kennan to develop a realistic set of proposals for dismantling that division through an

---

see Gabriel Gorodetsky's fascinating account, *Grand Delusion: Stalin and the German Invasion of Russia* (New Haven, CT, 1999) regarding his diplomatic maneuverings in relation to Hitler during 1940–41. One can argue, of course, that Stalin (or Moscow) "caused" the cold war because, in his realism, he failed to grasp the nature of US foreign policy and that by playing the game in traditionally cynical fashion he ended up triggering the cold-war policy he actually dreaded. Yet, this argument misses the real "origin" of the cold war, whose fundamental condition of possibility is the United States itself.

6 I draw here on my *Kennan and the Art of Foreign Policy* (Cambridge, MA, 1989); and "Kennan's Abendland: On Nationalism, Europe, and the West," chap. 10 of the present volume. I have also benefited from conversations with Patrick Jackson.

agreement with Moscow on Germany. Tragically, for him and for Europe, a simplistic version of his own containment policy was pursued instead, thus (in my view) not only postponing for decades the unification of the region but also rendering infinitely more difficult the positive development of the Soviet Union.

Though neither of Kennan's two ways of being toward the world had any extensive sanction in US traditions, his erstwhile account of fanatical Soviet expansionism lent itself to immediate appropriation within the universalist vision of the Truman Doctrine. Oddly, one facilitating factor here had to do with Kennan's Western culturalism, or, more precisely, its analytical effects. Culturalism traditionally tends to imagine that societies are integrated wholes and that these are also, metaphorically or literally, organic substances, bodies. (Contemporary culturalism is an interesting mirror inversion of this view since it perceives society as being purely a construction.) For Kennan, then, the real body, the body that matters, is the West. When he worries about this body—and he worries a great deal—it is consequently in the analogical terms of health and disease. The healthy body is already threatened by disease, from within as well as from without. The Soviet regime constitutes just such a disease: an external parasite that can become a cancerous growth (to muddle up the medical metaphors) if it finds suitably degenerate tissue inside. The parasite/disease, it stands to reason, can be studied and understood only when fixed under a microscope. Once scientifically illuminated and mapped, the disease can then be treated by appropriate measures: isolated rather than ignored, contained if you will. For in the absence (I suppose) of some injected gene therapy of sorts, the only possible countermeasure short of killing it by a vast violent smacking move was to prevent it from finding feeding grounds. Then, deprived of nourishment for growth, it would eventually die. The parasite, though active and alive, is to be treated throughout as an object—an object of knowledge and an object of action. It would be absurd to treat it as a subject or to recognize it as a dialectical other.

As it turned out, Kennan's morphological image of the object-parasite was immensely compelling to the Truman administration. Its particulars fit especially well into the grand narrative of freedom and totalitarianism: fanatical, devious, inherent expansionism understood as a malignant parasite, it was a creature whose behavior was innately predetermined. This nondialectical, diagnostic view, moreover, was easy to grasp in the United States and could accommodate, indeed explain, existing and seemingly irrefutable facts. Again, when combined with the totalitarian trope and the references to Munich and Pearl Harbor, it became a massively powerful ideology: it became Truth. The fact that Kennan's own frame featured a very different set of coordinates, constituting a sharp contrast to the universalist precepts of the Doctrine, was occluded by momentary political coincidence. Once, however, the analysis of the particular had served its universalizing purposes on behalf of the free world, Kennan's divergences began to manifest themselves and his political usefulness began to diminish. From then on there was no more need to delve into the peculiarities and possible internal dynamics of the Soviet Union. Ironically, though the universalizing policy of the Truman administration and its Republican successor was structured on the idea of winning a cold war against the Soviet regime, the essence of the actual policy turned out to be nothing other than a version of the early Kennan's policy of isolation by containment. The Soviet Union itself became an axiom, a nonproblem. Typically, none of the major policy documents after 1948 feature anything but the most perfunctory and sterile rhetoric on the subject. Accordingly, the experts in the field, while sometimes remaining prominent figures, found themselves largely overlooked when they offered any views of substance.

Whatever the analytical issues, a powerful material factor in this development was found in the fact that the nondialectical aspect allowed the Truman administration to resolve a colossal problem of structure: how to put the United States and its unexampled power into the world on a permanent, sustained basis. Only on the basis of the twin assumptions of a global, mortal threat, on one hand, and the impossibility of appeasing it by political, that is, diplomatic, means, on the other, could this be accomplished. That is not to say that the threat was manufactured for some more fundamental and sinister reason. It is to say, however, that the cold war made it possible for the United States to ascend to the position of leader of the free world, together with allowing for a restoration of order in the capitalist West and the imposition of order elsewhere outside the communist world proper. The last-named exercise was hardly a success but the achievement overall was formidable and makes it perfectly clear why there was never any great urgency in reevaluating the ultimate premise and basis of the whole edifice, why in fact such attempts made little sense and were dismissed, if not outright silenced.

Now, too, the road had opened up for what may be grasped as the Americanization of the totalitarian thematic, a transmutation illustrated nowhere more eloquently than in NSC 68, the voluminous and foundational policy document produced by the State Department during the spring of 1950.[7] Sometimes dismissed as nothing new, as insubstantial rhetoric, or (simply) as a crass pitch for mobilizing huge increases in military spending, NSC 68 actually expresses the cold war posture in its highest form. Paul Nitze, Kennan's successor as head of the Policy Planning Staff (PPS), was in charge of the document's overall composition, but other members of the PPS were responsible for the effusively ideological style and much of its actual content. The central feature in this regard was the return to the wartime allusions of the Roosevelt administration, that is, allusions to the American Civil War. NSC 68 dwells obsessively on the opposition between freedom and slavery, doing so in an idiom lifted directly, it seems, from the abolitionist movement of a century earlier. Once again, the idea of the world as a house divided writ large gained currency. Freedom was permanently endangered on a global scale by the enslaving, despotic conspiracy, the latter by virtue of its nature, turning it into a struggle to the death. Just like the Southern slavocracy of the 1850s, the Kremlin too could not tolerate the existence of freedom elsewhere. Evil communism, consequently, is inherently condemned as destroying all vestiges of freedom by every means at its disposal. The opposition is not dialectical (to put it differently, it is not Manichean) for the two sides are not equals: they do not symmetrically presuppose one another. Freedom is posited as the natural condition of humankind, a condition of complete independence and autonomy that needs no other. Slavery, by contrast, has no independent existence. While certainly the opposite of freedom, it is a subversive perversion rather than a dialectical other. Slavery, therefore, can only exist parasitically, as an attempt to destroy freedom. It follows, then, that its exponents have no possible legitimate interests or concerns: their entire raison d'être is to engage in formidably ingenious "designs" to undermine the plural "purposes" of the free world, by definition the

---

7   All quotations from NSC 68 as reproduced in United States Department of State, *Foreign Relations of the United States* [*FRUS*], 1950, 1:237–92.

only realm invested with legitimacy. It also follows (in another Rooseveltian revival) that until everyone, everywhere, is free, freedom will be in peril, which is to say there could be no relaxation of effort on the part of the fortunate free in combating this savage enemy across the board in what was (as NSC 68 says) "a real war." The document, predictably, climaxes in exhortations on behalf of a huge expansion of such efforts.

This language had sources of inspiration beyond the abolitionism of the 1850s and the ferocious struggle to force sinful slave drivers into unconditional surrender, sources indeed reaching back beyond the American revolution and toward the radical Protestantism of the English Civil War. In 1950, however, this is a thoroughly American language, impossible to imagine in any other political culture. It made good American sense, however, and more existential sense perhaps, than did talk that was solely restricted to totalitarianism, which was not only itself alien but also somehow gave rise, as a name, to alien abstraction. Abolitionism offered archetypes and a reenactment of timeless truths, the sort of universalism that Kennan had already condemned internally in the spring of 1948 as "escapism," as avoiding "the national peculiarities and diverging political philosophies of foreign peoples, which many of our people find confusing and irritating."[8] Thus, NSC 68 realized a sort of apotheosis of the nondialectical view: abolishing degraded and degrading evil by means of an uncompromising, herculean struggle. While paying formal homage to the concept of containment, the paper is in substance already pervaded by the spirit of rollback, the next great spatial metaphor, which also presupposed a line already drawn. Containment is symptomatically translated as "a policy of calculated and gradual coercion," and there are more than subtle hints that Kennan's version of it implied something altogether too passive (perhaps limited?). "Frustrating the Kremlin design," a phrase soon to be borrowed by the Republicans, necessarily entailed more offensive action, using the "current Soviet cold war technique" against the Soviet Union itself and taking "dynamic steps to reduce the power and influence of the Kremlin inside the Soviet Union and other areas under its

---

8   Kennan's point is made in the wide-ranging policy paper PPS 23. See *Foreign Relations of the United States*, 1948, vol. I: 2 (Washington, DC, various dates), 526. His target is legalist versions of universalism but the argument is applicable to any form.

control" so as to create "friendly regimes not under Kremlin domination." This was because the status quo, what NSC 68, in a key phrase, calls the "diplomatic freeze," was morally and politically intolerable as such, tilting the situation, in fact, in favor of evil. To put it more plainly, the cold war was putting the free world itself in increasing danger while liberating none of the enslaved. More of the same (that is containment as hitherto practiced) had to be replaced by a policy whose foundation was military escalation, presumably in order to intensify the said "calculated and gradual coercion."

One could argue that this signified nothing more than a shift in coloration and certainly no real break with traditional containment, which had always presupposed a strong military component. One could argue, in short, that Nitze and the PPS were just reformatting the original, nondialectical concept of containment to new and somber strategic realities (China and the Soviet atomic test), giving it a supposedly more adequate activist and, above all, military tinge, all in preparation for the real object of the paper, namely, military expansion. This is true. Yet the abolitionism of NSC 68 raised the bar qualitatively and turned Kennan's particularist reading of the Soviet problem into a universal, global quest for the eternal victory of freedom. Whereas even the nondialectical Kennan of 1946–47 had allowed, in a minor key, for the possibility of a mellowing Moscow with which one could deal—an image that, curiously, left it up to the policymaker to decide subjectively when that moment had arrived—and the Kennan of 1948 had decided on other grounds (indeed, somewhat paradoxically, in part because the very opposite of mellowing was taking place) that dialectical diplomacy was now fine and proper, NSC 68 in effect offered no such scenario. On the contrary, the document constitutes an emphatic reaffirmation of Lippmann's earlier verdict that the Truman administration had begun to rule out settlement of outstanding issues left over from the war. Another way of putting the matter is to say that NSC 68 had effectively reissued in amplified form Roosevelt's wartime matrix, with a reorganized concept of order and policing. The historizing concept of order and the attendant idea of freedom had now been exclusively transplanted into the noncommunist world. Hence, the realm of freedom soon came to include a range of very orderly right-wing dictatorships: Roosevelt's idea about the Soviet regime as applied to oppressive regimes whose anticommunism (and authoritarianism to order) made them potentially free in some imaginary future. And so it came to pass that, by the early 1950s, General Franco's fascist Spain was turning into a valued member of the free world.

As for the leader of that free world, the authors of NSC 68 insisted (this was Nitze's own chief point) that the United States had "a wide gap of unactualized power" and had "scarcely begun to summon up its forces." Herein lay, of course, the fundamental divergence with the ensuing Eisenhower administration, for which such unbridled summoning up also meant unbridled statism. Yet, at the same time, the Republicans had upped the ante by committing themselves in no uncertain terms to the very same logic of invigoration as contained in NSC 68, indeed rendering explicit the latter's sotto voce criticism of containment as passive and as reinforcing the status quo. Thus the Eisenhower campaign in 1952 casts (and castigates) containment as a policy of merely holding the fort, as de facto appeasement and, to use the clever slogan of the time, as a surrender on the installment plan. Containment was a disgraceful failure, forcing the United States to such deeply un-American stalemates as the one vividly demonstrated in Korea.

The imaginary resolution to the Republican dilemma of more activism and less statism was, of course, less people and more things nuclear. But this was no more than tinkering. The basic orthodoxy of NSC 68 remained in place. Perhaps the best index of that is the continuing inability to come to terms with the issue of negotiation. If sticking to the existing line (containment) was really appeasement, then actual negotiation was clearly far beyond the pale. Moreover, the overdetermining project was crucially about the noncommunist, as opposed to communist, world, and negotiating with the latter would only jeopardize the axiomatic divisions that enabled the project in the first place. Nonetheless, it proved impossible to entirely avoid the issue. NSC 68 wrestled with it, on the whole disingenuously, always tellingly. Mention was made that one ought to develop a negotiating position. After all, world opinion might be in favor of negotiations, in itself a supposedly good and Western thing to do. The truth of the matter, however, was that to negotiate in the given circumstances could only mean one of two alternatives, the one worse than the other: recognition of the status quo or compromise and concessions. Neither was acceptable since the existing House Divided was a moral outrage and a historical impossibility—again, one does not compromise with Satan. As NSC 68 wistfully admitted in passing, the only politically correct kind of negotiation would be one concerning "a settlement which calls for a change in the Soviet system." This is then correctly dismissed as an absurdity, leaving negotiations as either tactical propositions designed to make Moscow look bad or a simple registry for expected successes in the "policy of gradual and calculated coercion." The Eisenhower administration inherited the frame, the quandary and the fictional solutions. It is amusing to note the handwringing and unease that arose whenever the issue came up during the frequent seminars Eisenhower used to run in the form of National Security Council meetings. Once in a blue moon, some cabinet member from the Republican heartland, someone not exactly in the international know, would unwittingly reveal the nature of the game by thinking aloud that maybe there was no use in "trying to kick Russia in the shins" or, with reference to personal experience of domestic labor relations, that the United States "could no more bully the Soviet Union than we could bully the labor unions."[9] Typically followed by Eisenhower's waffling about essential agreement amid confusing abstractions and some tactically soothing words from John Foster Dulles, the matter would expire in vagueness and indirection.

The central Republican policy document of the period, NSC 162/2, appearing, symbolically enough, under the rubric "Reduction of the Soviet Threat," is thus remarkably wishy-washy on the topic.[10] Negotiations did of course happen at times, but as Dulles said in a moment of candor regarding the cases of Berlin and Geneva, "We did not actually desire to enter in either negotiation, but felt compelled to do so in order to get our allies to consent to the rearmament of Germany."[11]

By now a third moment in the development of my argument is discernible, one which raises the question about nothing less than the sources of US conduct. Having followed a certain pattern of nondialectical rejectionism, one would proceed to ask if there was historically something in the formation and development of the United States that was conducive to such a posture. D. W. Meinig has suggested in his

---

9 These pronouncements were made by Secretaries Humphrey and Wilson, respectively, at the NSC meeting on December 21, 1954. See *FRUS*, 1952–54, 2:837, 840.
10 NSC 162/2, finally passed on October 30, 1953, can be found in ibid., 578–96.
11 *FRUS*, 1952–54, 2:1, 843. Dulles made the remark on December 21, 1954.

monumental historical geography that the development of the United States was peculiarly nondialectical, a process of quantitative addition rather than any genuine "situatedness."[12] Its astonishing success, a product of unrepeatable historical circumstances, could thus be structured and imagined as the final world empire, a "*Weltreich*" in Otto Hintze's sense of a power that, while knowing there is an outside beyond its actual control, cannot conceive of itself as having any equal, or that the outside is in fact ever essentially similar to it.[13] In other words, while the United States is the world, the world is not the United States. That gap opens up the space for a potential decision to act or not to act: the actual, degraded world outside can be redone or rejected, in both cases because of the same logic of difference. US expansion and expansionism have moved within both frames, sometimes simultaneously. Their initial phase (from 1789 until the Civil War), the "Empire for Liberty," was thus an expansion that resembled a cellular replication of the same: an ongoing addition of states reproducing an originary essence while ignoring the outside as much as possible. The second phase, civilizational empire (from 1898 to 1910), featured European-style imperialism as filtered through the ideology of civilizational uplift typical of Progressivism; this was a case of continuous connection to Europe and of reforming an objectified outside. The third phase was the brief but world-historical interlude of Wilsonianism, the United States as a Mosaic lawgiver to a putatively grateful world. The cold war, finally, is abolitionism on a global scale, a metaphorical reenactment of the American Civil War, a thrust that provides the possibility of becoming the hegemonic leader of the only world that could be deemed genuine and proper. It ends in failure, in concessions and recognition of the enemy, in a nuclear stalemate of balanced terror where nothing much of substance can be abolished. Yet, in a way that I am tempted to describe as curiously dialectical, that very recognition of failure eventually gave rise to the abolition that abolitionism could never achieve.

---

12   D. W. Meinig, *The Shaping of America: A Geographical Perspective on 500 Years of History*, vol. I: *Atlantic America, 1492–1800* (New Haven, CT, 1986), and vol. II: *Continental America, 1800–1867* (New Haven, CT, 1993).

13   Otto Hintze's formulation in his *The Historical Essays of Otto Hintze* (New York, 1975), 468.

4
Cold War Degree Zero

Ronald Reagan, it is well to remember, would have denied with indignation in the early 1980s that he was reviving the cold war. In his view, it had never gone away, contrary to the egregious delusions of détente—that shameful era of Western passivity and appeasement that had permitted such vast Soviet advances toward world communist dominance. A good many historians today reflect this general frame, if not its politics or the idea of appeasement. They accept, in short, the notion that the cold war never went away and that it came to last as long as the Soviet Union lasted, as Reagan himself had indeed always insisted it would.

The reason for this agreement is not hard to divine. The Reagan era of drastic cold-war mobilization by the United States was followed by the extinction of the Soviet empire and so the end of an epoch in world politics. Something fundamental did in fact come to an end. The sheer obviousness of this end is overwhelming. By any measure, the expiration of the Soviet Union was a world-historical event. Given the reality of that end, there has to be a period that really and truly corresponds to it, that adequates it, so to speak. As that end game, too, takes place in the wake of Reagan's intense cold-war rhetoric, it is not surprising that the conventional name for the obvious period now laid to rest is "the cold war." The name worked. It still works. Thus we are now in an epoch "after the end of the cold war," the introductory phrase of a million policy articles since the early 1990s, along with that other cliché about "the only superpower." More recent events have put that latter designation into question, but the obviousness of the cold war remains in full force. Though the period itself is now fading into the distant past, no name of comparable rhetorical power has been invented to describe the ensuing period. We seem to live perpetually after the cold war. Ronald Reagan's view of the cold war still, in effect, holds sway. The notion that he was the one who essentially ended it with such success is only slightly less common.[1]

With little reflection, serious scholarship left and right has thus fallen into the superficial usage of Reagan's continuity thesis, which in turn is grounded one way or another in a set of systemic criteria, that there was somehow something inherently cold-war about the very difference between the United States and the Soviet Union or solely about the Soviet Union. There, however, the similarities end. Cold-war conventionalism may be said, for analytical purposes, to fall into three ideal types.[2] First, there is what one might call neoorthodoxy, the position of Reagan's faithful admirers, notably more numerous today than during his own controversial presidency.[3] Their preeminent historian is John Lewis Gaddis.[4] For Reagan's parishioners, nothing much about the cold war is problematic or difficult to grasp. In the spirit of their political authority, they believe that the cold war was a civilizational war that the West, under reinvigorated leadership, won by revealing the naked

---

[1] Melvyn Leffler's most recent monograph on the subject, notably, casts a wider net in this regard: the end is a collaborative effort on the part of Mikhail Gorbachev, Ronald Reagan and George H. W. Bush. The narrative is structured around degrees of "reasonableness" in circumstances that are systematically tense and difficult for both sides after 1947. Leffler, *For the Soul of Mankind: The United States, the Soviet Union and the Cold War* (New York, 2007). Resolution (and so the end) appears once the circumstances and the personalities involved allow reasonableness to be victorious. What needs then to be addressed is that that reasonable end is followed by another end, namely, the end of the Soviet Union. For a remarkable critique of Gorbachev's end game—how he gave away the farm, as it were—see Vladislav Zubok, *A Failed Empire: The Soviet Union in the Cold War from Stalin to Gorbachev* (Chapel Hill, NC, 2007).

[2] The trinity is necessarily crude and nonexhaustive but, with that proviso, useful for the sake of the argument.

[3] Barack Obama's express and typically pragmatic admiration for Reagan is a good index of the now dominant and highly refracted image of a Benign Communicator who revived America as opposed to, say, a far-right ideologue who initiated a massive assault on the working poor.

[4] See, conveniently, Gaddis, *The Cold War: A New History* (New York, 2005).

decrepitude of the perverse empire on the other side. The origins of the war have to do, then, with the nasty doings by the intrinsically nefarious Soviet Union, the end of which will therefore also be the end of the war. Subperiods of the war will then be read in terms of a continuing totalitarian threat and the variable adequacy of the Western response.

This, in all its essentials, is also the official US position from 1946–47 into the 1960s. Such a view, centered on communism and totalitarianism, was easier to propound then than now, given, for one thing, the subsequent Sino-Soviet conflict and China's de facto alliance with the United States. Nonetheless, neoorthodoxy does have a specific account of what made the cold war a cold war, in which regard it compares favorably with the other two conventional tendencies, which evince no very precise idea about that matter and rarely address it. These two positions share the basic, minimalist view of the cold war as a geopolitical period dominated decisively by the United States and the Soviet Union, with the added ingredient (enter the variable chill factor) of intense rivalry or abnormal tension. No normative judgment is necessarily involved. What differentiates the two, however, is the extent of the conceptualization and the importance accorded to the war itself.

One—let us call it neorealist—is chiefly interested in bipolarity as an overdeterminant system and its functional effects on state actors, with particular reference to the stability of the whole.[5] The domestic character and ideology of the antagonists, then, are largely irrelevant. So are the origins of the structure. No great mystery attaches to them in any case, just two massively powerful continental states of diverging interests bound for conflict after World War II, thus setting the stage for the subsequent stability of the duopoly. Exact origins and causes may be left hazy and are at any rate secondary. Notoriously, this position has no

---

5 This view is represented with typical clarity by Kenneth Waltz, *Theory of International Politics* (New York, 1979). "Competition" here is a function of structurally identical positions in a system that is itself not ideological. The cold war qua cold war is virtually absent. Gaddis at mid-career was heavily influenced by this kind of neorealism and wrote some of his best analysis in that mode, roughly the moment between *Strategies of Containment: A Critical Appraisal of American National Security Policy during the Cold War* (Oxford, 1982) and *The Long Peace: Inquiries into the History of the Cold War* (Oxford, 1987). Seeing the cold war as a long peace was a suggestive but limited idea, characteristically single-minded and forcefully expressed. Above all, however, it was badly timed. Gaddis the neorealist, it should be added, dealt with the cold war as actual history, as was not always the case with the political scientists who inspired him.

convincing account of the end, having disregarded the domestic aspect without which that event is largely incomprehensible, indeed rather a nasty surprise from a conceptual standpoint. The cold war, more importantly, is not fundamental to the proceedings. It is a semantic convenience (or unavoidable inconvenience). What matters is the range of possible effects and derivations from the concept of a structure of limited competition. Periodization itself, in fact, is not crucial: the object (since we are chiefly dealing with political scientists) is to produce a timeless, predictive theory wherein the postwar epoch serves as raw material; temporality, historical time, is mainly a disturbance and not a basic concern. The rights and wrongs of that theory, featuring (dubiously) electromagnetic metaphors of polarity but actually grounded in economic theories of limited competition, are not relevant for my argument here. What is relevant is the constitutive lack of interest in the cold war as a cold war. Neorealism is really more interested in the structural features that (I will argue) turned the cold war into something else.

The final position—amorphous, historically orientated, and more defined by what it avoids and dislikes—may also be concerned with bipolarity and the like but not in any theoretical sense. It emphasizes the existential realities of nastiness and massive threats. Neoorthodoxy in pure form is wrong, accordingly, because of its politics and lack of detachment. Neorealism, insofar as one acknowledges it, is wrong for the opposite reason: it is too detached; it is also ahistorical and hovering on the brink of amoral model-mongering. For amorphous convention (I am unable to find a fetching name), events of the cold war matter in themselves, so to speak. They are not the metanarrative expressions of some underlying evil empire or functional system. Historical variations within the epoch are thus genuine and profound. "Bipolarity in trouble," for instance, features a unique sequence of events of intrinsic historical interest: China breaks away, Western Europe begins to show signs of independent geopolitics, third world developments are increasingly hard to control, and so on. The outline and the props are familiar—very familiar—but generally the perspective seems credible enough. As in the case of neorealism, it permits a logical account of the place of the People's Republic of China. Semantically, meanwhile, "the cold war" is more than a terminological convention; it is an expression of something real, if not quite in the essentialist manner of Ronald Reagan (a philosophical realist, if not a political one). It is a term, then, with a great deal of historical resonance and for good reason. People used it. There was tension. Sometimes there was even terror, the terror of being on the brink of nuclear war. The cold war is a pretty good description. It makes sense. It makes obvious sense.[6]

The cold war thus serves as shorthand for an amorphous epoch of enormous span, variably defined, if it is defined at all. The geopolitical polarity is sometimes backdrop, sometimes immediately determinant, but works overall as a frame for investigations of all kinds of events and processes. At its blandest, amorphous convention turns the cold war into little more than an empty container of time, a homogeneous stretch when sundry things happen in sundry places for sundry reasons, nothing much apparently following from it: the cold war here and there and yonder. Even when it is supposed to carry explanatory weight, the actual studies are conceived of, in effect, as filling in empirical voids, areas and topics not yet covered. The cultural domain, especially, offers a potentially unlimited range of cold-war studies. Particular histories of substance are possible here, though the cold war adds nothing much to them and they in turn add little to it as an object of inquiry. Where amorphous convention makes direct claims about the cold war, where the periodizing device supposedly tells us something significant about the subject at hand, where it is not the backdrop but the stage itself as it were, the cold war still remains no more problematic than in either of the other two accounts. The aim is judicious elaboration and extension, not conceptual challenge. The approach is, however, not intrinsically vacuous. No one can deny that some kind of epoch comes to an end with the Soviet Union; and amorphous convention does represent a coherent periodization, however minimalist, that can also yield empirical knowledge. Because it is both specific and infinitely capacious, it permits distinctions between its object and other kinds of processes and temporalities. The cold war is not necessarily everything that happens in the cold war. Other histories and periodizations are, in principle, possible.

---

6   This ideal type, then, is less than ideal: it has no paradigmatic statement so to speak. It is more of an assumption, an implicit frame, than a clear concept. Much of diplomatic history in the United States operates within its compass.

Beyond the Continuity Thesis

So what is wrong with this view? A great deal, actually. Slipshod periodization aside, it would seem to ignore, in the first instance, the extent to which actors of the 1960s and '70s thought the cold war had indeed come to an end and acted accordingly. Richard Nixon must have been talking nonsense when, grandly but earnestly, he declared the cold war over in Moscow in 1972, when he envisaged something more traditional by way of Great Power rivalry. That Nixon was talking nonsense was of course precisely Reagan's belief; and thus neoorthodoxy now thinks justified Reagan's deep, not to say visceral, anger at détente and his subsequent restoration of a grand policy that recognized cold-war truth. For the less ideologically inclined, however, the experience of détente as an end and qualitative break is rather a retrospective curiosity, to be registered but of no deeper significance, easily submerged as a mere phase within the fundamental cold-war continuity. Alternatively, it can even be seen as the intensification of the rivalry and the cold war. The conclusion, whether explicit or not, is in any case identical to that of neoorthodoxy. The cold war, in fact, continued.

And, indeed, it may be that Reagan and the conventional cohort are right: Nixon was in fact mistaken. Though the appearance of such talk in 1972 can scarcely be ignored as a historical phenomenon, there is no reason to take it at face value either, or for that matter to take at face value the panoply of actions that manifestly did not conform to cold-war concepts. These acts, then, might have been misconstrued by contemporaries, or perhaps seen as a case of devious recasting of old categories into new form, a performance for the galleries. In short, one might choose, on methodological principle, to treat as immaterial or of very limited pertinence the phenomenological aspects, how events were experienced and defined. While, consequently, it is correct to insist on some kind of account of why participants ceased to think in classical cold-war categories, this does not, obviously, make it incumbent on latter-day amorphous convention to agree with them.

My initial objection is thus of limited scope, the conventional tendency to flatten out what actually happened notwithstanding. The related denigration of the category of the cold war itself is more difficult to ignore. By treating it as self-evident, convention of the detached variety turns the cold war into description and leaves aside its potential as explanatory concept. I realize that the distinction is not absolute: there is no pure description or explanation. Even so, amorphous convention treats the cold war more as description of something self-evident than a concept to be produced and used to explain the nature of the period. At most, it is a concept without movement.

One major reason for this is the negligence of how "the cold war" became a term in the first place and its various subsequent meanings. This is certainly improper procedure. How it emerged in the immediate postwar years, the specific references that made up its conceptual ground, how it became a semantic field, are elementary components of any historical inquiry that makes claims about the cold war as a period. The historian (and the odd political scientist) must give a critical, indeed historical, account of the basic terms deployed—subject them to some minimal degree of interrogation. Geopolitical dominance plus intense rivalry here does not equal such an interrogation. The problem is compounded because the term in question is not merely a name we now give to a distinct period ex post facto. It is not an analogue of, say, "the interwar period" for the years 1919 through 1939, a term that is certainly disputable in making the two World Wars into obvious bookends but surely not as politically and ideologically loaded a term as "the cold war," nor one that carries with it the weight of explanation, nor one that contemporaries actually used since it was hard to imagine oneself (generally) as living between two wars. The cold war, by contrast, seems to tell us something quite powerful about what went on: it was invented by contemporaries and used from the outset, then battled over continuously by politicians and public intellectuals, in due course also by historians in the many polemics about who caused the war, and then used retroactively when, presumably, the obvious end had occurred. This sedimentation of meanings, this mess of political and scholarly controversies, demands some account if the inquiry is to earn its critical credentials. Yet historians have next to nothing to say about it.

I find this strange. One would think that, regardless of politics, such a strikingly polyvalent term as "the cold war" would occasion excessive fascination rather than drone-like acceptance. Each of the three words that make it up may in fact be put into question. The cold war: was there only one or can there be others? Is it a historical form or type such as for instance holy war or civil war? If it is, then any systemic interpretation (for example, democracy/totalitarianism or capitalism/communism) would have some elaboration to do. If it is unique, are all other uses metaphorical analogies, and in what sense? The cold war: Why this particular metaphor, and what does it do? Cold is a relative description on a scale, a continuum; it is a condition of degree. This is in fact a fundamental reason it works so well. One can account for variations: increasing chill, a warming thaw (though there is a problem with heating up). Moreover, cold already has a wide metaphorical register before it becomes a specific one in "the cold war." When one refers to a personal relationship as cold, the word means unfriendly, hostile, limited in range and expression. A cold person is similarly so, the opposite of warm. The metaphorical register here is grounded in the temperature of water (as is the Celsius scale) and its qualitative states, as well as in the related, more encompassing domain of weather and climate. Ice, frozen water, embodies several disagreeable features: rigidity, exterior blankness and unresponsiveness, physical threat to the normal state of the human body. Frosty relations are thus bad but not quite as bad as frozen ones, in which nothing moves. If things warm up and relations improve, a thaw is said to be underway. The rigidity is loosening up, opening up for tactile interaction, a diversity of actions and reactions.

As long as one thinks along these analogical lines of the human body (warm is good) and its environs, and, metaphorically, the relations between them (warm is good), the semantic field seems predictable enough. One might even consider the optimum (warm is good) as some Aristotelian mean between two deviating extremes, hot and cold. There, however, the exercise threatens to go astray because a hot war is infinitely worse than a cold one. This cannot simply be resolved by projecting the referential temperature onto climate and weather, the environs of the human body—a mild and temperate climate being the best because it permits the widest range of life, a world where people can flourish in a way that is impossible in the arctic or the desert. When pushed further, the climatic sense can then turn the cold into a sign for the outside, to be contrasted with the warmth of the inside. Thus we have entered a world not of frozen immobility and stasis but of action, speed, and dissimulation, the cynical world, in short, immortalized in the novels by John le Carré, the looking glass war of essentially identical antagonists, a space represented directly by the divided city of Berlin on a typically nasty winter day.[7] Berlin may otherwise serve as symbol for the kind of freeze that is encapsulated in the very line of rigid demarcation that marks the cold war in its European frame, what Winston Churchill famously referred to as "the iron curtain" (he was recycling an old metaphor originating in the construction of British theaters).[8]

These may seem idle musings on a word (cold) that happens to be endlessly suggestive. I think not. For the chain of signification had real historical effects. It is not difficult to see, for example, how the notion of a cold war could by transference be associated in the United States directly with the Soviet Union itself and the totalitarian system. What is this system imagined to be (not entirely without reason) but a rigid, immobile, and unfriendly one, the very essence of coldness? The identity is obvious—too obvious.

The third word, "war" in "the cold war," is the trickiest. What kind of war was this? The two sides never went to war with each other. There is no obvious beginning, no single moment of initial aggression, no declaration of war, no crossing of a certain line, and no open military engagement. Is war then perhaps also a metaphor, not an actual war but an image of something warlike? Contemporaries at the outset used the term "cold war" (predominantly) as a category for a new kind of warfare, new but real, as real as hot war. I myself will argue below that there is an essential element of truth in this. In particular, one must ask oneself, historically, what kind of peace it posited. Soon, in effect, that question came to be bracketed along with the whole issue of metaphor. One reason was indeed its potent range of meanings and possible uses: it lent itself to instant metaphorical extension for journalistic purposes. In September 1947 "the cold war" enters public discourse; a month later the term is used in the *New York Times* to describe relations between rival football leagues.

Overall, then, "the cold war" is a designation of the greatest elasticity and range of use. It can be used relatively to describe variations, degrees

---

7   Le Carré "resolves" this identity ultimately by annulling it in some individual and typically quixotic act of heroism that breaks with the systemic altogether. Witness Alec Leamas on the Berlin Wall in the climax of *The Spy Who Came in from the Cold* (1963), a novel whose spirit and appearance are of the greatest interest when it comes to periodization.

8   On Churchill's metaphor (which had a long and not always honorable lineage), see Patrick Wright, *Iron Curtain: From Stage to Cold War* (Oxford, 2007).

of hostility, or the mere impressions of such variable states since there is no objective way of measuring them. Because the condition and the activities it implies are indeed indistinct, almost an absence (of hot war), any number of things can appear in it. Recognizing these difficulties, one might of course eliminate the problem by eliminating the term itself, or reducing it to triviality. One might replace it, for instance, with "the postwar epoch" or some such neutral or anodyne designation. In the best of cases, this could then be developed into a genuine concept along the lines of what happened in the 1980s with the analogous category of postmodernity, where the simple chronological notion of "after" was transformed to the point of explanatory power.[9] Evading the cold war as a proper concept of periodization would turn it into a purely historical object, to be studied by those so inclined as one way among others that contemporaries thought and acted in the world, as a historical conception of a certain condition or series of events. Such an investigation is indeed indispensable but not enough. I am myself opposed to the evasive move. For one thing, the ideological uses of the cold war are everywhere in evidence and operation. More fundamentally, it is my contention that the cold war, if treated as a concept, actually tells us something real beyond the archaeological, second-order understanding of contemporary understandings. Its history is also the history of a genuine historical movement. If this is right, then avoidance serves only to obscure that historical movement. It is imperative, in particular, to counteract the tendency to normalize the end and reinscribe that normality in the beginning. It is altogether too easy because of the massively obvious end, to normalize the United States, the victorious antagonist, and inversely to turn the pathological Soviet Union into the constitutive factor, the abnormality that actually caused the whole thing. The real historical conditions of possibility for something called the cold war thus vanish along with the fact that the cold war was a US project.

Such an argument will require a positive account rather than a critique, an alternative that shows that the cold war can provide rigorous

---

9   Jean-François Lyotard originated this with *The Postmodern Condition: A Report on Knowledge* (Minneapolis, 1984 [original in French, 1979]), but for me the best conceptualization remains Fredric Jameson, *Postmodernism, or, The Cultural Logic of Late Capitalism* (Durham, NC, 1991); the original article by the same name appeared in 1984. Jameson's Althusserian understanding of what it is to produce a concept has been decisive for me.

periodization, which is what historians do or are supposed to be doing.[10] I will attempt a sketch of this kind below. The gist of it may cause unease, even irritation. I shall claim, then, that the cold war was from the outset not only a US term but a US project; that it began as a contingently articulated policy that eventually generated a system, static and dynamic at the same time; that this system was qualitatively transformed in the early 1960s into something else. This is not a moral argument, much less a moralizing one. I am not, in short, inverting neoorthodoxy by claiming that the United States equals the cold war. The United States, from a systemic standpoint, did not need the cold war.[11] I am proposing, however, that the cold-war frame is structural to the extent that it made abundant sense in distinctly American terms for the dominant internationalists who articulated the US approach to the world between 1946 and 1950; and that they used it to considerable effect the global purpose of putting the United States into the world once and for all. This, I reiterate, was not a necessity: it did not have to happen that way. Once my account reaches the 1970s, I will shift gears again by turning to a fourth version of the continuity thesis, Odd Arne Westad's ambitious *The Global Cold War: Third World Interventions and the Making of Our Times*. Westad propounds the thesis that the cold war was, or became, largely about third world interventionism and that détente signified its extension and deepening. Westad's thesis is an ambitious attempt to break with amorphous convention that nevertheless ends up reinforcing it because the alternative concept of the cold war is empty.

---

10   Vulgarly put, historians chop up time and give names to the ensuing entities or periods, offering accounts in the process of origins and causes of expiration. Space is a complicating factor not always recognized.

11   I disagree, therefore, with the many left-wing accounts of the cold war that see the need for capitalist expansion as central. The cold war was a political move, a strategic way of putting the United States into the world in no uncertain terms, a way of rendering global engagement irrefutable. This is not unrelated to capitalism, of course, but at the same time not reducible to it. An argument could well be made that a better solution for capital in 1947 than the cold war would have been extensive cooperation or at least geopolitical agreement with the Soviet Union; but such a view would also be politically ahistorical.

Emergence and Periodization

I must begin, for archaeological and conceptual reasons, with a couple of classical realists. Walter Lippmann's symptomatic reading of George F. Kennan's X article under the rubric of the cold war in the fall of 1947 placed the term into common usage and also offered the beginning of a genuine concept. By reinforcing the media obsession with containment as the essence of Kennan's original article, Lippmann's critique condemned Kennan to the fate of having his historical accomplishment perennially summarized in that truly tiresome attribute "architect of containment," and to the fate of being forced into half a century of fruitless denials. (Containment was not all there was to Kennan's argument and was arguably not even its central aspect, but let us leave that inexhaustible question aside.)[12] For a month, in fourteen columns no less, the pundit of pundits subjected Kennan to a critical scrutiny that sometimes verged on ridicule. Many things caused his displeasure but above all two. He considered the notion of containing the Soviet Union across the globe a "strategic monstrosity"—a position that would leave the initiative entirely up to Moscow while saddling the United States with the obligation to prop up all manner of unsavory and unreliable allies, satellites and clients, on the sanguine hope that frustration of the Soviet Union's initiatives would eventually cause its internal destruction or at any rate a qualitative mellowing. In accordance with the universalist spirit of the Truman Doctrine of March 1947, containment was thus utterly devoid of that basic aspect of any proper strategy, namely, a realistic ranking of priorities. Kennan actually agreed, but the formulations of his article left him (and the Truman Doctrine) open to the charge.

Lippmann's second complaint, more pertinent in our context, had to do with diplomacy, or more precisely its absence. His point, a correct

---

12   Though only mentioned more or less in passing, containment was important in expressing Kennan's notion of a predetermined, unresponsive Moscow. Lippmann spotted this. The idea, however, that containment was a strategy is incorrect. It meant nothing more than counteracting in various ways at various points. Kennan would spend the next half century trying to explain why this was presumably not grasped. The literature on the alleged meaning of containment is enormous and still growing. A recent example, typically streamlined and simplified for prescriptive purposes (well intended in themselves) is Ian Shapiro's *Containment: Rebuilding a Strategy Against Global Terror* (Princeton, 2008). Containment functions here chiefly as a fantasized counterpoint to the excesses, real enough, of George W. Bush.

one, was that Kennan appeared to exclude the normal workings of diplomacy in dealing with the Soviet Union. Lippmann objected specifically to the notion of incommensurability, the notion that somehow the vast chasm, cultural and ideological, between the Soviet Union and the West, the central referent here both for Kennan and Lippmann, rendered agreements impossible in the manner of some thwarted Wittgensteinian language game. Historically there was nothing in difference as such (or lack of intimacy) between powers that militated against agreements and settlements. In his ideological fixation, moreover, Kennan had forgotten (said Lippmann, a bit unfairly) that the Soviet regime existed in the same geopolitical setting as the old czarist empire, a setting that was eminently translatable and meaningful in traditional categories of power. Lippmann's primary example was the presence and place of any given army. An army is either there or it is not. An army is recognizable in any language game, so to speak. Hence, given that the primary problem for the West (in 1947) was the presence of the Red Army in Central Europe, one might usefully investigate what, if anything, Moscow would be willing to accept by way of bargaining to retract its military line. One would engage in actual diplomacy to adjudicate interests.[13]

Kennan, like Lippmann a realist of sorts, was not, on reflection, averse to such ideas. His disagreement with Lippmann had to do with the conception of the Soviet Union: Stalin's regime was beyond the realist pale. Kennan's realism was notably bounded by a certain civilizational sense. Interests attach to every form of power but the world is differentiated according to the ways in which these interests are pursued. To be realistic vis-à-vis third world nationalism (to name one of Kennan's later horrors) was thus something altogether different from being so in a Western context, a context, by the way, that for him was not about democracy but a certain kind of order and tradition. To be realistic vis-à-vis Moscow was to ignore it or, when that was impossible, vigorously to counteract it. In no way, however, was it a regime with which it was possible to enter into any kind of agreement or deal.[14] Perhaps the

---

13 Lippmann, *The Cold War: A Study in Foreign Policy* (New York, 1947). The articles appeared from September 2 to October 2 in the *New York Herald Tribune* and the *Washington Post* (and were syndicated elsewhere). "Strategic monstrosity" was used in his column on September 6.

14 The closest analogue, analytically, is in fact FDR's conception of Hitler's Germany: one could do business with unpleasant dictators, even fascist ones such as

closest analogue here is Edmund Burke's conception of revolutionary France and the threat to Europe, which is to say essentially Christendom. Containing and eventually crushing the revolution in the name of this civilization of Christian particularities did not assume that the world was unitary or binary, that it represented the quintessence of humankind. So while the French had committed treason against the ruling Christian regime of Europe, the outside of that order was a differentiated, multifaceted series of realities. Meanwhile, the place of Russia within this imagined European community had of course always varied: inside, on probation, after 1721; outside again in 1917.

In 1947, then, Lippmann did not find this Burkean argument persuasive. With piercing clarity, he had diagnosed the undialectical nature of Kennan's diagnosis, that it was really a kind of medical diagnosis of an object under a microscope, the analysis of a virus, an organism, a parasite, a tumor, in short something to be surrounded, contained, suffocated, denied its feeding grounds, forced into submission or, better still, killed off. For Lippmann, this was a serious misreading leading to a potentially disastrous strategy of perimeter defense, a posture singularly ill-fitted for the kind of power that the United States wielded: mobile, specific, firmly Western. The Soviet Union, for its part, wielded power almost exclusively because of its mighty army and on its perimeter. Communist parties elsewhere, however devoted to Moscow, could not become a lasting problem in the absence of that power. Hence it was in the Western interest, indeed paramount for the West, to negotiate with Moscow for the withdrawal of all alien armies from Europe (meaning the armies not only of the Soviet Union but also the United States and Britain).[15]

Mussolini, but not with the Nazi regime, whose gangster nature made all agreement impossible. On the civilizational aspect, see Patrick Thaddeus Jackson's stimulating *Civilizing the Enemy: German Reconstruction and the Invention of the West* (Ann Arbor, MI, 2006). See also John Lamberton Harper, *Visions of Europe: Franklin D. Roosevelt, George F. Kennan, and Dean G. Acheson* (Cambridge, 1994).

15 I have developed the analysis here at greater length in chap. 1. See also Anders Stephanson, *Kennan and the Art of Foreign Policy* (Cambridge, MA, 1989), 17. Compare Nicolas Guilhot, ed., *The Invention of International Relations Theory: Realism, the Rockefeller Foundation, and the 1954 Conference on Theory* (New York, 2011). Realism was far from a single political position. Reinhold Niebuhr's Christian realism was eminently compatible with a cold-war posture. Morgenthau's realism, of course, continued to exert a powerful academic influence, not least because he was the author of the standard textbook.

Lippmann was largely right, but both Kennan and he turned out to be wrong in the end, displaced as they were by the metarealism of Dean Acheson. By the time Kennan had grasped the truth of Lippmann's objections in the late spring of 1948, his erstwhile position, or what passed for it, had become unshakeable orthodoxy: no real diplomacy with the evil empire, compromise now defined as appeasement. Both Lippmann and Kennan, in fact, found their contributions selectively appropriated for other purposes. The invention of a term and its subsequent uses are, as Nietzsche famously insisted, quite different phenomena. Lippmann's barrage, published under the rubric of the cold war, did not explicate the term; in fact, he never once mentioned it in the actual articles. It was present in its absence. In subsequent columns, he did deploy it, sparingly, in the spirit of his earlier pieces to designate, matter-of-factly, a mutual condition, a situation of cold as opposed to hot war that applied to East and West alike and that could be overcome by a more appropriate US policy, namely, a policy of real diplomacy. The term, however, began to appear daily in the press to indicate, quite differently from Lippmann's account, just the current manner of Soviet totalitarian aggression; in which regard a heavily reduced version of Kennan's Soviet Union became axiomatic, condensed into the single proposition that here was a fanatical force committed to the destruction of the West (or "freedom") and impervious to any reasonable or traditional consideration from the outside. From then on, the cold war is what the Soviet Union is and does, specifically the strategy it deploys to destroy the Free World since it is (as yet) not strong enough to launch a hot war.

Classical realism, from then on, passes to the margins of the mainstream as it were, ultimately un-American in its assumption that policy must start from the realization that there is no overarching normative order in the world beyond interests; and that it is both daft and counterproductive to operate on the belief that the values of the United States apply everywhere. If so, then it is also the case that actors in the field of international relations are for analytical purposes identical, a view that is completely at odds with the notion of a salvational agent such as the United States embroiled in world-historical, global struggle against a mortal enemy. Scattered leftists aside, the only vocal critics of cold-war thinking in the early 1950s are in fact some of the classical realists, outstandingly Kennan himself.[16] Cold-war

---

16 Compare Guilhot, *Invention of International Relations*.

orthodoxy, meanwhile, became enormously effective. To see how, we need a brief word about the semantic field and contextual politics in which Lippmann's idea was formulated, more precisely how the term might have appeared to him as a proper name for something deeper.

It is largely to do with the understanding of the 1930s. Beginning when the Japanese Kwantung Army created the incident at Mukden in 1931 and subsequently invaded Manchuria, the 1930s seem to be about flagrant violations of traditional legal definitions of war and peace. States, according to the norm, would either be at peace or war with one another, and a war could not properly begin unless openly declared. A string of fascist aggressions (Japan, Italy and Germany) then made that distinction and notion of propriety nigh-on meaningless. No war is declared. No legal niceties apply. Instead a gradated sequence of possible actions, more or less violent, replaces the old division. This is allowed to go on because traditional powers have more pressing matters to handle, above all the Depression; but the end result is of course World War II, fought not only to extinguish fascist illegality for all time but also to institute a machinery that would not merely establish the status quo ante but make even traditional, legal war virtually illegitimate. Lippmann's critique, then, is articulated when that project, the notion of one world of peace and stability, appears to have capsized, not because there are differences between the West and the Soviet Union but because of the way in which those differences are grasped. For Lippmann, it makes sense to call this condition a cold war. He means a condition that is warlike by the old standards in not permitting or exhibiting the normal diplomatic means of peace but at the same time does not involve any overt military engagements.[17] Clearly, too,

---

17   Lippmann does not, in my view, think of the term "cold war" as a metaphor but rather as analogous to what the French writer Georges Duhamel had referred to in 1939 as *la guerre blanche*, Hitler's bully tactics against the French, a war of terror, one might say, without the actual violence. Lippmann later claimed indeed that he had picked it up in France in the late 1930s: I have never found it, however, in the form of *la guerre froide*. The term was used on a couple of occasions in the spring and summer of 1947 by Bernard Baruch but not in any sustained way. George Orwell first used the term in 1943 without any deeper significance and then in 1945 to describe, more suggestively, a typically dystopian future of superpower domination, internally coherent imperialisms in a system of constant but cold external hostility. The *Chicago Tribune* characterized Truman's "Doctrine" address in March 1947 as "cold a war speech" as any; and the *India Times* in turn recast that expression into the more succinct "Cold War Speech." It is easy to demonstrate, however, that Lippmann's acerbic series inaugurated the public use of the term. By November–December, it was in daily use.

he finds such a posture to be contrary to the interests of the United States and, more important, the West.[18]

In this last notion, then, Lippmann proved interestingly off the mark. For the errors of containment and the underlying misapprehensions about the Soviet regime he had pinpointed proved extraordinarily successful for the promotion of the interests of the United States in the world. The cold war became a matrix that made unarguable, indeed imperative, a truly globalist role for the United States, a role it was to play to great advantage for quite some time. In practice, as the policymakers were perfectly aware, the universal struggle for freedom meant quite specific interests in specific places; but the globalist frame was an absolute precondition for that specificity. The whole point of the exercise was in fact not to engage the Soviet Union in the trenches of any war, real or imagined, but to establish Washington's license to act everywhere else. In short, error was productively serving ends of the greatest ambition. It would take Kennan almost a decade of frustration before he realized this, partly courtesy once again of Lippmann (and Raymond Aron). Kennan was dumbfounded.[19]

The basic features of the US matrix are well known and can be summarized quickly: a literal translation of the appeasement lessons of the 1930s, the world war as a result of totalitarian aggression and wanton disregard for traditional standards of peace and war, now in the face of a much more insidious version requiring a huge and global effort on the part of the only power capable of leading the Free World. That the cold war passed into general usage was partly, as intimated, because it fit the Soviet Union itself, a very cold place run by a very cold dictator, who, on closer inspection, had turned out to be drastically different from his avuncular wartime image; and partly too because it allowed one to think the intratotalitarian difference between Stalin and Hitler, the difference between using a wide range of cynical, sly, and subversive measures, depending on the circumstances, and the brash, reckless open warfare

---

18 Compare chapter 1 in this volume.
19 In his *Memoirs II* (1972), Kennan credits Raymond Aron together with Lippmann with his enlightenment in the late 1950s after the disengagement controversy. It is hard to accept that he remained blind to the functionality aspect of the cold war for so long; but it seems plausible, given that he is still, in his famous Reith Lectures of 1957, proposing diplomacy and disengagement rather along the lines of Lippmann's critique in September 1947.

of the Nazis: Stalin in contrast not only to the open and warm politicians of the West but also to the "hot" dictator Hitler, hysterically angry and keen on hot wars. The end result however is identity: two totalitarian regimes on a quest for world domination. Moreover, there is now a sense that Stalin's strategy of cold war is more effective, more rational if you will, in this quest than Hitler's hot war.

The cold war, then, is what the Soviet Union is and does, destruction of the Free World by any means necessary. The matter need not be analyzed any further. Not much by way of analysis did in fact follow, either. What is peculiar in retrospect about the dichotomy (a dichotomy in the true sense of the word) is that it is not in fact Manichean: freedom being the natural state of affairs, the real world is the free world whereas the totalitarian sphere is inherently incapable of independent existence, always taking the parasitic form of an attack on freedom. With this netherworld of world-conquering aggression and subversion, accordingly, there can be no compromise and certainly no traditional diplomacy. Here, then, in all its essentials is the structure Reagan thinks never went away. The axiom is explicit: the cold war, being an effect of the very nature of the Soviet system itself, can only end when that system too has ended, when the Soviet Union has ceased to be the Soviet Union.[20]

What are the auxiliary conceptual effects? Initially this: an exhaustive distinction of such a binary kind renders it incumbent on the keeper of the faith to arrange every phenomenon taxonomically on one side or the

---

20 Compare chap. 2. The model here is of course Augustine's solution to the problem of evil amid the omnipotence of God: evil is a perversion of good, not a quality of independent existence. Nietzsche's transformation of this is also pertinent: the infection of the strong by the slave mentality, which can only exist parasitically and not in its own right. The political consequence is the essential point. Had the structure been properly Manichean (which is often wrongly assumed), the possibility of a modus vivendi and all manner of deals would have at once been opened up. On the aspect of unconditional surrender, see NSC 68, the most authoritative US policy statement after Kennan's articulations of 1947–48, which says in April 1950 that "we can expect no lasting abatement of the crisis unless and until a change occurs in the nature of the Soviet system," and that any diplomatic settlement "can only record the progress which the free world will have made in creating a political and economic system in the world so successful that the frustration of the Kremlin's design for world domination will be complete." It is hard to think of a more resolute rejection of the kind of diplomacy and strategy Lippmann had in mind. There can be no agreement unless it is a matter of registering the destruction of the Soviet system. This is an offer one must refuse in Moscow, as indeed was also the intention.

other. There can be no place for neutrality: "You are either with us or against us," to echo a more recent reinvention of the reinvention. (In the early 1960s, Kennedy will respond to previous innovations in Soviet policy by visualizing good neutrals, but these are neutrals who, being free, are really objectively not neutral at all but inherently resistant to, and subversive of, the other side.) In short, there can be no distribution of entities along a line of continuity or within clusters based on variable criteria—such as for instance Kennan's alternative (by 1948) to cold-war binarism, the notion of five military-industrial centers of potentially open-ended internal configuration, where the US strategy would be devoted negatively to keeping the Soviets, one of these centers, from seizing control of any of the remaining ones. The rest of the world, then, was essentially of limited or no importance.

Such differentiation, such a principle of nonidentity, is thus illegitimate within the binary cold-war division; but there is another set of divisions, secondary seemingly but crucial, once the overarching divide has been set forth and territorialized. First, there is a certain differentiation on the totalitarian side. Totalitarian space is occupied space, illegitimate, impermanent and unreal. It is a netherworld of slavery, an unnatural space harboring captive people whose natural freedom is entirely denied. Thus there is a difference between the dictatorial regime and the people. In practice, however, differentiation is erased precisely because totalitarianism means total domination (which also paradoxically makes it brittle). Reform is inconceivable. Slaves, being slaves, are unlikely meanwhile to liberate themselves. The other order, then, must be abolished in toto for liberation to take place. Hence any deals with the regime are inherently counterproductive, serving only to strengthen the system and to recognize its validity. The immediate reference here is the analogy to the Munich Pact and appeasement. A much deeper domestic grounding, however, will be found historically in the abolitionism of the 1850s and the ensuing Civil War, a posture expressed with tremendous rhetorical force in NSC 68. The problem with abolitionism, alas, is that while self-evidently true, it is also impossible to implement, either by open war or subversion.[21]

---

21 This is the notorious problem with rollback, the Republican counterpoint to containment in the early 1950s. Republican critics were right to say that if international communism is all the things that the Truman administration says it is, then it is inherently immoral by American standards to leave it in place, as containment would seem to

What remains, then, is to bracket the other side while vigorously protecting and fortifying the free world. This is where a second and decisive differentiation enters the proceedings, having to do with the map of the free rather than the totalitarian netherworld. Another line of demarcation is drawn, auxiliary but in fact decisive, namely, the line between the United States and the rest of the Free World. The United States is both part of the Free World and absolutely different from it. For, as guarantor, the United States is invested with unlimited power to act across the board. The (messianic) agent here is thus a precise place and identity, freedom achieved; but the extent and whereabouts of the free world are always up for grabs, under constant construction as it were. Freedom, in short, must everywhere be asserted, inscribed, established, clarified. It must be made legible. In making it legible, one has to posit that it is always already under threat. The free world, then, is a perpetual and unlimited security problem while the other side of the fence is a nullity that should, all things being equal, be unlocked and naturalized, totally cleansed of its totalitarian system. While striking a defensive note, then, this posture is in actuality relentlessly offensive. The world, in principle, is a natural whole but perversion happens temporarily to rein in a specific area. History, plainly, is now calling upon the one agent capable of global action to defend existing freedom and eventually root out perversion, the one agent that is not only totally free but also, not accidentally, massively powerful.

It will then be remarked that the Soviet position mirrored the US binary exactly, certainly by the time Andrei Zhdanov had established the two-camp delineation in September 1947. This is not quite true. For there are two crucial and related differences. First, the two-camp theory (democracy/peace versus imperialism/aggression) is grounded in the Stalinist version of the Marxist-Hegelian notion of contradiction, which, unlike the (Augustinian) polarity of good/real/natural versus evil/unreal/unnatural, constitutes a dialectical unity of

---

imply. Logically, then, this system of slavery had to be abolished, or rolled back, instead of merely contained. Logic then falters: even without the threat of nuclear war, it would have been hard to find a workable rollback strategy short of outright war, which is to say another world war, at which point one had good reason to flinch. Logic also falters, however, for the same reason that Kennan's contrary position failed as a critique of containment: what the Truman administration and cold-war thought said about the Soviet Union was only a premise, an enabling condition, for something quite different.

opposites, always by definition locked in struggle, but a struggle of "equals" so to speak. The difference here between a parasite and a real enemy is essential because the latter allows for real deals on the basis of real interests (or interests imagined to be real). That the revolutionary principle is antithetical to this precisely in its refusal to deal is ultimately less important than the reality of the unity of opposites and the reality of interests. Long-term transformation here always entails realist recognition of objective interests: the enemy is at once legitimate and not, historically passé, to be superseded and annulled at the most general level but at the same time actually existing in the present, representing interests pursued in accordance with their identifiable nature and so open to calculation of losses and gains. While capitalists as a class are on the verge of becoming historically reactionary, individual capitalists (such as Averell Harriman in the 1920s) may well have interests that coincide with those of the Soviet Union, thus giving rise to mutually profitable and highly realistic relations.

By the time we get to Stalin the hyperrealist, in any case, revolution had undergone drastic reconceptualization. This is the second difference. For the decisive main contradiction in Stalinism had been territorialized (that is, horizontalized) after 1928 such that the line between the Soviet Union (and its auxiliaries) and the outside now incarnated the old vertical and deterritorialized opposition between capital and labor. Instead of a dual, international set of classes, then, there is now a socialist headquarters in a well-specified place with a well-specified leadership, the survival of which overshadows every other concern. Territorialization is then wedded to the historical vision of capitalism in its last, monopoly stage and the inverse notion of rational construction of socialism in one country (and its vicinity); in which case the central object, again, is always by definition the survival and protection of space already gained by the socialist mother/fatherland. Altogether, this is an eminently strategic view, a view featuring a quasimilitary conception of space that is itself not a very farfetched reworking of the quasimilitary conception of politics found in Lenin (but that is another story). It was also, in fact, an eminently defensive conception, one in which there could be no room for any idea of launching a cold war against an enemy that was by all measures infinitely more powerful.

This is why the Soviet response takes the tactical form, not of socialist confrontation, but an appeal to national independence supposed to attract sundry bourgeois elements, complemented later by the universal appeal to peace—both measures designed to thwart what appears to be in the Stalinist perspective an embryonic, protofascist threat from the United States, as embodied in the policy of the cold war (which Stalin always imputed directly to the United States and the United States alone). The notion of protofascism is significant here. The United States as such is not inherently either fascist or protofascist, because the Stalinist concept of fascism has been, since 1933, at once extraordinarily narrow and arbitrary, locating the phenomenon in the most reactionary part of finance capital, a very small, imaginary class fraction that may be in power but apparently not necessarily so (as evidenced by the highly praised Roosevelt and the wartime alliance). In reality, of course, the index of fascism had nothing to do with actual class analysis and everything to do with the degree of perceived hostility toward present Soviet policy. Soviet and auxiliary space is accordingly defined as liberated, democratic and free, while the imperialist outside is differentiated, to various degrees and at various levels, sometimes but not always under the control of "the most reactionary circles of monopoly capital," thus requiring by way of response an equally differentiated policy designed, above all, negatively to split the forces on the other side so as to prevent fascization. Degrees, then, are vitally important: fascism full-blown is equal to war, preeminently targeting the rising embodiment of socialist achievement and so forth, while fascization is a scale measuring the concrete bourgeois posture toward the Soviet Union and its interests. Spaces and maps can be inscribed correspondingly.[22]

Moscow and Washington, in short, both laid claims to the legacy of 1945, the War that was supposed to have created One World but evidently had failed to do so. From the Soviet standpoint, the war had been a class coalition at the state level in the name of antifascism, a massive attempt to root out the sources of fascism. Now, in late 1947, it appeared that residual forces of this kind had not only survived but were indeed flourishing in new guise in the post-Rooseveltian United States. From the US standpoint, the war had been a struggle for freedom everywhere. Owing to appalling mistakes (see Yalta) and dark treachery (see

---

22   The two best analyses of this Soviet complex remain Nicos Poulantzas, *Fascism and Dictatorship: The Third International and the Problem of Fascism* (London, 1974); and Fernando Claudin, *The Communist Movement From Comintern to Cominform* (Harmondsworth, UK, 1975).

Soviet actions in Eastern Europe and elsewhere), the war effort had turned out in reality to advance hugely the interests of another and potentially much more dangerous version of totalitarianism, the very antithesis of freedom. What followed from these two different conceptions of the one world that, unexpectedly, had turned into two, were two very different strategies: renewed antifascism in the one case, a defensive move amid retrenchment and continentalism; renewed struggle for global freedom in the other, an offensive move. As it happened, this mirrored the actual power capabilities of the two sides.

The cold war, then, was the manner in which the United States was able in peacetime to enter into the world of international politics on a global scale in the name of conducting a war short of actual war that had allegedly been declared by international communism. Domestically, the cold war as an always already assumed structure of aggression imposed by totalitarian Moscow worked magnificently, again, to render virtually impossible any opposition to Washington's license to act everywhere. A Republican Congress reluctant, all things being equal, to go along with governmental largesse in peacetime found itself flummoxed by the cold-war logic. The Truman administration knew this and instrumentally exaggerated without compunction the worldwide threat. This is why Acheson can be considered a metarealist. He saw quite lucidly that the cold war was a way to stamp out once and for all any postwar tendencies to isolationist reversal. To deal with the realities of domestic politics one could not be entirely true to the realities abroad. In a word, one had to be ideological.[23] From that angle, the concept had the signal virtue of making it impossible to dissent and still remain politically viable. Argument could only be about a cold war more or less vigorously and successfully pursued. Here there was a political price to be paid down the line. If the threat was indeed an immediate matter of life and death on a global scale, then no incumbent could possibly do enough to meet

---

23 Thus, in a way, the cold war is an invention, but the dynamic is certainly not reducible to any functionalist creation of useful myth. Acheson ultimately believed in the essentials of the cold war, the idea of the global threat and the necessity of a commensurate US response. It should be noted that officialdom, as opposed to mass media, used the term "the cold war" sparingly. Until NSC 68, internal policy documents did not feature it either. One reason was that one did not wish to be seen as warlike, as participants in a war, the implication being identity and similarity, perhaps. This is contradicted, however, by NSC 68, which speaks approvingly of fighting the cold war.

it. One was always, therefore, acting with a certain deficit. Inadequacy, failure, was inherent. Hence of course the Republicans would soon come back with a vengeance after the Truman administration had failed in China and then failed by not winning in Korea. Cold-war ideology, by being unanswerably true, is also ipso facto politically rigid. There is no way of moving beyond orthodoxy.

After the Korean War fizzled out and Stalin died in 1953, a mutually reinforcing system was emerging, marked by warlike hostility under ostensible conditions of peace, nonrecognition of the other side's legitimacy coupled with unremitting propaganda, an intense arms race, and the imposition of an increasingly bipolar structure on international politics, and, in qualitatively different ways, suppression of domestic dissidents. The Soviet Union, though sharply opposed to US cold-war hegemony overall, began to recognize, too, the advantages of physical separation, the potential for recognition of the status quo. The real is rational. Notably, nothing by way of actual head-on military conflagration takes place: Korea was close and dangerous enough. The cold war became not a strategy but a geopolitical system, set in place and dominated by the United States.

The Dénouement

Three developments made the US matrix historically unsustainable from the early to mid-1960s. First and most important, nuclear weapons turn out to be very effective ideology killers. The best early indication is the development of nuclear strategy in the United States from the mid-1950s onward, which involved the articulation of various logics whose fundamental premise is that the calculation of costs and benefits apply to both sides equally, that there is indeed a positional identity, a sameness, here; and that the game is a dialectic of sorts. In short, there is no deep freeze but competition and interaction, a game involving two sides with identical premises. This is precisely what cold-war thought denied. The philosophers of escalation are thus not the quintessential cold warriors immortalized by Stanley Kubrick but, unbeknownst to themselves, harbingers of change. More immediately, the heroic "better dead than red" bravura of cold-war culture is hard to maintain amid the increasing awareness that any postwar world would be devoid of life as we know it. Dwight D. Eisenhower was uncomfortably alive to this (along with, sotto voce, John Foster Dulles); but he was typically incapable of breaking with the existing frame, his great achievement really being the negative one of preventing lunacy. After the Cuban Missile Crisis, however, the issue became chillingly concrete and explicit. Nothing is worth the ultimate price of nuclear war, a hot war, the kind of war that amounts to the very erasure of value itself. The Cuban Missile Crisis adds to this intellectual realization the vital, existential experience of the actual abyss and the untruth of the cold war. In the immediate aftermath, the days of October 1962 may have looked like a fabulous cold-war victory but no responsible observer, and certainly not Kennedy himself, could miss the fundamental lesson that the world no longer made sense in those terms. Instead of hovering on the edge of total destruction, there had to be management, order and predictability, some kind of normality. The Missile Crisis is the cold war degree zero.

Second, the very notion of "international communism" is rendered increasingly phantasmagoric because of the Sino-Soviet split: first an internal fight about revisionism, then an open cold war bordering on all-out war after the Maoists have decided that the new czars are the new main enemy within imperialism. The Titoist break in 1948 could be integrated into the cold-war frame as a minor anomaly, but the Chinese defection could not. The idea of a territorialized monolith and simple binaries is blasted asunder. The dichotomy is dead. The unavoidable corollary begins to emerge: preserving the cold-war frame is denying oneself the marvelous chance of playing the two communist antagonists off against each other. When none other than Richard Nixon begins to articulate this in 1967, he is saying the unsayable but obvious. Even if some notion of intracommunist quarrels can be maintained within the cold-war orthodox view at the outset, it certainly cannot be so once the PRC and the United States move into de facto alliance, to the point where the Maoist regime becomes a fervent supporter of Chilean fascism because it happens overall to serve anti-Soviet interests. The orthodox argument indeed capsizes here: if the Soviet Union was the cold war, how could one with suave ease align with a regime that fulfilled much more accurately the original criteria of what made the Soviet Union the Soviet Union? It makes no sense whatsoever, which is why Ronald Reagan did not like it (yet would maintain the alliance once in power).

The Cuban Missile Crisis and the Sino-Soviet conflict destroy the cold-war matrix. A third event then ratifies this historical rupture. For, if one needed no other proof, the Vietnam debacle was every day demonstrating in living color the absurdity of cold-war shibboleths, leading indeed, by 1968, to something approximating a legitimacy crisis at the very top echelons of the US state apparatus itself. The timing here is subject to debate. Ideology does not change overnight. Lyndon B. Johnson, unlike his mercurial, mobile (and, in a way, more cynical) predecessor, is still operating rudimentarily within Munich memories when he imagines what Vietnam is about, not to mention the Dominican Republic in 1965. However, already amid the great escalation of 1965–66 in Vietnam, he is beginning to sense that the whole endeavor is about face, prestige and credibility, as defined by some now defunct categorical frame. Vietnam is not the end of the cold war but the most graphic evidence conceivable that its historical moment has already been over for some time. The decisive change from 1963 onward is recognition: recognition of the other side's legitimacy as a geopolitical actor, if not its domestic system; recognition of the mutual interest in avoiding nuclear war at all costs. It is not recognition of the status quo across the playing field; but neither is it, metaphorically or really, a cold war. It becomes, one might say, a rivalry rather than a war where winning and losing are presumably about total destruction of the other's system.

The cold war, then, was a grand policy on the part of the United States which eventually becomes a system of sorts, involving both sides. Yet from another vantage point, it is not systemic at all. Almost all versions of the conventional view are grounded in some kind of systemic conflict. This position can, to reiterate, take two distinct forms: either it locates the cold war as an integral part of the nature of one of the two antagonists (chiefly the Soviet Union), or it locates it in the very difference between the two. Both versions will then have to decide whether the cold war actually began in 1917 with the appearance of the Soviet Union and if Rooseveltian wartime alliances and all the palpable variations in the relation are subordinate phases of the cold war as systemic difference. I think this is altogether mistaken. Neither of the two sides was constituted in such a way as to give rise necessarily to the cold war, nor was their difference in itself enough to produce one. Neither side needed the cold war for its domestic reproduction. Moreover, there was nothing in the existence of two completely different social and political systems, however antithetical in structure, that in itself would have led to a cold war or *the* cold war. Though opposed to one another on principle in a wide range of areas, there was no intrinsic reason that the two could not have recognized territorialized demarcation and a more traditional rivalry. Moscow would certainly have gone along with that in 1947; Washington, for specific historical reasons, found it impossible to do so, choosing instead a radically different route. This choice, to be sure, was not a mere whim. Without the systemic differences, the US matrix would have made no sense and so would have been impossible. Yet a choice it remained, a deliberate decision that was not necessary.

Here one wonders, futilely but unavoidably, what would have happened had Roosevelt not died. For the license of the US presidency to create its own foreign realities is extraordinary. Witness the mind-boggling shift in US attitudes that took place with regard to Mao's China in a matter of a year or two in the early 1970s, all against the backdrop of the minutely managed Nixon-Kissinger opening. Roosevelt, in any case, had a very different view of politics and how one conducts international relations from that which obtained after 1946. He was interested in management, order, and predictability, preconditions for Progressive change.[24] Instead there was a cold war and eventually a structure to go with it, or, to be more precise, two massive, analogous structures, each devoted to outrageous levels of military expenditure and unremitting ideological hostility. Notably, the dissolution of traditional categories of war and peace, the whole notion of a cold war in effect, fitted the United States quite well: the inherent power in the executive could be deployed in full force, the cumbersome separation of powers was overcome, various forms of intervention launched, if need be, global military installations established, all on the old premise that this war, like any other war in modern US history, would take place elsewhere, outside the body politic and its sacred territory. Domestically, meanwhile, it allowed a version of the corporatism of the 1930s to be institutionalized: science, capital, labor, the state, all devoted irrefutably to a single monumental struggle.

---

24 FDR, representing in many ways the last gasp and generation of the Progressive Era, always insisted on the worldliness of the United States, that one had to recognize that America was in time and history, part of a larger whole and irrevocably called upon to act in it. His singularly cavalier attitude to the finer points of the Constitution was indicative: there was nothing sacred about the United States as a tradition. This is also why he had no trouble in seeing the United States as part of a genuine alliance.

After 1963, this ends when the conservative potential of that duality of structures becomes not only visible but recognized. The military machines, with their domestic deformations, do not go away; on the contrary, their lethality is continuously expanded and much improved. Place and meaning, however, are radically different. Neither side assumes that meaningful peace, if not bliss, is a matter of the disappearance of the other. Because the cold war is not an outright war that can be seen and touched, its transformation is not immediately obvious or easily determined. The problem is readily grasped if we consider present-day Korea, which is at one and the same time a continuing issue of (i) World War II, (ii) the cold war, (iii) the Great Power conflict, and (iv) above all, local conflict. The historical temporalities of all enter directly into the concrete case. By the same token, it is not necessary to declare the end of the cold war in any definitive manner. It can fade away, recede, cease to be a way of thinking and doing. Indeed, residual cold-war action can take place, as I noted in the case of Johnson's Dominican intervention. By the early 1970s, however, the Nixon-Kissinger moves against Salvador Allende in Chile are unmistakably of a different logic and order, based on recognition and geopolitical spheres of influence. That qualitative break occurs in 1963.

This is the point where convention registers very firmly a diverging opinion. That something does happen to the relationship and so to international politics in 1963 and roughly on the grounds that I have outlined is not generally disputed. What is disputed is that it signifies any end to the cold war. My thesis, indeed, faces the problem of what happens next, how one is to conceptualize and periodize it. There is, initially, the problem of naming. Nothing comparable in rhetorical power to the cold war presents itself. Great Power management? I think not. Détente? Yes, for a while, but then again that designation leaves the opening to China aside. Détente is not what happens with regard to the PRC. Bipolarity amid increasing tendencies to multipolarity? Descriptively not without its virtues, but unless we want to pursue the neorealist solution, it is not an explanatory concept, in addition to which the whole semantics of polarity is fraught with difficulties, imported as it is from physics. In the end, no single logic dominates or overdetermines the coming era in the same way as did the cold war. Resurrecting a term once peddled by Acheson on Capitol Hill, one might perhaps call it a "cold peace."[25]

---

25 *New York Times*, June 11, 1950, 125. Acheson's remark was uttered a couple of weeks before the outbreak of the Korean War.

Historically, the best way concretely to approach this is through Mario Del Pero's revision of the conventional account and his emphatic insistence that Henry Kissinger's approach (Nixon's being less transparent) is never about the recognition of multipolarity but about the attempt to reimpose bipolarity. The conventional account, of course, sees détente as a relaxation of tension, relative cooperation between the two superpowers, and, on the part of the United States, the famed triangulation marked by the move on China in 1971. In a larger context, the period is typified by the aforementioned multipolarity that begins in the 1960s and now gains recognition: Beijing's break from Moscow, Charles de Gaulle's partial move away from NATO and the United States, Willy Brandt's Ostpolitik, the Czechoslovak Spring in 1968, Japan and West Germany's rising economic power within the West, the later beginnings of Eurocommunism, and so forth. As Del Pero argues, Kissinger's design is not based on any acceptance of multipolarity and the need to manage it; on the contrary it is about the reassertion of US power in the framework of bipolarity, that is, within the polarity of the real superpowers.[26]

This, in my view, is largely right, with the proviso that Kissinger is only pragmatically interested in bipolarity. His aim, after all, is not bipolarity for its own sake but the reassertion of US power—indeed, all things being equal, the achievement of US hegemony, if not (unrealistically) supremacy. Even so, it is also clear that his hyperdiplomacy is not situated within any cold-war frame. In short, the bipolarity in question is not to be confused with any dichotomous division of the world in terms of good and evil, or freedom and totalitarianism. Bipolarity is about a certain power relationship and how one conducts it to the best of one's interests. Kissinger is decidedly indifferent to political coloration. This is why he can find Zhou Enlai so congenial, the most impressive kindred spirit he ever encounters in geopolitics. This is why his idea of the Chilean coup in 1973 as a model for dealing with legitimate Eurocommunist power in Western Europe should not be grasped in cold-war terms. In the privacy of his chamber, Kissinger might well have agreed that the Italian Communist Party would have been the best administrator of local capitalism; but it was simply an irrelevant consideration along with the general principle of Italian democracy. In Chile

---

26 See Mario Del Pero, *The Eccentric Realist: Henry Kissinger and the Shaping of American Foreign Policy* (Ithaca, 2009).

and Western Europe, policy is a matter of superimposing geopolitical order, reasserting the line. Similarly, Kissinger's sundry actions to subvert and destroy Soviet and Cuban allies in Africa are a matter of making life difficult for the opponent who is getting out of bounds. At no time, however, does Kissinger challenge the right of the Soviets, all things being equal, to control their own sphere.

Kissinger's hyperdiplomacy was thus a recognition of certain realities having to do with the relative loss of US power and an ingenious attempt to recuperate that power by novel means. That the material underpinnings of the cold war had crumbled was one of those realities. It was Kissinger's misfortune, however, that cold-war ideology had not evaporated along with its foundations. It survived superstructurally, so to speak, always lurking ideologically in the background should things go wrong. The surviving element of bipolarity itself was similarly open to such potential reinterpretation. Hyperdiplomacy in the name of the balance of power, then, was always going to be a position that lived on borrowed time. By the end of the 1970s, things had gone very wrong indeed, which is why Ronald Reagan, for a period, could reinvent the cold war with such success. Yet it is significant that Reagan's cold war remained a policy, that it never became a structure. The policy could never be translated into the kind of international system that characterized the cold war in the 1950s or even lastingly mark the US posture. The very brevity of the exercise demonstrates how weak were its material underpinnings, even with the extraordinary regeneration of the military machine. The brevity, alas, is mostly forgotten now because of the massive, world-historical contingency that actually followed. What is in fact also mostly forgotten is that Reagan's cold-war phase had essentially ended before the Soviet Union ended, before the cold war itself, according to convention, had ended.[27]

Foray into the Third World

Here, I must confront a common argument for the continuity thesis that also happens in a way to be true, to have empirical validity, while self-consciously breaking with convention in other ways: the notion that the

---

27 Leffler's *For the Soul of Mankind*, it should be said, recognizes this discrepancy.

cold war continues by means of direct intervention and use of proxies in the third world, that it is really about third-world interventionism. As the 1970s amply illustrate, client struggles do continue and sometimes intensify in the third world. This is a cogent viewpoint. I will respond by examining Odd Arne Westad's tome on the subject, *The Global Cold War*, which is certainly the most far-reaching attempt, from a detached standpoint, to think the cold war in the third-world frame.[28] Sympathetic as he is to those on the receiving end, Westad is still detached in not setting out to demonstrate interventionism as the natural expression of US imperialism, or for that matter Soviet imperialism. In very much less detached form, the argument could otherwise be traced back as far as Gabriel and Joyce Kolko who dismissed the cold war in the early 1970s as an "egregious" obfuscation of the actual counterrevolution that the United States inflicted on the world at large and the third world in particular.[29] In Westad's version, interventionism is not the exclusive property of either superpower but a systemic function of the cold war as it developed from the 1960s onward.

Empirically, the novelty has chiefly to do with the Soviet side and its particulars, but the periodization is the decisive aspect: the 1970s mark the intensification of the cold war, not the easing or the end of it.[30]

---

28 Westad, *The Global Cold War: Third World Interventions and the Making of Our Times* (Cambridge, 2006).

29 Gabriel and Joyce Kolko, *The Limits of Power: The World and the United States Foreign Policy 1945–1954* (New York, 1972), 6; see also 2–5, 709–15; and Gabriel Kolko, *The Politics of War: The World and the United States Foreign Policy, 1943–1945* (London, 1969), 3–6, 619–22.

30 Westad's delineation is commendable on specific events and interventions, going all the way back to the Iranian crisis of 1946, where he reminds us that Stalin, far from pushing any communist agenda, typically sold out his political friends for limited and narrow Soviet interests. Westad's treatment of Africa (Congo, Angola, Mozambique, South Africa, Ethiopia, Somalia, and the Horn) is a series of outstanding analyses of local struggles, superpower arrogance, and the ubiquitous revolutionary enthusiasm of the Cubans. Similarly, the ensuing chapters on "the Islamist defiance" and the events of Iran and Afghanistan are superb histories, especially of the fateful Soviet decision-making process on Afghanistan and the subsequent disaster, all the more poignant a story because Moscow's policymakers were so aware of the dangers involved. It is striking to see, in fact, how often Soviet analysts had a highly realistic view of third-world events and allies. Yet policy change was doomed because the given framework did not allow it. Or, as in Afghanistan, letting go was also to let the newly aggressive United States into one's backyard. Westad's treatment of the United States, by contrast, is much weaker than the comparable considerations on the Soviet Union, the PRC, and the third world. He is less interested in the United States and has nothing very probing to say about it.

Détente and stability in Europe, in short, allow the superpowers to play out the cold war to devastating effect in new third-world areas, especially Africa. Where amorphous convention sees a thaw and management, Westad sees huge expansion in space and greater ferocity. He also insists that the confrontations are central because both superpowers, not only the United States, are now capable of projecting power on a global scale and do so. That the frozen fixity of the cold war in its European area of initial confrontation should have generated client warfare (of sorts) in the third world is itself not a new idea. Westad's privileging of third-world events, their centrality in the cold war, is, however, unusual: "The most important aspects of the Cold War were neither military nor strategic, nor Europe-centered but connected to political and social development in the Third World."[31] Consequently, this is in no way a history of the global cold war. Willy Brandt does not appear in it. Nuclear arsenals are absent. Even the missiles in third-world Cuba are referred to only in passing. Europe, refreshingly in a way, is nowhere to be seen except insofar as it has effect on the third world.

The constitutive concept here is not the cold war in any determinate sense but the notion of the three worlds, more particularly, the United States, the Soviet Union and the third world. Auxiliaries do play a role (above all Cuba); but the essence is superpower confrontation in an area that is largely created by that confrontation itself. The narrative, in its bare essentials, is as follows. In 1945 two major powers with universalist pretensions confronted each other by providing two radically alternative ways of coming to grips with modernity and modernization. The Soviet Union, however, was at the time largely defensive while the United States moved actively to check what it perceived as the advance of international communism. US interventionism in a way created the third world, a differentiated space for battle outside the Eurasian heartland proper. This eventually coincided with decolonization and liberation movements, at first mainly nativist and nationalist in orientation but, partly in response to US power, gradually more radical. After Stalin, the Soviet elite woke up to the possibilities here but had few means to mount a real challenge. That challenge came instead from the experiences and revolutions in Vietnam and Cuba (and the solidaric export of the latter revolution). In the 1970s,

---

31 Westad, *Global Cold War*, 396.

then, the Soviet Union is caught between two apparent imperatives: to manage, through détente, the relationship with the United States while at the same time supporting the spreading and increasingly radicalized movements in the third world, above all in Africa. Throughout, third world elites, for their part, had found themselves both courted and repressed by the superpowers, faced with a choice of developmental models and political alliances that might provide opportunities and material support but often, too, interventionism and unwanted, engineered conflict.

These games are played out through the 1970s with mixed results: the Soviet Union (assisted and pushed by the more enterprising Cubans) scores some apparent victories, in southern Africa for example, but is ultimately dragged down, the disappointment of the Ethiopian "revolution" being only a faint omen of the disaster that would await in Afghanistan. The main cost is not material or even strategic. The Soviet Union could have gone on for a long time in Afghanistan. Yet the Afghan morass and third world moves generally were a decisive part of the growing legitimacy crisis within the elite. Conversely, the United States in the 1980s is able to reconstruct global capitalism and crush revolutionary challenges in Central America. And thus it went, the cold-war victims in the third world mostly forgotten along with their countries and the very idea of the third world itself.

This vivid history of the 1970s and '80s restores the importance of that conjuncture and the importance of the third world within it. Why, however, we should forget nuclear strategy, and why we should accept that bipolarity did not weaken, is not obvious. Conflict certainly spread into new areas (whether it intensified is another matter); but how did client warfare differ qualitatively from the kind of jockeying that went on, say, between Russia and Britain in the arc from Turkey to China in the nineteenth century? And did the interventionism result from intensified, globalized bipolarity? Westad himself shows with great clarity the degree to which the thrust of Soviet interventionism in Africa was directed not at the United States but at the People's Republic of China, a rival power that it openly clashed with militarily in 1969 and feared a great deal. As one of the few Western historians outside the ex-Soviet bloc with a command of both Russian and Chinese, Westad knows that conflict better than most, but what we get is description, ample description, but nothing but description.

It is easy to see the intention. Westad wants to dislocate or decenter the cold war from its Euro-Western theater. "Decentering" seems to be code for rewriting the cold war in the spirit of social history, where the "Euro-centric" comes to stand for rarefied, old-style political history and third world interventionism for the uncovering of a more genuine history from below and beyond, a properly archaeological investigation of the real workings of the cold war, so to speak. My own view is the exact opposite: relentless and rigorous centering. I leave aside the fact that interventionism in the third world is hardly what the chief antagonists themselves believed the cold war was about, nor where they spent their preponderant resources: one might argue that they were mistaken about the real. To center the concept and period of the cold war, however, is not to ignore the third world or any other world for that matter. On the contrary, it is only by being insistently specific about the overdeterminant structure that one can see its contradictions and, crucially, how it operated by projection. Third world interventionism would not have happened without the cold war, but it should not be conflated with it.

Westad's whole, in that sense, is false. For what is this cold war that is being played out to such catastrophic consequences in the third world? Westad has no single concept here. Initially, he thinks, conventionally, that the cold war is just the period when the United States and the Soviet Union dominated international affairs. That dominant relationship became a confrontation because the two happened, for various historical reasons, to be ideologically universalist and thus necessarily interventionist in orientation; and the confrontation became a cold war because of "the American ideological insistence that a global spread of Communism would, if not checked, result from the postwar extension of Soviet might."[32] So it is perhaps not rival universalism as such but one particular form of it, the US variety, that really generates the cold war. However, there is also the interventionist nature of their respective ideologies to consider: they cannot not intervene. And intervention amid the tripartite structure of the world, not the cold war, is Westad's central concern. He is not interested in the cold war as a cold war: he is interested in the ruinous effects of Western interventionism and modernization (Western here meaning both the United States and the Soviet Union). He is, to coin a phrase, interested in the Clash of Modernizations. Thus, in his concluding remarks, he begins to imagine

---

32   Westad, *Global Cold War*, 25.

the cold war as merely the Clausewitzian continuation of colonialism by other means, the latest but not the last form of a process that may have begun, not in 1945, not in 1917, but in Berlin in 1878 when the Europeans divided Africa. Indeed, he says, why not date the beginning to 1415 and the first Portuguese colony?

Indeed, why not? So, at long last, we have arrived at the point where the meaning of the cold war has been reduced to nothing, where all conceptual value has been lost in a historical fog: the cold war as another name for Western colonialism as it began in 1415.[33] The difference between Westad's position and the customary continuity thesis, namely his foregrounding of the triangular in contrast to the simple binary, is in short less radical than it seems. In insisting that the cold war was a condition, a relationship between two equal entities, Westad differs fundamentally, to be sure, from the neoorthodox idea of the cold war as Soviet aggression against freedom. His triangulation, however, is really the binary confrontation writ large, a confrontation emptied of political meaning. Dislocating the cold war in Westad's fashion makes it disappear. An unconventional account of intense third-world conflicts and their increasing geopolitical significance in the 1970s does not in fact require the conventional scaffolding of the cold war in the 1950s. Westad does not need the cold war and, after a fashion, he comes to see this: the otherwise absurd reference to 1415, even if half in jest, reveals that his is not a history grounded in any cold war.

None of the above takes care of my own problem with the meaning of that other end, the end of 1989–91. What is it that comes to an end with the end of the Soviet Union, beyond, obviously, the remnants of bipolarity? The short answer is the epoch precipitated by the Bolshevik Revolution in 1917. There is one extant way of thinking about the epoch from 1917 onward that shows both systematic precision and explanatory value. I am referring to Francis Fukuyama's once famous thesis, now widely disdained, concerning the end of history, his quasi-Hegelian notion that the passing

---

33   The Iberian reference brings to mind the suggestive idea that the originator of "cold war" as a term was the Castilian grandee Don Juan Manuel, who, earlier in the fourteenth century, had pondered the nature of the conflict between Islam and Christianity on the peninsula as (so it is said) a kind of cold war. Don Juan Manuel, interestingly concerned with irregularity and ideological incommensurability, is however not talking about a cold war but a lukewarm one, a metaphor of rather different implications. See chap. 1, note 4.

of the Soviet Union also signified the end of a certain historical principle or spirit/Geist, leaving liberal, democratic capitalism (reverse the order of the terms as you please) in place as the final legitimate order for the ages to come. The last proposition was a bit of a wager on Fukuyama's part; but if some new negation was to emerge, it was certainly unimaginable at the time. Meanwhile, Perry Anderson's Marxist variation on Fukuyama's theme held out the possibility of such a new oppositional moment but not for the foreseeable future.[34]

This Hegelian motif is of the greatest interest, though it has faded in prominence, perhaps because in desiccated form it has become common wisdom, or because it is no longer meaningful, or both. In any case, I think it may well be right. It allows for different periods and phases within its formal compass, the cold war being one of them. It also allows for other processes, other principles, other temporalities, other periods so to speak. It does not treat (or necessarily treat) the entire epoch as a unified, expressive totality. The cold war, however, in the Fukuyama-Anderson frame is never a problem. It is subsumed under the general contradiction. In principle, this is compatible with my account, with the notion that the cold war has a specific genesis, meaning, function, and place in postwar US policy; but, tendentially, it is easy to miss its salience amid the grand Hegelian narrative.[35]

---

34 Fukuyama originally proposed the argument in "The End of History?," *National Interest* 16 (Summer 1989) and expanded it (in more ways than one) in his subsequent book, *The End of History and the Last Man* (New York, 1992). Perry Anderson's perceptive critique, dealing extensively with the conceptual history of the whole idea of the end, appeared in his volume *A Zone of Engagement* (London, 1992).

35 Anderson recognizes that something decisive did happen in 1963, indeed putting an end to the cold war stricto sensu. He insists, however, that the antagonism between the United States and the Soviet Union was systemic, grounded in the conflict between capitalism and communism. Anderson to the author, December 26, 2008. A roughly similar view is espoused by Fredric Jameson in his *The Hegel Variations: On the Phenomenology of Spirit* (London, 2010), wherein he refers to "the Long Cold War" (1917–89). My objection, to reiterate, is this: once territorialized and stabilized, there is nothing about that conflict that in itself would lead to any cold war, nothing systemic in short that would force either capitalism or communism to do anything in particular vis-à-vis the other. The two systems side by side are certainly "incompatible" in that neither can work in the same space (though the PRC today shows that capitalism is eminently commensurate with the political dictatorship of the Communist Party; but then again we always knew that capitalism had no inherent political form beyond the legal sanctity of property). Such an incompatibility does not in itself translate into any determinate relationship or foreign policy.

I have argued this view of the cold war, the salience and the specificity of the cold war as a US project, in different ways since the 1980s with little or no success. Convention rules OK. The reason for resurrecting the argument in revamped form is the recent eruption of US global power in a unilateralist spirit as expressed above all in the Iraqi operation. Whatever else it did, the presidency of George W. Bush certainly served to concentrate the global mind on the nature, conditions, and possible limits of US power. Hence his presidency also revived the spirit of all those organic intellectuals of US power whose fortunes had dwindled so dramatically in the 1990s, the unheroic era of more and better capitalist globalization along with, in a minor key, humanitarian diplomacy and intermittent war. After the massive shift of 2001, predictably, there were numerous tracts on the United States and empire, typically featuring some potted history of what was imagined to have been the cold war. Once again the period was put to good ideological use. Once again one had to object to the obvious and the self-evident. Once again we were after the cold war. The ensuing "war on terrorism," soon widened to the more nebulous "war on terror," was indeed in some ways a postmodern play on the cold war or what the cold war was supposed to have been about, its pivotal shortcoming being that it had no proper political enemy on which such a war (whether real or metaphorical or both was always unclear) could be waged. We have now entered a new phase, another version of the postmodern, where large concepts and large names are purposely left aside, if not entirely forgotten. It is the heroism of the low-key. Whatever its immediate political virtues, such a pragmatic emphasis on the particular easily renders the cold war historically invisible, invoked if at all as a conventional shorthand for something once useful but now passed. Conventional appropriation or sidestepping is however not always the best way to transcend the Grand American Narrative. The ferocious return of the repressed is not hard to imagine, at which point one had better be prepared.

II
On Diplomatic History

5

Writing the Cold War Circa 1950–90: A Triptych Extended

The historical telling of the cold war used to be a highly politicized field centered on the inflammatory question as to who was to blame for causing it: the traditionalists or orthodox blaming the Soviet Union, the revisionists blaming the United States. Interest in the nature of the cold war as such, was, however, lacking. "Extreme global tension between the two superpowers, threatening nuclear extinction in less than half an hour" or some such generic description would probably have satisfied most. The question, then, as in many historiographical controversies about war, was who caused it. As passions cooled in the 1970s, there were attempts to move beyond the given parameters, displacing, at least ostensibly, the question of blame while appealing to the empirical and so becoming less immediately political. My account here will follow this scholarly political conflict in writing the cold war into that moment when the original antithesis was being transcended (or not, as the case may be) by post-revisionism and corporatism, two moves in different registers that expired, as it happens, in the same epoch as did the Soviet Union. Since then, the politicized aspect has greatly diminished and the field itself branched out in multifarious directions. Much of the historiography I shall examine here, then, will be *dead and gone*—or so it may be felt. My own view is that this lineage and the politics that informed it should be known or at least not forgotten. Nothing compares to it.

A few preliminary notes should be made. First, the historiography is lopsidedly about the United States and is of US provenance. It is a large body of work because the United States is a large place with a large university world but also because its distinctive educational apparatus features college curricula and liberal arts which in turn, luckily, produce history departments of considerable size and breadth. The field, quaintly known as diplomatic history, formed part of the US field overall, thus giving it a certain reputation for parochialism, broken only in a minor way in recent years by the emergence of international history (I leave aside whether the "international" is actually a real object of inquiry) on the one hand, and by abandonment of the archaic diplomacy in favor of the US in the world on the other, a blander and less jarring category in the eyes of a profession that operates under multiple anxieties about names and naming.[1] A second feature, odd on the face of it, is the separation from the adjacent subfield of political science known as international relations (IR). Devoted to model building with predictive pretensions or, in its more policymaking aspect, producing advice to various administrations, IR has had little use for history except, fairly crudely, as raw material and data (there are exceptions). Conversely, history being constitutionally averse to prediction, if not always theory, there has been almost no interest in IR from the other side, though diplomatic history would in fact have gained from an engagement at least with the current of critical IR. This demarcation between history and international relations has been sharp in the case of the Americanists, much less so for, say, historians of East Asia, the Middle East, or any other field that falls within what is known as area studies. It was in fact the cold war and the global commitments it entailed that gave rise in the 1950s and '60s to the

---

[1] Christopher Thorne, a British historian, once described the result as a "paradigm which places the United States at the center and draws out from there simply a series of bilateral links, like the spokes of a rimless wheel." See his "After the Europeans: American Designs for the Remaking of Southeast Asia," *Diplomatic History* 12:2 (1988), 206. For responses, see the symposium in *Diplomatic History* 14, no. 4 (1990). In a more wide-ranging attack, Charles Maier underlined how the Americanist fixation forced historians of other areas to stick more to the company of foreign colleagues. Charles S. Maier, "Marking Time: The Historiography of International Relations," in Michael Kammen, ed., *The Past Before Us: Contemporary Historical Writing in the United States* (Ithaca, NY, 1980), 355–87. Meanwhile, the substitution of "US in the World" for "Diplomatic History" opens things up but sometimes loses sight of foreign relations and power at the center.

huge growth in such policy-oriented and partly interdisciplinary institutions within the university. Sovietology, for obvious reasons, became especially close to the state and its need for knowledge and intelligence.[2]

---

2   For the history of international relations, see Stanley Hoffmann, "An American Social Science: International Relations," *Daedelus*, 106 (Summer 1977) and Steve Smith, "The Development of International Relations as a Social Science, *Millennium* 16 (Summer 1987). A representative collection of critical texts in IR is James Der Derian and Michael J. Shapiro, eds., *International/Intertextual Relations*, (Lexington, MA, 1989). John Lewis Gaddis is the great exception here. Roughly speaking, from the late 1970s to the late 1990s, he interacted widely with mainstream IR, which he knew well and used (for example, Alexander George and Kenneth Waltz). The interest was reciprocated. For the interim Gaddis, taking diplomatic historians to task for their "spatial and temporal parochialism" while he still operated in the environs of mainstream IR and neorealism but was on the way somewhere else, see his "New Conceptual Approaches to the Study of American Foreign Relations, *Diplomatic History* 14:2 (July 1990), 405–23, quotation on p. 411. His chief concern throughout, however, was politics rather than theories as such. Impatient (and with a Nietzschean capacity for forgetting), Gaddis put the neorealism of *The Long Peace* behind him and went on to new and better things, among them in the 1990s complexity theory and the geology of plate tectonics. Indeed, given accolades to the Long Peace and his flirtation with IR, Gaddis had some recalibration to do after 1989. As he rightly put it himself in 1992, "One might as well have relied upon star-gazers, readers of entrails and other 'pre-scientific' methods for all the good our 'scientific' methods did" in "anticipating the most significant event in world politics since the end of World War II." The answer to this embarrassing shortcoming, then, he found (momentarily) in complexity theory: weird stuff happens. What complexity did for Gaddis, however, was not complexity but, characteristically, simplicity: it allowed him to explain the event without being locked into any single model. Hence, too, the attraction of plate tectonics, geology rather than geopolitics if you will: the truth of change and direction building up slowly, imperceptibly, for a long time and then coming to a crisis (fill in the blanks). Science itself, in fact, as he emphasized, no longer did the kind of modelling IR tends to imitate as scientific. See his laborious inventory of IR theories and their failure to forecast, "International Relations Theory and the End of the Cold War," *International Security* 17, no. 3 (1992-93), 5–58 (quotation on p. 18). For his salvaging job on *The Long Peace*, see his "Great Illusions, the Long Peace, and the Future of the International System," in Gaddis, *The United States and the End of the Cold War: Implications, Reconsiderations, Provocations* (Oxford, 1992), chap. 10. The "illusions" here are a reference to Norman Angell's book of 1910, *The Great Illusion*, famously predicting there would never be a great war. Calling himself a "consumer" of theory, Gaddis thus found US-centric IR modelling wanting and went shopping elsewhere. Notably, he stayed away from two obvious alternatives: the English School of traditional skepticism and historical particularity, on the one hand, poststructuralist linguistics on the other. Nor did he do anything much with the thriving field of historical sociology, though he dipped into it. Complexity theory notwithstanding, the destruction of the Soviet Union soon pushed Gaddis back into ideology of the most orthodox kind. Another exception is Marc Trachtenberg, who actually migrated from history—partly by way of policymaking schools—into political

However parochial, the Americanist tilt has not been an unmitigated ill. For it freed the profession from any too onerous imperative to serve the powers that be and allowed, in the 1960s and '70s, a critical edge seldom found in international relations—one reason this moment should not be forgotten. Incidentally, placing one's work politically was not only true for leftist historiography. Some of the earlier, mainstream historians had participated one way or another in the events they described, and so they had an irreducible stake in their histories, or they were simply committed cold-war liberals. Sovietology, meanwhile, included some emigres, with all the passions and interests attached to that difficult position. Moreover, virtually all these historians, from left to right, were deeply marked by the experience of Vietnam. From that traumatic, extended and divisive war there was no personal escape; and though it now seems as distant as the 1960s, its shadows are still inescapable.[3] Vietnam, however, was in a sense only symptomatic of what made cold-war history and the issue of its origins so *fundamental*. Not to put too fine a point on it: How did we get to this potentially earth-ending condition of nuclear obliteration, and what was (and is) the role of the United States in that process? Are we sustaining, indispensably, the world and its freedom—the now much vaunted seventy years of the liberal world order—or actually leading the way to its desolation, ruining lives and inflicting violence in the name of ideological falsities? These were and are urgent questions.

I need also to say something about the system of the cold war in the 1950s and early '60s, as it settled into a recognizable set of features, a typology, that may serve as a reference when we think about periodization and concepts. Thus, laying no claim to originality, I consider the cold war to have been marked by these characteristics:[4]

---

science and IR proper, generally from a realist angle. His important *A Constructed Peace: The Making of the European Settlement, 1945–1963* (Princeton, 1999) is compatible with my periodization (1963), though on different, realist grounds, which is to say minus ideology. He may disagree with this assessment.

3 By "experience," I am not referring to participation of course but the *existential presence* of Vietnam everywhere and anywhere. It is not now present in the same way as it remains present in, say, the US Army—even some generations removed from the actual war, it is an ever-present reference and institutional memory for the officer corps.

4 This typology (it is only that) and its inversions are taken from Michael Mann, *States, War, and Capitalism* (Cambridge, 1988), 177–8. Though his periodization is different from mine, see also Gaddis, *The Long Peace* chap. 8. Gaddis, interested in periodization, usefully points to the emergence of rules of engagement.

(a) warlike hostility, carried on by means short of war;
(b) diplomacy, consequently, being turned into militarized thinking and a kind of warfare itself;
(c) denial of the opponent's legitimacy as a regime, resulting in intense propaganda attacks;
(d) increasingly bipolar structure of international politics through the superimposition of the conflict onto the rest of the world;
(e) intense military buildup in the arms race;
(f) suppression of internal dissidents (much more so in the Soviet Union).

The cold war differed, then, in important ways from the classical balance of power structure of the eighteenth and nineteenth centuries. It was a true polarity and static as opposed to multifarious and shifting. It had no place for any balancer to equilibrate the balance, such as Great Britain had traditionally done. It also tended, by being ideologically charged, to deny the other party's right to exist and participate in the comity of nations. In that sense it was a return to the absolute enmity and hatred typical of the religious wars before the European state system evolved in the seventeenth century.[5] It became an extreme polarity in which victory meant total annihilation of the opponent as a political regime. The conflictual element inscribed in the very separation between states hence assumed the antagonistic nature traditionally reserved for moments of total war, as distinct from peace.

This is why it makes sense to call the period in question a cold war. This is also why it makes much less sense to use it, in the now commonly accepted manner, as a description of the whole postwar era. Soviet-American relations have in fact been largely strained ever since 1917 but in very different ways and with different effects. The cold war, as conceived of here, actually underwent in the 1950s a series of changes that turned it into something else after 1962; and we need a way to describe this without diluting the usefulness of the cold war as a concept, without losing its specificity. The resultant system (of sorts) entailed:

---

5 This is in part inspired by Hans Morgenthau's classic *Politics Among Nations* (New York, 1948, 1985 [with Kenneth W. Thompson]), chap. 21.

(a) de facto recognition of the other's legitimacy and consequently de-emphasis of the irreconcilable ideological differences;
(b) mutually, if tacitly, agreed spheres of influence, the American sphere being both far looser and far larger;
(c) no direct military conflict between NATO and Warsaw Pact forces in Europe or elsewhere, so that the major wars involving the two (Korea, Vietnam and Afghanistan), were fought indirectly or by means of proxies;
(d) agreement, again tacit, not to use nuclear weapons except as ultimate resort on the vital assumption (true or not) of MAD, mutually assured destruction.

Elements of this qualitative easing of tensions—détente—had been present ever since Stalin's death, in some instances even before, but had not dominated the relationship. It took the (apparently) final division of Germany in 1961 and the near hit of the Cuban Missile Crisis of 1962 to achieve that. The new situation then found very clear expression the following year in the limited Nuclear Test Ban Treaty (and, less often noted, the wheat trade). The dialectic had transformed antagonistic to agonistic relations, a rivalry in competition but involving too mutually beneficial geopolitics of hegemonic control over the two halves of Europe, competition narrowed down to the arms race, space projects and maneuvers in the third world, eventually and more dangerously involving the People's Republic of China. The cold war *stricto sensu* was thus over in its European context, though it experienced a phantasmagorical and brief return during the late 1970s and early '80s. What was coming to an end around 1990 according to this periodization, then, is the whole postwar order itself, an international order dominated in the last instance by the relationship between the United States and the Soviet Union but not to be conflated with any cold war. (And now the whole seventy-year period after World War II is being touted as the Liberal World Order, the enabling condition of which has been the indispensable United States.)

A Note on Hegel

Cold-war historiography, before it dissolved, was often told in the form of a Hegelian triptych. First there were the traditionalist or orthodox accounts of the 1950s and '60s that on the whole supported the official American position: the totalitarian Soviet Union started the cold war by its expansionism while the democratic United States, initially reactive, eventually moved to stop this and so defended the free world. Then, antithetically, along came the revisionists of the 1960s and '70s, for whom the all-powerful United States initiated the cold war for ideological and economic reasons, while the Soviet Union was cautious, reactive and nationalistic, limited in its security claims rather than messianically ideological and expansionist. Finally, the disciplinary resolution arrived with the postrevisionists of the 1970s and '80s, emerging from the preceding confrontation to create a superior synthesis by choosing the best elements of both schools: a transcending *Aufhebung*, in other words.

This caricature of the Hegelian dialectic is not without heuristic value. The labels it employs cannot of course be created except after the fact. The traditionalists did not know that they were writing traditionalist work; only when the revisionists appeared was this slightly derogatory term invented. And the postrevisionist imprint is in some ways a self-serving construct by postrevisionists themselves; they might just as well be dubbed antirevisionist or neorealist. Finally, the whole picture was complicated by the emergence in the late 1970s and early '80s of a seemingly rival school of corporatism. For this new antithesis cast itself in the form of a critique of the new postrevisionist orthodoxy and considered the cold-war problematic of the preceding schools, if not a dead end, at least something whose terms should be sharply revised. Consequently, it had very little to say about the origins of the cold war as such. With the passing of intensity there was indeed a diffusion of perspectives, such that schools could no longer be distinguished. Nonetheless, with all due misgivings, my analysis here will follow the general contours of the would-be Hegelian structure, with suitable additions. The emphasis will be on interpretation and explanation, not on empirical detail and exhaustive lists of names.

Traditionalism

The traditionalist historians of the 1950s and '60s ranged from straightforward apologists to critical realists.[6] Most of them agreed, however, that the Stalinist regime was exceptional and not just an ordinary Great Power. Cooperation (a supposedly neutral concept seldom investigated) was therefore doomed. The genesis of, and hence blame for, the cold war lay in the unilateral moves of the Soviet Union, initiated even before the end of the war, to impose its rule on the areas of Eastern Europe liberated from Nazi occupation: "Thus the cold war grew out of the interactions between traditional power politics and the nature of the Soviet regime. The power vacuum created by Germany's defeat provided the opening for Soviet power to fill, and Communist ideology made a clash inevitable."[7]

Traditionalists disagreed over how important communist ideology was in Moscow's expansionism, but not about the moves of the Kremlin blatantly to disregard the established consensus of the wartime coalition. The Polish question is often brought forth as an egregious example: Stalin broke the Yalta accords on free elections, ruthlessly rolling onto center stage his stooges, the "Lublin" regime, to the exclusion of other forces. By the fall of 1945, continues the argument, it was abundantly clear that Moscow would allow no democratic, free states in Eastern Europe, as had been implied in the Atlantic Charter of 1941 and agreed upon at Yalta in the Declaration of Liberated Europe.

The United States, according to this account, played a comparatively passive role, preoccupied during the war with military affairs and assuming postwar cooperation with the Soviet Union within the future United Nations. Still, in the months immediately before the German collapse in May 1945, events in Eastern Europe were beginning to cause serious alarm. Washington, having expected to play the modest role of

---

6   For good overviews, see Thomas Hammond, "Introduction" in Hammond, ed., *Witnesses to the Origins of the Cold War* (Seattle, 1982); Geir Lundestad, *America, Scandinavia and the Cold War 1945–1949* (New York, 1980), chap. 1; and J. Samuel Walker, "Historians and Cold War Origins: The New Consensus," in Gerald K. Haines and J. Samuel Walker, eds., *American Foreign Relations.* (Westport, CT, 1981). For archetypal traditionalist works, see the oeuvre of Herbert Feis, in particular his *From Trust to Terror* (New York, 1970).

7   John W. Spanier, *American Foreign Policy Since World War II* (fourth rev. ed., New York, 1971), 28.

mediating between the imperial Britain and the radical Soviet Union, found the former tottering and the latter hostile. The Soviets proved intransigent in the Council of Foreign Ministers, the periodically convened forum for negotiations about the postwar order. There followed, even more ominously, Soviet thrusts in 1945–46 into the Near East: the resurgence of communist-instigated civil war in Greece, imperious demands on Turkey, and the refusal to leave northern Iran as previously agreed. The appearance, meanwhile, of illegitimate communist regimes in Eastern Europe continued apace, a progression reaching its brutal end with the Prague coup of February 1948, which eliminated the last noncommunist vestiges in Czechoslovakia.

Under the impact of these ever-more evident Soviet transgressions, the Americans finally began vigorous counteraction. Eastern Europe was more or less lost, but Washington was able to shore up the threatened Iran in 1946, to shoulder Britain's responsibilities in the eastern Mediterranean through the Truman Doctrine in the spring 1947 (offering primarily military assistance to Greece and Turkey on grounds of universal defense of freedom), and, most important, to prop up the vital Western European area by economic assistance (the Marshall Plan, announced in summer 1947), supplemented by military ties through the establishment of NATO in 1949. In occupied Germany, where cooperation had broken down as a result of Moscow's obstinacy, the United States found it necessary in 1946 to cease the eastward flow of reparations from its occupation zone and to merge it with the British one into the so-called Bizonia. In the absence of agreement with the Soviets, the Western powers announced plans in June 1948 for a new West German state and an immediate currency reform. The Soviet Union responded with an illegal blockade of divided Berlin but was thwarted by an immense Western airlift; and in 1949 a democratic West Germany came into being that would serve as an engine for European recovery. Thus Western Europe was saved from Soviet expansionism and domestic communism. A somewhat similar turn took place in Japan.

These, then, were the chief ingredients in the traditionalist histories. The predominant theme is an ideological one: the democratic, hitherto isolationist United States reluctantly assumes its objective responsibilities as leader of the free world and major opponent of the totalitarian and ruthless Soviet Union. Traditionalists of a more realist bent typically made less of a morality tale out of it. For the realists (as distinct, in their own eyes, from idealists), the world of international relations is a Hobbesian jungle, a space unlike the domestic one in featuring few common norms and no ultimate sanction of force for those that do exist, a field in which every state does whatever it can to keep up with the competition for power, a world defined by the "might makes right" logic of Thrasymachus. Accordingly, it may well prove a fatal mistake to project one's own standards of morality on the outside. Indeed, argues the realist, one will have to violate those internal standards when engaged with the outside world. The role of ideology/morality is thus characteristically given short shrift in realist explanations of international events. Louis Halle expressed this when, in a famous formulation, he compared (1967) the cold war to putting a "scorpion and a tarantula together in a bottle." No obvious sense of morality can be imputed to such a conflict between (presumably) innately deadly, *equally* deadly, insects: it is a predicament, requiring mortal battle.[8]

For the realists, the question was, however, chiefly not one of outright battle but of reestablishing a workable balance of power: a naive and inexperienced American regime comes to understand the realities of power and act with suitable acumen. At this point, however, the realists began to differ. Some considered the increasing ideological fervor that accompanied the new activism as necessary to break the isolationism once and for all; they also defended much of the expanded American role. Others, notably Kennan, thought the universalist discourse disastrous in the long run because it confused the issues, thus clearing the way for the limitless and ultimately impossible American commitments that were to follow. Indeed, for Kennan the realistic period lasted only until 1948, after which the rhetoric took over and there was a growing gap between means and ends.[9]

The ideologically charged apologia seemed by the end of the 1980s to be mostly of archaeological interest but it was energetically revived after the end of the Soviet Union. The realist narrative, meanwhile, survived in pristine form in various post-revisionist accounts. This future

---

8 Louis Halle, *The Cold War as History* (New York, 1967), p. xiii. Halle was a former member of the Policy Planning Staff turned historian and writer. Given the timing, one wonders where China would fit in.

9 See George F. Kennan, *Memoirs* (Boston, 1967). On the most straightforward realist historian, see Jerald A. Combs, "Norman Graebner and the Realist View of American Diplomatic History," *Diplomatic History* 11:3 (July 1987), 251–84.

connection is already evident in what is often taken to be a quintessentially traditionalist piece, Arthur M. Schlesinger Jr.'s article in *Foreign Affairs* in 1967, "Origins of the Cold War." To the extent that it is the first serious attempt to rethink the traditionalist position after the revisionist onslaught, it is in fact a precursor of post-revisionism. Schlesinger seems willing at the outset to do away with orthodox villainy: what is crucial for him is instead the conflict over spheres of influence. Whereas the USSR doggedly pursued an exclusive sphere in the East, the United States was committed to one-world universalism. Both misunderstood the other's moves as an offensive against vital interests, the Soviet Union in Eastern Europe, the United States in the western parts. A clash was inevitable, for "each side believed with a passion that future international stability depended on the success of its own conception of world order." Schlesinger then reverts, crucially, in the final part of his article, to the ideological explanation: the Soviet Union was not a normal nation-state but a totalitarian one, run by an intermittently paranoid dictator. The American reaction was consequently legitimate and understandable.[10] The contours of this analysis were to reappear in post-revisionism.

Revisionism

The 1950s had been placidly quietist. A high degree of agreement had reigned between historians and officialdom; historiographical debate on foreign policy was correspondingly narrow.[11] Revisionism, to paraphrase Walter Benjamin, would blast this serried conformism apart.

Several moments in American historiography have earned the label revisionist: the debunking attacks after each of the World Wars

---

10   Arthur M. Schlesinger Jr., "Origins of the Cold War," *Foreign Affairs* 46:1 (October 1967), 22–52. The same issue commemorating Red October included George Lichtheim on the question of "what is left of Communism" in view of "the dying sun of the October Revolution." Clearly, Lichtheim says, such "an increasingly conservative and stratified society" would consider any "commitment to world-revolutionary utopianism . . . a prime danger" to relations with the United States.

11   On American historiography in this period and generally, see Peter Novick's classic *That Noble Dream: The "Objectivity" Question and the American Historical Profession* (Cambridge, 1988).

on the official accounts of the American entry are two instances.[12] In the 1950s, very much in the spirit of the times, there was something called business revisionism, whose basic claim was that the robber barons of the late nineteenth century, in their exemplary capitalist greed, had been essential producers of the material wealth that now enabled the United States to lead and fund the Free World against the totalitarian danger; thus they were not robber barons at all.[13] By revisionism in the present context, however, I am referring to that extraordinary reversal of conventional cold-war wisdom that took place in the 1960s and '70s.

This reversal should not be considered simply a result of the New Left of that period. The importance of Vietnam has already been mentioned. Yet, reinforced as they were in their views by the burgeoning antiwar (and civil rights) movements, most revisionist historians were products of the late 1950s and early '60s, the first New Left by contrast to the second countercultural left that followed. The historians of the latter generation, though also mainly Americanists, inclined in their practice toward social rather than diplomatic history, toward E. P. Thompson rather than William Appleman Williams.[14]

It is indeed with Williams and his Wisconsin group that any delineation of revisionism must begin.[15] The prevalent interpretation of American history in the 1950s was the so-called consensus school. Against the older Progressive thematic of clashing interests and upheaval, these historians emphasized basic pragmatic continuity and integration: conflict there was, but chiefly over status, not economic interest. The United States was portrayed as one big middle-class society with a minimum of ideological dissension; the very term "ideology" became badly tainted.[16] Progressive history survived primarily at the

---

12   See Athan G. Theoharis's useful survey, "Revisionism," in Alexander De Conde, ed., *Encyclopedia of American Foreign Policy* (New York, 1978).

13   Ian Tyrell, *The Absent Marx* (Westport, CT: Praeger, 1986); Gabriel Kolko, "The Premises of Business Revisionism," *Business History Review* 33, no. 3 (Fall 1959), 330–44.

14   Novick, *That Noble Dream*, 445.

15   The following account is, unless otherwise noted, based on Novick, *That Noble Dream*; Tyrell, *The Absent Marx*; Jonathan Wiener, "Radical Historians and the Crisis in American History, 1959–1980," *Journal of American History* 76, no. 2 (September 1989), 399–434.

16   See Lloyd Gardner, "Consensus History and Foreign Policy," in De Conde, ed., *Encyclopedia*. Major exponents included Richard Hofstadter, Louis Hartz and Dennis

University of Wisconsin under the auspices of Merle Curti, Fred Harvey Harrington and others. Williams, who had done his graduate work at Wisconsin, returned there in the fall of 1957 to teach. Several eminent revisionists would come out of Williams's circle. His first teaching assistants, Lloyd Gardner, Walter LaFeber and Thomas McCormick, would all become leading diplomatic historians.

Williams was actually a deeply patriotic man, a navy graduate outraged late in life by the misdeeds of the prominent midshipmen in the Reagan administration (Oliver North, Robert McFarlane and John Poindexter). He had a Midwestern suspicion of the Eastern elite but combined this populist sensibility with wide-ranging intellectual pursuits outside his field. He was anything but parochial theoretically.[17] Unlike his associates, he never wrote a monograph on the cold war; his forte was the extended interpretative essay, a narrative framework in which the cold war typically became a phase of a longer trend.[18] Here, effectively, Williams tried to wed the insights of the consensus analysis to the older Progressive emphasis on economic interests. Thus he saw consensual continuity, but a consensual continuity of economic expansionism: there had always been a constructed identity between expansion and well-being in American history, first in the form of the westward-moving frontier, then, after 1900, through the increasing globalism of corporate capitalism, resolving internal problems by means of external expansion. It was this general interpretation that came to be known as the Open Door thesis.

Potter but conspicuously not Arthur M. Schlesinger Jr. and C. Vann Woodward. Anti-Beardism was dominant throughout, as was anti-communism.

17 I base this sketch on several remembrances offered at the Williams memorial conference, held in Washington, DC, on June 10, 1990, especially those by Wendy Williams, Lloyd Gardner, Walter LaFeber, Gar Alperovitz and Thomas McCormick. See also Paul Buhle's sympathetic *William Appleman Williams: The Tragedy of Empire* (New York, 1995).

18 On Williams's writings, see further Bradford Perkins, "The Tragedy of American Diplomacy: Twenty-Five years After," *Reviews in American History* 12, no. 1 (March 1984), 1–18; J. A. Thompson, "William A. Williams and the American Empire," *Journal of American Studies* 7, no. 1 (April 1973) 91–104; David W. Noble, "William Appleman Williams and the Crisis of Public History," in Lloyd Gardner, ed., *Redefining the Past* (Corvallis, OR, 1986); and Noble, *End of American History* (Minneapolis, 1985). Generally, see Charles S. Maier "Revisionism and the Interpretation of the Cold War Origins," *Perspectives in American History* 4 (1970); and Stanley Hoffmann, "Revisionism Revisited," in *Reflections on the Cold War*, ed. Lynn H. Miller, Ronald W. Preussen (Philadelphia, 1974).

Launched in Williams's now classic but then largely ignored *Tragedy of American Diplomacy* (1959), the Open Door thesis essentially maintained that Americans had replaced territorial notions of national interest with a market conception, propagating unfettered international competition, an open door for capitalist penetration. In theory this would then be beneficial to all but in fact it would reward the economically strong, in this case the United States. Such a self-interested approach, or Weltanschauung as Williams preferred to think of it, was not a product of crass ruling-class manipulation but honestly felt views. The tragedy, then, lay in the fundamental divergence between ideal and reality, or rather in the dialectical irony that realizing the ideal subverted the ideal. Pragmatic and tolerant encouragement of self-determination everywhere, for instance, was in reality an attempt to impose the American system and ideology on others:

> The tragedy of American diplomacy is not that it is evil, but that it denies and subverts American ideas and ideals. The result is a most realistic failure, as well as an ideological and a moral one; for in being unable to make the American system function satisfactorily without recourse to open-door expansion (and by no means perfectly, even then), American diplomacy suffers by comparison with its own claims and ideals, as well as with other approaches.[19]

This was an *immanent* critique using the given ideals to show that reality did not live up to them. The cold war was seen as a result of the American move after 1944 to replace cooperation with the defensive Soviet Union with an imperial Open Door system. The frost that followed was, so to speak, the icy condensation of this move. The original utopian ideal of American democracy had mutated into global counterrevolution.

Williams's account suffered, as many observers have noted, from a basic indistinction between system and ideology.[20] It was not clear if

---

19 William A. Williams, *The Tragedy of American Diplomacy* (rev ed., New York 1972), 219.

20 This was a critique from both left and right. See for example Eugene D. Genovese, "Beard's Economic Interpretation of History," in Marvin Swanson, ed., *Charles Beard: An Observance of the Centennial of his Birth* (Greencastle, IN 1976); Genovese, "William Appleman Williams on Marx and America," *Studies on the Left* 6 (January–February 1966); and, from the opposite side, Robert W. Tucker, *The Radical*

American corporate capitalism actually needed economic expansion for its survival as a system (which, at any rate, was hard to demonstrate historically), or if it merely tended to expand, or if expansionism was an ideological misconception, false consciousness, on the part of its representatives. To a degree this confusion had to do with Williams's reliance on the concept of Weltanschauung, which he appropriated from Wilhelm Dilthey, Georg Lukacs, Karl Mannheim and German idealism. There is on the whole more of the last-named than Marxist materialism in Williams. A worldview, a Weltanschauung, forms a totality in which any given part expresses the truth of the totality, and vice versa. The Weltanschauung of the Open Door expresses such a total truth in the sense that, in Williams's words, "[it] integrates economic theory and practice, abstract ideas, past, present, and future politics, anticipations of utopia, messianic idealism, social-psychological imperatives, historical consciousness, and military strategy."[21] In short, everything.

This epistemological maneuver made possible a characteristic tendency to concentrate, not on actual economic systems and processes, but on economic ideology (as a partial yet simultaneously total truth). The field thereby opened up for his followers to move into ideological research. The result could be outstanding, as for instance Lloyd Gardner's symptomatically entitled *Architects of Illusion* (1970). In this collective biography of early cold-war figures, Gardner argued that the American disagreement with Moscow over Eastern Europe was the result of an Open Door–inspired opposition to exclusive spheres and blocs:

> Against the fear of revolution, the United States erected a barricade built upon the Bretton Woods system and anchored by the British loan. Economic opportunity in Eastern Europe was not essential to American capitalists, but an open world was—especially after twelve

---

Left and American Foreign Policy (Baltimore, MD, 1971), 55–57. See also Thompson, "The "American Empire." There are occasional systemic formulations in Williams, for example his classification of the cold war as "the confrontation between the United States, the Soviet Union, and the People's Republic of China, between 1943 and 1971," which in turn is "only the most recent phase of a more general conflict between the established system of western capitalism and its internal and external opponents." Williams, *Tragedy*, 10.

21 William A. Williams, "Open Door Interpretation," in De Conde, ed., *Encyclopedia*, 201–02. For his most poignant statement on theoretical references, see "A Historian's Perspective," *Prologue* (Fall 1974).

years of depression and war. The world could not be divided without being closed to someone, so it had better not be divided.[22]

The United States, then, was held more responsible than the Soviet Union for the manner in which the cold war developed. There had been alternatives. Washington could have avoided playing politics with economic aid; it could have offered Moscow an agreement in 1945 on German disarmament and a security treaty; and it could have tried to approach Moscow directly on the control of atomic energy instead of pushing through an unworkable plan in the United Nations. This, argues Gardner, might not have eliminated the conflict itself but its "worst moments."[23]

If the systemic problem was partly evaded by the Wisconsin School, the other major vein of revisionism, Gabriel Kolko's, dealt with it simply by postulating a direct causal link between economic interest and policy. The Wisconsin School had revised traditionalism chiefly by focusing on the United States and its early activism: instead of naive but decent Americans operating on the assumption of cooperation, there were self-conscious capitalist expansionists meddling with cautiously formulated and on the whole understandable Soviet security concerns. In believing this sort of Open Door expansionism necessary, these capitalist ideologues may or may not have been mistaken (Williams's followers are more systemic here than he is); but expansionism was nevertheless a fact. For Kolko and his sometime collaborator Joyce Kolko, however, capitalism as a whole had not only been counterrevolutionary ever since the Bolshevik Revolution but also systemically rapacious and expansionist. By World War II, the United States was the leading power within this constellation. Afterward, having suffered no devastation, it was ready to impose its will "to restructure the world so that American business could trade, operate, and profit without restrictions everywhere."[24]

---

22 Lloyd Gardner, *Architects of Illusion* (Chicago, 1970), 319. The other outstanding Wisconsin work in the area is Walter LaFeber, *America, Russia, and the Cold War* (New York, 1967) [multiple editions]. LaFeber, ranging broadly in the history of US foreign relations, should be the object of historiographical study outside the cold-war framework.

23 Gardner, *Architects*, 318–19.

24 Joyce and Gabriel Kolko, *The Limits of Power: the World and United States Foreign Policy, 1945–1954* (New York), 6–7; also 2–5, 709–15. Gabriel Kolko, *The Politics of War: Allied Diplomacy and the World Crisis of 1943–45* (London, 1969), 3–6, 619–22.

Yet Washington was clearer on its economic goals than on how to achieve them politically. And here, in addition to the problems of the Soviet Union and Britain, the United States found itself confronted by a more serious threat in the form of the left, emerging out of "the disintegration of the prewar social systems and the growth of revolutionary movements and potential upheaval everywhere in the world." This had nothing to do with Moscow, which "had long since abandoned revolution elsewhere in Europe on behalf of national security, and had embarked on a policy of minimizing political risks." In Eastern Europe, for example, the Soviets followed a "conservative and cautious line wherever they could find local non-Communist groups willing to abjure the traditional diplomacy of the cordon sanitaire and anti-Bolshevism." Far from simply Sovietizing the region, Moscow's order reflected to no little degree existing social forces, though none of the three Great Powers would generally allow "democracy to run its course anywhere in Europe at the cost of damaging their vital strategic and economic interests." In Western Europe, Moscow actually gave "capitalism the critical breathing spell" by making the communist parties follow a policy of class collaboration. For Kolko, then, the left denotes a radicalized European working class (distinct from both communists and social democrats), as well as the rising anticolonial movement. The war, in short, had unleashed a crisis of the old order and the emergence of powerfully antisystemic forces. The reaction came in the form of American-led global counterrevolution, "vast quantities of violence" as the Kolkos put it.[25]

In light of his concern with the third world and the forces outside the basically conservative framework of Great Power politics, it is logical for Kolko to refuse the whole cold-war problematic as too centered on the bipolar conflict between the United States and the Soviet Union. For him and for Joyce Kolko, the term is actually "egregious" because it is "a static concept which conditions us not to probe further the real character of the forces of intervention and expansion—therefore violence—in our times. It minimizes the nature and causes of humankind's fate today, leading us to believe that conflict and violence are accidental rather than inevitable consequences of the objectives of American foreign policy and the imperatives it has imposed on movements of social transformation throughout the world."[26]

---

25   Joyce and Gabriel Kolko, *Limits*, 714.
26   Ibid., 6.

We have come a very long way from traditionalism here. It is almost a case of incommensurability: events are analyzed in radically different frameworks, which allow no empirical adjudication between rival claims. The Marshall Plan, in the orthodox view the savior of Western European democracy, becomes for the Kolkos a tactical American move to subordinate European capitalism and destroy any tendency toward autonomy. What seemed good turns out, on closer inspection, to have been bad. But the Kolkos also deviate from other revisionists in finding the determinant factors of the postwar epoch to have little to do with the emerging cold war, which for them is nothing but a side issue, an obfuscation. They face a problem, nevertheless, in explaining it. For if the Soviet Union was in reality a conservative and appeasing (if not outright counterrevolutionary) power, the American-induced freeze would seem incomprehensible or at least illogical, except possibly as a kind of shield for the overall US drive toward open markets. And the Kolkos do indeed tend to resort to a notion of the cold war as invented expedience: the usefulness of crisis diplomacy would thus explain why the Soviet Union was not allowed its security zone.

In the new remarks that frame his republished *The Politics of War* (1968, 1990), Gabriel Kolko tones down his views considerably, now claiming that the United States "missed comprehending the richly textured, infinitely complicated web of factors that had gone into producing the postwar international order" and, in the ensuing frustration, mistakenly blamed Moscow: hence the confrontation. Then, alas, we seem to back in the realm of false consciousness, the distance to the Wisconsin School correspondingly reduced.[27]

The notion of a systemic conflict between revolution and counter-revolution after the Bolshevik Revolution is also problematic in that it is never clarified when and why the Soviet Union ceased to be part of the antisystemic left, an abstraction which functions symbolically in Kolko's narrative as a concept of moral foundation and means of regeneration. The threat posed by the left is also considerably exaggerated, at least in the European context.[28] However, it is too easy to be critical of Kolko:

---

27 Gabriel Kolko, *The Politics of War: Allied Diplomacy and the World Crisis of 1943–45* (New York, 1990), xxii.

28 On the European point, see Maier, "Revisionism." See also Hoffmann, "Revisionism Revisited."

the apocalyptic tone, the absolute certitude, the often simple determinism are immediately suspect, while the claims are often empirically questionable or one-sided. Yet he and Joyce Kolko attempted something highly unusual. Much of the preceding historiography, traditionalist or revisionist, had been locked into a bilateral fixation, centered affirmatively or negatively on American policy. Other actors often seemed to be plastic matter or did not exist, except of course the Soviet Union in the early parts of traditionalist histories. There was very little context. The Kolkos transcended this and actually dealt with the local circumstances, the constraints, in which intervention and policy took place. The attempt was in that respect far more dialectical and complete than any other. Few have tried to emulate its scope. *The Politics of War* is by any standard an extraordinary work.[29]

There were other early revisionist works, of which should be mentioned D. F. Fleming's *The Cold War and Its Origins*. This pioneering narrative focused on crisis events as told by an old Wilsonian internationalist for whom Truman represented a sharply negative break with Roosevelt's cooperative policies.[30] Fleming thereby encouraged interest in what has proved an endless question: Was there in fact a basic change between the two presidents, and would things have been different if Roosevelt had lived? This question is not without interest. In its simple form, however, it is unanswerable. The material precondition for it is of course the accidental fact of history that Roosevelt's death virtually coincided with the end of the war, with the end of an obvious period. There could, accordingly, be both a traditionalist and a revisionist case for either side. Both could take the position that (a) there was no fundamental change (Roosevelt and Truman were of the same cloth, the differences being only tactical shifts depending on the demands of moment), or (b) there was such a change (Roosevelt was naive and Truman realistic; alternatively, Roosevelt was farsighted and Truman was the cold warrior incarnate).

A later and more scholarly work that in some ways extended Fleming's thread (without its Wilsonian streak) is Daniel Yergin's *Shattered Peace*.

---

29   Gabriel Kolko continues this in his history of Vietnam, *The Anatomy of War* (New York, 1985), wherein the Vietnamese side receives unusual and proper attention.

30   D. F. Fleming, *The Cold War and Its Origins* (Garden City, NY, 1961), two volumes.

Also featuring events and personalities, it elaborates the thesis of a qualitative break by delineating two sets of competing American axioms about the Soviet Union: a cooperative one dominant under Roosevelt and a noncooperative one under Truman, resulting, during the latter's reign, in the national security state. This has been criticized as altogether too neat an account. The objection is valid but the very symmetry here, the almost stylized clarity, is also a virtue in that it generates argument in the same way that simplified social science models can do in the best of cases. Yergin's axiomatics, from that vantage point, have actually aged surprisingly well, however overdone the starkness of his models.[31] Roosevelt as a historical figure is not easily pressed into an axiomatic model. Nevertheless, Warren Kimball's treatment of him, the most authoritative we have from a sympathetic but critical angle, argues that his style and substance differed essentially from that of such close advisers as Averell Harriman, advisers who would later not only advise Truman but make his policies. In Kimball's view (and I think he is right), Roosevelt's nonconfrontational style might have led to a less acute kind of conflict with the Soviet Union.[32]

The revisionist critique, then, did not suggest a single argument, except insofar as it saw the general causes of the cold war in American actions.[33] The internal diversity can best be seen in the reception of what became perhaps the most notorious revisionist work, *Atomic Diplomacy* (1965), written by a former undergraduate from Wisconsin, Gar Alperovitz. The standard traditionalist on the subject, Herbert Feis, had argued that the atomic bomb was deployed, justifiably, at the end of the war in August 1945 because it saved lives, though he acknowledged

---

31 Daniel Yergin, *Shattered Peace* (Boston, 1977). Yergin is scarcely a revisionist and does not claim to be one. Having published his book at the tail end of détente, he was indeed quick to deny any relation when détente was henceforth replaced by renewed cold war. His work is better characterized as a neorealist attack on the realist Kennan, articulator of the negative Riga axioms, for not being realistic. The connection with Fleming is from that angle tenuous: for Yergin, Truman is a neo-Wilsonian idealist. Interesting early critiques of his work are Carolyn Eisenberg, "Toothless Revisionism," *Diplomatic History* 2 (Summer 1978) and Daniel F. Harrington, "Kennan, Bohlen, and the Riga Axioms," *Diplomatic History* 2 (Fall 1978).

32 Warren Kimball, *The Juggler: Franklin Roosevelt as a Wartime Statesman* (Princeton, 1991).

33 Michael Leigh's "Is There a Revisionist Thesis on the Origins of the Cold War?," *Political Science Quarterly* 89, no. 1 (March 1974), 101–16, demonstrates the internal differences but misses the unifying political theme.

that Japan probably would have surrendered anyway shortly thereafter. Alperovitz put forth, by contrast, the scandalous view that the bomb had been dropped to impress the Soviets. Truman, knowing that the bomb would be militarily unnecessary, had reversed Roosevelt's cooperative policy but delayed confrontation with Moscow until the bomb had been tested, thus making possible a tougher line against the Soviets in Eastern Europe and conceivably an end of the war against Japan before Stalin could enter it as agreed. This tactic also rendered existing alternatives to deploying the bomb meaningless. After Potsdam, then, the atomic monopoly became the foundation for a harsh posture versus Moscow. The bomb, in short, was central to American maneuvers in 1945, ipso facto also in the emergence of the cold war.[34]

Alperovitz's view, reiterated unrepentantly, with more evidence, on the fortieth anniversary in 1995, was contested not only by traditionalists but also some revisionists.[35] Thus Kolko, agreeing here with the traditionalists, argued that the tactical changes on the American side could not be tied directly to the bomb and that the atmosphere was simply not conducive to restraint. Hence he minimized the political aspect of the question. Gardner also criticized Alperovitz, on somewhat similar grounds. Barton Bernstein, finally, has shown the astonishing extent to which the deployment was just never the object of the sort of sustained consideration and evaluation that we, retrospectively, would expect from a world-historical event that was planned and engineered. The historiographical debate has intermittently been vigorous and the public counterpart inflammatory. The empirical evidence is open to argument and speculation. J. Samuel Walker, however, summarizes the preponderant view well: "The bomb was used primarily for military reasons and secondarily for diplomatic ones." This is obviously not Alperovitz's argument, but it concedes an important part of it, above all the very posing of the question.[36]

---

34 Gar Alperovitz, *Atomic Diplomacy: Hiroshima and Potsdam: The Use of the Atomic Bomb and the American Confrontation with Soviet Power* (New York, 1965, rev. ed., 1985); Herbert Feis, *Japan Subdued: The Atomic Bomb and the End of the War in the Pacific* (Princeton, 1961).

35 Gar Alperovitz, *The Decision to Use the Atomic Bomb and the Architecture of an American Myth* (New York, 1995).

36 J. Samuel Walker, "The Decision to Use the Bomb," *Diplomatic History* 14, no. 1 (January 1990), 111. The debate, however, will never end. For a measured and in my view persuasive evaluation that gives proper consideration to Alperovitz's argument, see

Post-revisionism

As the archives progressively opened and the political atmosphere cooled, there was a clearing for a new historiographical moment—an empirical reconsideration of the whole cold-war problematic in light of revisionism but without its political commitment. This has been labeled post-revisionism. It is not an altogether happy choice of term. Strictly speaking, it merely implies that one is writing after the revisionists, a purely temporal as opposed to substantial designation. Some historians included in this category would perhaps have difficulty recognizing what precisely it is that has earned them their membership. The concept owes its strength chiefly to John Lewis Gaddis, its most eminent exponent and the most visible American historian of the cold war. Post-revisionism became for this and other reasons an accepted concept, widely deployed until the 1990s. What did it entail?

In its early stages post-revisionism can be seen as an attempt to come to terms with revisionism while remaining within the political mainstream. Hence its deliberately neutral tone and apparent impartiality. It tried to determine the validity of traditionalist and revisionist claims by empirical means, while preserving a pro-Western realist version of the traditionalist narrative. The best taxonomy of post-revisionism has been made by one of its most solid proponents, Geir Lundestad.[37]

Post-revisionism, for him, is first of all not interested in the question of war guilt that so exercised both traditionalists and revisionists. If anything, Americans and Soviets were both to blame. Post-revisionism agrees with revisionism that the United States had an active policy much earlier than 1947 and indeed showed hostility toward the Soviet Union as early as 1944. Nevertheless, the revisionist picture of compact

---

Barton Bernstein, "The Atomic Bombings Reconsidered," *Foreign Affairs* 74, no. 1 (January 1995), 135–52. Bernstein shows that though atomic diplomacy came into play, the really surprising aspect of the planning is the absence of planning, the absence of any deeper strategic consideration. This squares with the attitude toward the horrific firebombings of Japan in March 1945—no limits of any kind, laws of war or not.

37 The distance of post-revisionism as an impulse, so to speak, was congenial to Lundestad's own view of the US polemics. Lundestad is Norwegian but has published extensively in the United States and intervened vigorously in the debate. It would be wrong, therefore, to exclude him from the purview of this essay. (There is indeed a Nordic contingent in the field perhaps worthy of an essay someday—among others, Lundestad, Westad, Fredrik Logevall, Jussi Hanhimäki.)

anti-Sovietism is considered overdrawn. As Lundestad's own research reveals, Washington had no coherent policy in Eastern Europe. The United States worked here with inconsistent energy for democracy and free trade, in effect to gain power in the region at the expense of the Soviet Union, but without ever resolving how much to sacrifice for these aims. Eventually the Soviet-controlled regimes were recognized: Poland in June 1945, Romania and Bulgaria the following December. Contradictory impulses and policies thus render any single model along the lines of the Open Door inadequate as an explanation for the American posture.

There was further agreement with revisionists that there was a hostile element in the abrupt stop in lend-lease aid at the end of the war, but post-revisionists also emphasize the constraints of congressional law and domestic politics. Gaddis, in particular, was wont to criticize revisionists for having a reductionist view of domestic politics and not understanding the internal limitations. Post-revisionists conceded, however, that the Truman administration sometimes consciously exaggerated the Soviet threat to get certain legislation through Congress. The contours of the Marshall Plan, moreover, had been visible for a while and this famous move was therefore not the sharp break postulated in orthodox accounts. And, as the revisionists had argued, the United States did establish a kind of sphere of influence of its own by excluding the Soviet Union (and Britain) from the occupation of Japan and the Philippines. Finally, there were also early plans for a global chain of overseas military bases. In short, the United States was not innocently naive; it moved to defend its own interests, and it did so long before 1947.[38]

On the other side of the balance sheet, revisionism was found to have exaggerated the uniformity and universality of American expansionism. Some areas were more important than others. Washington refused, for example, to offer massive support the Nationalist regime in China; and interests in Eastern Europe were given up de facto in exchange for a free hand elsewhere. The Soviet actions in its zone were therefore not the

---

38 Geir Lundestad, *America, Scandinavia and the Cold War 1945-1949* (New York, 1980), chap. 1; Lundestad, *The American Non-Policy Towards Eastern Europe 1943-1947: Universalism in an Area Not of Essential Interest to the United States* (Tromso, 1978); John Lewis Gaddis, "The Emerging Post-Revisionist Synthesis on the Origins of the Cold War," *Diplomatic History* 7, no. 3 (July 1983), 171-90.

result of any American meddling. Stalin acted unilaterally, not on account of any messianic ideology but chiefly for security reasons. Nevertheless, these moves were expansionist when measured against the status quo ante 1941 and certainly cause for legitimate Western concern. Nor, continued the post-revisionists, could capitalism be the privileged explanatory device, as revisionists believed; economics was merely one factor among many. For one thing, the United States did not depend on external trade. In explaining American policy, much more emphasis should instead be put on geopolitical concerns of security. Post-revisionists underlined, consequently, that the United States frequently acted with the complicity and encouragement of the various overseas regimes with which it dealt. Thus, in Lundestad's now celebrated phrase, the "empire by invitation."[39]

Many of these arguments, sustained by extensive archival research, represented decisive advances. Epistemologically, however, the post-revisionist theme of a bundle of complex circumstances and motivations lent itself to accusations of eclecticism: presenting simple aggregations of factors without any explanatory power. Over time, partly as a response, there was less eclecticism and more of a reversion to traditionalism in its realist form. This was particularly discernible in the trajectory of John Lewis Gaddis mid-career. His early, much acclaimed work *The United States and the Origins of the Cold War* (1972) had concluded that the cold war was unavoidable because domestic political constraints would not allow deals with dictators such as Stalin. This was a rather lame ending to an otherwise nuanced book that had paid proper attention to revisionist arguments. During the following decade, Gaddis was to develop a more sophisticated neorealist understanding of the issue and rework the traditionalist standpoint into a plausible geopolitical narrative centered on the concept of security.[40]

---

39   Geir Lundestad, "Empire by Invitation?," *SHAFR Newsletter* 15 (September 1984). Lundestad's piece made a big impact and duly reappeared in various guises, including books, forever after. See for instance Lundestad, *"Empire" by Integration: The United States and European Integration, 1945–1997* (Oxford, 1998).

40   John Lewis Gaddis, *The United States and the Origins of the Cold War* (New York, 1972). The criticism for being fuzzy was evident already in some reviews of this first major work. See Barton Bernstein, "Cold War Orthodoxy Restated," *Reviews in American History* 1, no. 4 (December 1973), 453–62; and Robert Schulzinger, "Moderation in Pursuit of Truth Is No Virtue; Extremism in Defense of Moderation Is a Vice," *American Quarterly* 27, no. 2 (May 1975), 222–36. Gaddis's eclecticism was first

Relying mainly on Vojtech Mastny's work *Russia's Road to the Cold War* (1979), Gaddis began to argue that Stalin was never actually interested in basic cooperation with the West, at least not cooperation on grounds acceptable to any reasonable Westerner (which had been the unspoken revisionist assumption). Roosevelt had pursued a kind of containment of integration, an attempt to bring the Soviet regime by means of sticks and carrots into the American project for a new international order. The attempt failed because the Soviet Union was not susceptible to outside influences. When in doubt, Moscow always relied for its security on unilateral action.[41] Truman understood this:

> Repeated demonstrations of Moscow's callousness to the priorities and sensibilities of its former allies had by this time virtually drained the reservoir of good will towards the Russians that had built up during the war. American leaders had been inclined, for many months, to give the Kremlin the benefit of the doubt: to assume, despite accumulating evidence to the contrary, that difficulties with Moscow had arisen out of misunderstandings rather than fundamental conflicts of interest. But such charitableness could not continue indefinitely.[42]

So the United States got going after the strategic uncertainty that had originated in the novel sense of vulnerability induced by Pearl Harbor. The old continentalist sense of security had given way to a more expansive view according to which the chief objective now was the "preservation of a global balance of power." However, this notion emerged before any identifiable "challenges to that balance had manifested themselves." It remained an abstraction in search of concretion: the Soviets were not yet there to fill the role of an enemy. But "Soviet

---

emphasized by Warren Kimball in "The Cold War Warmed Over," *American Historical Review* 79 (October 1974).

41 Vojtech Mastny, *Russia's Road to the Cold War* (New York, 1979); John Lewis Gaddis, *Strategies of Containment* (New York, 1982), 9, 18; Gaddis, "The Insecurities of Victory" (1984), republished in his *The Long Peace: Inquiries into the History of the Cold War* (New York, 1986). Gaddis characterizes Mastny's work as "a striking and powerful new interpretation" ("The Emerging Post-Revisionist Synthesis," 176). To me it is a useful map of Stalin's misdeeds in Eastern Europe but thoroughly in the old framework of traditionalism orthodoxy.

42 Gaddis, *The Long Peace*, 34.

unilateralism, together with the conclusions about the roots of Soviet behavior that unilateralism provoked, had by 1947 created a credible source of danger, with the result that American strategy now took on a clearer and more purposeful aspect."[43] The structural void had been filled.

Gaddis's functionalism here is peculiarly reminiscent of Kolko's notion of the cold war as an instrumental invention, though for the former, Washington was really right anyway about not wanting cooperation on Stalin's conditions. More fundamentally, Gaddis was proposing a geopolitical reading. He envisioned the genesis of the cold war in terms of improperly scaled and executed security moves by the Soviet Union, the mammoth "heartland" power, against the European "rimland" powers. The logic of Soviet expansionism was neither ideological nor totalitarian but "imperial." Nevertheless, Moscow's security needs were expansive and ill-defined and the manner in which it tried to satisfy them was nasty. This impropriety, as it were, caused alarm in the West and eventually vigorous countermoves ensued, quite rightly, in the form of "containment." If anything, the implementation of containment had been a bit late. The object was not "American hegemony" but resurrection of Western Europe as one of a series of "independent centers of power." Indeed the Europeans themselves were desperately eager to prevent the US from leaving the region to its fate. In 1947 the means to achieve Western aims were economic as opposed to military, but economics was precisely a means to a geopolitical end, not the other way around. Capitalism was secondary and strategy, primary.[44] Propriety, it seems, had been restored by a new version of the old balance-of-power system, the difference being that the United States replaced Britain—albeit not as balancer but permanent supporter of one side.

To reinstate the geopolitical in this manner was a healthy corrective both to ideologically primitive forms of traditionalism and the economic determinism of some revisionism. It is to insist that geopolitics is a discrete sphere with its own logic. But to identify American policymaking in the early cold war with strict balance-of-power thinking is in my view to superimpose altogether too clear a vision on the events, in some

---

43   Ibid., 40.
44   Ibid., 44, 43, and chap. 2 and 8 *passim*. See also Gaddis, "The Emerging Post-Revisionist Synthesis."

ways as reductionist as the systemic capitalist expansionism in Kolko's account. Like all realist stories, it tends to downplay ideology, for example the visceral anti-communism that permeated much of the American policymaking elite. And like all realist stories it tends to subordinate objective economic processes to voluntarist moves of more or less deft strategists. Ideology (anti-Sovietism, Wilsonianism) was for the Gaddis of this moment (the end in 1989-90 would see him move successively back to orthodoxy) something that served chiefly as an *ex post facto* rationalization and legitimation for directions already in place. Soviet ideology is similarly displaced by the reference to the imperial.

A basic tension thus marked Gaddis's causal reasoning. The geopolitical is a realm that takes as its premise unified states and polities, territorialized entities inherently in more or less overt conflict: the system is determinant. Yet, following Kennan, Gaddis had also been apt to underline the constraints of domestic politics, the seemingly unending difficulties of the American polity in getting things across at home, in brief, the impossibility of letting the geopolitical logic run its course. Thus, at the very end of his fine survey of postwar America, *Strategies of Containment* (1982), Gaddis suddenly reintroduces, much along the lines of his 1972 work, the "remarkable degree" to which "containment has been the product, not so much of what the Russians have done, or of what has happened elsewhere in the world, but of internal forces operating within the United States." And he is further surprised by how much strategy has been determined by domestic considerations of economy (problems, to be sure, of a fiscal nature and not the revisionist economics of surplus capital and markets).[45] Whither then the causal effectivity of the international system? It has to be specified.

Gaddis's narrative was also less critical than Kennan's original, its source of inspiration. In Kennan's periodization there was a golden moment between the twin errors of naivete and anticommunist crusades, a period between 1946 and 1948 when Washington actually managed to conduct policy intelligently and in the national interest (a moment when, not coincidentally, his own authority was also at its peak). Ideological fog and cold-war fixation then took over. In point of fact, Kennan had had a deeply disheartening experience with clever American policymaking precisely when he had tried in 1948 to implement the idea

---

45 Gaddis, *Strategies*, 357.

of independent balancing centers in Germany and Japan. He got nowhere. The world, he found, was supposed to be black or white, no shades of gray. He should not have been surprised. It was actually the American refusal to construct a decentered balance of power system that made Kennan by 1949 an alienated and marginalized presence in the administration. For Gaddis, on the contrary, the defensive strategy of containment was outstandingly successful in Europe and Japan, and vis-à-vis the Soviet Union. That no third force actually developed was really a good thing: the Europeans did not want it, and the system that evolved proved remarkably stable. The period might then be better understood as a long peace than a cold war. On the negative side, to be sure, there was in the fullness of time a tendency, as in other imperial systems, to lose the critical distinction between vital and peripheral areas. The results were overcommitment and serious setbacks, exemplified most graphically by the Vietnamese debacle.[46]

It was characteristic of Gaddis in this period to think of the loss of criticality as a product of some transhistorical "imperial" tendency and not, in Kennan's terms, as the result of American universalism. One might well enquire, then, as Gaddis rhetorically does himself,

> just how post-revisionism differs from traditional accounts of the origins of the Cold War written before New Left revisionism came into fashion. What is new, after all, about the view that American officials worried more about the Soviet Union than about the fate of capitalism in designing the policy of containment, about the assertion that Soviet expansionism was the primary cause of the Cold War, about the argument that American allies welcomed the expansion of US influence as a counterweight to the Russians, about the charge that the government responded to as well as manipulated public opinion?[47]

In responding, he points principally to the recognition of an American empire as the distinguishing mark. But it is of course an empire by invitation and so implicitly benevolent. Moreover, the *kinds* of

---

[46] Anders Stephanson, *Kennan and the Art of Foreign Policy* (Cambridge, MA, 1989), chap. 4; Gaddis, *The Long Peace*, chaps. 2, 3 and 8.

[47] Gaddis, "The Emerging Post-Revisionist Synthesis," 180.

Europeans that actually do the inviting are rarely subject to systematic scrutiny. When all is said and done, then, we are essentially back to blaming Stalin, not necessarily for being an evil totalitarian but for lacking imperial competence. Gaddis's post-revisionist synthesis could thus be grasped as a kind of strategy of containment: it contained the revisionist critique within the overall boundaries of a realist form of traditionalism.

This, as such, does not diminish its validity or interest, and it remains a powerful analysis. Yet Gaddis moved increasingly into writing history inside the operative sphere of policymaking, writing history for the purpose of providing guidelines for American officialdom by answering relevant questions about what was to be done. Here, since the cold war for Gaddis in the 1980s turned out to have been a long peace in the European theater, the question naturally arose what could possibly follow except something worse. From there it was but a short step to look back on the cold war as rather a good thing. The timing (*The Long Peace* appeared in 1986) of this argument was not good, of course, as it turned out that the whole thing was about to go belly up and in a way that none of Gaddis's friends in IR, realist or neorealist, could have predicted, thus leaving him momentarily floundering.[48]

In view of the sharp rightward trend of the 1980s, it is not surprising that some post-revisionists would reinvent the revisionist inversions of the 1960s. In no case is this as evident as in Robert Pollard's *Economic Security and the Origins of the Cold War, 1945–1950*. Revisionism had confronted traditionalism head on, setting out methodically to revise (invert) what was perceived as an omnipresent, asphyxiating mythology. The scope of their findings was therefore shaped by the nature of the target. Still, revisionism had given an economic flavor to the

---

48 Aside from *The Long Peace*, chapter 8, see also his speculative piece "How the Cold War Might End," *Atlantic* (November 1987), overtaken like so many other things by the events themselves, but interesting precisely in that light. The 1987 article should be compared with his "Coping with Victory," *Atlantic* (May 1990), where he pleads (persuasively) for the preservation of Russia as a great power. The conservative implications of the "long peace" argument were then drawn out with stark clarity in John J. Mearsheimer, "Why We Will Soon Miss the Cold War," *Atlantic* (August 1990)—it has taken a couple of decades of Vladimir Putin to give that view a certain plausibility. Leftists, primarily from the third world, express similar views from a wholly different premise, arguing that the imperialist United States, in being the only remaining superpower, is now free to intervene at will in the third world.

proceedings that was distinctly its own. Pollard straightforwardly appropriated this element and turned it around.

Calling his book the "first synthetic 'post-revisionist' interpretation of Truman's foreign economic and security policies," Pollard essentially accepts the Open Door argument and adds a strategic twist. The difference is that he finds the resultant policy "one of the great success stories of the twentieth century, not just for the United States but for the Western world as a whole." The basic American goal, long before the cold war, had been an "interdependent economic system." Then, after the war, bearing "the long-term need of American business for an open worldwide economic environment" clearly in mind, the United States "captured, for itself and its allies, control over the most important sources of strategic minerals in the non-Communist world." Particularly helpful here in sustaining the West was "the vast expansion of cheap overseas oil supplies." The policy pursued was good since the alternative was protectionism and the system served the West as a whole (if not the third world) exceedingly well for a long time. Hence we are not dealing with any "imperialist elite bent upon aggrandizing power in the service of world capitalism or narrow US interests," but with a "largely enlightened and responsible" polity, "willing to sacrifice short-term national advantage to long-term gains in Western stability and security."[49]

Yet Pollard refuses to link this "American quest for multilateralism" causally to the cold war. The Truman Doctrine was certainly meant "to reduce American inhibitions about establishing a sphere of influence in Western Europe to counterbalance the Red Army's presence in Eastern Europe." But multilateralism had not been incompatible with Soviet security earlier on: "Agreements with Moscow, a reconstruction loan, and Lend-Lease were all possible before the Soviet crackdown in Poland." Alas, Moscow refused to play along, opting instead for "extreme hardship." The cold war, then, was a conflict over Europe and geopolitical security, induced by the Soviet actions.[50]

The disagreement with revisionism here seems mainly of a normative kind. The facts, aside from the strategic aspect, are not so much in dispute as is the way of approaching them. Williams might have found much to

---

49 Robert A. Pollard, *Economic Security and the Origins of the Cold War, 1945–1950* (New York, 1985), 3, 9, 246, 249, ix.
50 Ibid., 247–48.

agree with empirically in this quite illuminating work. If strategy is seen as part of a Weltanschauung, he might even have concurred in privileging that as a more comprehensive totality than economics. In a certain sense Pollard's work represents the highest stage of post-revisionism, the point indeed at which the whole notion ceases to be meaningful.[51]

Corporatism

At the very moment that the new synthesis was being celebrated in the early 1980s, it was challenged by a school or approach called corporatism. Long since passed into historiographical obscurity, it set itself explicitly apart from the state-centric neorealism of post-revisionism by arguing for a socioeconomic or decentered approach. A major theme in the corporatist manifestos was the need for a truly new synthesis, by which was meant, of course, not the kind of simple aggregations that post-revisionism put forth but a genuinely synoptic way of looking at the periodization of foreign policy, beyond the limits of the immediate postwar moment.[52]

---

51 Pollard comes close to "Hurrapatriotismus," D. C. Watt's somewhat unfair description of Arthur M. Schlesinger, Jr. See Watt's "Rethinking the Cold War: A Letter to a British Historian," *Political Quarterly* 49 (October 1978), 456. Watt otherwise takes a supremely patronizing view of American cold-war debates, contrasted of course with the indisputable soundness of British historiography. See for example, "Britain and the Historiography of the Yalta Conference and the Cold War," *Diplomatic History* 13 (Winter 1989). This is, on the whole, a sharp piece but it makes the fantastical claim that much of the "intellectual lumber" of revisionists such as Alperovitz and Kolko originated with the Frankfurt School exiles (83). Nothing in their writings indicates that this is so: no Adorno, no Horkheimer, no Benjamin, no great interest in the culture industry, no reference I can recall even to the widely disseminated Marcuse.

52 For corporatist manifestos, see Thomas McCormick, "Drift or Mastery? A Corporate Synthesis for American Diplomatic History," *Reviews of American History* 10, no. 4 (December 1982), 318–30; Michael J. Hogan, "Corporatism: A Positive Appraisal," *Diplomatic History* 10, no. 4 (October 1986), 363–72; Joan Hoff-Wilson, "symposium," *Diplomatic History* 5, no. 4 (October 1981), 377–82; Hoff-Wilson, "The Future of American Diplomatic History," *SHAFR Newsletter* 16 (June 1985). To the extent that the desire for synthesis means that one thinks there are too many monographs around and not enough interpretation and periodization of the general it is of course quite praiseworthy. Otherwise talk of the need for synthesis, for some all-embracing agreement on interpretation, fact and method, is strangely popular in American diplomatic history. What is really needed, one would think, is more and sharper competition between different, explicitly theorized frameworks of explanation.

Corporatism, in a historiographical context, had two separate but partly overlapping origins. On the one hand, it came from a set of economic historians with a particular interest in organization and modernization. They were not always conservative but still far from radical. On the other hand, it had roots in Williams's Wisconsin seminar, in his own periodization of American history on the basis of the emergence of corporate capitalism, as well as in his student Martin Sklar's analysis of Wilsonian Progressivism. This genealogy is perhaps not so odd: behind each strand will eventually be found the Weberian problematic, however mediated, of rationalization, stability and order.[53]

In social theory, corporatism has been a conceptual rival to pluralism as a way of describing capitalist societies. Rather than a plurality of individual actors competing in the neutral arena of the state, there is a determinate set of embodied interests, associations or corporations. These seek representation before and within the state, a state that is consequently an actor in its own right. This development is generally seen as the result of the transition from competitive, preindustrial capitalism to the corporate age, usually dated to around the turn of the twentieth century. To bring order and regulation into these new conditions, liberalism thus responded in the American case by trying to find a golden mean between the alternatives of laissez-faire and welfare statism. One paradigmatic solution here was the voluntarism of the associative state attempted by Herbert Hoover in the 1920s, bringing interests voluntarily together in cooperation to eliminate waste and inefficiency. In the realm of foreign relations, this period was not as commonly believed one of isolationism; instead it featured an activist,

---

53   See aside from the preceding references, Ellis W. Hawley, "The Discovery and Study of a 'Corporate Liberalism,'" *Business History Review* 52, no. 3 (Autumn 1978), 309–20; Martin J. Sklar, *The Corporate Reconstruction of American Capitalism, 1890–1916* (Cambridge, 1988), 18–19; Michael Hogan, *Informal Entente: The Private Structure of Cooperation in Anglo-American Diplomacy, 1918–1928*, (Columbia, MO, 1977); Joan Hoff Wilson, "Economic Foreign Policy" in De Conde, ed., *Encyclopedia*; Gabriel Kolko's partial auto-critique, "Intelligence and the Myth of Capitalist Rationality in the United States," *Science and Society* 44 (Summer 1980). Kolko's earlier work (his dissertation) on the Progressive Era, typically inverting the image of liberal reform into one of conservative regulation for corporate interests, is together with Sklar's the critical counterpoint here to Hogan (see Gabriel Kolko, *The Triumph of Conservatism: A Reinterpretation of American History, 1900–1916* (New York, 1963). The indigenous counterpart, meanwhile, to Weberian rationalization is that of Thorstein Veblen (more engineering than Protestant spirit, to be simplistic); but I am unclear on the precise connection.

corporatist policy aimed at an international order in the American image.[54]

That American image is then said to have pivoted increasingly around the concept of productionism: escaping the traditional nature of politics as necessity/scarcity by means of constant growth. The originator of this notion was Charles Maier, also the first to rethink the two postwar epochs within a single conceptual framework. As a Europeanist, however, his work was situated at a certain remove from the internal debates on corporatism, a concept he did not in fact feature. For Maier, productionism was the essential element in American postwar strategy to eliminate ideology from politics, since it turned the latter into a question of economic growth. In short, politics was reduced to a problem of output and efficiency. It was in this light, he argued, that one must understand the American restoration of Germany and Japan as geo-economic rather than geopolitical powerhouses, a transformation facilitated to no little degree in the German case by the prewar Nazi destruction of working-class organization.

The cold war fits into Maier's scheme only in a secondary manner. While it "had a decided influence on internal outcomes" and "imposed a framework on international politics," it "did not exhaust the issues." On the contrary, "viewed over the whole half century, the American international economic effort of the era of stabilization centered on overcoming British, Japanese, and especially German alternatives to a pluralist, market-economy liberalism." The state of Soviet-American relations, in short, was not the best place to find out what the postwar era was chiefly about.[55]

---

54 On corporatism particularly, see Birgitta Nedelmann and Kurt G. Meier, "Theories of Contemporary Corporatism Static or Dynamic?," and Phillippe C. Schmitter, "Still the Century of Corporatism?," both in Schmitter, ed., *Trends toward Corporatist Intermediation* (Beverly Hills, CA, 1979). For the American 1920s, see Hogan, *Informal Entente*; and Ellis W. Hawley, "Herbert Hoover, the Commerce Secretariat, and the Vision of an 'Associative State,' 1921–1928," *Journal of American History* 61 (June 1974). Hoover is a central figure in Hawley's version of this (Hawley was Hogan's teacher).

55 Charles S. Maier, "The Two Postwar Eras and the Conditions for Stability in Twentieth-Century Western Europe," *American Historical Review* 86, no. 2, April 1981, republished in his *In Search of Stability* (Cambridge, 1987). The quotations are from the latter (on pp. 180, 183). See also his important companion piece in the same work, "The Politics of Productivity: Foundations of American International Economic Policy after World War II" (originally 1981). I have simplified, perhaps unduly, Maier's nuanced analysis.

This perspective has been highly influential; parts of it, for example, appear in more celebratory form in Pollard. To understand its implications for corporatism, however, we must turn to the most consistent member of that tendency, Michael Hogan. Like most historians of this persuasion, he began by doing work on the 1920s, but it is his magnum opus, *The Marshall Plan* (1987), that is of interest to us. Here he wanted "to cast the Marshall Plan in the context of America's twentieth-century search for a new economic order at home and abroad . . . rather than in the context of the Cold War." From that angle the Marshall Plan was "a logical extension of domestic-and foreign-policy developments going back to the first American effort to reconstruct war-torn Europe." The domestic origin, according to Hogan, lay in the "New Deal coalition" and its combination of "the technocorporative formulations of the 1920s with the ideological adaptations of the 1930s in a policy synthesis that envisioned a neo-capitalist reorganization of the American and world systems." Marshall aid, then, aimed at "economic growth, modest social programs, and a more equitable distribution of production," which "would immunize participating countries against Communist subversion while generating the resources and mobilizing the public support necessary to sustain a major rearmament program." In this project the United States was enormously successful. Though clearly a vast, self-interested expansion of power into Western Europe, the Marshall Plan was also "far less heavy-handed than the concurrent interventions in Greece or the subsequent interventions in Central America, Southeast Asia, and other parts of the globe." Hence it was "a reasonable defense of American interests, one in which the means used were largely positive, largely scaled to the interests involved, and largely applied in collaboration with reliable local elites." Foreign policy, then, was essentially brought into line with the systemic shifts of the preceding decades in the United States.[56]

Hogan's massive study has been criticized empirically by the British historian Alan Milward, whose earlier, equally massive study had maintained that the Marshall Plan was never the critical intervention it is almost always considered to have been. In his later critique of Hogan, Milward argued that the models for the Marshall Plan did not originate

---

56 Michael Hogan, *The Marshall Plan: America, Britain, and the Reconstruction of Western Europe, 1947–1952* (Cambridge, 1987), 3, 18, 427, 429, 443.

so much in the interwar period as in the wartime system, and that the expansive policies pursued by the European governments were in large measure a product of political expectations from below. Western Europe, as William Diebold has pointed out, also had closer traditional ties between state, capital and class than the United States, which renders dubious the notion that the neocorporatist solution was simply an export item.[57]

Roosevelt, it may be said in passing, was always enthusiastic about schemes to internationalize the New Deal. It is important to note, however, that the cold war was virtually nonexistent as a problem in Hogan's account. This was what separated him from Gaddis and post-revisionism. For there is nothing, surely, in Hogan's analysis of the Marshall Plan itself that Gaddis would seriously disagree with; the disagreement concerned mostly the corporatist tendency to disregard geopolitics (that is the international system) in favor of domestic derivation of policy.[58] For corporatism, as a scholarly inquiry, was typically more interested in the complexities of economy and society than in geopolitics.

Despite high hopes early on, the corporatist thrust fizzled out as a coherent methodological movement, if not as individual research. In part this had to do with the extravagant claims that were made for the concept at the outset. The desire to establish an explicit approach of some sort was laudable. The extent to which it led to enquiries into the social origins of policy, investigations of clashes and compromises of interests inside and outside the state, was also laudable. The danger was a certain lack of demarcation and a subsequent open-endedness in potential research topics, detrimental to the conceptual rigor of the problematic. More seriously, corporatism was taken to be an explanatory category. In fact, it was chiefly descriptive, on par, say, with expansionism. As a description it is not without its uses, though the

---

57 Alan Milward, *The Reconstruction of Western Europe, 1945-1951* (London, 1984); Milward, "Was the Marshall Plan Necessary?," *Diplomatic History* 13, no. 2 (Spring 1989), 231-30; William Diebold, Jr., "The Marshall Plan in Retrospect: A Review of Recent Scholarship," *Journal of International Affairs* 41, no. 2 (Summer 1988), 421-35.

58 For a Wisconsin critique of Hogan's earlier work, see Carl Parrini, "Anglo-American Corporatism and the Economic Diplomacy of Stabilization in the 1920s," *Reviews in American History* 6, no. 3 (September 1978), 379-87. For Gaddis's assessment of the subject, see his "The Corporate Synthesis: A Skeptical View," *Diplomatic History* 10, no. 4 (October 1986), 357-62.

United States strikes me as singularly devoid of corporatist elements in any traditional sense: disorganized and heterogeneous, with a porous state machinery marked historically by complete domination of various sections of capital, and lacking the strong working-class organizations that are a precondition for a truly reformist (as opposed to fascist) corporatism, the United States was therefore not at all the relatively autonomous entity implied by the concept. Moments of corporatist class strategies, notably in the New Deal, do not in my mind outweigh the overpowering mastery historically of the bourgeoisie and its entirely rational way of treating the state as its possession, as an administrative shell to be populated and put to good uses.[59]

These problems can be followed in Thomas McCormick's work of the 1980s. McCormick welcomed corporatism enthusiastically as a way of rejuvenating revisionism, assuming that it would allow a kind of "social history" of foreign relations, a move away from narratives of crisis-events toward questions of power and domination over the *longue durée*. He stressed the ecumenical virtues of corporatism, but his agenda, as behooved a veteran of the Wisconsin School, was unapologetically left wing. What he wanted to analyze under the umbrella of this new synthesis was really corporatism as an American form of hegemony and social imperialism. By the mid-1980s, however, McCormick was already having difficulties in defending the concept against an attack from another leftist, John Rossi, who argued that corporatism covered up the dominance of capital over labor and was confused with "ordinary state/capital interaction." And in *America's Half-Century* (1989), McCormick's excellent survey of the postwar epoch, he had completely abandoned corporatism in favor of a more congenial world-systems model, inspired by Fernand Braudel and Immanuel Wallerstein.[60]

This work tells a familiar cold-war story in somewhat new language. The United States, notes McCormick, finished the Second World War

---

59   See Robert H. Salisbury, "Why No Corporatism in America?," in Schmitter, ed., *Corporatist Intermediation* for an argument that supports this impression. Schmitter's own powerful work has typically centered on Latin America.

60   McCormick, "Drift or Mastery?"; John P. Rossi, "A 'Silent Partnership'?: The U.S. Government, RCA, and Radio Communications with East Asia, 1919–1928," *Radical History Review* 33 (1985), 32–52 (quotation on p. 45); McCormick, "Corporatism: A Reply to Rossi," ibid., 53–9; McCormick, *America's Half-Century: United States Foreign Policy in the Cold War* (Baltimore, MD, 1989).

determined to accomplish the "hegemonic goals, awesomely global and omnipresent in nature" of integrating "the periphery" (the Pacific rim, the Mediterranean and Latin America) into an American-led "global market economy" and to prevent any other core power from dominating "the Eurasian heartland." The cold war (left undefined) was caused by the Soviet refusal to go along with the implementation of these goals, though there were also great problems with the Europeans right after the war. Eventually, there was "bipolarization between Russia and America" over the future of Europe and the Middle Eastern periphery. Stalin, more of a Peter the Great than a Marx, had been faced with the choice of integration into the world system or isolation and had not surprisingly chosen the latter. The iron curtain then closed off Poland, Bulgaria and Romania, but the domination was one of expediency rather than doctrine, much in the manner of the United States in the Caribbean. The ensuing American offensive McCormick sees, ingeniously, in three stages: the short-, medium- and long-term moves of, respectively, the Truman Doctrine, the Marshall Plan and NATO. The fundamental link, however, in his causal chain is constituted by the particularist class interests of a domestic elite orientated toward "long-term globalism," an elite apart in this regard from congressional opinion as well as from large sections of the business community.[61]

This causal aspect is the corporatist residue, an attempt to retain some notion of policy as a mediation between the inside and the outside. For McCormick seems otherwise to be joining what I think was the dominant trend of the 1980s, the shift toward geopolitics as *the* explanatory category. This shift was by no means unique for diplomatic history. Between 1945 and 1975, there appeared not a single work in the Anglophone world with the word "geopolitics" in the title; since then there have been numerous ones. There was thus widespread renewal of interest in geopolitical discourse, especially on the new right.[62] Corporatism, by contrast, was largely alien to geopolitical notions of

---

61   McCormick, *America's Half-Century*, 33–4, 23, 48–76, 16, and *passim*.
62   Peter J. Taylor, *Britain and the Cold War: 1945 as Geopolitical Transition*, (London: Guilford, 1990), 1. Colin Gray's oeuvre exemplifies the geopolitical discourse of the right, for example his *The Geopolitics of the Nuclear Era: Heartlands, Rimlands, and Technological Revolution*, (New York, 1977). The reason for the absence of the term during the postwar period was of course that it was equated with Germany and German *Geopolitik* and *Lebensraum* that is with ideas of brutal territorial expansionism.

territorialized balances, since these presuppose the very unified state actors that it wanted conceptually to discard.

McCormick's slide toward strategy was perhaps influenced by Melvyn Leffler, a historian sometimes also billed a corporatist but actually more interested in geopolitics, the place of policymaking and the policymaker. When the post-revisionist synthesis was being declared, he too was in the process of challenging it.

Reaching for "Security"

In 1984, Leffler initiated what would become the sharpest polemics of the decade by claiming that "the American conception of national security" involved a unilateral desire already in 1943–44 to establish a globalist system of defense; and that that move had little to do with any projected Soviet actions. Pearl Harbor, new air technology, and the rising popularity of geopolitical commonplaces about the "Eurasian landmass" and its importance combined to create a sense of vulnerability, which eventually would express itself in a grandiose strategic vision:

> This conception included a strategic sphere of influence within the Western Hemisphere, domination of the Atlantic and Pacific oceans, an extensive system of outlying bases to enlarge the strategic frontier and project American power, an even more extensive system of transit rights to facilitate the conversion of commercial air bases to military use, access to the resources and markets of most of Eurasia, denial of those resources to a prospective enemy, and the maintenance of nuclear superiority.[63]

Meanwhile, the American assessment of Soviet strategy underwent a basic change in 1945–46. Initially, security as opposed to ideology was presumed the central concern. Soviet expansionism was noted but so were the difficulties it faced and the potential for agreement. These notions then altered so that, while immediate aggression was still ruled

---

63 Melvin Leffler, "The American Conception of National Security and the Beginnings of the Cold War, 1945–48," *American Historical Review* 89, no. 2 (April 1984), 346–81, quotation on p. 379; and "Reply," ibid., 391–400, quotation on p. 399.

out, the long-term Soviet goal was assumed to be a communist world. The cluster of American moves initiated in late 1946, however, had less to do with this change of perception than with "appraisals of economic and political conditions throughout Europe and Asia," more specifically the "prospects of famine, disease, anarchy, and revolution." The possibility seemed great that the Soviet Union might come to dominate vital areas without having to do very much. Hence "the Truman administration assumed the initiative by creating Bizonia in Germany, providing military assistance to Greece and Turkey, allocating massive economic aid to Western Europe, and reassessing economic policy toward Japan."[64]

The Marshall Plan, as Leffler argued in a later piece, was the decisive factor "that brought about the final division of Germany and Europe and institutionalized a stable balance of power in the Old World." It also extended American interests to the periphery since these areas were deemed crucial to the European core powers and therefore

> encouraged American officials to look beyond Europe to safeguard markets, raw materials, and investment earnings in the Third World. Revolutionary nationalism had to be thwarted outside Europe, just as the fight against indigenous communism had to be sustained inside Europe. In this interconnected attempt to grapple with the forces of the left and the potential power of the Kremlin resides much of the international history, strategy, and geopolitics of the Cold War era.[65]

This was not, Leffler argued against Gaddis, an initially sensible effort to bring about an end to the cold war that eventually lost sight of its objective. On the contrary, it was intended to accomplish the goals of national security unilaterally, "regardless of the impact on the Cold War or on the Soviet Union." Indeed, one was aware at the time that these initiatives

---

64 Leffler, "The American Conception of National Security and the Beginnings of the Cold War, 1945–48," 363, 371.

65 Melvyn P. Leffler, "The United States and the Strategic Dimensions of the Marshall Plan," *Diplomatic History* 12, no. 3 (July 1988), 278, 306. But see Michael Hogan, "In the Shadow of the Left: The Postrevisionist History of American Economic Diplomacy," *Reviews in American History* 13, no. 2 (June 1985), 276–81, for a critique of any overvaluation of the strategic. As Hogan insists, there was a direct conceptual connection between the danger of autarky and the danger of aggression: the former was assumed to generate the latter. The question, then, is whether all of the above can be conveniently subsumed under security.

would increase Soviet insecurity and thereby hence also the risk of war.[66] As he puts it in his landmark study, *The Preponderance of Power*, "the cold war and division of Europe were regrettable prospects but not nearly so ominous as the dangers that inhered in economic contraction, autarchical trends, Communist gains, and the prospective erosion of American influence throughout the industrial core of Western Eurasia." It would have been better, Leffler concluded in another article, to have raised the question of whether there were other ways of defending one's interests that diminished "Soviet perception of threat, aligned the United States with popular nationalist movements, curtailed the dependency on nuclear weapons and air power, and circumscribed American commitments."[67]

Leffler was criticized by Gaddis and Bruce Kuniholm—by the former for confusing hypothetical military contingency plans with real national policy, by the latter for underestimating the initial Soviet thrust into the Near East and hence not giving proper credit to the Truman administration for its judicious response of containment. For Kuniholm, the aims of the Soviet Union in the Near East, though in the tradition of Russian geopolitics, were "far in excess of its reasonable security requirements." To have caved to Stalin's intimidation might have put the area within his sphere, and the American response was consequently a legitimate restoration of the balance of power. Because "the mood of the American public was uncertain," continued Kuniholm, it may indeed have been necessary to couch containment in the admittedly less than perfect form of the Truman Doctrine.[68]

The disagreement between Leffler and Kuniholm hinged largely on the empirical question of Soviet behavior in the Near East (especially toward Turkey) and the related problem of what in fact constitutes legitimate security concerns. Leffler maintained forcefully that Soviet pressure on Turkey was negligible, to the point where it was eminently difficult for American officialdom to find any justification at all for aid; and, consequently, that it was the far-reaching strategic interests

---

66 Leffler, "Reply," 398–9. Gaddis's original argument, essentially that the form took over the substance, can be found in *Strategies*.

67 Leffler, *Preponderance of Power: National Security, the Truman Administration, and the Cold War* (Stanford, CA, 1992), 504; Leffler, "Reply," 399.

68 John Lewis Gaddis, "Comment," Bruce Kuniholm, "Comment," *American Historical Review* 89, no. 2 (April 1984), 382–90. For Kuniholm's quotations, see 387–88.

of the United States rather than Moscow's moves that put bombers in Turkey.[69]

Leffler, on balance, got the best of that disagreement. Nevertheless, as Gaddis rightly pointed out in his reply, Leffler was rather circumspect about the Soviet side of things.[70] To remedy that, Leffler's *Preponderance* (1992) offered a more explicit reading. Cooperation in the manner that it was offered by the West would have run counter to the most crucial security needs of the Soviet Union. Moscow could not "accept popular elections, self-determination, open trade, and the free flow of capital in the countries on their immediate periphery" or "defer reparations payments and provide raw materials and foodstuffs to the western zones of Germany." Hence "it was unreasonable to expect any Russian leaders to comply with such priorities."[71]

Soviet actions during 1945–46 did not form a uniform picture, but in Leffler's judgment in *Preponderance*, the moderate element was not sufficient to quell American apprehension. For at the same time there was serious erosion in the Western situation: the strength of communist parties in France and Italy, the civil wars in Greece and China, economic distress in Western Europe, and surging third world nationalism. While the Kremlin was not responsible for these developments, the United States felt obliged to act. There followed the Truman Doctrine, the Marshall Plan and the decision to divide Germany. The Kremlin, broadly speaking, was on the receiving end. The central question for Leffler, therefore, was "not whether American actions triggered the cold war, but whether they were intelligent responses to real and perceived dangers." Here, he thinks Washington could not have avoided "provoking the Russians" in 1946–47 if a "tolerable configuration of power" was to be achieved. *The risks were too great.* Hence, "prudently conceived and brilliantly implemented" American initiatives brought about the cold war. Alas, the Soviet response to these was not such as to warrant the enormous follow-on in the form

---

69   For further materials on their disagreement, see Kuniholm's *The Origins of the Cold War in the Near East* (Princeton, 1980); Leffler's review of it "From Cold War to Cold War in the Near East," *Reviews in American History* 9:1 (March 1981), 124–30; and his "Strategy, Diplomacy, and the Cold War: The United States, Turkey, and NATO, 1945–1952," *Journal of American History* 71, no. 4 (March 1985), 807–25.

70   Gaddis, "Comment."

71   Leffler, *Preponderance*, 512, and *passim*.

of rapidly expanding arsenals and perpetual interventionism in the third world.[72]

This, then, is Leffler's general answer to the query he posed so powerfully in 1984: Was there an alternative? Apparently not, he seemed now to be saying. His perspective, *in effect*, had coalesced with Gaddis's: both were strategic in nature, with emphasis on security as a total concept. Leffler, like Gaddis, was now also writing from the subject position of an ersatz policymaker. The question was again the instrumental one about what the United States should and should not do. Leffler's three aspects of judgment are indicative: wisdom, prudence, foolishness, prudence proving the dominant mark, foolishness predictably pertaining to exaggerated moves in the third world. Notably, the spirit of Leffler's empirical history was far more critical: *Preponderance*, between the introduction and the conclusion, remains the most devastating synthetic account we have of the globalist aims of the Truman administration. Gaddis was not particularly interested in counterrevolution; Leffler was quite explicit about it.[73] For Leffler, who looked beyond the State Department, especially beyond Kennan, the case was closed: the United States was more powerful and took the initiative, Soviet Union was defensive. This was what separated him from Gaddis: his was not a story about restoration of any independent centers. It was about an American game. The question, then, was whether the game was a good thing. For Leffler, all things considered and excesses noted, it was reasonable and rational.[74]

---

72 Ibid., 513, 516.

73 *The Long Peace* contains virtually nothing about the third world except reflections on the extent to which the United States tried to split the communist world. The long peace refers, of course, to the European and industrialized world.

74 My original version of this chapter was based on Leffler's introduction and conclusion, which he had kindly sent me in manuscript form, as *Preponderance* was yet to be published. The disjunction with the actual book is striking. The verdicts of Leffler's conclusion made it easy for Gaddis now to agree with him. Thus Gaddis called the book (with justification) "a masterly work of synthesis," and "the best book anyone has yet written on the United States and the origins of the Cold War." See John Lewis Gaddis, "How Wise Were the 'Wise Men'?," *Atlantic* 269, no. 2 (February 1992), 103. Leffler should not have been surprised at these effusive accolades.

Brief Note on Other Contributions

To speak of schools and tendencies, as I have, obviously marginalizes a whole host of significant contributions and developments that do not quite fit. One thinks, for example, of Ronald Steel's work in the 1960s and '70s: deeply critical of Wilsonian internationalism and American globalism, unmistakably limitationist in tone, yet not influenced by Wisconsin revisionism but by the impression of Gaullism and, later, the folly in Vietnam. One thinks, too, of Thomas Paterson's contributions, from the early, revisionist works to the recent centrist ones. His and Les Adler's essay on the American conflation of Nazi Germany and the Soviet Union under the sign of totalitarianism was especially influential.[75]

With the exception of a few remarks on Mastny, I have also ignored Sovietology. Something more must now be said of it. As a subfield it was marked by its many emigre scholars, its role as a virtual service organ to the state, and the paucity of archival sources for the Soviet side. These were not propitious conditions for wide-ranging debate. Stephen Cohen's judgment is telling: "The profession lost the purpose, vigor, and scope" because of "scholarly consensus on virtually all major questions of interpretation." More precisely, the totalitarianism school became totally dominant. A revisionism of sorts began to appear in the late 1960s that challenged notions of an unchanging monolithic essence marching through history; but this concerned mainly the nature of the domestic Soviet system, and the discipline seems to have remained largely untouched by the continuing revisionist controversy in American historiography on the cold war itself.[76]

The result earlier, however, was not always American apologia. Marshall Shulman's work in the 1960s, for example, was in certain respects compatible with erstwhile revisionist notions of Soviet

---

75 See for example Ronald Steel, *Pax Americana*; Les Adler and Thomas G. Paterson, "Red Fascism: The Merger of Nazi Germany and Soviet Russia in the American Image of Totalitarianism, 1930's–1950's," *American Historical Review* 75, no. 4 (April 1970), 1046–64. Among Paterson's notable and incisive works are *Soviet-American Confrontation: Postwar Reconstruction and the Origins of the Cold War* (Baltimore, MD, 1973) and *On Every Front: The Making and Unmaking of the Cold War* (New York, 1979).

76 Stephen F. Cohen, *Rethinking the Soviet Experience: Politics and History Since 1917* (New York, 1985), 4 and chap. 1 *passim*.

defensiveness and caution. Adam Ulam, in the same period, while sharply critical (as Mastny would be in the 1970s) of revisionism as well as of the ineptitude of American policymaking in 1944–45, also underscored how the emerging conflict gave rise to such simplistic and unfruitful questions as "Was Soviet Russia out to conquer the world or was Stalin going to abide faithfully by the charter and spirit of the United Nations?" The ensuing "grandiose rhetoric" would, in Ulam's realist view, form the background for both "would-be magic solutions" (massive retaliation) and revisionist evocations of American guilt.[77]

A more recent feature of cold-war historiography, hitherto also neglected, must now be acknowledged: several significant studies that transcended the bipolar fixation on US-USSR relations, studies of areas and countries not as mere objects of action but, so to speak, as live matter. Thus there emerged a better picture of the concrete context and effects of the cold war in such diverse places as Latin American, Italy, Scandinavia, Britain, the Near and Middle East, Africa and East Asia (a particularly vibrant area of scholarly inquiry). Though this essay is chiefly concerned with the US historiography on the cold war in the European context, something more should at least be said of the East Asian sphere.

No single area has indeed produced such a rich scholarship as that of East Asia, a field with its own forms of traditionalism and revisionism and a synthesis that is more neo- than post-revisionist. For the traditionalist moment, marked by cold-war zealotry, has not survived in any recognizable form. Robert McMahon, in an excellent survey of the literature, has described the old position thus: the American occupation of Japan benignly pushed the country along on the path toward "peace, democracy and free enterprise." In China, the communist victory was an unmitigated setback for the United States, rendering diplomatic reconciliation unthinkable. The ensuing reaction to the developments in

---

77 Marshall D. Shulman, *Stalin's Foreign Policy Reappraised* (New York, 1966 [1963]); Adam Ulam, "Re-Reading the Cold War," *Interplay*, March 1969, 51–3. Ulam is a curious figure, more heterodox than one might think. More professedly heterodox works could be mentioned: William O. McCagg, *Stalin Embattled* (Detroit, 1978) and Albert Resis, *Stalin, the Politburo, and the Onset of the Cold War* (Pittsburgh, 1988). For a more mainstream (and important) work to be read alongside Mastny's, see William Taubman's *Stalin's American Policy: From Entente to Détente to Cold War* (New York, 1982).

Korea and Vietnam was legitimate; and, generally, the United States was in congruence with nationalism in the area, assisting decolonized states on their route of independence. Against this idyll, revisionism stressed imperial extension of the cold war and the counterrevolutionary suppression of national liberation. After impressive research, several of these questions have been elucidated. It is clear that before the Korean war there were US notions of Mao as an Asian Tito and of normalizing relations. How strong these ideas were is still subject to diverging opinions. Everyone agrees, however, that the Korean War ruined whatever there was along these lines and served to militarize the American posture. There is agreement, too, that the administration was convinced in the immediate postwar years that China was not a place worthy of full-blown American intervention. Finally, as regards Japan, the view is that there had been a decisive alteration in occupation policy by 1947, away from attempts at reform and toward restoration of a strong power that would play the critical economic role in the anticommunist implementation of American-led containment in the region, a role that would serve the familiar dual purpose of reviving the overall economic system and prevent communist penetration. The occupation has in fact been the object of particularly interesting work, underlining the extent to which traditionally dominant class interests survived the initial reform moves only to become vital components, by 1949, in a reworked containment version of the old Co-Prosperity Sphere that would include Southeast Asia. Pre-occupation decisions of American policymakers to preserve the imperial and other government institutions after the surrender have also been emphasized. This imposed determinate limits on thoroughgoing reform and laid the foundation for the reversions after 1946.[78]

---

78 See Robert J. McMahon, "The Cold War in Asia: Toward a New Synthesis?," *Diplomatic History* 12, no. 3 (July 1988), 307–27; Howard B. Schonberger, *The Aftermath of War: Americans and the Remaking of Japan, 1945–1952* (Kent, OH, 1989); Michael Schaller, *The American Occupation of Japan: The Origins of the Cold War in Asia* (New York, 1985); Schaller, "Securing the Great Crescent: Occupied Japan and the Origins of Containment in Southeast Asia," *Journal of American History* 69, no. 2 (September 1982), 392–414; and William S. Borden, *The Pacific Alliance: The United States Foreign Economic Policy and Japanese Trade Recovery, 1947–1965* (Madison, WI: University of Wisconsin Press, 1984). A good historiographical view, aside from McMahon's, can be found in Carol Gluck, "Entangling Illusions: Japanese and American Views of the Occupation," in Warren Cohen, ed., *New Frontiers in American-East Asian Relations*

The most radical change of vision has occurred on the Korean issue. Here Bruce Cumings, writing with the authority of a Koreanist, has shown that the war can no longer be grasped as *simply* an attack by the North but must be placed in the setting of a drawn-out and bloody civil war that began already at the moment of the Japanese surrender in 1945. The United States came to align itself here by necessity with extreme right-wing domination. Cumings has also cast doubts on any significant Soviet part in the North's decision to launch the conventional attack of June 1950—though this is still a contested matter. All in all, Cumings has put into severe question a whole mythology by actually studying the local circumstances.[79] A central theme in the literature across the board has indeed been the extent to which local forces (classes, elites, parties, and individuals) played an active and in some cases crucial role in the unfolding events. As a result, the Western European part in NATO's genesis is now much better understood.[80]

Conclusion: The Ends of Geopolitics

The appearance of Melvyn Leffler's *Preponderance of Power* in 1992 marked the end, one can now see, of a long cycle in which diplomatic history centered on the crucial decade from the early 1940s to the early 1950s when the United States became a global power once and for all. The returns on (unevenly and briefly) opened archives in the East have been rather less than expected, as Soviet policy was not the mystery its devotion to secrecy and control seemed to indicate: Moscow had a line and followed it. In fact,

---

(New York, 1983). On Japan, see also John Dower's powerful *Embracing Defeat: Japan in the Wake of World War II* (New York, 2000). Since I wrote this in the early 1990s, there has also been a very considerable body of work on Vietnam that goes beyond the already existing massive literature on the US aspect.

79 Bruce Cumings, *The Origins of the Korean War, Vol 1: Liberation and the Emergence of Separate Regimes, 1945–1947* (Princeton, 1981); and Cumings, *Origins of the Korean War, Vol. 2: The Roaring of the Cataract, 1947–1950* (Princeton, 1992).

80 Fraser Harbutt, in the same vein, quite properly restored the trilateral aspect, Britain's position as a Great Power in the wartime coalition and immediately after. In emphasizing this he corrected distorted back projections of exclusive bipolarity (though Harbutt then goes on to exaggerate the importance of Britain and especially Churchill in the immediate postwar period). Fraser Harbutt, *The Iron Curtain: Churchill, America, and the Origins of the Cold War*, (New York, 1986).

there was no way of being Moscow without having one. More important, as the cold war—or what counted for it—receded into something self-evident with the disappearance of the Soviet Union, the historiography moved on. Whither is less obvious. It deserves saying: *No problematic and no controversy equal to that of the origins of the cold war has emerged.* A proliferation of studies connected to the cold war in a loose way, chronologically and spatially distant from its supposedly defining, original conflict, has certainly occurred; but here the cold war serves more or less as an enabling device for wider concerns, fueled to no little degree by Odd Arne Westad's influential work on the global cold war (I discuss Westad in chapter 4 of the present volume). Declassification, the supreme material condition of the field, has of course also moved on (every new decade being "crucial" once research gets there); but the more fundamental reason for the dissipation is the loss of political focus and engagement, in turn a reflection of the end of world-historical conflict in a Hegelian sense, the pages of history becoming empty (till further notice).[81]

Leffler's frame, if not his content, signified a realist (rather than neorealist) shift in the 1980s, its narrow form a concern with security and the policymaking rights and wrongs: an orientation rather than any too rigorous application of concepts and theories appropriated from the outside. So it is only proper to conclude with a (speculative) elaboration of my own contrasting view that the cold war is not reducible to questions of security. This is not to say that it was irrelevant, so let us determine what such an account can and cannot explain.

Social theory (and this is true both of Marxism and liberalism) tends to center on time and society, internally conceived of, rather than on space and societies.[82] Yet states and the polities that govern them

---

81 Odd Arne Westad, *The Global Cold War* (Cambridge, 2005). Endism was of course initiated here by Francis Fukuyama's diagnosis in 1989. As much as the end of history, his quasi-Hegelian thematic, has been derided and dismissed (not least by Gaddis), Fukuyama had a point, though the last thirty years have caused him to waver a bit. Perry Anderson, from a very different political stance, has offered a critique of Fukuyama's position—preserving and transcending it—in a long article delineating the history of the concept of an end. See Francis Fukuyama, "The End of History," *The National Interest* (Summer 1989), 3–18; Perry Anderson, "The Ends of History," in his *A Zone of Engagement* (New York, 1992), 279–375. Westad, meanwhile, succeeded Gaddis at Yale and historiographically is now the senior scholar of the cold war in an international frame.

82 On this, see the critical reflections of the geographer David Harvey, *The Condition of Postmodernity* (Baltimore, MD, 1988).

function in a geopolitical realm and employ the tactical and strategic technologies more or less appropriate to them. The consequent concerns of the state might then be summed up in the problematic term "security." To that extent, then, the initial postwar confrontation was certainly played out in the geopolitical domain: two huge and hitherto peripheral powers took the center stage and, on unfamiliar ground, failed to establish a *modus vivendi*, each probing for security in its own decisive manner. Acute conflict ensued, creating a situation short of war and more reminiscent of a truce than peace. Hence the cold war.

The "radical" Soviet Union was indeed far more traditional in that regard than the United States. The phenomenon of Stalin's geopolitics has always vexed American analysts: Marxism or *Realpolitik*? The either/or form of the question was misconceived, for the Leninist tradition saw no contradiction. Politics here had always been conceived of in military-strategic terms: leading one's forces from terrains won against the opposition by means of tactical and strategic moves. With the Bolshevik Revolution, this class perspective became state logic, reaching its apotheosis under Stalin. For Stalin combined an internal concept of progressive time and transformation (stages) with an external sense of spatial control (geopolitics). But by 1935 (and certainly by 1945), his class and state logic had become carefully nonrevolutionary, while remaining Marxist (of a sort) and military strategic. The object was to secure what had been won, not to jeopardize it with any adventurism.

The United States, meanwhile, vastly better off, vastly better positioned, enjoyed the dominant's peculiar privilege of being able to follow its inclinations without any too precise calculation of interest. Underneath the Wilsonian generalities, however, the calculation was quite precise, as Leffler shows in some detail. All things being equal, the US position in *pure* form, arranged under the notion of one world, was a market as opposed to a territorial conception of interest: an American-induced world system would ensure peace and prosperity throughout.[83] In actual fact, the US approach from 1943 onward was never reducible

---

83 See Michael Mann, *States, War, and Capitalism: Studies in Political Sociology* (Oxford, 1988). On the United States and Wilson in particular, Carl Schmitt, Mephistophelean figure of the extreme right, is a better critic here than the Marxist counterpoint: the typical displacement of politics proper into economics and ethics. See his *The Concept of the Political* (New Brunswick, NJ, 1976). This theme of depoliticization is somewhat similar in tenor to Maier's argument about postwar productionism.

to that market conception; the ideal type was itself subsumed under a larger, new globalist notion of interest qua security. Roosevelt's personal way of being toward the world should be kept analytically distinct here, as his approach was his own and, despite his legendary skills at communication, one he kept rather close to himself.

After his death and a certain interregnum of diverse movements and events, the US position became resolutely clear. Washington did two things: it escalated already existing efforts to open up a capitalist world system outside the boundaries of Soviet control, and it broke with tradition in moving vigorously to secure this system by asserting its military-strategic presence wherever possible (the embryonic project during the war). Against that offensive Moscow had very few defensive options except fortress vigilance, coupled with attempted Western peace alliances of the most diluted kind. Eventually the Soviet position did improve as a result of independently anti-Western movements in the third world and herculean efforts internally at achieving military parity with the United States; not coincidentally, that is also the moment, roughly speaking, when the relationship with Washington was transformed. The world, geopolitically, had turned into two superpowers with sharply diverging internal systems and a third heterogeneous area in which contradictions could be played out in an extreme, direct form that was otherwise impossible.

Up to this point, geopolitical categories are on the whole adequate: power, space, interests, movement, force, tactics and strategies, decision-making elites. Yet what must be explained here is not just an ordinary state conflict, however globalized, but the anomaly of annihilation of the Other in a period of ostensible peace. That there would be antagonism between the US and the USSR in a geopolitical sense after the war is scarcely surprising: they were, literally, on the river of Elbe. What must be explained is why it took the extraordinarily nasty form it did, why it became a *cold war*, why it nevertheless did not become a hot one and why indeed it came to transcend the geopolitical.

An obvious initial answer would be to refer to the systemic aspect, for the cold war was at once a socioeconomic, ideological-cultural and military-political conflict. Neither side, one might then argue, could tolerate the other, because its very existence meant the inversion of one's own system. This is mistaken: the two systems had coexisted before 1947, and they continued to coexist after the recognition of the early 1960s. They could do this because they were not locked into any vertical master/slave or capital/labor dialectic. Their relationship was horizontal across space. From a functional viewpoint, neither side needed for its own survival the destruction of the other. Each could, in principle, have gone on indefinitely without having to change its system as a result of the other's existence.[84] To use Louis Halle's metaphorical image again, the scorpion and the tarantula were not in fact locked in a bottle and so, functionally, did not have to kill each other. The fact that the Soviet side imploded and was transformed on Western conditions had less to do with any systemic conflict and more to do with its internal dynamic. In particular, it had to do with the historical limits of the model of accumulation that Stalin introduced in the 1930s and with his creation of a ruling technocracy, the descendants of which would eventually be highly attracted to the more advanced models of efficiency visible across the border: and so the Soviet Union, contingently, ceased to be. This is supremely ironic, but history is after all ironic. Marx always insisted it was.

Yet if the cold war was not systemic in this sense, it clearly became so in another. For it remains that it was launched in fiercely ideological terms as an invasion or delegitimization of the Other's social order, a demonology coupled of course with a mythology of the ever-lasting virtues of one's own domain. Once unleashed, ideology allowed little leeway.[85] The moment it was obvious that the two powers would not be able to work out a bargain in areas of common interest, the geopolitical

---

84   Fred Halliday delineates the systemic model, based on the capital/labor analogy, quite clearly in "The Ends of the Cold War," *New Left Review* I, no. 180 (March–April 1990), 5–23. He got an earful in response from E. P. Thompson, "The Ends of Cold War," *New Left Review* I, no. 182 (July–August 1990), 139–46. Thompson, going back to his banned Dimbleby lecture of 1980 for the BBC, cites Boris Pasternak's apothegm about history, "the consequences of consequences," to describe a system that has no other rationale than its own existence, whatever its origins. The disagreement between the two, not surprisingly, has to do with identity and difference: Thompson finds the cold war, after its originating moment, largely one of functional identity; Halliday finds the cold war constitutively to be about what it seemed to be about, capitalism and noncapitalism, each wanting to kill each other off (hence, in 1990, he thought history had shown him to be right, as indeed one side seemed to have won). My own view is closer to Thompson's—though he retains the notion of cold war for a system that I think (and he shows) had become something quite different.

85   I am using "ideology" here in the traditional and limited sense of relatively coherent political discourse.

boundaries had automatically been transgressed. Once that crucial break had been made, the unique systemic aspects of each side had to be given free play, but pre-eminently *in the realm of ideology*. I think this moment occurred around 1947–48. From then on, there were no intrinsic limit to the proceedings. What ensued was not a normal diplomatic dialogue but the simultaneous declamation of two monologues, separated in space. This dominance of the ideological was possible—indeed necessary—because of the project of securing, in different ways, one's own socio-economic systems in the two halves of Europe and anchoring the whole thing in a military deadlock. Elsewhere, the effects were lethal. The cold war was a conflict of total symbolic annihilation, its millions of actual casualties primarily suffered by the third world.[86]

Geopolitics, then, can give an account of the military-political but has little or nothing to say about the ideologico-cultural and socio-economic spheres; typically they become auxiliary functions of strategy, or generalship. To the extent that the privileged domain of interstate conflict has been the military-political, this is justified: states historically have been organizations of war and the preparation for war.[87] But the totalizing nature of the cold war is inexplicable without elucidation of the other two domains. For there was from the outset a rigid territorialization of ideology and economy, the paradoxical effect of which was to catapult to the forefront the only thing that could move, namely the mutually exclusive ideological aspect. Everything was thereby put on the table. The legitimacy of one's domestic social order could no longer be taken for granted as an unproblematic spatial whole. International politics was not simply a function of some spatially set and largely

---

86 The argument is not that third-world conflict was merely a product of the cold war. In some instances it was, but the chief point is that various local conflicts were unnecessarily intensified and prolonged. See again chapter 4, where I discuss Odd Arne Westad's work.

87 Geopolitics, I should underline, is not the same as realism—it is a larger concept. It is hard to be a realist without a geopolitical aspect but the reverse is not necessarily so. The charge here, then, is more directed at realism than the geopolitical as such (privileging space, crudely put, and spatial configurations of power, deducing policy flows from them). Space, beyond its physical aspect, is a social construct, a product of determinate social relations; and geopolitical reason is itself a discourse. There is no geopolitics, and certainly no account of it, that is not at the same time discursive and ideological. On geopolitics as practice and discourse, see Gearoid O'Tuathail, *Critical Geopolitics: The Politics of Writing Global Space* (Minneapolis, 1996). See also Henri Lefebvre, *The Production of Space* (Oxford, 1992).

atemporal realities (for example the size and location of states, their resources and organization), supposedly outside ideology and discourse.

I must then reiterate that Soviet ideology, even at its most harshly monological, always assumed that the conflict was about antifascism, preventing the United States from becoming, so to speak, a totally reactionary force devoted to the total destruction of the socialist fatherland (and so on and so on). Moreover, Moscow always saw the conflict itself as a dialectical one. Ideological limitlessness thus took different, asymmetrical expression. The legitimating master signifier in the cold war was freedom for the United States, peace for the Soviet Union: offensive in the former case, defensive in the latter.[88] The cold war was itself in fact an asymmetrical counter-concept invented by the United States: a world divided into a natural side of freedom with an indispensable leader on the one side, and a perverse, degraded and limitlessly evil force on the other. This asymmetry, and the huge disparity in power that underpinned it, is the key to the origins and nature of the cold war.

---

88 E. P. Thompson spotted the difference in master signifiers (though of course he did not use, and would never use, that expression). He was less interested in the asymmetry. See his expanded version of the Dimbleby Lecture, *Beyond the Cold War* (London, 1982), 6. His attack on the cold war as a structure was precisely that it ruled out putting peace and freedom together. In 1981 he imagined only war or transcendence in the form of a new, reunified European culture—forcing both sides to relinquish their grip—could end the cold war. That the eventual reunification of Europe (minus Russia) would take place under US auspices and rigid free market ideology, he could not envisage.

6
Considerations on Culture and Theory

When, in 1784, Johann Gottfried Herder began his vastly ambitious and predictably unfinished philosophical history of humankind, he did so by expressing deep dissatisfaction with reigning notions of culture: "Nothing is more indeterminate than this word and nothing more misleading than its application to whole nations and ages."[1] He also ridiculed the idea of history as a linear, unified process destined to end in European culture and civilization, the idea indeed that there was no culture elsewhere. On the contrary, his was a vision of several relatively independent cultures, and thus it would not be extravagant to claim that he was the first multiculturalist.[2]

Yet Herder went on to use "culture" in ways that violated the spirit of his remark, which is a good indication that this is a term that satisfies few but is hard to avoid. Having undergone several changes, its meaning now ranges from "every human artifact" (the opposite of nature) to "opera" (elite bourgeois sophistication). The usual academic view, that

---

1 Johann Gottfried Herder, *Ideen zur Philosophie der Geschichte der Menschheit* in *Werke in zehn Bänden* (Frankfurt, 1989), 6, no. 12. The quotation is also to be found in Raymond Williams, *Key Words: A Vocabulary of Culture and Society,* rev. ed. (New York, 1983), 89; and John B. Thompson, *Ideology and Modern Culture* (Stanford, CA, 1990), 126. My translation is a modified version of Williams's.

2 Herder is also oddly contemporary in his insistence on the identity of language and action. For a good introduction to Herder see Isaiah Berlin, *Vico and Herder: Two Studies in the History of Ideas* (London, 1976).

of a way of life or a symbolic system, is scarcely more precise. Culture is thus perhaps a kind of *semantic field* rather than a designation or concept; it enables one to say a variety of things.[3] Reflection on cultural studies and its possible importance for diplomatic history should include, therefore, some rudimentary sorting out of how the avowed object of inquiry conceptually emerged. One would want, in short, to historicize the matter and so elucidate how cultural studies came to relate to, and in some cases contest, other disciplines that also claim to investigate something called culture. Particularly interesting here is the uneasy relationship with history, more precisely the older kinds of cultural history, whose civilizational, all-encompassing thrust is really inimical to the deconstructions of cultural studies. One would want, finally, to ask if culture can (and should) be delimited vis-à-vis the political, the traditional domain of diplomatic history, in brief, to examine whether cultural studies has brought forth new events and processes that our subdiscipline ought to recognize.

The initial guess on that last score is that, as the thirty-year rule carries us further into the moment of transnational economies and mass culture, diplomatic history will decreasingly be about the history of diplomacy. Yet what is at stake is, of course, not only areas of jurisdiction but also the nature of the inquiry itself. Our "long crisis" is as much about laggard methods and approaches as it is about the relevance and boundaries of what we study.[4] There used to be a discomfort in this respect about social history, presumably an area of more important and innovative concerns. The discomfort is now about the new cultural history, to use its own epithet. This field, a younger cousin of cultural studies, is fast replacing social history as the general source of excitement and vibrancy. The very name diplomatic history conjures up by contrast the image of something old and not a little dusty, almost suggesting self-irony and defiance. Evelyn Waugh's ear trumpet comes to mind. So one must ask, too, if there is anything to learn by way of method.

These intentions are immediately faced with the difficulty that cultural studies is not especially interested in defining any specific object

---

3   Raymond Williams and Thompson both offer conceptual histories.
4   See Michael H. Hunt's incisive overview, "The Long Crisis in U.S. Diplomatic History: Coming to Closure," *Diplomatic History* 16 (Winter 1992): 115–40.

to be investigated, much less how. Its strength is indeed precisely a marked openness on both accounts. It is, as one critic has argued, more of a "desire" than any "floor-plan for a new discipline."[5] To make my argument more useful, therefore, I shall put the desire in the context of that larger development of the 1970s and '80s one might refer to as the advent of theory. I have in mind the migration of a particular cluster of European thought into a whole range of disciplines in the American academy, the "traveling theory" (in Edward Said's celebrated phrase) that has achieved institutional presence in such unlikely and disparate areas as jurisprudence and architecture. These currents, for which poststructuralism is a convenient if inadequate shorthand, are in my view more important for diplomatic history to evaluate than the specific phenomenon of cultural studies. Put differently, the question of theory itself is as crucial here as the future place of culture and certainly more crucial than the appearance of cultural studies.[6]

Although there were antecedents, cultural history emerged in late eighteenth-century Germany but was superseded in the nineteenth by the kind of political history illustriously represented by Ranke (and, less strictly, to this day by *Diplomatic History*).[7] It survived, nevertheless, so that a fairly straight lineage is discernible from Herder to Hegel to Burkhardt to Huizinga. What they have in common is the assumption that societies are functional organic wholes whose every part is an expression of a single principle or spirit. It is easy then to move on and privilege cultural production, or some aspect of it, as particularly expressive of this spirit/system, a condensation or microcosm in which the whole can readily be understood. Hegel, for example, believed that architecture was particularly expressive of the zeitgeist, because it was the most "material" of art forms.[8] The polarity drawn by Herder is revealing: "From a study of native literatures we have learned to know

---

5 Fredric Jameson, "On 'Cultural Studies,'" *Social Text* 34 (1993): 17.

6 Terry Eagleton, *Literary Theory: An Introduction* (Minneapolis, 1983), remains one of the best, and certainly most entertaining, surveys. "Deconstruction" is sometimes used as a term for the whole of poststructuralism, but Jacques Derrida's concept in fact fits badly or not at all with the work of Michel Foucault, the other icon of French theory.

7 Peter Burke, "Reflections on the Origins of Cultural History," in *Interpretation and Cultural History*, ed. Joan H. Pittock and Andrew Wear (New York, 1991).

8 See E. H. Gombrich, *In Search of Cultural History* (Oxford, 1969). Hegel, the most influential of the four, ultimately identified the state as the index of how far the world spirit had unfolded, though the state was for him also a work of art.

ages and peoples more deeply than along the sad and frustrating path of political and military history. In the latter we seldom see more than the manner in which a people was ruled, how it let itself be slaughtered; in the former we learn how it thought, what it wished and craved for, how it took its pleasures, how it was led by its teachers or its inclinations."[9] Said's *Culture and Imperialism* has a curious affinity with this tradition, his particularist claims to the contrary notwithstanding: a certain art form, the nineteenth-century novel, is taken to be *the* cultural locus where one can find out about the construction of imperial subjectivity.[10]

It may not be immediately apparent that the expressive model of cultural history is central to the most influential work of any postwar diplomatic historian, but it is. The whole oeuvre of William Appleman Williams revolves around the notion of an American way of life that can be read and understood in the domain of ideology and culture (the Weltanschauung) because a single, dominant principle pervades every part of the social totality. That reading will then, on the same grounds, be able to tell us something about foreign policy: the Weltanschauung of expansionism is the American Spirit, the unifying principle that expresses itself in different ways in different times, as the social totality unfolds in history. The power and ingenuity of Williams's performance are often overlooked among the many misleading accusations of economic determinism.[11]

There was, too, in cultural history an emphatic concern with the importance of *form*, aesthetic or social. What mattered chiefly was not so much concrete cultural content as its extended underlying shapes, structures not subject to constant fluctuation, the "deeper, general themes," to use Huizinga's formulation. Political historians concerned themselves with surface events; cultural historians, on the contrary, had to be configural "morphologists."[12]

---

9 Quoted in Berlin, *Vico and Herder*, 169.

10 Edward Said, *Culture and Imperialism* (New York, 1993), xii. His general view of culture is dualistic: on the one hand, the world of representation and communication; on the other, the most refined and advanced elements of arts and letters.

11 Williams's model (whose chief source of inspiration is Wilhelm Dilthey) is more open to the charge of idealism than that of economic determinism.

12 Johan Huizinga, "The Task of Cultural History" [1926], in his *Men and Ideas* (London, 1960), 28, 59. Closer to home, Warren Susman typically identifies as the proper domain of cultural history "the *forms* in which people have experienced the

Cultural history bequeathed this morphological aspect to anthropology along with the notion of culture as a total system. Anthropology was in fact founded on the concept, emerging as the discipline did in the guise of ethnographic classification of non-European (that is, "primitive") ways of life in the imperial heyday of the late nineteenth century. Debate about the status of culture has not ceased since. The two main positions even found organizational expression in the separation between cultural and social anthropology, the former centering attention on the matrix of behavior (but not behavior itself) as symbolically conveyed, the latter on the morphology of social relations. The social approach was thus unwilling to accord any constitutive role to culture and consequently also to see much value in interpreting it. But both positions reproduced what has always been an elementary part of debates about culture, the distinction and possible relation between the mental and the material. Both also stressed the need to study societies as totalities.[13] Marshall Sahlins and Clifford Geertz, the most eminent cultural anthropologists of recent times, have in different ways tried to transcend these limits. For instance, in the latter's view, culture is "a web of significance" that can only be understood through interpretation of meaning and then rearranged and deployed through "thick description." The task, then, cannot be carried out by formalizing a purely symbolic system. For culture is ultimately the "informal logic of actual life," the site where "cultural forms find articulation."[14]

---

world—the patterns of life, the symbols by which they cope with the world." Introduction to Susman, ed., *Culture and Commitment, 1929–1945* (New York, 1973), i. The mentalities studied by Annales historians are of the same order: durable structures of popular consciousness and subjectivity that are centered on the collective, the implicit, and the categories and matrices that render experience intelligible. See Peter Burke, *History and Social Theory* (Ithaca, 1992), 91–93.

13 See the entry for "culturalism and culture" in Raymond Boudon and François Bourricand, *A Critical Dictionary of Sociology* (London. 1982), 93–100. See also Shirley Robin Letwin, "Culture, Individuality and Deference," in *Culture et Politique/Culture and Politics,* ed. Maurice Cranston and Lea Campos Boralevi (Berlin, 1988), 73–85; the entry for "culture" in the *International Encyclopedia of the Social Sciences* (New York, 1968), 3:527–47; and R. B. J. Walker, "The Concept of Culture in the Theory of International Relations," in *Culture and International Relations,* ed. Jongsuk Chay (New York, 1986), 3–17.

14 Clifford Geertz, *The Interpretation of Cultures: Selected Essays* (New York, 1973), 5, 17. His "thick description" (conceptually borrowed from Gilbert Ryle) has been highly influential, not least within the New Historicism in literary criticism. A related

The social sciences have otherwise taken a rather dismissive attitude toward culture. One has tended to see it as "that residual realm left over after all forms of observable human behavior have been removed."[15] Those seriously interested in it generally conceived of it as the basic value system of any given totality/society. This allowed, then, for a culturalist (as opposed to a functionalist or structuralist) analysis of how individuals or collectivities are socialized to these norms—or, alternatively, deviate from them. Such a framework has the obvious advantage of lending itself to quantification. One can operationalize the model by breaking up the system into a whole range of subsystems: political culture, strategic culture, agency culture, computer culture, football culture, and so on. The classic American text here is Gabriel Almond and Sydney Verba's The Civic Culture. Following Talcott Parsons, the authors focused on the "cognitive, affective, and evaluative orientations to political phenomena," that is, a set of psychological dispositions vis-à-vis a specific object that lead people tendentially to behave in certain ways. Thus, Almond and Verba investigated and compared attitudes toward the political system in five different countries and found, very much in keeping with the cold-war liberalism of the time, that Anglo-American political culture was best suited to ensure both stability and democracy. Not surprisingly, their findings came in for a great deal of subsequent criticism; but as a model of inquiry, they remain in play.[16]

---

approach is to be found in the microhistory of Carlo Ginzburg. It would be amusing and probably educational to see this applied to some single moment of diplomatic history. Marshall Sahlins's seminal *Culture and Practical Reason* (Chicago, 1976) is the most sustained argument against instrumentalist conceptions of culture. With customary verve, he writes: "Nothing in the way of their capacity to satisfy a material (biological) requirement can explain why pants are produced for men and skirts for women, or why dogs are inedible but the hindquarters of steer are supremely satisfying of the need to eat" (207).

15 Robert Wuthnow et al., *Cultural Analysis* (New York, 1984), 4. See also his *Meaning and Moral Order: Explorations in Cultural Analysis* (Berkeley, CA, 1987).

16 Gabriel A. Almond and Sidney Verba, *The Civic Culture: Political Attitudes and Democracy in Five Nations* (Princeton, 1963). For retrospective assessments, including critical ones, see Almond and Verba, eds., *The Civic Culture Revisited* (Boston, 1989); and Michael Brint, *A Genealogy of Political Culture* (Boulder, 1991). See also Richard J. Samuels and Myron Weiner, eds., *The Political Culture of Foreign Area and International Studies: Essays in Honor of Lucian W. Pye* (Washington, DC, 1992). Pye is the third important figure in the field. For an early, highly ambitious, and unusual study in a more overtly cold-war vein, see Adda B. Bozeman, *Politics and Culture in International History* (Princeton, 1960).

It is against this background that one might position the only diplomatic historian who has done any extensive work along cross-cultural lines, Akira Iriye. Iriye opposes wide and narrow constructions of culture alike, extensive anthropological notions as well as limited concepts typified by strategic culture. In fact, however, his own view is roughly coeval with standard anthropological accounts and also compatible with a psychological or dispositional paradigm. Culture, for Iriye, forms an exhaustive societal trinity together with economy and power. It "is the creation and communication of memory, ideology, emotions, lifestyles, scholarly and artistic works, and other symbols," or, as he also says, it is "the sharing and transmitting of consciousness within and across national boundaries."[17]

Such an unapologetically mentalist conception can produce work of great worth, as evidenced by Iriye's own endeavors. Culture, however, operates here both to describe and to explain. The question, then, is what has actually been explained, and what happens when one begins to inquire into the foundations and place of this culture. Iriye himself recognizes the danger of reifying the concept, and the danger that it can serve to conceal internal domination and hegemonies of values. His own trinitarian model typically contains no account of causal connections (or, for that matter, how power can be understood outside of values). Once the aspect of domination appears, the culturalist approach faces the enduring problem of explanation. Is culture an enclosed sphere and, if so, what are its relations with the noncultural?

The haunting shadows here are Marxist theories of ideology, whose determinist and reflective flavor the notion of culture is often supposed to eliminate. Culture, in effect, becomes a substitute for ideology. Conservative versions of this move evoke deeply embedded traditions of a seamless social fabric devoid of conflict. The virtues of slow, organic change can then be extolled. The trope is well known. A plausible argument can indeed be made that culture always tilts in the direction of conservative wholes. Cultural studies is in a way the radical answer to that charge.

---

17 Akira Iriye, "Culture and International History," in *Explaining the History of American Foreign Relations*, ed. Michael J. Hogan and Thomas G. Paterson (New York, 1991), 214–25. It should be read together with Michael H. Hunt's "Ideology," in the same volume (193–201).

The field emerged in Britain in the mid-1960s, chiefly through the now legendary Centre for Cultural Studies at Birmingham. Central sources of support and inspiration for this project of understanding popular culture were the extensive tradition of Marxist social history, the strong links with adult education, and the pioneering work of Richard Hoggart (*The Uses of Literacy* [1957]), Raymond Williams (*Culture and Society* [1958] and *The Long Revolution* [1961]) and E. P. Thompson (*The Making of the English Working Class* [1963]). Over time, the distinctly British heritage here was transformed under the powerful dual influence of Antonio Gramsci (introducing the pivotal concept of hegemony) and Louis Althusser (whose structuralist Marxism undermined the humanist or subjectivist notions of agency exemplified by Thompson). This was then followed in the 1970s by a massive incorporation of poststructuralist theory, most of which had a deeply troubled relation to existing Marxist traditions. For if any single thing characterized this motley series of philosophical positions, aside from their French provenance and hostility to humanist traditions, it was the attack on totality and master narratives; and no theory fit that bill better than Marxism (especially Sartrean Marxism).[18]

The fundamental concerns, then, of British cultural studies had been Marxisant, revealed indeed in the pledge to unearth and give voice to popular groups marginalized by ruling-class culture. Three themes or arguments marked this project: (i) culture as a product of social relations, especially class relations; (ii) culture as a system that creates and maintains iniquities of power; (iii) culture, therefore, as "neither an autonomous nor an externally determined field, but a site of social differences and struggles." By contrast with existing radical critiques of the culture industry, however, the emphasis was not on a massive, single message of mind-numbing commodification and its institutional

---

18 This potted history is crude and simplified. For more historical context, see Patrick Brantlinger, *Crusoe's Footprints: Cultural Studies in Britain and America* (New York, 1990); Stanley Aronowitz, *Roll over Beethoven: The Return of Cultural Strife* (Middletown, 1993); Richard Johnson, "What Is Cultural Studies Anyway?," *Social Text* 16 (Winter 1986/87): 38–80; Tom O'Regan, "(Mis)taking Policy: Notes on the Cultural Policy Debate," *Cultural Studies* 6 (October 1992): 409–23; and Stuart Hall's retrospective remarks, "Cultural Studies and Its Theoretical Legacies," in *Cultural Studies*. ed. Lawrence Grossberg, Cary Nelson, Paula A. Treichler (New York, 1992), 277–94. For the interesting history of cultural studies in Australia, where it has achieved policymaking status, see O'Regan's piece and the special issue of *Cultural Studies* in which it appears.

underpinnings, but on how the popular classes resist and rework such messages to their own advantage, how they maintain a certain autonomy that is not to be understood as merely deprived, how they form their own culture in the process. Hence the attempt both to investigate actual lived experience on shop floors and to analyze working-class soap operas on television, not only semiotically but also as they were received, read, and imagined in a multiplicity of ways. None of this entailed, therefore, any one method or approach. Cultural studies, in the words of one of its founding spirits, remained "a kind of alchemy for the production of useful knowledge."[19]

An additional comment is necessary in this regard about the two canonical figures of Raymond Williams and Antonio Gramsci. Williams, who remained an inspiration, spent a lifetime wrestling conceptually with culture, never really succeeding in determining its limits. But whatever the specific definition, it always served two important functions for him. First, it was a way, against the absolute separation of spheres in bourgeois society, to insist on interrelatedness, to insist in particular that culture was not merely something spiritual but indeed part or essence of a material whole. Second, it was a way to get out of overly reflectionist Marxist models of base and superstructure, as well as narrowly construed notions of ideology as false consciousness. This fit well with the Gramscian legacy, rediscovered and introduced in the 1960s. For Gramsci, too, emphasized the importance of culture for any oppositional movement in the West. The concept of hegemony, bandied about everywhere today, was in Gramsci partly predicated on the distinction between Eastern and Western Europe. In the East, civil society was undeveloped, the state commensurately more pervasive, repression consequently the chief means of class rule; in the West, with its extensive institutions of civil society, coercion was conversely far less important, active consent instead the dominant aspect of maintaining the hegemonic order. A political strategy, therefore, would be successful in combating the existing normative system only if it paid proper attention to various cultural institutions, or sites. The object would be to create counter-hegemonies, as it were.[20]

---

19 Johnson, "What Is Cultural Studies Anyway?," 39, 38.
20 On Raymond Williams see Lesley Johnson, *The Cultural Critics: From Matthew Arnold to Raymond Williams* (London, 1979); and *Social Text* 30 (1992), a special issue

It is this amalgam, then, that forms the central point of departure for what would become in the United States an academic growth industry. The American setting is of course profoundly different and the appropriation inevitably marked by it. The clear-cut class aspects of British politics and society are not at all clear-cut here. Popular culture in the United States is not so much class based as mass-based. Socialist components are, needless to say, famously absent. The state apparatuses are far less developed and certainly afford less room for progressive links. The distance between academia and the popular classes (in themselves much more heterogeneous) is greater. Academia as such is an enormous, sprawling network, whose peculiar admixture of college education (as a direct extension of high school) and professional and research institutions has made possible, fortunately, an expansive world for the humanities. In this fluid world there is a professional premium on new things to say and so a material ground for the importation of theories that will facilitate such a development. When cultural studies migrated to the United States there was in fact already a growing presence of French and German theory and European philosophy that flourished, not in the rigid philosophy departments, but in the more open field of literary criticism. Relatedly, the cross-disciplinary problematics of feminism and various minority identities were also emerging, creating what in retrospect one might call "cultural area studies."

Finally, there was in the United States an established, wholly indigenous tradition of exploring mass culture: American studies, which partly overlapped with cultural history. Yet American studies was obviously more limited in scope than cultural studies, its mission in fact having been to detail and explain American exceptionalism. In this respect, it could take both a right and a left form, celebratory accounts by Daniel Boorstin, critical ones by F. O. Matthiessen, Merle Curti, Warren Susman, and now T. J. Jackson Lears and Michael Denning (in

---

devoted to Williams (wherein Catherine Gallagher's "Raymond Williams and Cultural Studies," 79–89, is of particular interest). Gramsci's argument can be found interspersed in *Selections from the Prison Notebooks of Antonio Gramsci*, ed. and trans. Quintin Hoare and Geoffrey Nowell Smith (New York, 1971). See also Perry Anderson's classic critique, "The Antinomies of Antonio Gramsci," *New Left Review* I:100 (November 1976–January 1977): 5–78. There is, too, considerable work in IR theory on hegemony, but only some of it is of Gramscian provenance. See Stephen Bill, ed., *Gramsci, Historical Materialism and International Relations* (Cambridge, 1993).

generational succession). Oddly, as Denning has argued, even the "anti-American studies" route was a response to the presumed Marxist failure to account for American "uniqueness." Yet on both sides of the fence there was a critical attitude toward the advent of crassly commercial mass culture, an impulse to counterpose to it the recuperation of some more genuine culture.[21]

These preconditions of reception affected cultural studies in several ways: It became heavily cross-fertilized and merged with other fields, more academic, more geared toward the purely semiological aspects of mass culture, and, above all, less Marxisant. The Gramscian counter-hegemonies tended to remain intramural: spaces within the academy, largely lacking connections with movements outside, such as they are. Conceptually, there was a concomitant drift toward making the sign stand for the social and thus letting the analysis of the sign replace the analysis of the social. Hence the gravitational pull in the direction of what might be dubbed the politics of representation, opposition then taking the form either of a critique of hegemonic discourses or an analysis of how various forms of cultural production or signifying practices constitute subjectivities and identities. Representation being everywhere, there is no end to the deconstructive possibilities. Theory can thus turn into a domestic machine for the production of academic discourse about discourse, a tool to make new statements about old, familiar subjects, like, say, eighteenth-century landscape painting. Idealism, philosophical as opposed to political idealism, would thus seem a distinct danger.[22] Despite the emphasis on culture as practice,

---

21 Michael Denning, "'The Special American Conditions': Marxism and American Studies," *American Quarterly* 38, no. 3 (1986): 356–80, terms appear on 358. On "anti-American studies," Denning is invoking Kenneth Lynn's bookreview of Jackson Lears's *No Place of Grace*.

22 Cornel West emphasizes this in his polemical (and extemporaneous) remarks regarding class, race, and inequality in *October* 61 (1992), an issue entirely devoted to identity politics: "Now of course there's a cultural dimension. This is where poststructuralists can teach us much. But we have to begin with talk about resources and the way they are linked *to* cultural identities . . . [If] we don't talk about resources, and bodies and land and labor and corporations, then we remain inscribed within a very, very narrow kind of discourse, one that chimes well with professional managerial space" (116, 117). Judith Butler responded that what counts as a resource is also a construction. Another type of danger is obeisant celebration of the joys of commodity consumption: anti-intellectual intellectuals who see in consumption a source of mass creativity and attack any critical thought of it as elitist. See Simon Frith and Jon Savage, "Pearls and

the claims of having overcome the old dualism of mental and material ring a bit hollow amid the proliferating constructivisms.

As regards theory generally, there was the additional temptation, especially in more formalized disciplines, to fall into a kind of pure negativity by engaging in a perpetual of dismantling of hegemonic models within the field. This has plagued the opposition in international relations theory, outstandingly so its leading figure Richard Ashley. Confronted with a compactly serried discipline that takes discipline very seriously indeed, Ashley and others have assumed an entrenched, defensive posture from which they issue a constant stream of metatheoretical critiques of the established clergy as well as—alternatively and to better effect—analyses of the semiological aspect of American foreign policy.[23]

Lest one fall into a comforting but all-too-easy attitude of dismissal of the foreign and the fashionable, it must be stressed that some poststructuralist themes conformed with the arguments of solidly American pragmatism. I am thinking especially of the critique of foundationalist epistemologies, notions of some ultimate ground or secure court of appeal for knowledge. All in all, three basic philosophical shifts took place during the 1970s and '80s: (i) a move away from the correspondence theory of truth, the proposition that language simply refers to something outside and that truth can thus be measured by the degree to which description accords with that outside; (ii) a move toward stressing linguistic instability or indeterminacy, that language has no fixed meaning but is intertextual, relational; (iii) the radical questioning of established Cartesian concepts of the human being as an identical self.[24]

The potential effect of this on cherished rules of the historical craft is easily imagined. The text or document no longer has any set boundaries

---

Swine: The Intellectuals and the Mass Media," *New Left Review* I, no. 198 (March/April 1993): 107–16. They are referring to a British type that emerged during Thatcher's market totalitarianism.

23 See, for example, Richard Ashley's well-known early article, "The Poverty of Neorealism," *International Organization* 38, no. 2 (Spring 1984): 225–81. There is now, however, a burgeoning critical literature within IR theory and more to come. For an interesting recent example that vigorously asserts its status as empirical research, see James Der Derian, *Antidiplomacy: Spies, Terror, Speed, and War* (Cambridge, MA, 1992). See also R. B. J. Walker, *Inside/Outside: International Relations as Political Theory* (Cambridge, 1993).

24 This sketch draws on conversations throughout the 1980s with Cornel West, who likes to divide things in three.

or foundation. Language, infinitely creative and opaque, has to be problematized beyond mere argument about context and authorial intention. The canons of evidence are subverted, evidence that in fact consists of, to use Geertz's pointed formulation, "explications of explications." The very distinction between history and story becomes fuzzy.[25] Yet none of this had any immediate impact on the historical profession, profoundly suspicious of attempts to infuse the discipline with theory and abstraction. Whether it is quantification or deconstruction is really irrelevant. If all observation is theory laden, history is perhaps "a philosophical discourse that is unaware of itself."[26] There is inscribed, however, in what I like to call the historical mode of production a certain reductionism that militates against any Derridean-inspired play of the sign. Historians gather enormous archival sources and must then necessarily summarize, reduce, condense, and privilege the central over the marginal, at the end of which procedure they must put some sensible whole together. It stands to reason that one might become a little strapped for analytical time.

Intellectual history, not surprisingly, is the exception: text and meaning here are a basic concern, as distinct from a merely documentary one.[27] Aside from the important exchanges that have taken place in that field, theory is having a strong impact on women's history and in other areas where the construction of identity is a central concern, not least then, as mentioned, the new cultural history.[28] Less well known is the vital dialogue about poststructuralism and history generated within South Asian historiography, particularly that of the Indian group around *Subaltern Studies*. Starting from a neo-Gramscian view, this interdisciplinary outfit has produced work of great sophistication and depth, the exemplary text here being Ranajit Guha's *Elementary Aspects of Peasant Insurgency in Colonial India* (1983). The poststructuralist element has

---

25 Geertz, *The Interpretation*. 9. On histories and stories see Hayden V. White, especially his excellent essay "The Context in the Text: Method and Ideology in Intellectual History," in his *The Content of the Form: Narrative Discourse and Historical Representation* (Baltimore, MD, 1987), 185–213.
26 Michel de Certeau. *The Writing of History* (New York, 1988), 12.
27 Dominick LaCapra has been a driving force in this debate. See, for example, *Soundings in Critical Theory* (Ithaca, 1989); the essay "Culture and Ideology: From Geertz to Marx," 133–54, is especially pertinent.
28 For an example see Richard Wightman Fox and T. J. Jackson Lears, eds., *The Power of Culture: Critical Essays in American History* (Chicago, 1993).

become stronger over time, fueled by the need to understand identity and difference in a colonial and postcolonial setting. A vigorous debate, across continental divides, is now going on as a result, a debate of general interest not least because it is about something more than merely theory: there is an actual body of historical work to discuss.[29]

On that note we may return to diplomatic history and ask what is at stake in the matter of culture and theory. Let us begin with the least controversial aspect: no one would probably dispute the value of general investigations of traditions. These works are, if nothing else, of empirical interest and offer a basis for understanding how foreign policies of different states can clash unintentionally. Michael Haas, for instance, has shown central divergencies between Asian modes of conducting geopolitics and typically Western concepts of interest calculation. Benedict Anderson's fascinating exploration of Javanese conceptions of power and territory is another example. Richard Slotkin has delineated a more familiar tradition, the extraordinary violence of American culture, an account of which should appear in every diplomatic survey.[30]

Quasi-anthropological culturalism of this sort falls largely within the older, contextual approach I have counterposed to the newer, discursive position. In the first case, culture forms a wide base upon which policy

---

29 Useful references here are Gyatri Chakravorty Spivak, "Can the Subaltern Speak?," in *Marxism and the Interpretation of Culture*, ed. Cary Nelson and Lawrence Grossberg (Urbana, 1988). 299–307; and Gyan Prakash, "Writing Post-Orientalist Histories of the Third World: Perspectives from Indian Historiography," *Comparative Studies in Society and History* 32, no. 2 (1990): 383–408. For an extremely sharp critique of Prakash's (Derridean) poststructuralism, see Rosalind O'Hanlon and David Washbrook, "After Orientalism: Culture, Criticism, and Politics in the Third World," *Comparative Studies in Society and History* 34, no. 1 (January 1992): 141–67. Prakash responds in the same issue (185–200). Ironically, while theory is making inroads in odd places, the theoretically minded are clamoring for more history, either in the form of increased awareness of the origins of theory itself, or as information, real knowledge so to speak. Political science, meanwhile, sees historical work as empirical raw material to be used in case studies, which in turn are supposed to prove or disprove models. The appropriation of history is often astonishingly naive.

30 See Michael Haas, "Asian Culture and International Relations," in Chay, ed., *Culture and International Relations*, 172–90 (the same work also features Johan Galtung's singularly acerbic "U.S. Foreign Policy as Manifest Theology"); Benedict R. O'G. Anderson, *Language and Power: Exploring Political Cultures in Indonesia* (Ithaca, 1990); Richard Slotkin, *Regeneration through Violence: The Mythology of the American Frontier, 1600–1860* (Middletown, 1973); and Slotkin, *The Fatal Environment: The Myth of the Frontier in the Age of Industrialization, 1800–1890* (New York, 1985).

formation and other activities take place; in the second it cuts *across* these other domains. The difference can be concretized in the following way. Herder and Huizinga argued for the primacy of cultural analysis on the grounds of greater penetration, deeper systemic knowledge. They did not deny the specificity of political history. Discursive proponents, on the other hand, extend the boundaries of culture at times to encompass, as one exemplary text puts it, "the amalgam of processes whereby *all* aspects of society are constructed." The author goes on to conclude that "*all* history is cultural history, since there can be no processes, whether economic, social or political, which are not mediated through ideas, concepts, theories, images or languages."[31] This seems to me a simple transposition of the well-known theme from yesterday, namely, that everything is political. If culture is everything, it is nothing, at least nothing analytically meaningful. To argue (as I myself have) the omnipresence of ideology is not to argue that everything is ideological.

What, then, are the uses of cultural history? First, improved theoretical acumen, of whatever kind, can only make history better, more subtle, more discerning, more conceptually interesting. This has always been true and so ought not to be a contentious proposition. Second, new theories of subjectivity and identity formation, both cause and effect of the critique of conventional conceptions of "man," are of obvious relevance, indeed unavoidable, in historical investigations of race, class and gender as well as of any groups in conflict. Third, the Western world has seen an immense explosion of the cultural sphere in the postwar era, a process supported by rapidly expanding modes of capitalist accumulation and concomitant advances in communication technology, the result of which is precisely to put the politics of representation at the center. This transformation, sometimes theorized as postmodernism, is marked by profound alterations of time and space, generating a whole new world of disjointed intensities and images in which the very nature of politics itself is put into question.[32] Poststructuralist theory is quite

---

31   Ludmilla Jordanova, "The Representation of the Family in the Eighteenth Century: A Challenge for Cultural History," in Pittock and Wear, eds., *Interpretation and Cultural History*, 118.
32   See Fredric Jameson, *Postmodernism, or the Cultural Logic of Late Capitalism* (Durham, NC, 1991. Jameson's panoramic work suffers from one weakness: it has no account of the political or the state as such. His analysis tends to posit only two spheres, the economic and the cultural/ideological. R. B. J. Walker alerted me to this. Jameson,

useful here. It is, as stated, well suited to semiological analyses of representation and subjectivity, for example, the mediatization of foreign relations, or aspects of gender and identity. It will be exceedingly difficult, one would think, for future diplomatic historians to write about the Reagan presidency or the Gulf war without first understanding postmodern theories of discourse and representation.[33] It will, similarly, be difficult to write about the United States and the Third World without reflection on constructions of the Other. The growing concern with Americanization and cultural influence in the wake of Emily Rosenberg's pioneering work will doubtless also generate interest in theory. No one, in any event, will seriously propound now that the archives of the State Department are going to elucidate our present epoch to the degree that they elucidate the late 1940s.

The postmodern turn is thus not merely fancy theoretical footwork. It is a reflection of historical change. Consider, for instance, how national character has gradually been displaced by concerns of national identity. Perry Anderson has conceptualized this change in an astute assessment of Fernand Braudel's final musings on the history of France. Character, as Anderson sees it, was a product of national culture in the imprecise nineteenth-century sense of "sociability, morality, creativity and consumption." Assuming, then, a distinction between social structure and national culture, he observes that differences in the latter can remain profound even as the former becomes increasingly homogenized in the advanced capitalist countries: "No one would confuse Belgium with Japan." Yet, as evidenced by Western Europe, the market is undermining differences in "the object-world" of consumption at a fierce rate, creating "a single time-zone of the imaginary, bounded by the optical fiber." With the added pressure of increasing ethnic mobility and migration, the national self as a specific character is thus put into question, replaced by a preoccupation with identity that can easily sink into rabid

---

however, sees it as a strength. Just as Hegel, and for the same reason, Jameson singles out architecture as a significant place to read historical transformation. Postmodernism has generated a problematic of space (or *spatiality*) and territory that will be increasingly important for historians, whose usual trade is in chunks of time.

33 Der Derian's *Antidiplomacy* explores the Gulf war in this way. As a counterpoint see Christopher Norris, *Uncritical Theory: Postmodernism, Intellectuals, and the Gulf War* (Amherst, 1992), wherein overly media-centered accounts of "the war that never was" are properly scrutinized.

assertiveness. For the difference is that, whereas character is self-sufficient and needs no external counterpart for its definition, national identity is something far more brittle and aggressive, marked by the need for a mission and an outside opposite, hence also by self-awareness and symbolization. "Issues of citizenship and sovereignty," as Anderson encapsulates his argument, "touch the nerves of national identity in a way that consumption and diversion do not."[34]

The most readily available presence in the current theory pantheon is Michel Foucault. He wrote histories, he wrote about power and security, and he wrote penetrating things about method and understanding. As a good neo-Kantian, he was always inclined to ask how rather than what questions, questions about the conditions of possibility for any given practice or discourse. From his earlier archaeological phase, with its considerations on rules of formation for knowledge, to his genealogical analyses of institutions of normalizing power, he never fetishized any analysis method because he was chiefly interested in objects of discourse, how things come to be constituted as targets of knowledge and power. Here, against the predominant Annales tradition, he wanted to reinstate the importance of events, discursive or other events that change our ways of thinking about what counts as historically significant. Such investigations would have to break at the outset with established assumptions and search for the strategies and operations that served to found that self-evident understanding, that truth-game. Conceptualization along those lines is clearly relevant for historiography in general, but Foucault's work on technologies of power, the kinds of knowledge and discourse that make certain policies possible, is especially pertinent in the subfield of diplomatic history.[35]

I must then go on, however, to remark that most of what I have called theory here has very little to say about society, the economy, or the state;

---

34 Perry Anderson, "Fernand Braudel and National Identity," in *Zones of Engagement* (London, 1992), 252–78; quotations 266, 261, 270. Anderson is skeptical of the concept of postmodernism, but his argument fits the general tenor of that debate.

35 I am benefiting greatly here from conversations with John Rajchman, whose *Michel Foucault: Philosopher of Freedom* (New York, 1986), is an excellent and very clear introduction. For an intelligent critique of Foucault and poststructuralism as a whole see Peter Dews, *Logics of Disintegration: Post-structuralist Thought and the Claims of Critical Theory* (London, 1987). Another relevant theorist (but no poststructuralist) is Pierre Bourdieu, whose sociological work on habitus (dispositions), cultural capital, and power relations is useful in analysis of policymaking.

nor is it particularly conducive to analyses of such subjects. Work at once historically and theoretically sensitive in our field requires that one widen the horizon beyond the politics of representation toward, for example, the critical traditions within geography, historical sociology, and political economy. But that is another story.

7
War and Diplomatic History

The Second World War is the most significant event in the history of US foreign relations. It accomplished what Woodrow Wilson believed, mistakenly, had already occurred through the Spanish-American War (to use its conventional designation), namely, to push the United States irrevocably into the world of great powers, indeed making it the most powerful of the only two that now really counted geopolitically as such powers. The Second World War was also the most extensive and successful mobilization of the nation as a whole, generating a massive output by a capitalist machine that was being reconstructed under state auspices, thus reestablishing confidence in a system whose credentials had come into question during the devastating Depression. While other powers suffered (none more so than the Soviet Union), the United States remained remote from the sites of war and witnessed a boom that was as unexpected as it was astonishing, propelling the country into economic preeminence in the postwar world. No single event, simply put, has changed the geopolitical position of the United States in the world to the extent that did the Second World War.

And yet this monumentally important moment or epoch has proved to be of very limited interest to diplomatic historians. It is now conceivably the case, for example, that the colonial war known here a century ago as the Philippine Incident is receiving greater scholarly attention—rightly or not—than the (nearly) global conflagration at midcentury. It would be wrong, however, to imagine this lack of concern as a story of decline and fall from some putative golden age. Relative neglect, if that is indeed the proper term, is in fact not a recent phenomenon. One scans in vain the classic tomes of diplomatic history for anything remarkable by way of substance, analysis, or even unusual attention devoted to the world-historical conflict in question. Peruse, for example, the fifth edition (1965) of Samuel Flagg Bemis's *A Diplomatic History of the United States* and you will find about twenty-five pages out of more than a thousand devoted to "American Diplomacy During the Second World War," as the relevant and not especially exciting chapter is called. Thomas Bailey, on his part, spends approximately thirty pages out of nine hundred on the topic in the seventh edition (1964) of *A Diplomatic History of the American People*. Notably, his fifth edition (1955) gave almost as much space to the Korean War. This is impressionistic evidence but I would hazard a guess that the high mark of scholarly work on the Second World War is of comparatively recent origin, distinctive not only against the present decline but against the historiography of diplomacy overall.

Listlessness here is a product of both contingent and structural factors. Significance notwithstanding, the Second World War exhibits among US wars a historic peculiarity that tends to make it analytically invisible, as it were. On the structural level, meanwhile, the absence of interest can be accounted for in a radical manner: war as such is not a proper object of inquiry in diplomatic history, for war is the end of diplomacy, the history of which must thus be about something else. In elucidating, elaborating, and revising these two arguments, especially the second one, my subsequent remarks will necessarily take on an abstract air here and there, for what interests me, above all, are the conceptual conditions under which an object such as the Second World War may appear in the field of diplomatic history and the explanatory effects that occur when it does. This involves, in turn, tricky issues having to do with periodization. Diplomatic history, to anticipate matters, is predicated on an initial division of time into two kinds of periods, war and peace, the latter of which is then subjected to further investigation and periodization. The distinction between war and peace, one might say, is the premise of the whole exercise but not its content. Yet we have learned since 1945 that war is less of a transhistorical phenomenon and less of a self-evident period than it seems. I will argue that the Second World War constitutes a break in the whole structure of war; that it is a moment in which the older European concept of a sharp distinction between war and peace is attenuated; that the central reason for the transformation is the US entry into the conflict; and that war consequently becomes a different object of analysis, all of which then also puts into question what a history of diplomacy might be about. This chapter, perhaps over-ambitiously, will be at once procedural (on periodization and explanation), substantial (in making concrete historical arguments), and demonstrative (in exemplifying one modest way of breaking with the confines of established practices).

I will begin, then, by asking why the Second World War is hard to see. The immediate answer is obvious, indeed almost a platitude. The Second World War was a popular war and so it has remained. Ipso facto, not a great deal of controversy attaches to it. Across the political spectrum, among the public and historians alike, it was and is a deeply legitimate war against very bad regimes bent on destroying by colossal aggression an existing order that, whatever its faults, was certainly worth defending. No serious scholar argues that a fascist victory would have been a good thing and it is hard to argue that the United States should not have become involved. To be sure, there are controversies. One may quarrel about the entry into the war, about (say) Roosevelt's manner of maneuvering the country into a position where, arguably, war with Japan became inevitable. One may quarrel about the discrepancies between the official posture of a democratic war and the actual conduct with regard to race and related aspects, as revealed in the egregious internment of Japanese Americans. One may quarrel with the framing, execution, and strategic view of the conflict. One may certainly quarrel over the vision of the Grand Alliance. And one may quarrel very hotly indeed about all things atomic. But regarding the heart of the matter, the actual war against fascism as such, there is and can be little controversy.

The Second World War is historically unique in this respect. Perhaps the Revolutionary War is comparable; but insurrectionary violence to create a republic is of a different order from that of a war conducted in the name of an already existing regime. Every other war (from all the Amerindian wars to the more conventional War of 1812 down to the war in Afghanistan) has been contestable on grounds that it was either unnecessary, morally wrong, or politically imprudent—or all of the above. The effort to crush fascism was none of these things. The room, accordingly, for historiographical disagreement of the elementary kind is rather narrow. The various historiographies on the formerly fascist side illustrate the difference most starkly: wrenching questions of national responsibility for aggression and murder on levels of unfathomable magnitude.

The uncontested nature of the war is also, one should add, what has opened it up recently for heroic memorialization. There has been relentless popular botany in sundry aspects of the war. Perhaps this is not surprising. War, after all, is a matter of life and death, a matter of existence itself; and, the Second World War (along with the Civil War), because of the massive commitment of the entire body politic, offers an inexhaustible source of epic tales. This is not incompatible with genuine knowledge; but at its most extravagant and uncritical, such remembrance has turned into serialized odes to the selflessly sacrificing generation, the generation that, after suffering the crushing decade of Depression, was confronted with global war and rose stirringly to the occasion, thus saving civilization in general and the United States in particular, after which said generation was able (one might imagine) to enjoy a well-deserved moment of the good life in the suburban 1950s, only to be faced with a tragically misconceived war and a lot of ungrateful, countercultural protesters in the 1960s. The implicit or not so implicit counterpoint to the good war is thus the bad war, which is to say Vietnam, distinct as it is not only for having been lost but also (and this is the decisive dimension) for having occasioned profound dissent across the land of the free about the very goodness of America itself. Memorializing the good war cleanses the body politic from lingering memories of the bad war and its attendant ills.

I am exaggerating a bit but the larger point is important. What makes the Second World War available to popular memory is conversely what renders it less compelling for scholarly analysis. For what drives diplomatic history in the United States is political controversy. Without it, the field has no direction, no character, no shape or form, no vivacity. This central feature is ultimately grounded in the fact that any analysis of the relationship to the outside world puts into question the very identity of the United States as an entity and a project. One might object that this is true of all countries. Yet the ideology of exceptionalism and the constant obsession with the world-historical role of the United States (indeed the very idea of the nation as a project) has served to accentuate in extraordinarily profound ways the meaning of the borderline, the meaning of the foundational distinction between inside and outside. To have an account of any given question of foreign policy is by implication to have an account of what the United States is and ought to be. It is to take a personal position on a certain political terrain. To see this dynamic more plainly, one may consider a counterexample conveniently near to hand: Sweden. Lack of Great Power aspirations, neutrality and not a single war for two centuries have constricted the scope for historical interest in foreign relations.[1] One can only write about the extent to which neutrality was more or less successfully carried out—though this compact, sometimes smug, consensus has now begun to break down against the backdrop of entirely new geopolitical conditions within the variable space called Europe. Political controversy, then, is inescapably what generates interest in the history of US diplomacy and its individual episodes. The Second World War as antifascism was a necessity and it is hard to argue with necessity.

The preceding comments, a sociology of knowledge of sorts, can account for a certain absence of historiographical exploration, but they offer no conceptual reason to neglect the period as a period. Thus, we should return to my opening thesis (or hypothesis) that war has no place in diplomatic history; and, by extension, that neglect of the Second World War is no neglect at all but a quite legitimate exclusion. For the beginning of war is the end of diplomacy, as war is the continuation of politics by overtly violent means. War is thus, bluntly put, of no interest to historians of diplomacy. More precisely, it is of interest only as a problem of diplomatic failure or impending peace. Small wonder, then, that historians have been inclined to analyze the Second World War either as the end of the sorry 1930s or the beginning of what is usually referred to as the cold war.

A brief sketch of the historical background of this argument is useful before we go on. War and peace, as they were defined by conventional European rules after the seventeenth century, are two mutually exclusive moments of state affairs, clearly demarcated and officially acknowledged. A precondition here is the prior demarcation of the state itself as a territory of clear borders and absolute internal sovereignty, mutually recognized by every other member of the system. This new formation

---

1 In 2024, Sweden abandoned those two centuries of neutrality for membership in NATO – with minimal debate.

had emerged, in part, to eliminate as rightful grounds for warfare, within and between states, the appeals to suprastate principles—quelling, in effect, politically debilitating disputes over Christianity. Thus, in due course, the state was turned into its own justification and legitimating principle; and to complement the transformation there emerged a kind of technology of statecraft, in which warfare and diplomacy were now two instruments of some larger policy (or grand strategy) designed to maintain and expand the security and well-being of the state qua state. Hence diplomacy became the legal and historical obverse of war, the promulgation of the national interest by peaceful means, mainly in the form of negotiation and bargaining—negotiation being, figuratively speaking, the equivalent of battle. On closer inspection, the relation turns out to be more complicated. While the outbreak of *actual* war spelled the end of diplomacy, the omnipresent *possibility* of war, the possibility of external state violence on a massive scale, was decisive throughout. Yet as concrete historical moments, war and peace remained distinct.

Analogously, then, diplomatic history eventually became the counterpoint to military history. Inverse mirror images, they are constitutionally grounded in the same sharp distinction. Thus the discursive place of war in diplomatic history is typically located around the condensing couplet origins/consequences.[2] How this operates to squeeze out war itself can be gauged by another example taken from Bailey's revealing tome: the First World War warrants no individual chapter at all, as the account moves directly from "The Road to World War" to "Negotiating the Treaty of Versailles." An event can only become an event in Bailey's work because it is something that leads to war or because it is a phase of the negotiated end of war. The difference between the historiography of the Second World War and Bailey's prototype is merely that, while the road to war is similarly present, the expected analogue of Versailles becomes the nonevent that produces the long permutation or interregnum in international relations known as the cold war. Had the Second World War been exceedingly controversial,

---

2 Here, diplomatic history is generally at one with the corresponding subfield in political science known as international relations, which is also uninterested in war itself as opposed to its origins and consequences. Otherwise there is little in common since international relations aims to determine in ahistorical ways the answer to the ahistorical question of why do states do what they do, a rather futile exercise.

then, the scholarly focus would have stayed on causes and effects rather than the war itself. For diplomacy and its history pertain preponderantly to foreign relations as they are played out in a state of peace.

This view may be challenged on several grounds, but I will restrict myself to two. The first and most obvious is that even the most conventional war usually entails simultaneous diplomacy vis-à-vis allied and neutral powers, a whole range of moves that falls squarely within the domain of diplomatic history proper. Such is the central terrain of Warren Kimball's extensive work on the Second World War, a string of peerless studies of Roosevelt and (in the main) Anglo-American diplomacy. What happened diplomatically, in that limited and strict sense, was crucial for the conduct of the war and in deciding the geopolitical future of vast parts of the globe, sometimes literally on the back of the proverbial envelope. Moreover, the absence of any comprehensive peace settlement left contentious issues stemming directly from those wartime decisions, issues in some instances still outstanding.

To ignore the historical situatedness of these wartime dealings is evidently a mistake. The diplomacy of war, as it might be called, seems thus to constitute a period in its own right and ought to be studied accordingly. What does it mean, however, to analyze such a period in its own right? The initial response is very likely a minimal, negative injunction: the moment must not be reduced to some mere prologue to the cold war, moved into the background as a staging prop for, so to speak, more important things. One must not, in other words, fall for the common inclination to consider the past as mere origin of the present, the procedure according to which the present is seen as a germ in the past and so the identification of the germinating aspect comes to constitute the explanatory scheme. A crude example of such a teleology is the tracing of something called the Western tradition from the Greeks onward and upward, where every significant moment from then on is understood and analyzed only as another stage in a continuous movement of the West toward its final fulfillment. The end, in both senses of the word, determines the beginning. What does not fit the end is consigned to the rubbish bin of failure, marginality, contingency, error: in short, that which is without historical interest and importance. A similar procedure is at work in writing the Second World War simply as the origin of the cold war. This is to wreak genuine violence on the historicity of the former: one seeks to find those elements of the war that already contain within them the essentials of the ensuing conflict, all in order to contrive a simple, sequential type of explanation.

Such a methodological trap has been subjected to a range of critiques. Nietzsche's genealogy remains perhaps the most powerful: "The cause of the origin of a thing and its eventual utility, its actual employment and place in a system of purposes, lie worlds apart; whatever exists, having somehow come into being, is again and again reinterpreted to new ends, taken over, transformed, and redirected by some power superior to it."[3] Instead of looking for precursors, then, one might articulate the conditions of possibility for the appearance of what seems self-evident, conditions that are contingent in that they are products of historically unrepeatable circumstances, yet also conjuncturally (over-)determined. This is how I have tried (I emphasize "tried") to use Franklin D. Roosevelt in my delineation of the concept of the cold war. In situating the Second World War as a worldwide need to obliterate fascist lawlessness, Roosevelt played on the language of the Civil War, the language of freedom and slavery, the language of unconditional surrender. By means of a crucial redeployment of the concept of totalitarianism, Roosevelt's matrix then becomes available (taken over, transformed and recharged) around 1946–47 for the US project known as the cold war.[4] My argument is not a causal one, as conventionally understood, since the reappropriation of Roosevelt's basic concepts is only one ingredient in a conjuncture of unrepeatable circumstances. It is at once contingent and structurally determined (because Roosevelt's language is of course in some sense distinctly American). In short, the analysis is an effort to pinpoint what allowed the cold war conceptually to appear as truth and eventually something self-evident. Roosevelt's framing is analyzed in relation to what followed but not inherently as the cold war to-be. As so many others, I happened to be more interested in the emergence of the cold war—my own formative experience of the self-evident—than in the dynamics of the Second World War. As there are no absolute origins, however, I had to ask myself how Roosevelt (and Henry Stimson) came to use that particular frame, how it became available to them at that particular moment. The Second World War then becomes not a prologue but an episode of sorts.

---

3 Friedrich Nietzsche, *The Genealogy of Morals* (New York, 1969), 77.
4 Compare chapter 1.

Whatever the genealogical credentials of this line of inquiry, it is still situated within a cold-war problematic; it is not, positively, a study of what was historically distinct about the diplomacy of war. But the remarks about Roosevelt's contextualization of the war already point to one difficulty in that regard. There is something about the very stratospheric altitude of wartime diplomacy that limits what one can do with it, at least on the US side. One can spend a lifetime trying to figure out if there is any there there in the interior of Franklin Delano Roosevelt. The extreme privacy of his wartime dealings is inversely related to the extreme maximalism of his ideological framing of the war (unconditional surrender coupled with the four freedoms and so on), a polarity that opened up the space, domestically, for the overwhelming emphasis on efficient warfare, on creating beneath the vast political generalities a fantastically powerful war machine to obliterate the enemy. The displacement of geopolitical issues in the name of present war and future freedom narrows the spectrum of retrospective analysis; neither diplomacy, nor military execution really lends itself to much geopolitical reflection.[5] Hence the proclivity to fold the political aspect into some more basic context such as, say, the American way of war or identity and difference in the US conception of the outside world.

All of which anticipates the second major objection to the main thesis: if war is understood along the given Clausewitzian lines as a political means, it ought to be the case that the framing of military strategy, its priorities, targets, and methods, will be affected by some deeper (geo)political logic or grand strategy. The moment has thus come to examine in what sense the Second World War represents, as I have claimed, a decisive shift in the place of war and peace in international relations, or, to put it differently, the degree to which the arrival of the United States onto center stage served to negate and transform the Clausewitzian matrix I used as a shorthand for the European order. For what arrived here was not just any Great Power but a superpower: a power that saw itself, quite literally, as above (and beyond).

---

5 Compare Gabriel Kolko, who once talked with such forcefulness, about a "politics of war," a broader, more comprehensive concept than diplomacy. Yet even Kolko's famous work begins in 1943, when the war had turned and the organization of liberated territories had commenced, when political arrangements on the ground no longer could be evaded.

A cursory return to the issue of war as a period will serve to open the argument. Historians are in the business of periodization. They chop temporality into parts according to one principle or another, postulating the change of something over time and assuming that the object of history is to clarify how and why there is such change—or, as the case may be, no change. Some historians are interested in breaks and discontinuities, others in characterizing the essential nature of what they identify, accordingly, as a period. Diplomatic historians genuflect toward the former because of the systemic importance of the crisis in international relations, the always existing risk of a breakdown and eventual war. The premise of periodization overall is indeed the idea of continuity and discontinuity, a binary that is ontologically suspect in that the latter, in positing an originary unity, may be parasitical on the former; whereas in the beginning there was perhaps only difference and dispersal. I will gladly dispense with any further consideration of that problem; but periodization, it must nevertheless be said, does tend to impose an unwarranted totality on any given slice of time. Not only is the naming of periods notoriously a normative exercise, the very act of naming tends to confer an essential nature on them. The Second World War, however, seems not to be a particularly difficult case in any of these respects. As names go, it is relatively neutral and descriptive. It appears, of course, under other, more situated designations in many places, designations that are part of sharp controversies about responsibility and dating. One might wonder, too, about which world it really was, whether it was perhaps not the world of the northern hemisphere, indeed whether the world of the preceding war implicitly present in the naming did not really take place in something even smaller. Finally, there is the problem if it was in fact one war or (at least) two, an Asian and a European one. Depending on the answer, one might well come up with two different starting dates. As far as the United States is concerned, however, the Second World War looks like a fairly well-defined period, replete with a clear beginning and end. The sense, too, in which this war—this period—was in fact a war is not in doubt. It was all-out war. The significant aspect lies elsewhere. It has to do with the aforementioned framing and purpose: to eradicate fascist criminality, all in the name of unconditional surrender. These were no more the terms of classical geopolitics than were they mere Rooseveltian whimsy. Even if the US entry into the Second World War was normal in that it was officially declared, the orientation expressed in Roosevelt's frame was hard to reconcile with the precepts of international relations, as traditionally conceived of and practiced. A brief digression about this discrepancy is now necessary.

The US attitude toward the European system of international relations had always been problematic: surface acceptance amid relative geopolitical seclusion, punctuated by erratic and limited participation. One reason for this variance was that the United States, far more than the Soviet Union, was (and is) a world empire. Like Rome, it is in principle the world, or the world to be.[6] There is an outside, to be sure, but it is intrinsically not an equal (equality between recognized states having been the basic principle of the European order). The outside is either evil or simply undifferentiated, amorphous mass to be acted upon in some manner or other. Hence, America is not, and never can be, one among many powers; and so it can never really embrace any truly international order either. While the idea of a league or united front of nations may be appealing, the actuality always turns out to be a disappointment as it falls short of being the United States; and so there opens up an irreducible gap between the world empire, on the one hand, as the embodiment of the universal principles of humanity (to use Wilson's formulation) and, on the other, its supposed reflection in the actual world. The World Court offers an interesting historical illustration: as American a project as one can imagine, yet invariably castigated as un-American (that is, antiworld) when it tries to expand jurisdiction over that part of the actually existing world that is the United States.

What concerns me here are not the reasons for this posture but the manner in which it situates the phenomenon of war and what happened in that context with regard to the Second World War. It stands to reason that war can scarcely be grasped as a simple instrument of statecraft and grand strategy. It cannot be legitimate for any recognized regime in the system to employ it just because that regime happens to consider it profitable. Indeed, the whole idea and machinery of statecraft itself are improper, or at least suspect, ways of being toward the world, for that world is naturally one of discussion, juridical principles, and autonomous economic exchange. Grand strategy, within this structure, is

---

6 Compare Otto Hintze's formulation in his *The Historical Essays of Otto Hintze* (New York, 1975), 468. Rome, it should be said, understood the world as that which mattered.

ineradicably a sign of the old and corrupt European state system that had produced war in the first place. War, in short, is rendered effectively illegitimate, except as a kind of *antiwar*. It can typically be launched only as one of two things: either in drastically maximalistic terms as a crusade to end all wars or, more frequently, as policing operations designed to punish perceived criminality and transgressions against an always already existing natural order of laws and norms. Crusading and policing may be understood here as integral moments of a larger legitimating story of moving history along to its end, when the natural and the normal will everywhere reign supreme. All US wars, at least after 1898, have thus entailed the idea of punishing opponents who have committed something illegitimate, if not downright illegal.

This was the background of Roosevelt's conceptualization of the Second World War as liquidation of incorrigible gangster regimes and, in the greater scheme of things, a crucial part of the eternal struggle to preserve liberty against the enslaving subjugators of humankind. The principle of law and order was connected with the more fundamental principle of global freedom as the end of history, an eschatological narrative according to which there could be no security for anyone until the very last slave master on earth had been wiped out and freedom triumphed. This was not exactly a traditional message and so the disjunctions between the US conception of the world and the older European order came to the fore (Wilson's First World War had been a dress rehearsal). It is ironic, however, that Roosevelt himself combined this quintessentially American perspective with a far more European vision of a postwar concert of regional policemen in which the United States would be one of a foursome and in that sense unexceptional, continuous with the world rather than embodying it. Roosevelt's unorthodoxy here, very much in the spirit of his predecessor Theodore, was nonetheless pitched in a minor key, premised as it was on a pious hope that realities would somehow turn out well enough to allow redescription in domestic terms. When, after 1945, this proved not to be the case, the usable parts of Roosevelt's frame were predictably the larger American ones, now recast in aggressively exceptionalist ways—leader of the free world, etc., etc.

The result was a curious amalgam in which the ambiguities were suspended, or encapsulated, within the cold war against communism, a war that was metaphorical at the crusading level but very real indeed in the realm of policing. Essential aspects of the old European order remained intact, such as the principle of sovereignty: proliferating new states in the last decade or so are eloquent testimony to its continued role as the criterion of international identity and participatory eligibility. Yet the system overall was reordered because of the US quest for supremacy. What enabled this conceptually to take place was the appropriation of Roosevelt's new, maximalistic notion of security—for security in that sense could accommodate older forms of realpolitik, narrowly conceived policies of national interest, within a larger narrative of universal right, globalism, and indispensable leadership. Anywhere and anything was now, in principle, within the field of action. War, specifically, tended to be sheriff operations. Not a single war since 1945 has been officially declared. Not a single one of them, that is, has been a proper war according to traditional conventions. Korea was explicitly defined as a police move. Vietnam was counterinsurgency against subversion, military aid as it were, before it was turned militarily into another Korea. The Gulf War was punishment of a "rogue state" (one, let it be said, that had committed illegitimate acts of war even by the older European standards). These have been acts of pacification and punishment, maintaining law and order within a larger context of defending "the free world" against slavery. Such undeclared, limited wars to punish transgressors bear a superficial similarity to older European wars of suppressing colonial disorders, but policing in the historical service of (US) freedom is something quite different. The normative excess, so to speak, makes the operations vulnerable to savage criticism unless they happen to be short, surgical, and utterly successful. For what is at stake is not the security of the limited theater in question but (one can always argue at home) the future of the universe. If, as in Vietnam, the limited war drags out and shades of gray begin to appear, the whole grand narrative might indeed come into dispute. More to the point, such exercises cannot be grasped as the opposite of diplomacy. On the contrary, as the qualitative distinction between war and peace is erased or at least blurred, policing goes beyond simple repression to become a means of political pressure, even a form of diplomacy perhaps.[7]

---

7 Consider the attack on rump Yugoslavia: a computer war conceived of as a combination of policing and diplomacy. Another development, incidentally, that has served to dissolve the older Clausewitzian constellation is the enormous expansion of the visual and cultural domain, which has blurred the boundaries of what constitutes

Neither war, nor peace, was thus what it used to be. Diplomatic history, meanwhile, found amid the infinities of cold-war policy that its object of inquiry was losing fixity and clarity. A seemingly endless crisis ensued. The extent of it was obscured by the very political ferocity generated by the revisionist challenge. A diplomatic retrospective of the Second World War, in any case, was now hard to write for it required temporary suspension of cold-war urgencies and the recovery of a kind of war that no longer existed. The case here, not surprisingly, will then turn out to be a plea not so much for a return to what was but for a wider reflection on how, for example, the transformations of war and peace have pertained to international relations in general and the United States in particular. Such a history may include comparative investigations of the place of war in state formation. Apart from the work of such iconoclastic world historians as William McNeill, the most interesting analyses along these lines have appeared within historical sociology. This scholarly current, emanating chiefly from Max Weber and, beyond him, nineteenth-century German historiography on the state, always foregrounds war (and the preparation for war) in the emergence of state and society. Historical sociologists such as Charles Tilly and Michael Mann connect this formative aspect to changes in mode of production, classes, technology, and norms, as military power and its uses occur within any given social formation.[8] The current vogue, in another register, for culture may well be supplemented by investigations into the history of law and its peculiar status. As the judicial aftermath of the Second World War showed at Nuremberg, there is a fascinating and entangled history of the US relationship to international law and the whole idea of legal procedure, not least when it comes to war. Meanwhile, none of this is of course to argue that one should not engage in the most exquisitely traditional investigations of those rarefied diplomatic moments when the future of huge tracts of land and matters of life and death are decided by very few people in the highest of places.

---

power, influence, and policy in times of peace, indeed, the whole domain of politics as such. Sanctions, meanwhile, form another sphere of action that transcend the traditional distinction.

8 Hendrik Spruyt, *The Sovereign State and Its Competitors* (Princeton, NJ, 1994), is, however, a useful corrective to excessive emphasis on war in the emergence of the modern state system.

III

US Foreign Relations

8
An American Story? Second Thoughts on Manifest Destiny

In one of the many metaphors that marked his analyses, George F. Kennan once likened the United States to a huge "prehistoric monster" with "a brain the size of a pin."[1] He wanted to convey that the United States, when provoked in the world, tends to react slowly but then to wield its enormous power without much reflection or nuance. His point, as so often, was both right and wrong.

He was wrong, certainly, about provocation and speed. Long before the early 1950s, when the disgruntled Kennan made the statement, the United States had been very quick indeed to take umbrage at injuries real and imagined, and to act expeditiously and powerfully to redress them. Amerindians and Mexicans of the nineteenth century could readily testify to that. Kennan was right, however, that the governing concepts have not only been simple but simplistic. As a realist he believed that such lack of clarity was a recipe for disaster. He never recognized that the United States, precisely because of its massive power, did not have to be right to be successful. The intellectual grounds on which any given opponent is flattened matter less than the fact of the flattening.[2] Official and public opinion has been wrong factually and conceptually about

---

1 George F. Kennan, *American Diplomacy*, 59.
2 Eric Hobsbawm refers pithily to this feature of the US posture as "the power of knocking things down," recently more in evidence than the otherwise much vaunted soft power (Hobsbawm in conversation with the author, June 6, 2008, London).

lots of events, but being wrong has not prevented results of the most favorable kind. One might well think, for instance, that the spirit of Manifest Destiny in which the United States went to war against Mexico in the 1840s was mistaken, along with the specific allegations of Mexican wrongdoing. If so, it was an error that added vast territories by chopping off the northern half of that unfortunate neighbor to the southwest.[3] One has every reason, then, to take US errors seriously.

My own interest in such errors happens to stem from one instance (probably *the* instance) when an error actually generated a monumental defeat, namely, Vietnam. Getting things wrong in almost every way really did have disastrous effects. All manner of lessons were and are said to have been learned from this. Certainly, the US Army officer corps is still indelibly marked, negatively, by the experience, which is one reason there was but feeble enthusiasm in 2003 for the Iraqi operation.[4] One aspect of Vietnam and Iraq alike is the manner in which they were produced as places and events, how they were conceived of in such a way as to warrant the kind of actions they did. In turn, this has to do with the deeper problem of what might be called the sources of US conduct and, in particular, its ideological aspects.

Ideologically, the US way of being toward the world has been at once massively traditional and strikingly arbitrary. On the one hand there is the inclination to invoke master narratives about the nation's place in world history; on the other there is the tendency to abrupt changes and arbitrary action in actual policy. The constancy here, then, has to do with the necessity of placing public action within an account of what the United States has always been about, or is imagined to have been about, in universal history. The United States has been grasped throughout as a world-historical project, the fundamentals of which have not changed

---

3 See my *Manifest Destiny: American Expansionism and the Empire of Right* (New York, 1995). The present essay, while drawing extensively on this short book, is otherwise an attempt to rethink it, above all on two matters: space and messianism. The classical work (and still the best) is otherwise Albert K. Weinberg, *Manifest Destiny: A Study of Nationalist Expansionism in American History* (Gloucester, MA, 1958 [1935]).

4 A peculiar lesson of the debacle in Vietnam, however, was that the critical evaluation of counterinsurgency ceased within the US military, overtaken by a will to forget. I have benefited much here from conversations with Lieutenant Colonel Conrad Crane (retired). Meanwhile, it would be easy, all too easy, to retort that while the United States lost, it really won in the end, what with Vietnam turning into an efficient low-cost factory run by the Communist Party for the benefit of the capitalist metropolis.

since 1776 (or 1789). The United States, one might say, is the original end of history: nothing, qualitatively, can improve on the original idea. This is why all political attempts to reshape the place, inside or outside, perennially appeal to origins and tradition, to the truth of the beginning.[5] Tradition is then combined, intermittently, with extraordinary leeway and arbitrariness in concrete policy. Witness, in the given period, Thomas Jefferson's Louisiana Purchase and Polk's war against Mexico, two (largely) individual actions that resulted in staggering expansion.

Their material condition of possibility has to do, most immediately, with the constitutional division of power and the quasi-monarchical role of the executive, not least his (still his) power as commander-in-chief. Conceived of as deliberately dysfunctional, the federal system in effect opened up, unexpectedly, for the imperial presidency, as the mini-state model on the North American continent came to be embroiled spasmodically but increasingly, and after 1941 irrevocably, with the geopolitical outside. The constitutional aspect both produces and reproduces the fractured domestic and continentalist structure of the ruling class. The system, in the end, makes it difficult to do decisive things at home while permitting, at times, decisive things abroad. The White House, historically, has been at considerable liberty not only to choose which particular external policy to pursue but also the particularly American manner in which to situate it.[6]

We are familiar with this phenomenon in more recent times. George W. Bush chose to respond to the September 11 event with wars against

---

5   A good example, now hard to remember, was Newt Gingrich's so-called "Contract with America" (1994), according to which America had lost its way after years of Democratic waywardness and now had to return to its original truth. Much of Ronald Reagan's rhetoric of return was similarly situated.

6   Executive power everywhere tends to have a certain license, a certain geopolitical privacy, but the decentered structure of the US government lends itself especially to it. See Michael Mann, *States, War, Capitalism* (Oxford, 1988), chaps. 5–6. My nineteenth-century examples of Jefferson and Polk notwithstanding, clearly there is a qualitative change here after December 7, 1941: The Second World War marks the beginning of the permanent National Security State and a massive expansion of executive power in foreign affairs. The distance between Woodrow Wilson's travails in 1919 and the ease with which Harry S. Truman pushed through his Doctrine in 1947 is testimony enough. In the present, a cursory glance over the global map of the US military power is enough to see the point. One of the few to pay proper attention to the political implications is Andrew Bacevich. See for example his *American Empire: The Realities and Consequences of U.S. Diplomacy* (Cambridge, 2002).

Afghanistan and Iraq, suspension of international convention in the name of an alleged threat to freedom everywhere, promulgation of the salvational role of the United States, and so forth. The frame here was a general "war on terror." Concrete policy was thus grounded in an appeal that was outstandingly American. Bush, however, might have chosen another, equally American frame, that of law and legitimate order, where the terrorist deeds would have been defined exclusively as crimes and the perpetrators not as warriors but criminals. Such a legalistic approach would also have featured a properly world-historical role for the United States but the ensuing policy scenarios would have looked quite different. Executive license, it should be underlined, is not a product of modern (or postmodern) spin machines and mass media: consider, again, Polk's inventions in engineering the war against Mexico in 1846.

This license then operates within, and is overdetermined by, the fundamentals of America. Moments arise when these signifiers become controversial, or, more precisely, concrete application renders their actual meaning questionable. Is bombing Vietnam compatible with the universal value of freedom? Is colonial annexation of the Philippines compatible with the postcolonial identity of the United States? Is the opening of acquired territory to slavery compatible with the notion of a free society? Controversial policy not only connects directly to ultimate principle as mere appeal but also serves to problematize the principle itself. This is what happens in the 1970s with détente. It begins as an American policy of negotiation, stability and, above all, avoidance of nuclear confrontation, then turning into the closest the United States has ever come to geopolitical realism, only to disintegrate, denounced left and right as essentially amoral and so un-American, by the liberal left for its murderous effects in the third world, by the right for appeasement of the Evil Empire. Détente, as practiced by Henry Kissinger, illustrates the difficulties of conducting foreign policy in an idiom that is unequivocally realist: realism, a discourse on timeless identity and sameness in international politics and is in that sense un-American. Never properly legitimate, realism works only half disguised and momentarily, as long as it is an unequivocal success or at least not an unequivocal debacle.[7]

---

7 On realism in the United States, see Nicolas Guilhot, ed., *The Invention of International Relations Theory: Realism, the Rockefeller Foundation, and the 1954 Conference on Theory* (New York, 2011).

My remarks here will pursue the constitutive frame commonly referred to as Manifest Destiny, articulated explicitly in the nineteenth century but recast and reused on several occasions in the twentieth, expression as it is of that powerful mixture of Protestantism and liberalism from which there is no escape when one tries to think America. At first sight, Manifest Destiny appears a very crude piece of ideology. Originally, it was deployed to sanction territorial expansion across the continent by appeal to the putatively self-evident edicts of higher authority, namely, God, Providence and History. Lofty references corresponded to the astoundingly successful process itself, as the already sizable federation grew into a transcontinental one. What can be more obvious: a self-serving ideology for massive, material gain.

This is true enough, in a way. The simplicities, alas, turn out to be rather knottier than that and certainly more interesting. One must be quite precise, in fact, about the manner in which the United States imagined itself doing God's (and thereby History's) work, first on the North American continent and then many thousands of miles across the Pacific Ocean. For one thing, all Western powers in the nineteenth century would have insisted, if asked, that they were doing God's work in expanding their possessions, colonial or not. It would have been impossible to say otherwise, Western civilization essentially being understood as Christian. Initially, the distinctive feature of Manifest Destiny, as it turns out, is not the providential appeal itself but the absolute differentiation of that godly work from the rest of the West and the concomitant utopian dimension, especially as it pertains to democracy and space. That differentiation, to complicate matters, is then partly elided in the second moment around the turn of the century, the moment of classical imperialism overseas when the ideology becomes civilizational. Even in that moment, however, the United States remains essentially a utopian project of world-historical significance.

Arguments along these lines would seem to land me in the diffuse debate about American exceptionalism. However, I do not want to go through all the preliminaries and caveats necessary to say anything substantial in that context. Manifest Destiny is certainly an ideology that centers around propositions about the United States as a unique and anointed agent in the world, but its specifics, which are very specific indeed, tend to disappear if the analysis is immersed in the wide array of concerns and issues that typically fall under the rubric of American exceptionalism.[8] My intention, instead, is to offer some considerations on the two central episodes when Manifest Destiny gained currency as a political term, moments that are both about territorial expansion and so about a certain inscription of space as it relates to distinctions between inside and outside. I will also say something necessarily sketchy and episodic about what happens to the concept in the twentieth century and into the present.

Manifest Destiny became a political catchword in the 1840s courtesy of John O'Sullivan, a foreign-born New Yorker of murky Irish-English background, a young Jacksonian who had turned into a prominent organic intellectual of the movement by publishing the influential *Democratic Review*.[9] By the standards of the time, then, O'Sullivan was a Progressive. He certainly perceived himself as a pioneer of the new, open and democratic future, if not as a radical. This is why he liked expansion. To get the rhetorical flavor, by no means extreme for the period, an extended quotation from an early programmatic statement (1839) may be in order:

> We are the nation of human progress, and who will, what can, set limits to our onward march? Providence is with us . . . The far-reaching, the boundless future will be the era of American greatness. In its magnificent domain of space and time, the nation of many nations is destined to manifest to mankind the excellence of divine principles; to establish on earth the noblest temple ever dedicated to the worship of the Most High—the Sacred and the True. Its floor shall be a

---

[8] The topic of exceptionalism has invited a vast literature, much of it misplaced in my view. I am sympathetic to Ian Tyrrell's well-known intervention: "American Exceptionalism in an Age of International History," *American Historical Review* 96, no. 4 (October 1991), 1031–55.

[9] O'Sullivan was from a lineage of Irish-English mercenaries and adventurers. His mother ended up in the United States, where O'Sullivan eventually graduated from Columbia College. His subsequent life (he died in 1895 on the eve of the resurgence of Manifest Destiny) was as every bit as checkered as that of his forebears: after selling the Review in 1846, for instance, he became heavily involved in sundry conspiracies to acquire Cuba. See Julius W. Pratt, "John L. O'Sullivan and Manifest Destiny," *New York History* 14, no. 3 (July 1933), 213–34; Sheldon Harris, "The Public Career of John Louis O'Sullivan" (PhD diss., Columbia University, 1958); and most recently, Robert D. Sampson, *John L. O'Sullivan and His Times* (Kent, OH, 2003).

hemisphere—its roof the firmament of the star-studded heavens, and its congregation of an Union of many Republics, comprising hundreds of happy millions, calling, owning no man master, but governed by God's natural and moral law of equality, the law of brotherhood ... For this blessed mission to the nations of the world, which are shut out from the life-giving light of truth, has America been chosen; and her high example shall smite unto death the tyranny of kings, hierarchs, and oligarchs, and carry the glad tidings of peace and good will where myriads now endure an existence scarcely more enviable than that of beasts of the field.[10]

O'Sullivan's argument, then, is simple. Democracy, the end of history, had come to its culmination in "the nation of nations," the space for which Providence had evidently set aside in the Western hemisphere to manifest to the world the meaning of divine truth. Democracy and Christianity, two aspects of the same thing, had thus come to its resting place in "the great nation of futurity," the glorious example to the world known as the United States. Expansion, it followed, was intrinsically a good thing. Believing divine democracy inherently peaceful, however, O'Sullivan never thought war in the traditional sense was the way to do it. Militarism was monarchical, European and old order. Yet it was actually in the heady conjuncture of impending war against Mexico, conflict with Britain over the Oregon Territory and the inclusion of the gigantic republic of Texas into the Union that he actually introduced the expression "Manifest Destiny," the idea that the United States was predestined "to overspread the continent allotted by Providence for the free development of our yearly multiplying millions."[11]

As homogeneity of democratic institutions was basic to providentially decreed experiment, O'Sullivan came to have qualms about the Mexican venture and just how much of the continent one could include for the unblemished order of the same to stay the same. On similar

---

10 The quotation is from his seminal editorial in the *Democratic Review* (official [unused] name: *The United States Magazine and Democratic Review*) July–August 1839, 427, 430.

11 The last quotation is from O'Sullivan's editorial "Annexation" in the *Democratic Review*, July/August 1845, 5, which referred not to Mexico but the annexation of Texas and the dispute with Britain over the Oregon Territory. He used a similar formulation in the *New York Morning News*, December 27, 1845.

grounds and for the sake of his party, he was explicitly against all discussion of that great problem of difference within the Union, namely, slavery. Perhaps he had a dialectical inkling somewhere that providentially predestined expansion might well spell the end of the glorious example as he knew it, as new territories would exacerbate difference over slavery to the point of breaking the delicate internal balance apart.[12]

Though that conflagration was already being envisaged by some pessimists, it was still some distance away. For now, despite biting critiques (chiefly in New England), the whole complex of ideas articulated in the concept of Manifest Destiny held the day. Its very prevalence, in a way, was the novelty. For on many an occasion before, arguments had been voiced to the effect that God had some preordained layout clearly in mind for the United States that involved vast expansion. So, for instance, policymakers would muse intermittently that Cuba, given its position on the map, surely belonged naturally to the Union. The massive expansionist moves of the 1840s, however, entailed a much more centered politics of destiny. Destinarianism (to coin a phrase) became the very idiom of the whole project of expansion.[13]

What is its deep structure? Is there one? If Manifest Destiny is reduced to the few elementary propositions O'Sullivan typically voiced, it appears to be nothing more and nothing less than what it states. To reiterate: God, and so History and Nature, has evidently singled out the United States as the exemplary sanctuary for the final stage of history and thus opened up the continent for the expansive playing out of that mission of freedom. Expansion, ipso facto, is inherently good, opposition to it, inherently wrong. End of argument. All that remains then for us retrospectively is empirically to account for how this was carried out and

---

[12] The aforementioned "Annexation" editorial expressed very plainly the rationale for its structural silence on slavery: "National in its character and aims, this Review abstains from the discussion of a topic pregnant with embarrassment and danger" (*Democratic Review*, July/August 1845, 8).

[13] One prominent predecessor will suffice as illustration. In a letter to his father in 1811, John Quincy Adams wrote: "The whole continent of North America appears to be destined by Divine Providence to be peopled by one *nation*, speaking one language, professing one general system of religious and political principles, and accustomed to one general tenor of social usages and customs." Adams also thought Cuba and Puerto Rico natural parts of the future continentalist power. His abolitionist reorientation in the 1830s changed this attitude completely. *The Writings of John Quincy Adams* vol. IV: 1811–1813 (New York, 1914), 209.

explore how the thematic came to return in a different register during the expansionism of the late 1890s. Yet O'Sullivan's position, which condensed in particularly clear form the whole destinarian thrust, deserves further elucidation. Again, it is an error to be simple about the seemingly simple. At the outset, accordingly, I need to say something fairly abstract about its conceptual history.

Ultimately, of course, Manifest Destiny is a concept of religious derivation. More precisely, it is Christian, Protestant and Calvinist, though this can easily be overemphasized.[14] From its colonial beginnings, the United States had certainly entailed a broad streak of destinarianism, a strong notion, in short, of being involved in something decisive in the historical trajectory of true Christianity. This is what gives the posture its typical radicality, its tendency to either/or, the desire for the absolute and the conviction that, essentially, one really embodies it. The underlying perspective can readily be summarized. History has a rational direction toward a given purpose, planned and guided as it is by Providence. In this unfolding, comprehensible drama, all agents are called upon to perform certain set roles and missions, callings they can choose to live up to or not, as the case may be. Choice is thus central to the proceedings, the act of constantly choosing, not between a potentially open series of options but between doing what one has been appointed to do and turning away from it. This way of being toward the world is at once individual and collective: the mission, responsibility and choice are necessarily features of one's community in so far as it is conceived of as such. Strict, one might say puritan, versions generate strong boundaries and an aversion to contaminating contact with the outside. The pure is conceived of as exemplary and difference is absolute. Hence, too, the policy orientation becomes explicitly isolationist.[15]

Yet the very same axioms can result in quite the opposite stance: when the Calvinist trope is fused, as it easily was, with a vibrantly

---

14 O'Sullivan, for instance, was an Episcopalian but his family background was in good part Catholic. Nonetheless, the basic structure was always Protestant, radically Protestant.

15 See my *Manifest Destiny* for more on this highly condensed account. Among the numerous primary and secondary sources I have used, the one I would single out is Sacvan Bercovitch, *The Rites of Assent: Transformations in the Symbolic Construction of America* (New York, 1993).

secular and republican ideology, conceived around a spatiotemporal opposition between the New and the Old World, there opens up the possibility of a kind of interventionism drastically to redo the outside, to purify and clear it so to speak. In the nineteenth century, this solution to what the United States ought to be about in the world remains largely an obscurity; but it would begin to come to the fore in the imperialist moment at the turn of the century and, later, differently, in the figure of Woodrow Wilson and by extension what we know as Wilsonianism. Originally products of the same conceptual frame, the two opposing postures have since remained central reference points for all domestic controversies about the general US role abroad.

Notions of a world-historical Christian mission should not be conflated, as frequently happens, with messianism. On the face of it, the transformative function of redeeming the world clearly implies some affinity with the idea of the messianic. Surprisingly, however, Manifest Destiny in its nineteenth-century version is only thinly connected to it. Christianity, unlike Judaism, is obviously founded on the messianic notion, the coming of the savior being the central event of history after creation itself, the next event being his return. The space of the messiah in Christianity (again, unlike Judaism) is thus preempted, which is why imitators and substitutes should beware. That said, there is room for intrahistorical simulacra. The original Puritan-Calvinist undertaking had been modeled on the idea of the sacred remnant, a proto-Judaic project where God's purposes have come to reside in the particular doings and choices of a rigidly bounded community of the Elect whose role is thus decisive to the movement of history. Still, this is not to be confused with the messianic as such. The formative sense of election and mission is then expanded and tremendously reinforced, albeit in modified form, with the advent of the secular, liberal United States and the Empire of Liberty: here is not only a sanctuary for freedom but a model vehicle for its inevitable victory in historical time and space.[16]

Once history is thus conceived of as providentially designed Progress to be played out in exemplary form in the United States, the notion of

---

16 See Gershom Scholem, *The Messianic Idea in Judaism and Other Essays on Jewish Spirituality* (New York, 1971); Peter Duncan, *Russian Messianism: Third Rome, Holy Revolution, Communism and After* (New York, 2000); and Thomas L. Thompson, *The Messiah Myth: The Near Eastern Roots of Jesus and David* (New York, 2005); and chap. 12 in the present volume.

ultimate crisis also vanishes or is at least put in brackets. Intramundane redemption is then reduced to quantitative expansion of the universal principle of the United States, more of the same, in short. This is perhaps messianic in some attenuated form: redemption is taking place all the time under the auspices of the ever-progressing, outwardly mobile United States, anointed to demonstrate for humankind where history is heading and so redeeming it or at least providing the preconditions for that happy event. Playing out the purposes of providential democracy on the North American continent, then, is a necessary step for the liberation of humankind; without it, liberation could not take place. Concretely, however, this is about the extension of already existing freedom in the United States, not about some erupting intervention into the historical world to remake and save it so as to establish eternal peace. The destinarian will become clearly messianic, to be sure, at certain critical points in the future: Woodrow Wilson's attempt to recast international relations in 1917–19 and the early cold-war posture are two clearcut examples. The expansive mission in the 1840s in the name of Manifest Destiny is not essentially messianic.[17]

Hence, relatedly, Manifest Destiny is not apocalyptic either. It is obviously not apocalyptic in the conventional (and erroneous) sense of some massive cataclysmic crisis. Manifest Destiny represents no such upheaval. On the contrary, it represents democracy and property, as rationally consecrated in the principle and predictability of Law, inherently peaceful, indeed the very meaning of peace. People in freedom are restlessly moving ahead in rational pursuit of whatever happens to strike their fancy; and they do so in transparent conditions of peace and legal order. If, by contrast, the apocalyptic is taken more accurately as revelation, Manifest Destiny seems directly related. Yet, peculiarly, it both posits revelation and declares the end of it.[18] Truth, Christian and secular, has been revealed in history, more precisely in the United States. Rigid providentialism now proclaims that the ancient mystery with no

---

17   Nor is to be conflated with the related Puritan mission of the sacred remnant, the quasi-Mosaic trek across space to preserve truth in a new and promised land. The land is certainly promised and the providential mission is about eternal truth, but the democratic project is not about a chosen people in the Mosaic sense. What defines the chosen agent in this case is in a way that it is not a people.

18   On this thematic, see Malcolm Bull, *Seeing Things Hidden: Apocalypse, Vision and Totality* (London, 1999).

visible or at least certifiable solution has been replaced by self-evident clarity of purpose and agency.

Apocalyptic strands survive instead powerfully among some of the most ferociously anti-expansionist forces, the abolitionists, for whom the republic bears within it the unmistakable and sickening signs of destruction in the monumental sin of slavery, the very antithesis of freedom. These are the people for whom aggressive expansion seems a conspiracy of the slavocracy and its allies, indicating death and destruction and what not, the kind of catastrophic denouement that did in fact ensue. Manifest Destiny, in polar contrast, entails no room for such interpretative and contestational moves: its predictive certainty is absolute. The westward-moving limit in space is the line where history comes to a stop, not apocalyptically but rationally and peacefully.[19]

In a more concrete vein, I now want to connect this to the geopolitics of O'Sullivan's actual world. His operative frame here, evolved since the early Republic, is constituted by a polarity between the United States and Europe. Whereas Europe is marked by the "exterminating havoc" of the balance of power, by war and retrograde monarchy, the United States signifies peace, rationality and freedom. This polarity, one should note, is resolutely undialectical: the United States or the sphere of freedom, being the natural state of humankind, has no need of Europe, either conceptually or functionally.[20] The federation stands alone, founded on a logic purely its own. No interaction with the outside is presupposed. Yet, normatively and actually, the United States favors interaction of another kind, not with Europe specifically but, all things being equal, with everyone everywhere. A proper international system, exemplified by the United States and to a lesser extent by the Western hemisphere of which the federated republic is both the emblem and the guardian, is one of trade and peace. The axiom, laid

---

19 Richard J. Cawardine, *Evangelicals and Politics in Antebellum America* (New Haven, CT: Yale 1993), 146–57; Reginald Horsman, *Race and Manifest Destiny: The Origins of Racial Anglo-Saxonism* (Cambridge, MA, 1981), 257–71 (which deals with the more incisive moderate critique as well).

20 A similar aspect appears in the cold war: the Free World is thus the natural one which can stand on its own, the totalitarian one essentially parasitic and dependent. The difference is that O'Sullivan's democracy/freedom exists as an isolated space, whereas the cold-war vision assumes the lethal threat of the evil parasite.

out by Washington and Jefferson, is quite clear: as much trade as possible, as little politics as possible, which is another way of saying that international relations should be about economics, maximum openness for individual exchange, as regulated in the last instance by law. The United States provides a perfect republican model of how to do this, a federated model of freedom for the world: local self-determination but overall economic permeability and individual initiative across borders.[21]

The implementation of that model in the conquered "virgin" lands of North America that seemed to O'Sullivan so manifestly preordained was really a product of a great deal of chance and unrepeatable historical circumstances. Ironically, the material foundation was indeed industrialization in Western Europe, which provided immigrants and was the ultimate basis for the valorization of conquered land. The US economy, oddly enough, was more globalized in the agrarian nineteenth century than in much of the industrialized twentieth. Yet the destiny of the United States is experienced as radically different and removed from Europe, chiefly because of the overwhelming reality of continental expansion in relative geopolitical autonomy. That autonomy, to compound the irony, turns out also to depend ultimately on European factors: the British found it in their interest after 1815 to acquiesce and to use their naval supremacy accordingly.[22]

The Monroe Doctrine of 1823, or what gradually becomes known under that name, is symptomatic. The United States declares itself the self-evident guardian of the entire Western hemisphere, which is defined as a space of progressive republican principle in contrast to retrograde monarchy in old Europe. History on the western side of the Atlantic has moved irreversibly to a new and, by implication, final stage and the relation between the new and the old is one of political separation, a separation curiously enunciated in the name of an antipolitics of sorts. What is wrong with Europe is in fact that it is (geo)political. At no point is it recognized that the whole idea is actually unenforceable and is only

---

21   David C. Hendrickson, *Peace Pact: The Lost World of the American Founding* (Lawrence, KS, 2006) explores the origins of the United States as a model for international relations.

22   Generally, see D. W. Meinig's marvelous *The Shaping of America: A Geographical Perspective on 500 Years of History. Volume 2: Continental America, 1800–1867* (New Haven, 1993).

allowed to flourish imaginatively because the British choose not to demonstrate its unreality.

The unreality of the Monroe Doctrine is however part of a destinarian ideology whose effects in the continental theater itself are very real indeed. The rationality and efficacy of the process are devastating. Its organizational device, politically, is a fundamental reason destiny can be imagined in the way it was. I call this unique model cellular replication. Originally set forth in the Northwest Ordinance of 1787, it became in every way constitutional, though it predated the actual Constitution two years hence. A machinery was established here whereby new member republics could create themselves in extant US territories, citizens-to-be thus contracting with one another as constitutive power and after a probationary period entering the Union on a footing completely equal to that of existing member states. It was in part this novel system that Thomas Jefferson, a central figure in its genesis, had in mind when he was referring to the "Empire of Liberty" and the "Empire for Liberty."[23]

Once the distinction from Europe has been made, the space of the United States as America becomes curiously indeterminate. It was not evident where the mobile United States of America actually were and or at any rate where they would finally be (only the Civil War made the Union singular). No defined territory or land attached to the union as a national mission. No one imagined that the United States would eventually be coterminous with the world, very few believed the entire Western hemisphere would be a single union; and, before the railroads, many had logistical doubts about the possibility of a genuinely transcontinental republic. Still, if other unions came into being further afield, they would not constitute any essential difference: they too would be more of the same, an American union of true America. Meanwhile (and it was a very important meanwhile), the United States as actually existing freedom would go about its business of expanding as best it could.

By imperial standards a very odd bird, it was really an enormously effective, decentralized way of recreating identity in space: the original,

---

23 On Jefferson and the state system generally, see Robert W. Tucker and David C. Hendrickson, *Empire of Liberty: The Statecraft of Thomas Jefferson* (New York, 1990); Peter S. Onuf, *Statehood and Union: A History of the Northwest Ordinance* (Bloomington, IN, 1987); John Lauritz Larson, "Jefferson's Union and the Problem of Internal Improvements," in Peter Onuf, *Jeffersonian Legacies* (Charlottesville, VA, 1993).

consensual union of republics reproducing and growing by means of more of exactly the same, reiteration where historical time is frozen. In the democratic 1830s and '40s, cellular replication across the West, vigorous and open-ended, was still for most an unmitigated good. The expansion of the Empire of and for Liberty, the timeless, universal principles of Man, was by definition a good thing. How could it be otherwise? One might quarrel over the proper way of dealing with the Amerindians or the British, and about how far the existing Union could feasibly be extended. One could quarrel, in short, over means. But about the notion that expansion of the United States, as embodied in the unique principle of federative replication, was world-historically legitimate and fervently to be desired, about that idea there could as yet be no disagreement.[24]

It is useful to compare this replicating union of sameness with the concurrent notions of European nationhood (and quite similar ideas in Latin America). The United States is not a homeland: it has no myth of a single people inhabiting since times immemorial a single land and speaking a single language, supposedly reproducing vertically generation after generation, with all the attached genealogies, traditions and histories that go with that process. Moreover, there is none of the liberal vision of European nationalism one finds in, say, Guiseppe Mazzini, the idea of the world as a mosaic of equally worthy nation-states in peace, all reveling in their differences as peoples and cultures, indeed not only tolerating but celebrating each other's differences and peculiarities— one recognizes the argument in more recent odes to multiculturalism. In polar opposition, a clean and homogeneous space of absolute freedom, grasped as the indispensable vehicle for the world-historical future of that principle, can have no equals. For, absent any identical, adjacent federations, the United States as a concept does not permit any notion of equality with the outside. What is beyond can only be understood as a not-yet, mired in various degrees of retrograde unfreedom. That domain can and certainly will be liberated at some point, if not by actual inclusion into the United States, then perhaps by following its radiant example at some distant time, or, as mentioned, because the empire of liberty itself finds a way to undo the shackles. Nevertheless, at all given times, there remains between the United States and the outside a constitutive

---

24   See chap. 9 for a more extensive treatment of the idea of cellular reproduction.

gap of absolute difference, a difference of inequality in the name of equality, a difference ultimately between the free and the unfree. The United States is the world or the truth of the world, but the world is not the United States.[25]

The United States, then, comes to stand (incipiently in 1776 and certainly after 1800) metonymically for the whole of the New, the Republican, the Free, and the Western in the world, a place to be imitated and in fact the essence of the future. This is what O'Sullivan is referring to when he is imagining his nation as the essence of the world, though by his time, the condensing concept has become democracy. The future, then, has already arrived in the nation of futurity, the nation of nations. For the United States, equipped as it is "with the truths of God," the "arena" is exclusively about "the expansive future," an "untrodden space" to be entered "with a clear conscience unsullied by the past." Thus the European past has no meaning for O'Sullivan except as "lessons of avoidance," as a realm of error.[26]

When historical time has ceased to develop qualitatively on the inside and only pertains, as a series of stages, to the outside, it follows, critically, that outside opposition is irrational, if not downright criminal, while political quarrels on the inside can only take the form of an appeal to the principles and promise of the timeless, universal truth of the Origin. Authorized violence on the frontier, to name but one effect, is thus always conceived of not as war but as pacification, the repression of violators of the peace and the clearing of the way for the final transformation to order, independence and freedom for those who are eligible to participate. Others can legitimately be punished with large-scale violence. And so, to devastating effect, indeed they were.

The border, the line moving constantly outward, is accordingly invested with decisive importance. In the most immediate, concrete sense, it

---

25 Ibid.
26 The quotations are from O'Sullivan's "The Nation of Futurity," *The Democratic Review*, 426–27. For a stimulating account of the Protestant precedents, see James Simpson, *Burning to Read: English Fundamentalism and its Reformation Opponents* (Cambridge, 2007) chap. 6. The notion of creation ex nihilo in a pristine space was modified and indeed contradicted, depending on the day-to-day relation with Britain, by the element of Anglo-Saxonism, namely the United States as the preservation and fulfillment of ancient Anglo-Saxon (that is Teutonic, pre-Norman) liberty.

becomes, famously, the frontier, a zone of transformation where freedom is created from scratch, as it were, out in the open.[27] Land beyond, always by definition untouched, properly virginal, is turned into land proper when it has been cleared and subsequently surveyed. Wildness is eliminated. The settlement of what will become the United States is colonial in the true sense of the word. Land, then, is either not yet occupied or insufficiently occupied by people whose capacity to contract with one another and thus to be free and independent is next to nil. It is one of the signal features of the Empire of Liberty, accordingly, that it is keen on land but not on people, especially if the people in question happen to be different and already on that land. Amerindians, not being the Same and being irrationally in possession of the land, were thus an obstacle to be overcome by whatever means necessary. Contrary to a great deal of obvious evidence, the conventional justification assumed that Amerindians, being "naturally savage," were incapable of being American in the sense of fulfilling the criteria for what passed for a rational person.

Crass self-gain aside, the foundational argument here was forthright and ingenious: property, not vague possession, was the essential characteristic of true selfhood; property meant independence and the capacity to make the land productive; Amerindians had no property and were apparently incapable of production; hence they were not real selves; hence they had no intrinsic right to the land. To relieve them of their land, one should nevertheless (contradictorily, but as a sign of superior civilization) enter into the kind of purchasing contracts they were presumably unqualified to conclude. Amerindians, until well into the nineteenth century, were thus defined as sovereign nations capable of concluding (unequal) treaties at the same time as they were constitutionally unfit for sovereignty. Whatever the means, in short, law and exchange are the master signifiers of the process, the politically correct way of dispossessing peoples.[28]

Such theorizing is of course not particular to colonial North America and the United States, but it reached its purest and most lethal

---

27 On the spatial issues of expansion, see Meinig, *The Shaping*. See also Thomas R. Hietala, *Manifest Design: Anxious Aggrandizement in Late Jacksonian America* (Ithaca, NY, 1985).

28 The legal and political issues are analyzed with great rigor in Lisa M. Ford, "Settler Sovereignty: Jurisdiction and Indigenous People in Georgia and New South Wales, 1788–1836" (PhD diss., Columbia University, 2007).

expression here and it became an integral part of the larger destinarian schemes of the 1840s. By then, however, the Amerindians had ceased to be a major obstacle and, by their dispossession and expulsion, turned into evidence of the very freedom, independence, property and democracy that had presumably replaced them, all, again, plainly according to the irrefutable historical edict of Providence. Their destiny, so to speak, had already been established: graphically removed, legally subordinated, militarily reduced to a disturbance on the frontier.

If various earlier forms of destinarianism, not least as doctrines of natural right, had thus informed the uneven development of pacification, one must emphasize that when O'Sullivan and the Jacksonians begin to talk about Manifest Destiny, Amerindians are not the polemical concern. Geopolitically, O'Sullivan is concerned to contrast American space not with any indigenous world but with the distant European one of hierarchy and oppression. This opposition, again, is not a dialectical struggle in contradictory unity but nothing more and nothing less than a contrast, displaying an absolutely separate universe where the true purposes of humankind are manifestly to be shown. Europe, in short, is what needs to be discarded, the polemical enemy, though by the end of the war against Mexico, when O'Sullivan himself had gone on to other things, the enemy had become Europe as refracted through the supposedly degraded Spanish-Catholic legacy in that country. Conceptually, moreover, the governing Jacksonian notion of democracy (and, synonymously, freedom) evades the indigenous issue on the whole.[29] When Alexis de Tocqueville writes *Democracy in America* in this period, he notes with exemplary lucidity that democracy is heavily racialized in its actual content. The Jacksonian order is indeed massively white and in many ways far from democratic. It contains, in particular, a racialized component (of sorts) in the increasingly prominent imaginary Anglo-Saxon heritage, a component that is enormously reinforced through the war against Mexico. Manifest Destiny in that sense comes to the foreground in the 1840s ethnic essentialism over democratic principle.[30] Yet O'Sullivan's operative concept of

---

29 Sean Wilentz, *The Rise of American Democracy: Jefferson to Lincoln* (New York, 2006), elaborates well the democratic credentials of Jacksonianism, though perhaps he goes a trifle too far.

30 On the racial issue, see Michael Hunt, *Ideology and American Foreign Policy* (New Haven, CT, 1987); Patricia Nelson Limerick, *The Legacy of Conquest: The Unbroken Past of the American West* (New York, 1987); and especially Horsman, *Race and Manifest Destiny*.

democracy, the very essence of the providential dispensation, says nothing as such about race, much less slavery. Democracy in his conception is not a doctrine of conquest or displacement. Conquest enters into the proceedings only as a contingency and then preferably in the form of empty space to be settled, not as displacement or subordination of other people. Democracy, in effect, is a discourse of political community based on the principle of equality of its constituent members; it appears as it were in a vacuum. The crucial issue, consequently, is eligibility of membership. Who counts? Who is equal? On what grounds are certain categories excluded (Mexicans, Catholics, women, people of color, immigrants, individuals younger than eighteen)? The answer is subject to political struggle in the present. Exclusion, then, is intrinsic to constitutive inclusion. Displacement, however, is not. It is historically specific.

Displacement is latently problematic precisely in raising the issue of eligibility to the level of principle. Thus O'Sullivan liked to imagine Amerindian displacement as a vanishing act that had nothing inherently to do with the establishment of providential democracy. Insofar as Amerindians come into play, it is really as historical validation or prop of the basic truth of America, not in being displaced by conquering white settlers but as part of the objective process of receding wilderness and wildness, the opacity that is rapidly being turned into the translucent space of democracy. Indeed, it had become possible by O'Sullivan's time to feel a certain remorse and nostalgia about what was imagined as the Amerindian disappearance, if not extinction.[31] Even Andrew

---

31 Compare his passage in the *Democratic Review*, December 1842, 621, on Amerindians: "It is melancholy to reflect that, judging from the past, no future event seems more certain than the speedy disappearance of the American aboriginal race, when these now broken, scattered, and degraded remnants of a primitive and once cultivated branch of the human family, will scarcely be remembered, save in poetry and tradition." On other occasions, the *Review* articulated the more conventional view that it was all really Amerindians' own fault: "Doubtless the Indians have suffered in contact with us; but they have suffered, because of their own inherent vices of character and condition, such as their obstinate idleness and apathy, and their want of, and revulsion from all political institutions . . . rather than by reason of any fault of ours. It is our misfortune, quite as well as theirs, that they cling so tenaciously to their native degradation" (*Democratic Review*, September 1838, 129). By the time O'Sullivan left, the *Review* had become more overtly racist and vulgar: "The Mexican race now see, in the fate of the aborigines of the north, their own inevitable destiny. They must amalgamate or be lost, in the superior vigor of the Anglo-Saxon race, or they must utterly perish. They may postpone the hour for a time, but it will come, when their nationality shall cease" (*Democratic Review*, February 1847, 100).

Jackson, ruthless remover-in-chief, manages to persuade himself that he has actually been saving Amerindians by expelling them from the Southeast and sending them off, at the cost of enormous native suffering, to a Western wildness commensurate with their allegedly natural way of life. Henceforth, the Amerindian position becomes, by means of legal permutation and happenstance, a bizarre anomaly: domestic dependent nationals.[32] Their space, then, lies within but is excluded from America proper. America has no place for Amerindians. America and democracy are for eligibles and eligibles alone. It is utopian, it is total and it is homogenous.

In the Canadian provinces, perhaps the closest comparison, Amerindians were less vulnerable in theory and practice, ironically because of the supposedly retrograde and tyrannical imperial system: they were just one kind of imperial subjects among many other differentiated ones, ultimately covered throughout by the Royal Proclamation of 1763. Imperial authority performed a mediating role, then, that was missing in the pure and unadulterated space of freedom where everything was clearly taking place on direct authority of Providence, which is to say white democracy. The conceptual cleanliness of liberal, subsequently democratic, contractualism proved much worse for the indigenous peoples than the diversity of royal subjection.

The anomaly of an alien Amerindian space within fit the Manifest Destiny of Jacksonian democracy well because it allowed one to put brackets around the whole native problem without wreaking conceptual havoc on foundational principles. Moreover, as Amerindians do not constitute a systemic problem, they require only limited attention, rather like the present-day anomaly of Puerto Rico and numerous other US dependencies. For the ruling white order, slavery and free black people were problems of an altogether different magnitude, the functional silence commensurately more conspicuous. To put it a little too simply: democracy in the South liked slavery and increasingly came to see it as a foundation for (white) freedom, while democracy in the North disliked black people, thought them inimical to (white) freedom and so wanted to exclude them, preferably sending them off to some appropriately

---

32 On peculiar legal history here, see Lindsay Robertson, *Conquest by Law: How the Discovery of America Dispossessed Indigenous Peoples of Their Lands* (New York, 2005).

exotic location. As O'Sullivan knew (along with his sometime mentor Martin van Buren), Jacksonian democracy could harbor both of those positions only by means of another bracketing operation, hoping that somehow the problem would go away.

As it happened, the Manifest Destiny of continentalist democracy, the bracketing move itself, vastly exacerbated the problem by adding more territory and more inflammatory questions as to what exactly constituted a free, democratic and truly American space. In 1845, the Jacksonian task seemed simple: the purely quantitative one of creating, ex nihilo, pullulating democratic republics across the continental universe. The object of Manifest Destiny, then, has to do with space, not time. It has to do, specifically, with a certain theater or setting where the democratic purposes, hitherto hidden, are now revealed with complete clarity for the benefit of universal history. It is an irrefutable justification for the acquisition of that setting: Manifest Destiny is about a certain destination, the outer edges of the North American continent (though I doubt that O'Sullivan was clear on where those edges really lay). This is not only a unique project, it is the world-historical project to end all other political and civilizational projects. The dividing line between inside and outside is thus absolute. A single thrust, the war against Mexico engineered by James Polk, achieves the continental goal with apparent ease. Outstanding territorial issues with Britain in the Northwest, meanwhile, are resolved.

Stunning as this ratification of Manifest Destiny seemed to be, dialectical history would shortly stage an equally stunning reversal. Temporality returned in the form of staggering internal carnage. Continental success, Manifest Destiny, turned out to be a disaster just as the apocalyptic abolitionists had predicted. Contradictions over the authority of the center to decide whether Sameness would include or exclude slavery broke the union of freedom violently apart in one of the bloodiest conflicts in the nineteenth century. Not surprisingly, the Civil War gave simple expansionism abroad rather a bad name.[33]

---

33   The so-called Gadsden Purchase of 1853, which added some Mexican territory, turned out to be the last gasp, though no one expected this to be the case at the time. The Northern Whig and later prominent Republican William Seward, ardent expansionist and abolitionist at the same time, added enormously to the federation after the Civil War by buying Alaska, but his would-be Folly was widely conceived of as nothing but an

This was not the end of expansionism, however, as there was ample room in the already existing acquisitions for the astonishing capitalist accumulation and industrialization that had begun even before the Civil War. Demonstrating American purposes, sans slavery now, was still the order of the day, as was the continuous replication of new states within. Race, at length, was transformed into a pseudo-scientific category designed to legitimate the widespread institution of white supremacy after the end of Reconstruction. Such seemingly rational concepts of racial hierarchies allowed white society to congeal nationally once again at the same time as they served to curb much of the enthusiasm for expansion in places with lots of racially dubious people. Destiny did not disappear but it largely faded from visibility in the boom and bustle.

A would-be humanitarian exercise in 1898 to help the Cuban insurrection against imperial Spanish rule (or at least to quell its disastrous effects) unexpectedly brought Manifest Destiny back to public debate with a vengeance. Its context and use was, however, radically different. The democratic element, for one thing, had disappeared; space was historicized and race was everywhere. Most decisively, the United States was connected with Europe and the world in lines of continuity, thus replacing absolute distinction. What had happened?

Above all, empire, racialized, scientific empire. The last third of the nineteenth century had seen a formidable drive by the imperial powers of Europe to subordinate territories in Africa and Asia and to formalize their imperial systems. This process was conceived of in two divergent registers. Taken as a collective unit, European imperialism was grasped as a civilizational and thereby Christian project for the good of all—even when Japan entered the game seriously in 1895, it did so explicitly in the collective name of civilizational superiority (less the Christian element). Within, however, imperialism was conducted as competition, as a struggle in the name of national greatness, size and exclusivity. Navies increasingly provided the indexical measure here, the force that had made the British the hegemon of the century and now expressed

---

arctic waste; and so it raised none of the now-paramount problems of alien peoples and their threat to republican purity. Ernest N. Paolino, *The Foundations of the American Empire: William Henry Seward and US Foreign Policy* (Ithaca, NY, 1973) remains the best treatment of Seward.

more than anything else how well one could combine industrial and military prowess. Important figures in the United States worried about this competition and what appeared to them as a national failure, not necessarily the failure of the world's first postcolonial power to become properly colonial but certainly to maintain a geopolitical posture commensurate with its enormously expanded economic base. According to this view, while the United States was well on its way to becoming the world's largest industrial and agricultural producer, it was failing signally to translate that prowess into political advantage on the international arena.[34]

The vast majority of the public cared not one whit about this; nor did the majority of the politicians. The smoldering Cuban issue, however, served to bring geopolitics inadvertently to the surface. By going to war against Spain for the sake of Cuba, the United States ended up making the island into a protectorate and Puerto Rico, the Philippines and Guam into colonies, in addition to which Hawaii was annexed. At the end of 1898, the United States suddenly looked rather like one Great Power among a very select number of others, an impression deepened manyfold by the addition of the Panama Canal zone five years later. The historical particulars of this astonishing shift are of the greatest interest but not for my purposes here. What is of interest instead is how the United States could be recast in destinarian terms now that it was apparently doing exactly what every old-style imperialist power was doing. Whither, in short, essential difference?

The advent of imperialism, it will be remembered, coincided with the advent of what is usually referred to as the Progressive Era in the United States, a period of reform grounded in a certain (let us say) rationalist, middle- and upper-class sense that the country had lost its bearings and was urgent in need of better order and better management along scientific lines. The colonial break divided this movement. Some of the most articulate and unfaltering anti-imperialists were Progressives. Nevertheless, the predominant Progressive view was not only to acquiesce but to see in the US version of empire an opening precisely for quintessentially intelligent, enlightened reform, a project related to

---

34 Generally, see Stephanson, *Manifest Destiny*, chap. 3; for an argument about executive power, see Fareed Zakaria, *From Wealth to Power: The Unusual Origins of America's World Role* (Princeton, NJ, 1998).

other imperialist endeavors, yet profoundly different. Civilization was the conceptual terrain on which this problem was fought out and eventually settled.[35]

It became possible, in effect, to grasp the endeavor entirely in civilizational and humanitarian terms, as the bringing of peace, prosperity, health, education, and so forth, to needy natives, or at least eligible and capable ones. Humanitarian guardianship was always coupled with a liberal, scientific racism, a scheme of classification according to which certain allegedly inferior types would naturally be consigned to the dustbin of history, as had, however regrettably, the Amerindians at home. Evolution would take care of them, so to speak. Not coincidentally, the Progressive Era is one of those intermittent moments when America decides that the collective, ethnic, alien space of Amerindians is an irrational affront that must be abolished, and the natives individualized and expeditiously Americanized. All this is indeed put on brilliant display in the St. Louis world exposition of 1904: the extraordinary "Philippine Reservation" with its taxonomic exhibit of the new colonial possession and all the uplifting, intelligent reform imposed upon it; and the Indian model school, replete with women's basketball teams and other invigorating features for the mind and body.[36]

According to the Progressive view, then, to eschew guardianship over those indigenous elements that survived evolutionary rigors was to shirk from responsibility, duty and obligation, in short from one's Manifest Destiny. Essentially, in other words, one identified with the civilizational aspect of Western imperialism (only a few arch-imperialists in the United States would choose to accentuate the strictly geopolitical dimension). The United States, on this view, was the most advanced and sapient part of the most advanced and sapient part of Western civilization, namely, the Anglophone world. The modifier "most" here is crucial. It indicates that the United States, though different, was actually part of something larger, the vanguard, to be sure, as

---

35 For more on this, see chap. 9.

36 See Paul Kramer, "Making Concessions: Race and Empire Revisited at the Philippine Exposition, St. Louis, 1901–1905," *Radical History Review* 1999, no. 73, 74–114; on the taxonomic aspect, see Vincente L. Rafael, *White Love and Other Events in Filipino History* (Durham, NC, 2000); and Theresa Ventura, *American Empire, Agrarian Reform and the Problem of Tropical Nature in the Philippines, 1898–1916*, PhD diss., Columbia University, 2009.

evidenced for instance by the selflessly enlightened reforming and recreation of the Philippines, but nevertheless a project integrated in a line of continuity with other civilizational uplifters. The absolute divide, in other words, of the original Monroe Doctrine had been eliminated. Symptomatically, Teddy Roosevelt's famous corollary to it in 1904 situated the United States as the regional Great Power in the Western Hemisphere with the right to discipline and punish, all of which indicated that other Great Powers would not only be within their right but would also be obliged to carry out a similar role in other regions.[37]

The elision of absolute difference was in fact typical of the Progressive Era, one of the few in US history when it became possible to say in polite society that the Constitution really was rather an old and dated document in need of severe revision for modern times.[38] Continuity or not, talk of Manifest Destiny in this context was (again) largely a progressive or reformist concern: it was manifestly the destiny of the United States qua United States to help the little Brown brothers who, unforeseeably, had come under its benevolent jurisdiction. The project as such, the election campaign of 1900 notwithstanding, had far less impact on the political structure than the destinarian expansion of the 1840s. After the Panama events, the brutal repression of the Philippine insurgency and the celebratory excitement of the St. Louis Louisiana Exposition of 1904, colonial concerns faded from public purview.

Another fundamental problem of difference remained, however, a problem not in relation to Europe but to the new imperial possessions themselves. For it was clear that no person from, say, Guam, however radical the uplifting, would ever become a proper American, and that as long as the island remained within, it would also remain outside the United States proper. Cellular replication had come to an end (though it would take half a century of probation before Hawaii would mark the actual end.) The Empire of and for Liberty could now have territorial

---

37 Stephanson, *Manifest Destiny*, chap. 3.

38 Compare Teddy Roosevelt here with his distant relative and equally Progressive follower Franklin: neither had much devotion to the Constitution as an expression of timeless truth, both thinking presidential power should be stretched as far as it possibly could, which, in Franklin's case, was very far indeed. On the line of continuity with Europe in the Progressive Era, see Daniel T. Rodgers, *Atlantic Crossings: Social Politics in a Progressive Age* (Cambridge, 2000); and on the geopolitical aspect, Warren Zimmerman, *First Great Triumph: How Five Americans Made their Country a World Power* (New York, 2002).

possessions in a state of enduring inferiority. This was a fact. There was, alas, no immediately obvious solution to what these facts, these dependencies, really were in a legal sense, the simultaneous status of being both inside and outside. Not for the first time, it was the courts that eventually resolved the issue for the political system: with an invented category, the new territories were said to be "unincorporated," as distinct from "incorporated" acquisitions such as Alaska and Hawaii. To be unincorporated meant that one was in principle an instrument of the US Congress, a thing to be disposed as Congress saw fit. That the instrumental status is still very much with us is scarcely well known in the United States, though it certainly is in Guam.[39]

History, cast in evolutionary concepts, thus made possible a new inscription of space(s) and the peoples that inhabited them at the same time as it brought the nation of nations back into its fold. No longer was the United States a sacred space for the implementation and demonstration of providential purposes of democracy. The United States was still exemplary but chiefly in the role as pioneering, superior agent in the transformation of the imperial world. Progressive empire is not about democracy but about mastery of self and others; and governing the self is primarily a problem of being able to master the art of governing others and their unwieldy, irrational ways. One of those ways is actually excessive democracy. Progressivism is about supposedly intelligent management of the real. Destiny is about evolutionary development and the capacity to understand and direct it. It is about conquering spaces peopled by inferiors. In short, it is about difference, hierarchy and heterogeneity, not about identity, democracy and homogeneity. The corresponding advent of segregated, racial spaces within is a graphic expression of the same shift.

The colonial moment was thus a large-scale destinarian intervention in the outside world but not in response to any massive crisis of a world-historical kind. Apocalyptic sentiments, as in the 1840s, were more a

---

39 Generally, see Arnold Leibowitz, *Defining Status: A Comprehensive Analysis of United States Territorial Relations* (Dordrecht, Boston, 1989); on Puerto Rico, see *Foreign in a Domestic Sense: Puerto Rico, American Expansion, and the Constitution*, edited by C. D. Burnett and B. Marshall (Durham, NC, 2001); and the pathbreaking work of Efrén Rivera Ramos, *The Legal Construction of Identity: The Judicial and Social Legacy of American Colonialism in Puerto Rico* (Washington, DC, 2001).

mark of opponents, who predicted, wrongly this time around, that expansion would ruin the Union. The effects on the body politic were in fact limited, except insofar that it actually made that body into a body that could have extremities, though paradoxically unincorporated ones. The civilizational aspect entailed no messianic element. Rhetorically overblown as its antecedent, Manifest Destiny was now carried out in the name of providential, historical inevitability and the world-historical role of the United States in that process.

World-transformative uniqueness combined with the apocalyptic was, however, about to appear with unexpected power and speed in the shape of Woodrow Wilson, a prototypical Progressive at the outset who eventually comes to revolutionize the ordering process to entail the entire globe, imputing to the United States (and himself) the messianic role of accomplishing this mighty change in history. In epically destinarian but now also apocalyptic language, he articulated the absolutely decisive calling for the United States to seize the moment and change the world finally into something identical to the United States itself, that is to say, the democratic and peaceful end of history. The United States, then, is both agent and model.

Wilson failed. Yet he would also leave a curse on all his successors since. There is no way of escaping Wilson because he enunciated the ultimate American destinarianism, ultimate in scope of application and world-historical magnitude. Wilson became an unavoidable reference point, a navigational landmark even when his legacy was in fact eschewed. Thus Franklin D. Roosevelt, the ostensible Wilsonian, often invoked destiny but in fact espoused none of the messianic convictions, always remaining (after the Japanese attack in 1941 had put the United States irrevocably in the world of geopolitics) a Progressive committed to law and order, stability and predictability, all sanctioned by genuine commitment to wartime collaboration with allies of a quite different ilk. With the idea of absolute difference with the outside world, he had very little patience. When the wartime collaboration breaks down and is followed by the most intense antagonism conceivable under formal conditions of peace, there is also a return to the American matrix: a messianic response to an apocalyptic crisis, a perceived and perhaps artificial crisis. What is known as the cold war is indeed originally how the United States, more particularly the Truman administration, resolves the problem of legitimating peacetime globalism: perpetual US engagement everywhere in the name of war for the sake of saving the world from destruction. In creating the division between the Free World and the unspeakable netherworld that tries to invade it, the United States actually remains absolutely apart within its own sphere. The Free World is not uniform. To lead that world is not merely to be indispensable, it is to have absolute authority in the last instance to do whatever it takes to carry on the war.

Arguably, this version of Manifest Destiny expires around 1963, after the threat of nuclear conflagration came graphically close to effecting a truly apocalyptic ending for everyone involved. It is hard to be messianic—or, for that matter, destinarian—about mutually assured destruction. To be one superpower out of two is to engage in geopolitical management, not to be on a quest for transcendence. Nuclear parity implies similarity, if not identity. Neither Richard M. Nixon nor Henry Kissinger is any exemplary exponent of Manifest Destiny, however fateful the political career of the former. Reaganism briefly resurrects the cold-war format, almost as postmodern pastiche, but the very brevity of the exercise demonstrated how weak were its historical underpinnings. For one thing, behind the binary rhetoric of the Evil Empire and the Free World about to battle it out at Armageddon, Reagan's policy entailed intimate strategic relations with the other communist giant, the People's Republic of China. Yet, to repeat, the United States does not have to be right to be successful, and in a mindboggling twist of history, for reasons much more contingent than now recognized, the Evil Empire self-destructed, to the monumental surprise, certainly, of its erstwhile enemies.

The ensuing period, the cliched "after the end of the cold war," was not a propitious one for destinarian thinking. Destiny, so to speak, was over. Manifestly, destiny had happened. The role of the United States in the globalizing world of more and better markets, indeed more of the same everywhere, was certainly conceived of as indispensable; but the space for world-historical transcendence and massive intervention had obviously disappeared. What remained? Mopping up operations and brushfire wars? Improving the World Trade Organization? Not much heroic material to be found for the organic intellectuals of "the only superpower" (the other ubiquitous cliché of the era).

An eruption of unimaginable magnitude then opened up once more for the return of the destinarian formula. The "war on terror," modeled on the cold war, thus once again featured a United States manifestly destined by higher authority to combat the forces of evil in the world and assuming the right to do so in whatever fashion and wherever it might see fit: the messianic is inherently beyond the law because the present is by definition degraded, in need of transcendence. This marked the return, then, of the United States as a world empire proper. However, the open-endedness and deterritorialized nature of the project ensured its failure: there is no possible end to a war, at once metaphorical and real, against a historical phenomenon, terror, that has no territory and is not actually an existing enemy in the first place. It is one thing to carry on an endless war on drugs where relative failure is recognized from the beginning; it is quite another to fashion one's position in the world on an endless war on terror that one expects to win and to mobilize one's incomparable military machine accordingly.

There was however another side of the destinarian thrust of the George W. Bush administration, which O'Sullivan, Wilson and Truman would all have recognized. I am referring to democracy, self-determination, freedom and the auxiliary concept of free enterprise. This ideological assemblage posits that people (those who count as such) are everywhere the same and, if allowed truly to determine their own selves, will naturally be free. Rational people everywhere, when given a chance, will constitute themselves politically in parallel ways to the Land of the Free itself, the actions of which are therefore always greeted by true people everywhere as liberation, even if it actually means coming under US occupation and guardianship. Opposition, in this seamlessly circular argument, is thus at best mistaken or, at worst, subversive.

The century, then, that has passed since the imperialist surge, has seen, in fits and starts, the emergence of the United States as a world power. Manifest Destiny, which began as a spatio-temporal notion pertaining to the North American continent, was transformed into a global aspiration and became in the process messianic. As a political trope, it has had the advantage of being malleable and open to new content. Manifest Destiny, from that angle, is a function: it has no given concrete goal. Its axiom is world-historical, providential chosenness. The actual task of that function can vary. In a continental setting, it was not about intervention but contiguous expansion. In an imperial-colonial setting, it was about peerlessly enlightened uplifting of appropriate natives. At Versailles, it was about recasting international relations and letting people truly be people. In the cold war, it was about saving the Free World and vanquishing totalitarianism. In the current era (about to pass, as I write), it is about saving the world from terrorism and making it safe for democracy. From another angle, I have argued that Manifest Destiny, variations aside, did not become messianic until the object was the whole world and a catastrophic crisis was at hand; and that the messianic variant, once continentalism has been fulfilled and superseded, is the strongest conceivable one when it comes to separation between the United States and the outside.

Yet I have also argued that Manifest Destiny is not an ideological given or absolute feature of US history. Its use is not random, but it is certainly contingent. Manifest Destiny, to reiterate, is conspicuous by its absence in the massive global emergency of the Second World War: a combination of FDR's Progressive disdain for US separation ("isolationism") and the realities of the wartime alliance precluded destinarianism. In the end it must also be said Kennan was right about the peculiarities of the social and political structure of the United States: mixing a strongly decentralized and domestically orientated ruling class, politically expressed in the locally anchored Congress, with an equally strong nationally elected executive, who is also, monarchically, commander-in-chief, makes for a certain license in the choice of ideological framing that few other regimes can afford or even contemplate. What these frames are and how they are made is of monumental concern for the world outside the United States, regrettably often more so than for the United States itself.

9
A Most Interesting Empire

The United States is today the world's largest transoceanic empire. Innumerable islands under the American flag dot the Pacific and the Caribbean, the biggest and most notable being Puerto Rico. This is a colonial empire in the most conventional sense: far-flung territories and populations are held under the control of the center in a status of formal inferiority.[1] Beyond the normal purview of US politics, these old-style imperial possessions are rarely discussed or even acknowledged; they are set aside if not wholly forgotten. The centenary of the Spanish-American War, in which many of them were acquired, occasioned only sporadic interest.[2] The internments, illegal by international law, at Guantanamo Bay in Cuba served as a brief reminder, but chiefly in terms of legal peculiarities. The overwhelming reality of imperial power in the insular possessions, then, is mirrored inversely in the insularity of the imperial power itself.

In a range of other domains, however, there has been a strong resurgence of interest in the idea of empire and in thinking about the United

---

1 For an overview, see Arnold Leibowitz, *Defining Status: A Comprehensive Analysis of United States Territorial Relations* (Dordrecht, Boston, 1989). Denmark is arguably territorially a larger empire, but its chief possession, Greenland, is de facto under the geopolitical suzerainty of the United States.

2 Depending on time and place, this war has been known under a variety of names. The designation in the United States, "the Spanish-American War," symptomatically hides the Cuban participation. "The Spanish-Cuban-American War," as it is known in Cuba, is better but elides in turn the independent Philippine aspect.

States generally as an empire. The immediate reason is not hard to detect: empire was and is a readily available way of conceiving the geopolitical situation after the implosion in 1991 of the Soviet Union, which left the United States as, in a phrase endlessly repeated, the only superpower. Whether one chose to characterize empire as the immanent form of globalized capitalism or, more traditionally, as a form of domination (and indeed whether one found that domination congenial), the term "empire" was doubtless beginning to enjoy renewed currency from the 1990s onward. The US thrust to global power in the wake of September 11 amplified these imperial reverberations. Still, it is good to recall that there was growing investigation of empire even before the 1990s. Some of it can be traced, academically, to the confluence of cultural studies and its emergent postcolonial cousin, though empire here was less the concept of the exercise than its site, so to speak. Relatedly, if less visibly, there was also growing concern with ancient and peripheral empires in certain subfields within the social sciences. Indeed, the Soviet collapse itself (when not taken as simply irrefutable evidence for the perversity of socialism) could be conceived of in part as a problem of imperial disintegration.[3]

---

3   In the 1960s and early '70s, there was of course an explosion of interest in imperialism in general and US imperialism in particular. This came to a predictable end with the end of the involvement in Southeast Asia. In the mid-1980s, there began a rejuvenation of an older, sociological kind of academic inquiry, roughly descended from Max Weber's comparative concerns. A central work here was Michael Mann's *The Sources of Social Power, Vol. I: From the Beginning to 1760 AD* (Cambridge, 1986). Simultaneously, there appeared in the case-study method of mainstream US social science Michael Doyle's significant *Empire* (Ithaca, NY, 1986). Yet it was the entirely new phase in geopolitics after 1990, with its apparent unipolarity (an oxymoron) that turned empire into a field, if not a master signifier. Michael Hardt and Toni Negri's controversial and much debated *Empire* appeared from Harvard University Press in 2000. The separate strain through cultural studies to postcolonial studies originated to no small degree in Edward Said's *Orientalism* (1979); but the independent and sophisticated current originating in India now known as subaltern studies was already in existence and became influential as well. A good collection on empire from a comparative perspective is *After Empire*, edited by Karen Barkey and Mark von Hagen (Boulder, CO, 1997). Since September 11, there has been a veritable onslaught of arguments about the American Empire. Some conservatives, interestingly, have been highly critical. See for example, Andrew J. Bacevich, *American Empire: The Realities and Consequences of US Diplomacy* (Cambridge, 2002). Others such as Niall Ferguson foregrounding historically the British model, advocate US empire as a sensible contemporary way to run the world but doubts Washington is up to it. See his *Colossus: The Rise and Fall of the American Empire* (New York, 2004).

Although the term "empire" fills certain needs, what it actually explains is far from clear. In the case of the United States, its usage is often descriptive and metaphorical. There is a sense, for example, that somehow the aggregate discrepancies between the superpower and the rest must amount to something imperial. One is reminded of earlier tendencies in the historiography where the United States is almost but not quite an empire: a way of life perhaps, marked by a will to expansion, or, alternatively, protection and assistance at the eager invitation of potential recipient countries.[4] The more typical procedure, explicit or not, is to create a model of sorts, centered on domination or inequalities of power, and then to measure the extent to which any given relation, situation, or structure can be said to qualify. Lurking in the background is often some abstracted version of ancient Rome; but the historical reference is less important than the method of modeling itself, which allows for comparison of social formations and types of rule across time and space. The procedure can yield interesting results: the rich, comparative tradition of historical sociology is eloquent proof.[5] Yet the conceptual difficulties are undeniable. The Marxist tradition has wrestled mightily with them. Unlike, say, capitalism, empire is a transhistorical category, which can be applied, without much discrimination, in vastly different periods and places. Unlike, say, mode of production, it is a transhistorical category that permits little room for qualitative historical change. Lenin, famously, tried to historicize and theorize the concept by turning it (as imperialism) into a particular and final stage in the development of capitalism, a ripened, potentially stagnant and reactionary form dominated by monopoly. His rendition, composed in the midst of World War I to grasp the nature of that cataclysmic event and the antecedent frenzy of imperial expansion, turned out to be wrong in almost every respect. In canonized form, it was to exert a stifling effect on Marxist theory forever after.[6]

---

4 The allusions here are to William Appleman Williams, *Empire as a Way of Life* (New York, 1980) and Geir Lundestad, *American "Empire" and Other Studies of American Foreign Policy in a Comparative Perspective* (Oxford, 1990), though the original idea was put forth in Lundestad's article "Empire by Invitation" in *SHAFR Newsletter,* September 15, 1984.

5 One important, earlier presence here was S. N. Eisenstadt. See his *The Political Systems of Empires* (New York, 1963). "Empire" in historical sociology has otherwise been one of several forms of state, less an object of inquiry in itself.

6 Lenin's theorization became Soviet orthodoxy of the most entrenched sort, the frame within which all international politics was ultimately conceived of. That the

All description (or facticity) is of course in some sense theory-laden, but inscription in an implicit conceptual frame does not make empire into a real concept. Still, the term can be used to advantage. First, description is not necessarily bad. Empire actually exists. That the United States does indeed possess a colonial empire overseas, whose aquatic area equals that of the lower forty-eight states, may be a descriptive proposition; but it is also an interesting fact that demands exploration and explanation. Empire, on that view, signifies nothing but a legal and political form, and sometimes, with all the proper caveats, it is illuminating to describe a system as an empire. What is particularly interesting about the US variety is the obvious anomaly: persistent formal inferiority within a liberal framework, an official anticolonialism that both recognizes and manages not to recognize the colonial fact. Second, since September 11, one might well raise the eternally returning question, whether the United States was or is indeed sensibly described as an empire, above and beyond its undeniable colonial appendages. In what sense may the bid for supremacy amount to an imperial structure, either in terms of intent or results? Third, the historical uses of empire are always unavoidably ideological, symbolically significant acts that can sometimes tell us about something else. In the United States, "empire" has been used authoritatively and favorably as self-description in two periods, first intermittently in the late eighteenth century and nineteenth century before the Civil War, and then in the imperial moment around the turn of the twentieth century. With the conflagration of 1914 and the concomitant crisis of the Eurocentric ideology of civilization, "empire" became on the whole a term of opprobrium. After the Second World War, it appears either as radical critique of United States in the world or, in the rhetoric of officialdom, as a designation for Soviet domination. Only in the 1990s, then, can one detect signs of renascent, unabashed neo-imperialism, the kind of ideology of beneficent domination by a single power or civilization that marked the

---

"highest stage" went on and on never occasioned any basic rethinking until the days of Gorbachev. Hardt and Negri are partly a response to this impasse, an original attempt to rethink the problem by finding empire in the very form of decentered, globalized capitalism. Heavily theoretical though their work is, one still wonders in the end why this form is necessarily to be called empire. Perhaps it is meant as Brechtian estrangement effect. For another kind of reflection in the Marxist tradition see David Harvey, *The New Imperialism* (Oxford, 2003).

conjuncture of a century ago. These shifts reveal something about how the United States has understood itself in the world. In that ideological context, there is a fourth approach, a more specific one centered on Otto Hintze's notion of a "world empire," an empire such as Rome, whose self-constitutive feature is that it can have no equal in the world, that it understands its compass as identical with the world that really counts, as opposed to the actual one.[7] The messianic character of the United States, an overdeterminant ideological form that is anything but nebulous, is conducive to such notions. At this nexus between messianism (what often passes under the rubric "American exceptionalism") and empire lies a crack of considerable analytical interest.

These are vast issues. In this essay, I will explore in what sense Alexander Hamilton might have been right to think the United States "an empire in many ways the most interesting in the world"; but I shall only explore at certain moments when empire and (for lack of a better term) the identity of the United States in the world was raised, either expressly by contemporaries or by the actual historical situation. I begin with a delineation of the formation of the peculiar republican empire in the late 1780s, though I use Thomas Jefferson rather than Hamilton as a representative figure because his break with existing political models is sharper and coincides better with what actually happened in the following century.[8] I then periodize the crucial shifts in the nature of the body politic during the nineteenth and early twentieth century, against which backdrop I examine what some have seen as the imperial expansion of the cold war. I end with a consideration of the recent epoch when the United States, for a moment, decided that it would assume a very conventional form of imperial rule for the benefit of everyone. Since the

---

7 Otto Hintze, *The Historical Essays of Otto Hintze* (New York, 1975). The German term *Weltreich* is semantically not directly related to the Latin "imperium," but it makes sense: "By 'world empire' I mean those states of ancient times and of non-European civilization, which established a universal authority in an area they regarded as the known and inhabited world, and which recognized no other states as equal" (468n).

8 Hamilton's formulation comes from *The Federalist* no. 1. Almost all references to the United States as empire in *The Federalist* are to be found in his contributions. Empire in itself is neither good nor bad. It is used as a designation for rule involving many states and enormous size. See also John Robertson's interesting "Empire and Union: Two Concepts of the Early Modern European Political Order," in *A Union for Empire: Political Thought and the British Union of 1707*, ed. John Robertson (Cambridge, 1995).

matter under inquiry is political form, I shall deal only briefly with the religious dimensions. Having discussed them at some length elsewhere, I am fully aware how preponderant they are; but here they must chiefly be taken as givens.[9]

When Jefferson approvingly referred to the United States as an empire, he did not have the models of Britain or Rome favorably in mind. After all, this was arguably the first postcolonial nation, the result of imperial rule dissolved. For Jefferson, in fact, the United States was to be the sort of empire that the British should have been or perhaps indeed was thought to have been before despotism and tyranny presumably destroyed the rights of Englishmen who happened to live across the Atlantic. Empires for him (as far as anything determinate can be said of this voluble but mercurial character) rule over an extended territory that is not a single sovereignty, something large, powerful, and of world-historical importance. The crucial and unprecedented aspect of the United States as an empire was that it was to be free and devoid of any dominant, imperial center. This was not only an "empire of liberty," as he called it, but also an "empire for liberty."[10] Less often noted, his second formulation indicated a space that was intrinsically free and singularly designated to serve the higher purpose of freedom itself. Jefferson's innovation, contrary to all orthodoxy, was to make imperial expansion take place in the name of self-determination—the very essence of liberty as it was understood. Hence there was no contradiction when he spoke of the natural suitability of the United States for "extensive empire and self-government."[11] The two aspects went hand in hand. In fact, the

---

9 Anders Stephanson, *Manifest Destiny: American Expansion and the Empire of Right* (New York, 1995).

10 In the immense literature on Jefferson, see Robert W. Tucker and David C. Hendrickson, *Empire of Liberty: The Statecraft of Thomas Jefferson* (New York, 1990); Peter S. Onuf, *Statehood and Union: A History of the Northwest Ordinance* (Bloomington, IN, 1987); John Lauritz Larson, "Jefferson's Union and the Problem of Internal Improvements," in *Jeffersonian Legacies*, ed. Peter Onuf (Charlottesville, VA, 1993). Hamilton, it should be added, would not have disagreed with Jefferson, but his concern was chiefly how to achieve control and cohesion while avoiding despotism, rather than promoting any worldhistorical principle of liberty as such. I leave aside the ticklish issue of whether Jefferson as president turned out to be a Hamiltonian.

11 Letter to Madison, April 27, 1809. *The Papers of James Madison* (Presidential Series, vol. 1), ed. Robert Rutland et al. (Charlottesville, VA, 1984). All quotations except "empire of liberty" in Jefferson's letter to Madison on the given date in Rutland except

latter presupposed the former. Jefferson himself had played an instrumental role in rendering this concept possible through the Northwest Ordinance of 1787, which allowed the addition of new states into the original Union on an equal basis. The Ordinance defined the territories initially under federal governance as inherently destined to become states, the requirement being that each at a certain stage would reenact the kind of founding compact that was said to characterize the original membership in the federation. Each territory, filling up gradually through immigration from existing member states, would thus prove itself before gaining entry; but the concept of full and equal statehood was inscribed in the whole procedure from the beginning. Though the biological metaphor is not exactly right, one might call this "empire by cellular self-replication," a sort of serial process of constantly renewed sameness. Such a settlement, which endlessly reproduces the original moment and principle of liberty in an agrarian setting, is surely colonization in the strongest meaning of the word; but it is not a conventional empire (even if understood only as command and rule over something extensive).[12]

The moment when empire meets self-determination is a dialectical and quite radical break. It is worth noting that Jefferson, in typical anthropomorphic fashion, conceived of these new exemplars of self-government as analogues of eighteenth-century bourgeois subjects.

"empire of liberty," which may be found in Jefferson to Rogers Clarke, December 25, 1780 (founders.archives.gov/documents/Jefferson/01-04-02-0295).

12 The metaphor becomes paradoxical when the voluntarist component of the founding moment is taken properly into account: what is reproduced is not a biological code or essence but the act of proving one's ability to determine oneself freely, an act defined precisely by the absence of any outside or prior determination. My metaphor in any case turned out to be unoriginal. Robert Bartlett uses a similar one in describing the medieval Germanic colonization of Eastern Europe: "What they were doing was reproducing units similar to those in their homelands. The towns, churches and estates they established simply replicated the social framework they knew from back home. The net result of this colonialism was not the creation of 'colonies,' in the sense of dependencies, but the spread of a kind of cellular multiplication, of the cultural and social forms found in the Latin Christian core." Bartlett, *The Making of Europe: Conquest, Colonization and Cultural Change, 950–1350* (Princeton, NJ, 1993), 306. The process seems in turn rather similar to the successive waves of Greek colonization in the Mediterranean after the eighth century BCE. One basic difference with the United States, of course, is that Washington was a functioning federal center, albeit a weak one, in the nineteenth century.

To be a state and thus a member is to be a person in the sense of someone who is fully rational and autonomous. The concomitant idea of self-determination thus should not be taken lightly. To be a full subject-self, to be sovereign in a way, is precisely to be able to act without any external determinations. Yet at the same time any such new autonomous subject-self would naturally find it rational to join that which is already a compact of similarly free entities.[13]

This political union-republic, interestingly, is not at all a nation in the emergent European sense. For Herder, and later on Mazzini, the state presupposes a rooted people, a sequence of generations born in a particular territory, a homeland if you will, and a particular culture, something grown over a long time, to go with it. From the liberal perspective of the nineteenth century it was then possible to imagine that a fully free and developed nation of this kind would naturally want to see the development of other such free nations and live in harmony with them, the world becoming a series of autonomous polities filled with specific peoples, each with a unique character and a unique contribution to make to the glory of the world. This scenario, of course, failed to materialize. In the Empire of and for Liberty, one is confronted with something quite different: a perpetually growing space for the demonstration of the higher historical purposes of humankind as such, all in the name of self-determination and autonomy. It is a timeless, physically indeterminate space of movement and colonization. A homeland, however, it is not.

Spatially, then, this union is theoretically under perpetual construction both inside and outside its borders. As an expanding political form of no particular nationality, it has no intrinsic limit. The territorial growth of such a political entity would by definition extend the sphere of liberty. Moreover, expansion had the potential to cancel the historical cycle according to which, typically, rising republics eventually become

---

[13] Again there is a dialectic: free choice becomes its opposite, a foregone conclusion. Among the numerous works on autonomy and freedom I have used Quentin Skinner, *Liberty Before Liberalism* (Cambridge, 1998); Fred D'Agostino, "Two Conceptions of Autonomy," *Economy and Society* 27, no. 1 (1998); and David Brion Davis, *The Problem of Slavery in the Age of Revolution, 1770–1823* (Ithaca, NY, 1975). Autonomy as a criterion or precondition of selfhood (the capacity to determine rationally and freely without any outside influence) goes back of course to classical Greek thought.

corrupt and die. To maintain the original spirit of liberty, then, expanding the federation was, pari passu, a good thing and in accordance with the direction of rational history. There were admittedly actual limits to the United States as a federation: Jefferson happened to think Cuba the southern end because expansion beyond that island would require a big navy, something that in turn would undermine the republican nature of the original body politic. He was uncertain about other directions, but generally his vision was expansive. And if the existing union would face natural limits at some point, one could always imagine the creation of— essentially similar—unions adjacent to the original. Temporally, such spatial replication freezes time in a qualitative sense and removes the historical specter of decline. For there can be no new and better stage in history beyond the perfect union-republic. The idea can only grow or self-destruct.

As embodied universality, in fact, such a nation could tolerate no qualitative deviations. Mixtures and "blots," as Jefferson put it, must not be allowed. Heterogeneity, qualitative heterogeneity, could have no legitimacy and had to be eliminated from the space and project of rational freedom. The unfortunate Amerindians, certainly an anomalous presence, found out in no uncertain terms what this meant. Replication of the same was not an empty formula. For Jefferson, arguably, the more sinister danger always lurked within: dark forces that could lead the empire of liberty into corruption, regression and ultimately death.[14]

The structural answer to this historical problem of past, present, and future was thus dual: eternal vigilance against enemies within and constant expansion without. The initial formulation of the Monroe Doctrine might so be read as a statement about historical irreversibility: the Western hemisphere is declared to have entered a new stage and the United States assumes the task (in theory) to see to it that the decolonized states would not become colonies once again, or at least colonies

---

14 As Jefferson writes to Madison in 1801: "It is impossible not to look forward to distant times, when our rapid multiplication will expand itself beyond those limits, and cover the whole north, if not the southern continent with a people speaking the same language, governed in similar forms, and by similar laws; nor can we contemplate with satisfaction either blot or mixture on that surface." Quoted in Tucker and Hendrickson, *Empire of Liberty*, 160–1. Saint-Just, in a different register, expressed the same imperative more unequivocally in the French Revolution: "No liberty for the enemies of liberty."

of Europe. For the first time, a sphere of influence is thus invested with an explicit political principle.

In the course of the first half of the nineteenth century, the Union expanded transcontinentally in this manner. Even the war of conquest against Mexico in 1846 that cut that country in half was carried out in the name of the expansion of the principle of liberty, a justification that had been fused powerfully by then with the Protestant vision of providential election in the form of physical destiny. Thus the deterritorialized, timeless name of liberty was invested with physical meaning in actual geography. The dialectical result, however, was intensifying conflict. How could expansion of the free and self-determining also be the expansion of slavery? Could anyone be free if some were always unfree? Who possessed a self capable of being free? Was African descent actually compatible with having a self in the first place? How could one be free if slavery of those naturally condemned to it were not there to demonstrate the opposite of freedom? Was it not, moreover, the very mark of a free state to be able to withdraw from a compact freely entered? Regionalization of identity along these conflictual notions of liberty had to be adjudicated by means of one of the bloodiest wars in the Western world during the century between 1815 and 1914. The victorious North, having thus fought on the symptomatic basis that one could not live half-slave and half-free, proceeded to impose its own concept of universal liberty, indeed to make the United States into a single body without blots.[15]

This newly integrated body politic, consequently, could no longer be imagined in quite the old Jeffersonian manner. Still the embodiment of universal purposes, it nevertheless came to be seen as somehow complete, at least for the foreseeable future, in the territorial sense. Available objects for acquisition had become racially and politically suspect. The exception, Canada, showed no signs of wanting to follow the rational course of entry into the Empire of and for Liberty. Yet the full-grown body was only full in its contours. Within, of course, it was filling up at astonishing speed through the twin processes of immigration and industrialization. But cellular replication of the self was over (only to be reinvented in modified and

---

15   I am drawing here on my *Manifest Destiny*.

unexpected form in the early Union of Soviet Socialist Republics, but that is another story).

From now on, any additions would have to be conceived of otherwise. The humanitarian effort to liberate Cuba by means of war with Spain in 1898 could thus not initially be grasped in terms of any inclusion of the island in the Union, as Jefferson and others had envisaged a century earlier. Liberating Cuba in fact turned out to mean establishing a US protectorate over the Cubans, while the other acquisitions in the Treaty of Paris, from the Philippines to Puerto Rico, were classed as imperial possessions pure and simple. And so, in many instances, they remain. Guam, as the courts decided in 1985, is "an instrumentality" of the United States Congress, an instrumentality, one might add, extensively resurfaced with tarmac for the purpose of projecting massive air power.[16] Even Castro's Cuba has had to accept de facto the continued colonial presence of a US military base.

The Empire for Liberty thus became an empire of a conventional kind. This was duly recognized at the time and hotly debated, if only momentarily. The name, it should be underlined, was primarily invoked by anti-imperialists, indicative of a certain discomfort with the idea across the political divide. Was the very idea of the United States as embodied liberty in fact compatible with empire, especially in an epoch when imperialism, a movement and system, was so directly associated with the dominant European state order? A comforting answer along liberal and Christian lines was indeed available in the language of responsibility and obligation, parents and children. It was easy, then, to classify the newly acquired subjects as immature, childlike entities in need of proper uplifting and tutelage. The master signifier under which this project was carried out was of course civilization; but just as in Jefferson's days, the perennial and decisive question was who might count as a full and sovereign person, the foundation of any given sovereign liberal nation. At some future and unspecified date, then, these wards would become capable of governing themselves. The catch was law and order, the establishment of which might initially require large-scale exertion of military violence, or, to use another term, pacification.

---

16 On this development, see Leibowitz, *Defining Status*, passim. On Puerto Rico, see *Foreign in a Domestic Sense: Puerto Rico, American Expansion, and the Constitution*, edited by C. D. Burnett and B. Marshall (Durham, NC, 2001).

An obvious model for the whole concept and process was available near to hand in the treatment of the Amerindian population at home.

It was partly here, too, that the solution was found to a second, more specific problem, for which the Constitution offered no answer. Could the Union, whose reunited body had demonstrated its restored health and vigor in the war, add territory that was not meant to become a state, a real part of it? Not for the first time in American history, it was left to the courts to decide a politically difficult issue. Justice White, in the Insular Cases of 1901, came to invent accordingly the important distinction between incorporated and unincorporated territories, the latter to be designated for such purposes as Congress might find fit to determine, a view essentially confirmed, then, in the decisions of 1985. White's edict of 1901 verified that the body might now grow again but in a new fashion. Two separate but not necessarily incompatible concepts were at work. One the one hand, there was the ancient idea (first codified by Aristotle and given juridical form by the Romans) of instrumentality: tools of the sovereign self, be they things, human beings, or animals, to be used for whatever purposeful activity the master might choose. On the other hand, there was the curious idea of a body with appendages that are part of the body at the same time as they are not. The conceptual precedent, again, lay in the gradual subjugation of the Amerindians: a population that was both inside and outside the United States, subjects but not members of it. Even the pure externality of the instrumentalist perspective was ultimately compatible with the dominant liberal language of benevolence and uplifting of the retrograde or less fortunate. The central point, however, is that the United States now had a clear framework for keeping territory in subjugation in perpetuity and, accordingly, that people in these territories were not destined to become members of the Union of freedom or indeed necessarily ever free at all.[17]

Contrary to erstwhile hopes and predictions, the chief importance of these appendages turned out to be military rather than commercial, Panama perhaps offering the partial exception. The moment of

---

17   See, *passim*, references in previous footnote. See also the pathbreaking work of Efrén Rivera Ramos, *The Legal Construction of Identity: The Judicial and Social Legacy of American Colonialism in Puerto Rico* (Washington, DC, 2001) and "The Legal Construction of American Colonialism: The Insular Cases, 1902–1922," *Revista Juridica de la Universidad de Puerto Rico* 65 (1996): 227–328.

classical imperialism itself passed relatively quickly. After establishing the Caribbean basin as a de facto protectorate and an area of naval domination with rights of intervention, the United States assumed a more traditional posture of benevolent peace and rationality vis-à-vis the outside, often coupled with control, formal or informal, of the financial infrastructure, a "normality" punctured by sundry military interventions of the disciplining kind. There was no more direct territorial acquisition, the unprofitability of which had become obvious. After 1914 and the implosion of the entire world of "civilization," it was in any case impossible to speak fervently in favor of "empire." From now on, the term passes into the realm of the negative, though the liberal idea of tutelage would survive vigorously in the euphemistic form of "mandates" from the Versailles treaties to the UN system after 1945.

"Empire," then, went through two distinct phases as a political category and project. The initial "Empire for Liberty" was seen as a space of no determinate, stable boundaries, as a perpetual, open-ended colonizing process of republican reenactment in adjacent domains. This came to a crushing halt in the Civil War, which generated a kind of internal republican reenactment on the basis of a northern concept of liberty. The United States became a homeland, albeit a peculiar one. Eventually this consolidated body entered a second phase, which one might call the Empire of Civilization. The new colonial outside was grasped either as lastingly inferior (on racial grounds) or as subject (in the very distant future) to uplifting. The European Other, meanwhile, was deemed to be mired in various sclerotic states of declining civilization. This view was confirmed when Europe collapsed in conflagration, only to be saved to no little degree by the rising center of Western civilization across the Atlantic. In the first phase, "empire" signifies rule over extended territory with connotations of glory and world-historical significance, while in the second it becomes a sign of civilization and the obligation to engage in progressive control and direction of the uncivilized, a task that also entailed infusing them with the inherent virtues of commerce. This conceptual shift does not, however, take place on a continuous line: "empire" forms no coherent semantic or political field that can evolve over the entire historical period. In the antebellum period, the term is a convenient shorthand at times for the extraordinary process of border expansion. Its descriptive value then lies largely in its counterintuitive or even ironic qualities. The United States as empire is thus distinct because it is not imperial rule. This empire is homogeneous. In fact, it has no other object than the growth of the very principle of independence, the natural and proper system for the diverse desires of those capable of being free. What is outside the empire is either to be rendered identical with, and then included in, the homogeneity, or else only contingently and occasionally meaningful. In the second phase, by contrast, "empire" is reintroduced in ways that are conventional within Western standards at the turn of the century, that is, as *mission civilisatrice*. The object of the operation is now centered on subjugation and subjects. This is a bit troublesome, but not for too long.

Empire itself soon faded from the political horizon, the constituent issue of identity less so. Whereas the United States was of course absolutely different from the rest of the world in the first phase, the civilizational moment made it an integral part, although putatively the most advanced and enlightened, of the civilized world. As always, the notion of sameness and integration fit awkwardly within the political culture of the United States. It was only possible around 1900 because the development was quite distant and unimportant for the country as a whole. This was also why the potential contradictions and anomalies of the imperial edifice could be contained. None of it mattered very much. Though, to reiterate, the civilizational empire is still with us and an overpowering fact for those on the receiving end, Samuel Flagg Bemis was right in saying that its historical moment proper was brief and its ideological character suspect. It is another matter that the idealist vision of the United States he used as a measure of normality was a remarkably rosy one, if not a total fantasy. Uplifting and tutelage, in any case, have now gone on for more than a century, a fact that seems to trouble hardly anyone at all in the United States. With the partial exception of Puerto Rico, none of these insular possessions has had any organic impact on the body politic. Cuba, interestingly, began to have such an effect only at the moment when it broke militantly with the mold. Latterly, it has become absurdly important every four years because of the pivotal electoral votes of the state of Florida. Otherwise the lack of imperial concern is an expression of a rule so obvious that it is often ignored, insofar as it is even visible: the United States means more for and to the outside than the outside means for and to the United States.

Civilizational empire was succeeded by Woodrow Wilson's collective security, a project that could be (and indeed was) accused of un-American qualities on account of its multilateralism; but it actually preserved American exceptionalism in that the United States was conceived of as a unique mosaic lawgiver to the world. A failure but a grand one, Wilson's gambit also featured a vision of republican reenactment but now in the universal name of popular sovereignty understood as homeland. Collectively, these were to be assembled in a global compact of theoretical equality (though the firm leadership of the elect, in particular the United States and its political embodiment, Wilson himself, was presupposed throughout). Elevating self-determination to a universal principle, however, was entirely compatible with a revised version of *mission civilisatrice:* mandates for the benevolent development of colonial areas. Empire, in any case, had become a bad word and the United States made every attempt to call its relatively limited moves something else.[18]

World War II posed the Wilsonian question anew; but there was in fact nothing much Wilsonian about Rooseveltian grand strategy and nothing much Wilsonian about the cold war aftermath either. FDR himself was convinced that the historical time of European empires had passed, though as a good and orderly Progressive he was also as enamored with the idea of policing the unruly as he was with the idea of maintaining mandates. He can indeed be described as a second Bemisian aberration, for in his thinking, profoundly Progressive as it was, he presupposed no basic separation between the United States and the rest of the world, only a connecting line.[19]

The nature of the cold war is pertinent here to the extent that it served to recast and partly displace the issue of empire. A handy way of tracing this event is to begin with the incisive and always useful James Burnham, an intellectual of considerable political influence in the 1940s. Though "empire" had become politically incorrect as self-description, Burnham used it unabashedly in 1947 in calling for a global American presence in the fight against Communism. He wanted the United States, as he put it,

---

18   After World War II, sensitivity in this regard made even the word "possession" excessively blunt. See Peter C. Stuart, *Isles of Empire: The United States and Its Overseas Possessions* (Lanham, MD, 1999), introduction.

19   For more on FDR as an aberration, see chap. 12.

to become "world-dominating," by which he meant that it should be able to decide everywhere "the crucial issues upon which political survival depends." Keenly aware, however, that empire was now a suspect term, Burnham proposed to call his strategy something more pleasant-sounding, namely, "the policy of democratic world order." This approach, in all its essentials, was arguably the one adopted. In 1950, the foundational cold-war analysis of the Truman administration, NSC 68, took a position that was quite close to Burnham's, but without of course any reference to a US empire.[20]

The imperial referent tended to be reserved instead for the Soviet side and, in a very minor key, the older European empires in various degrees of decline. If the official line was not quite anti-imperialism (a term tainted by its featured place in Moscow's political lexicon), it was nonetheless against empire. To be against empire, then, meant chiefly to be against the Soviet Union. Though the language was that of liberty and freedom, it did not follow that one was against friendly empires (much less that one cared to remember one's own). Because they could be placed within the comforting historical narrative of gradual emancipation, empires of cold-war allies were not only acceptable but in some cases actually to be supported with heaps of aid. This was not an embarrassing contradiction. It followed from the cold-war matrix: everything that was not totalitarianism was freedom or potential freedom (freedom in the making). In consonance with the ideology of pacification and policing during the imperial period proper, it was easy to see that a stage of authoritarianism might well be necessary if the long-term interest of freedom were to be served in the zone of instability, which was indeed a very large zone of the free world.[21]

What was most analytically problematic for contemporaries in 1947 was not the Soviet empire but the rather more amorphous world of freedom, potential or real, and how one was to related to it. Two quite diverging concepts crystallized as to what this really entailed and the kind of world such leadership should or could create. By 1950 one of the two had emerged entirely victorious. As these positions, in their baldest

---

20 James Burnham, *The Struggle for the World* (New York, 1947), 53–5, 182–3, 221.
21 On the authoritarian/totalitarian distinction and the logic of supporting the former, see David Schmitz, *Thank God They're on Our Side: The United States and Right-wing Dictatorships, 1921–1965* (Chapel Hill, NC, 1999).

articulation, have a certain contemporary relevance, they deserve a word.

The first and losing perspective was represented by Burnham's central target within the Truman administration, the still powerful Kennan (but, let it be said, few others). Its essentials can be stated briefly. Kennan accentuated particularity. The United States, on this view, was only one nation-state among many others, though for historically specific and unexpected reasons it happened to be in a position where it was called upon to lead. To do so successfully, however, was to recognize the limited significance of the United States as an example for the world and the limited applicability of its particular norms for others. Imagining oneself as the embodiment of universal right was an error likely to cause serious policy mistakes, none more egregious than assuming the Wilsonian role of lawgiving (and, later on, the policy of militarization). The realistic object of policy, on the contrary, should be to build up the few traditional power centers in the world that could serve the equally traditional purpose of counterbalancing the Soviet Union. This, in turn, would initially necessitate a strong effort to make certain that these balancing centers would not in fact be open to Soviet penetration. Close allies such as Britain, meanwhile, were not newfound client states but equals fallen temporarily on hard times. Empire, in Kennan's scheme, was not a problem: it was a historical fact and as such beyond good and evil. Colonial powers civilizationally close to the United States should be supported against destabilizing nationalist opposition, though Kennan, as a meticulous reader of Gibbon, was also aware of the long-term difficulties in holding faraway provinces in subjugation. Some imperial cases were at any rate hopeless and better abandoned.[22]

The other view—let us call it universalist—was most forcefully expressed in NSC 68. Following Burnham, the analysis criticized (in muted form) containment for its allegedly passive qualities and, as mentioned, advocated a massively expanded US role in the world. Unlike the panoramic review of the world Kennan had offered in PPS 23 of 1948, NSC 68 was almost exclusively concerned with the United States and its monumental struggle against the Soviet Union. Other free

---

22 There is now a very substantial historiography on Kennan in this epoch. My own perspective, of which this paragraph is a condensation, may be found in *Kennan and the Art of Foreign Policy* (Cambridge, MA, 1989).

nations are mentioned in passing, mainly as supporting cast. They have no independent function. Moreover, the document places the struggle (to the point of obsession) within the global polarity of slavery and freedom.[23] To secure the space of freedom against the formidable world-conquering empire in the East, then, requires a commensurate exertion of effort, a sort of continuation of the successful mobilization of World War II against similar kinds of world conquerors: a total gathering of forces to fight the totalitarians. This, then, is a struggle to the death, a world war that, for purely contingent reasons, happens to take a cold form. To lead the embattled sphere of freedom in such circumstances is a call for command—imperium in the strictest sense of the word. Closer inspection thus reveals a second, internal distinction between the land of the free and the rest of the free world. The latter is conceived of not at all as a domain of autonomous, self-determining subjects but as clients in need of assistance (as indeed many of them successfully liked to portray themselves); or, alternatively, as troops to be called up, forces to be marshalled. This was entirely logical. If one declares (i) freedom to be the natural state of humankind, (ii) the perverse empire of slavery as the fundamental subversion of that state, and (iii) the United States as the (messianic) protector of the survival of true humankind as well as its the true embodiment, it follows that there can be no equals to that power even in the world of putative freedom. Amidst the larger dichotomous divide and the drawing of battle lines, it was impossible to accept as legitimate any desire on the part of free auxiliaries to choose anything but subservience. Choosing wrong was to turn away from right, as defined by a supreme power invested with the authority to correct waywardness. Having no equals, then, meant full assumption of the obligation to lead, protect and conquer, the right to command.

The vision of a final struggle between freedom and slavery was a good domestic strategy for the permanent mobilization of the United States abroad, but it had shortcomings as global prescription since, elsewhere, the cold war was not always similarly conceived of and the sundry interests of the free world could not be controlled according to the principle of command. There was accordingly an inherent discrepancy between the theoretical claim to command in a global war, the supreme right to decide, and the actual conflicts, indeed the actual structure of the world.

---

23 On NSC 68, see chap. 2.

In one respect, certainly, the thrust outward resulted in something rather like Burnham's ideal. For the creation of military alliances and base installations across the globe put the United States in the position of potential commander over immense areas. As conquering the citadels of evil proved impossible, what followed was in fact a version of nineteenth-century imperial pacification and policing, where, typically, no war was ever declared but put forth as corrections of a disorderly, diseased, and abnormal state. Yet even if there were in fact regions of utter domination (for example, Latin America), the totality was not an integrated imperial system proper but a complex, overlapping series of power networks with no single governing center or logic. Economic circuits followed quite different rules, ideology yet others. Thus international capitalism was reconstructed under US auspices but remained only partly under its adjudication. Immensely powerful economically and militarily, the United States could in fact afford to take a relatively generous view of the economic aspect as long as the military system remained intact. Witness the lenient and open attitude toward Japanese capital in the 1950s. Meanwhile, a diffuse sort of ideological power, chiefly in the form of commodified mass culture, proved hugely successful, even withstanding the moment of profound US delegitimation when the great effort to combat the Empire of Slavery bogged down on the uncongenial terrain of Vietnam and the truth of the thrust was revealed as its opposite. The enormous disparity between the United States and everybody else in the 1950s, then, was thus the condition of possibility for the differentiated system that combined, to put it simply, a militarist structure of domination with a managed, liberalizing international economy and a diffuse ideological culture of mass consumption.[24]

These complexities and the absence of any formal empire generate, as indicated earlier, the urge to rewrite empire as metaphor. The alternative, hegemony, is thus sometimes preferred because it allows for differentiated power and also for consent on the part of auxiliaries and

---

24 Here I am following Mann's concept of a differentiated and contingently combined set of power structures: economic, military, ideological, and political. He has used it to good effect recently in his incisive study of the United States, *Incoherent Empire* (London, 2003); but I note that he is still using "empire" as though the idea were not in need of problematization as such. The imperial aspect, so prominent in his first volume of *Social Power*, disappeared strangely enough in *The Sources of Social Power: Volume II, The Rise of Classes and Nation-States, 1760–1914* (Cambridge, 1994).

subjects. It is a more accurate description of how the structure looked. Consent tends, however, to eclipse the coercive component to the point of total obscurity. In less able hands, hegemony thus becomes a mere euphemism for Cicero's old idea that the imperium was really a patrocinium, a form of benevolence or guardianship for the benefit of everyone involved, an idea that James Harrington in seventeenth-century England would resurrect in an expansionist republican frame. Often, then, hegemony turns out merely to mean anointed leadership without the connotations of dominance encapsulated in the original Greek concept.[25] And ultimately the universal claims of the United States in the struggle to the death featured the right to decide on pain of immense violence.

Reiterating and revising Burnham's suggestive proposition, one might say that the United States was at very least claiming the negative right to decide how the crucial issues could *not* be decided. This, in turn, was but a permutation of the nineteenth-century invention represented by the Monroe Doctrine, as it developed from 1823 down to the Roosevelt Corollary of 1904: declaring an irreversible, territorialized political principle as well as the basic right to eradicate any threats to it. Leading the free world, then, was doubtless an imperial gesture, a declaration of sovereignty over sovereigns. It was not, however, an expression of any logic of empire. In other words, one cannot derive the will to supremacy from any imperial function. The effect was imperial but the sources of US conduct lie elsewhere.

---

25 Hegemony does have the advantage of allowing one to think the East-West division as a thousand-year demarcation down the Elbe and the kind of differences in modes of rule and dominance it has generated. Yet one should then recall that if Gramsci saw the absence of civil society and inverse dominance of the state in the East, he underestimated the coercive power in the West. Given the emphasis on the consensual dimension of hegemony here, it is interesting that US officials in the 1950s used the term to describe the evil Soviet empire: it appears for instance in NSC 68 and in the Solarium exercise of the early Eisenhower administration. On guardianship and patrocinium, see Robert M. Kallet-Marx, *Hegemony to Empire: The Development of the Roman Imperium in the East from 148 to 62 B.C.* (Berkeley, CA, 1995); James Harrington, *The Commonwealth of Oceana: A System of Politics*, ed. J. Pocock (Cambridge, 1992), 221–3; and Nicholas Greenwood Onuf, *The Republican Legacy in International Thought* (Cambridge, 1998), 128–31. I have learned much from David Armitage on this topic, specifically from his "The Origins of Anti-Imperialism in Early-Modern Britain" (unpublished paper).

And so Jefferson's Empire for Liberty, contrary to his every wish, ended up a belligerent power with massive military forces and corrupting interests everywhere. Of the eventual setbacks and gradual loss of clarity here, I will say little. Even in the West, at one point, imperialism gained credence as a designation for the foreign policy of the United States. The end of the cold war proper in 1963—the end, that is, of the struggle to the death after it had very nearly produced that death in global conflagration-combined with the continuing disaster in Vietnam, was also the end of the imperial gesture as a universal claim to sovereignty. Henceforth, the United States would make its moves on the grounds of more conventional interests, namely, the particular interests of a Great Power. The destruction of Salvador Allende's regime in 1973 and the interventions in southern Africa may stand as examples. Once again, however, particularism proved an unstable foundation, its limitations exposed with the greatest clarity by the succeeding popularity of Ronald Reagan's pastiche of a crusade in the early 1980s.

Reagan's reinvention of the cold war, replete with massive transgressions in the name of final battles, was of course predicated on the persistence of something that could be construed as an Evil Empire. The subsequent implosion of the Soviet counterpoint in 1989–91 thus served to radically confuse things. The absence of ideological polarity robbed the situation of any clear strategic meaning. Confusion, however, mattered little now. That neither of the two approaches the United States adopted toward the world in the 1990s had any extensive grounding in the political culture was of no great consequence. There was first George Bush the Elder's ill-fated New World Order, a very short moment of limited geopolitical realism in the name of international multilateralism and legality. It was followed by Bill Clinton's more and better globalization. Centered on the US economy, Clinton's policy was coherent and, for a while, hugely successful. When perpetual capitalist expansion ceased to be perpetual, the policy had run its course. Behind it, politically, was nothing. What followed instead after the spectacular terror of September 11 was a new line with very deep roots indeed.

What ensued was in fact a full-fledged version of the always-latent notion of the United States as a world empire; and the moment has come, in conclusion, to return to this suggestive notion of Otto Hintze's, not as self-description but as a way of thinking about the sources of US conduct. The material underpinnings for the thrust to global supremacy were of course already present in the 1990s: massive military superiority, economic and political hegemony on a global scale. No matter how indispensable the United States was supposed to be, there seemed to the unreconstructed activists to be something humdrum and petty-minded about ever-increasing doses of free trade. The alternative—a vigorous and invigorating form of imperial rule for the benefit of universal (American) values, centering initially on the Middle East and the surrounding regions but with the rather more ambitious ultimate aim of effecting regime change in the People's Republic of China, the one potential future threat—was facilitated enormously by the monumental event of September 11; but it is important to recollect that this vision was already well worked out by neoconservatives during the sordid, disappointingly successful days of Bill Clinton. It was a potent combination of secular and religious (or more precisely, Protestant, as some of the most vocal opposition to it originated in some Catholic circles) messianism: the notion that the United States has a historically or theologically grounded right and duty to remake or save the world according to its own universally valid, timeless principles. Just like Rome or for that matter the regime of the Celestial Mandate in imperial China, the United States can never have an equal in the world. Even regimes that are linguistically, culturally, and politically similar can never be conceived of as identical to the United States. The outside, in short, exists de facto but cannot be recognized as qualitatively equivalent. The difference here between Rome and China on the one hand and the United States on the other is that nonrecognition for the former means that the outside, however much of a nuisance in reality, is essentially meaningless, a conceptual nullity; whereas for the latter, it is something that is by definition always problematic in the sense that it must either be actively rejected or actively reworked.

The vast ambition, in any event, of the geostrategic rulers around George Bush the Younger to achieve global domination, the unapologetic revision of the Burnham model of empire from a negative right to disallow disagreeable decisions by minions wherever one might see fit to a positive right to change regimes in the biblical likeness of the United States—this ambition is already running afoul of its own systemic preconditions. For not only is the moment of such integrated empires long gone, so too is the very possibility of projecting an integrated form of universal power in the name of any particular power. The differentiated and highly vulnerable structure of twenty-first-century capitalism permits no such thing, as the United States is now discovering. Violent disruption on an unimaginable scale by small, mercurial forces is now an always-present threat. Meanwhile, the circuits of inexorably expanding capital require only the predictability of law and order, not the kind of violent disorder and illegalities brought about by the will to empire.

10
Kennan's *Abendland*: On Nationalism, Europe, and the West

Geography, writing the earth, is an activity of the greatest political moment. It begets boundaries, territories, claims and counterclaims. It names—sometimes with a vengeance. Less immediately, it also fashions our geopolitical imagination, the way we think the world as a series of spatial units that relate to each other in certain ways.[1] My concern here—or call it a curiosity—has to do with Europe and the West, two diffuse and sometimes discordant categories within this imagination.

It is often recognized that the West is not so much a place, or even a space, as a political and cultural aspiration, one side of a dualism that, however ancient, has shown great variations in its actual geographical referent. That Europe, too, is an uncertainly located place is less clear. Continents, our greatest territorial blocs, are also supposed to be the most natural ones and so devoid of any deeper political content. Yet Europe is arguably nothing more than an Asian peninsula, the product (crudely put) of faulty cartographical knowledge in antiquity and sundry prejudices since. Its boundaries have, now and then, been up for grabs, as indeed they are in our present epoch. The Soviet implosion and the letting loose of what, in bad metaphorical language, used to be called its satellites have put into question once again where Europe begins and what it might mean, thus wreaking havoc on, among other things, the

---

1 On space and politics, see Gearoid O'Tuathail, *Critical Geopolitics: The Politics of Writing Global Space* (Minneapolis, MN, 1996).

Franco-German project of making Europe synonymous with a judiciously expanded version of the European Union. Meanwhile, the notion of Central Europe, long since thought vanished, has reappeared, chiefly perhaps to allow former Eastern Europeans to rid themselves of a perceived geographical stigma. But what is East and West and European here is not at all clear anymore.

I shall pursue these issues through the odd vehicle of one of the most notable American policymakers and public intellectuals in the last century, George F. Kennan. Kennan fascinates because he seems so sublimely contradictory: the preeminent cold warrior who becomes a strong advocate of peace and nuclear disarmament while insisting that he never changed his views; the policymaker who argues for the division of Europe after the war and then becomes staunchly critical of it when this policy becomes reality; the opponent of US interventionism in the third world who is also a defender of colonial empires; the historian and intellectual who blames intellectuals for Bolshevism and for the uprisings of the 1960s; the defender of Western freedom who hates market society and favors rigid conservative hierarchy; a reactionary communitarian long before communitarianism in more anodyne form becomes voguish. Yet beneath the surface there are constants and coherences. One of them is Kennan's profound antipathy for nationalism and obverse attachment to something he liked to think of as the West, an entity anchored in Western Europe but geopolitically and civilizationally defined against a whole range of possible ills and enemies.

The spatiotemporal concepts of this orientation will be the starting point for more general considerations.[2] I place—and this is the crux—Kennan's position in the context of primarily German Catholic ideas in the 1920s about the West, the *Abendland*, understood as a supranational and symbolic space between Bolshevik Russia and capitalist America. My claim is that Kennan came to develop close affinities with this view, which was antimaterialist, antisocialist and antiliberal at the same time as it was hierarchical and organicist. Based on an idealization of medieval Christian Europe, *Respublica Christiana*, its organizing concept

---

2 Much of the contextual material on Kennan stems from Anders Stephanson, *Kennan and the Art of Foreign Policy* (Cambridge, MA, 1989). My original impetus for this essay was a realization that I had failed to do anything interesting with the problem of religion in that book.

was that of the premodern Catholic West and, partly for that reason, it could never easily turn nationalist, nor indeed fascist. As any truly Catholic position must be, it was contrary to nationalism without thereby becoming internationalist. In mutated form, this view then played an important role in the political revamping of Western Europe after World War II.

To those familiar with Kennan, such a Catholic connection may seem nothing less than bizarre. He was always a Presbyterian paragon, a Calvinist of brooding introspection and exemplary work ethic. Paucity of sources has indeed made my account one of inferences about affinities and resemblances rather than one properly sanctioned by empirical evidence.[3] Yet the connection makes sense if it is seen not as a matter of explicit theology but as a "symptomatic sensibility." I borrow the term from Lutz Niethammer. He uses it to describe the group of intellectuals of varying political persuasions who came to theorize what they perceived as the petrification or freezing of the West into an endlessly accelerating reproduction of sameness. In the 1930s, this dystopian vision of a techno-social megamachine moving fast toward hypertrophy (or posthistory) was encapsulated by Hendrik de Man in a string of suitably ugly nouns: "Massification, bureaucratization, depersonalization, autonomization and unmanageability of giant apparatuses."[4]

---

3   After writing the initial version of this article, I learned (through William Miscamble) that Kennan had just become a high Episcopalian—as close to Roman Catholicism as one can come and still remain a Protestant. The tone of the commentary on religion in George F. Kennan, *Around the Cragged Hill: A Personal and Political Philosophy* (New York, 1993) is pertinent. Roman Catholicism is to be respected "for its grandeur in scope and concept; for its very catholicity; for its paternal understanding for the needs of humble people everywhere; for its recognition of the values of order, and even hierarchy, in the spiritual guidance of great masses of people, etc." In short, the Roman church is "one of the greatest institutions of Western culture," and much of the same is true "for some of its partially rebellious children—outstandingly, the Church of England" (49–50). Interesting parallels and differences might also be drawn with the peculiar cultural politics of the Anglo-Catholic converts of the interwar period, the Evelyn Waughs, the Graham Greenes and the T. S. Eliots, especially perhaps the American expatriate, spiritually and physically twice removed as he was from the materialistic abyss of St. Louis, Missouri, not only to England but to *Catholic* England. There is another essay to be written about this angle.

4   See Lutz Niethammer, *Posthistoire: Has History Come to an End?* (London, 1994); De Man's quotation on p. 99. See also in this context Jeffrey Herf, *Reactionary Modernism: Technology, Culture, and Politics in Weimar and the Third Reich* (Cambridge, 1984).

The depiction may well serve, too, as a summary of Kennan's own, deeply pessimistic view of the industrial world, capitalist or socialist. "Massification" is indeed part of the problematic here, if not its point of articulation.

I will first outline Kennan's understanding of nationalism and how it fits into his political formation in the interwar period, noting its connections with the contemporary discourse on the Abendland. I then trace the alternative notion of Europe in its various versions up to the diverging political projects of Paneuropa and Mitteleuropa in the 1920s. Finally, I connect this to Kennan again in the context of what happened to these European/Western projects after World War II. The format is essayistic and not at all linear.

In the summer of 1953, when Kennan felt he had been unceremoniously fired by the new Eisenhower administration, he pondered whether "some relatively cheap part of Europe" would not be a better place to live. There was, however, an obstacle. "Children," he wrote wistfully to a friend, "insist on having some sort of nationality." He himself, then, was not about to insist on any such thing, much less fall into gushing sentiments of nationalism. Yet, as he would recognize later on, human beings appear to have "a universal need" to belong to "something larger than themselves." Why this upholder of the national interest so detested nations and nationalism is a question that must thus be followed by another and more interesting one, namely, to what sort of larger entity Kennan himself might belong, if not the nation.[5]

Nationalism is a subject about which, interestingly, Kennan has said fairly little in his long career. There are glancing references here and there; but only in *Around the Cragged Hill* (1993) does he finally offer a more sustained analysis. The relative silence is itself an expression of disdain, coupled perhaps with a recognition that the subject is fraught with danger and best left alone. But there can be no doubt: Kennan despised nationalism. What is more, his contempt included American nationalism (and its mirror image, universalism). He also found the United States too big for its own good and would have preferred, I think,

---

5 George F. Kennan to Charles Thayer, July 7, 1953, George F. Kennan Papers (henceforth GFKP), Box 3, Mudd Library, Princeton University, Princeton, NJ; Kennan, *Cragged Hill*, 74.

some form of regionalization of North American sovereignty. "People," he argued, "are not meant to live in such vast, impersonal political communities." The nation-state was not to be fetishized: here today, gone at some point, if not tomorrow then perhaps in a not too distant future. It was certainly not the end of history, or indeed any worthwhile end in itself.[6]

His pokes at the prevailing wisdom on the subject had three targets: right-wing nationalism (the most extreme being fascism); liberal (especially Wilsonian) ideas about peoples and linguistic groups having intrinsic rights to territorial self-determination; and, most saliently, revolutionary third world nationalism. He was most voluble about the last, which he referred to as "the fanatical and childish passion of native nationalism." His hostility here went far beyond the discomfort typical of other American policymakers after World War II when, as leaders of the free world, they confronted vexing issues of national liberation. Their dilemma, simply put, lay in having to combine the Wilsonian principle of national self-determination with the geopolitical imperative of keeping the anti-Soviet bloc solidly together amid allied colonial reassertion. The result, not surprisingly, was a mishmash. Kennan suffered from no such equivocation. To condemn colonialism was to engage in undue generalization, to distort the particular realities at hand. Believing in the right of natural rulers to rule, he also believed that there was nothing inherently wrong with colonialism. Hence there could be nothing inherently right in anticolonialism and national liberation movements. In fact, in virtually every case there was something wrong with them. Contrary to his nominalist claims, Kennan actually

---

6   George F. Kennan, *Democracy and the Student Left* (Hutchinson, 1969) 234–5. See also Kennan, "How New Are Our Problems," *The Illinois Law Review* 45:6 (January–February 1951), 718–30. As Kennan wrote to me: "I have come to the conclusion that the really great countries, such as China, Russia, ourselves, and perhaps India and Brazil as well, are dangers both to themselves and to others." Letter to the author, April 3, 1997. Perhaps his most eloquent denunciation of nationalism appears in *The Fateful Alliance: France, Russia, and the Coming of the First World War* (New York, 1984), 256–7: "In the view [the nation-state] takes of itself it is admiring to the point of narcissism. *Its* symbols always require the highest reverence; *its* cause deserves the highest sacrifice; *its* interests are sacrosanct. The symbols, causes, and interests of its international rivals are, by contrast, unworthy, disreputable, expendable . . . One sees how the myopia induced by indulgence in the mass emotional compulsions of modern nationalism destroys the power to form any coherent, realistic view of true national interests."

subsumed the phenomenon of third world revolutions under a general description, for he read them through a proto-Bolshevik prism—neurotic intellectuals incapable of dealing with their insecurities, compensating for their hopelessly jealous attitude toward the West by means of fanaticism and revolution. Just as was fatally the case with the Russian intelligentsia and educated classes toward the end of the nineteenth century, so nationalism in the colonial world was largely an artificial Western import, alien to the historical context of the colonial and pre-colonial world alike. In any case, the West had no reason—moral, political or historical—to accept claims for national independence on the part of palpably immature peoples. It made no sense to think that the "mere trappings of self-determination can imbue them with qualities comparable to those of the advanced states of western Europe."[7]

His second target had to do with what he always saw as the silly liberal principle of national sovereignty in international relations (and its universalizing modern concomitant, self-determination). Here he was an unflinching realist. States, many of which are not even proper nations, differ in size and importance. Any realistic concept of international power should recognize these objective differences. Having no liking for the classical nation-state as such, he also argued that it was foolish to accept (unrealistically) that states everywhere had an inherent right to do whatever they wished within their own borders. National sovereignty, which never acknowledges any "law but that of its own egoism,"

---

7   George F. Kennan, lecture, September 19, 1949, GFKP, box 17; Kennan to Bohlen, April 3, 1952, GFKP, box 18. "I have always been wary of attempts to place phenomena in categories. I have, for example, never had thoughts, so far as I can recall, about empires in general. I have always had to ask: which empire, how, and when?" Letter to the author, April 3, 1997. On Kennan and third world nationalism, generally see my *Kennan and the Art of Foreign Policy*, chap. 4. The chastising experience of having been completely surprised by Tito's disassociation from Stalin in 1948 led to a curiously divided viewpoint on nationalism within the communist bloc. On the one hand, he tended to see nationalism where others, more in dogged cold-war fashion, detected world communist revolution. Thus he came to understand Ho Chi Minh and the Vietnamese revolution as preponderantly nationalist. This was a central argument in his critique of the US intervention. He also grew to respect and like Tito's project (a kind of domestic multinationalism in the name of external nationalism) itself. On the other hand, he could never bring himself to advocate unequivocal support for putative "Eastern European nations" in the 1940s and '50s just because it might undermine Soviet rule. Accordingly, he was far from jubilant later about the breakup of the Soviet Union.

must thus not be recognized as absolute. "Could anything be more absurd," he would ask rhetorically, "than a world divided into several dozens of large secular societies, each devoted to the cultivation of the myth of its own unlimited independence?" The endless "multiplication of sovereignties" he found pernicious. It made intelligent, prudent and moderate operation in the national interest harder (for existing states or Great Powers, that is).[8]

If the phenomenon of sovereignty brought forth his realist credentials, the problem of nationalism in a Western setting revealed a historicist bent. It was a matter of historical stages and "immaturity." Once upon a time, there had been a national moment in the West, but "the cult of national glory" was now only "an undesirable hangover from a romantic past." Having originated in German idealism and the French Revolution, nationalism was then, in the course of the nineteenth century, fueled by a series of factors: free-floating Romantic intellectuals, industrialization, mass entry into political society and the education of people without property status. The mix proved lethal. Indeed, it would take two enormous bloodbaths to overcome the spirit of nationalism in the maturing West. "Nationalism is a heady and dangerous wine," he mused darkly. "The restraint and dignity necessary to permit stability of behavior in a great power come only by long familiarity with the sense of national power."[9]

The notion of intoxication with attendant delusions and hangovers belongs to a language of diagnosis. Similar thinking, though stripped of temporal dynamic, marks the analytical centerpiece of his more settled

---

8 George F. Kennan, "History and Diplomacy as Viewed by the Diplomatist," *Review of Politics* 18, no. 2 (April 1956); Kennan, address, October 17, 1956, GFKP, box 19. To Kennan, communism and third world nationalism were both "dangerous and revolting" and of "similar origins and traits," showing "debasement and medievalism of international practice" (Kennan to Bohlen, January 22, 1952, GFKP, box 18). His realism, as he himself insisted, was in part directed against the kind of realism centered exclusively on nation-state sovereignty. But, again, most of his actual anger came to the fore when third world sovereignty was at stake, as when the US seemed to him to accept Nasser's expropriation of the Suez Canal in 1956.

9 George F. Kennan, unused paper, September 1959, box 26; Kennan, draft of article on Germany, GFKP, Box 25, 1949; Kennan, notes, GFKP, Box 26, folder IV. The term "heady wine" reappears in his *Memoirs 1925–1950* (Boston, 1967), 416. On his view of nationalism in the nineteenth century in the Russian and European context, see Kennan, *Decline of Bismarck's European Order: Franco-Russian Relations, 1875–1890*, (Princeton, 1979), 417–19.

argument in *Around the Cragged Hill*. The fundamental premise here is a division between normal and pathological versions of national sentiment, the former being ordinary, fairly low-key feelings of patriotism that recognize faults and strengths alike, the latter a "diseased form" marked by "mass emotional exaltation," a sort of transference of the romantic glorification of the individual to a national scale. The pathological theme makes sense, given that the disease appears not only in the third world but in Western, democratic countries as well. If normality is Western to begin with, and the nation-state can be viewed as a normal part of its history, then contemporary nationalism must be a radical breakdown in the ordinary workings of the body, an abnormality. In non-Western settings, however, perversion can then very well become the norm.[10]

The tentative distinction between normal patriotism and abnormal nationalism may be Kennan's symbolic resolution of something essentially unresolvable, allowing as it does the antinationalist supporter of the nation to remain a solid citizen, to avoid the impossible choice between cosmopolitanism and nationalism. The same distinction, in any event, became Catholic dogma in the interwar period when Pope Pius XI denounced "*immoderatum nationis amorem*" but endorsed, conversely, "*caritas patriae*." The English rendition of these terms can be found, for example, in the tracts that Carlton J. H. Hayes wrote against nationalism at the behest of Catholic authorities in the 1930s. (Catholic scholars in the Anglophone countries, one should note, wrote critically about nationalism long before it came under the massive scrutiny we now see.) A convert and well-known historian, Hayes was soon to be Franklin D. Roosevelt's ambassador to Franco's Spain. Later, he served as president of the American Historical Association. In the name of "ethical patriotism," Hayes condemned "exaggerated nationalism" as "the seizure of the collective consciousness by demagogues and agitators." The historical preconditions for this delusion he found in the advent of modernity—industrialization, technological change, urbanized mass society and "the unrestrained rise of individualistic competition and capitalism." Typically, Hayes also denounced communism, polar opposite of "tribal nationalism" but also modern, as a "poisonous form of materialistic internationalism." The coupling was conventional

---

10   Kennan, *Cragged Hill*, chap. 4.

enough. Yet behind it lurked, in the American context, another enemy as well, for the anti-Catholic pursuits of the Ku Klux Klan in the 1920s will still have been fresh in Hayes's mind. It made political sense to invoke the duty "to love devotedly and to defend the country" where one was born (as Pope Leo XIII had said already in the 1890s) in order to protect oneself from nativist onslaughts, from accusations of un-Americanism. After the Second World War, this desire to belong, to prove national allegiance, opened up the space within American Catholicism for anti-communism on a grand scale.[11]

Kennan never fell into that trap, stemming as he did from a very different background and being entirely clear on the dangers of domestic anti-communism. Nor, of course, did all Catholics succumb, as demonstrated for example by the *Commonweal*, the liberal Catholic magazine in which indeed Kennan occasionally found a forum for his critical views on the cold war. His historical perspective, however, was actually quite similar to Hayes's. For all three of Kennan's targets could be traced in some way to the transformations of the nineteenth century, when nationalism and industrialism, twin evils, destroyed the old balance-of-power system and eventually produced World War I. For him, in fact, the Great War was the pivotal disaster that would govern the whole trajectory of the tragic twentieth century. The War dissolved the old polyglot Habsburg Empire; provided fascism with its climate of

---

11 Carlton J. H. Hayes, *Patriotism, Nationalism and the Brotherhood of Man*, (Washington, DC, 1937), 43, 23, 24, 33 and *passim*. On Hayes, see Peter Novick, *That Noble Dream: The "Objectivity Question" and the American Historical Profession* (Cambridge, 1988), 174n, 243–4, 322. As Novick points out, most prominent Catholic historians were converts. The profession, overwhelmingly Protestant, distrusted Catholic scholars. For a different view on Hayes, see Philip Gleason, "American Catholics and Liberalism, 1789–1960," in R. Bruce Douglas and David Hollenbach, eds., *Catholicism and Liberalism: Contributions to American Public Philosophy* (Cambridge, 1994), 45–75. On the politics of anti-communism, see Michael L. Budde, *The Two Churches: Catholicism and Capitalism in the World-System* (Durham, NC, 1992), chap. 4. See also Dorothy Dohen, *Nationalism and American Catholicism* (New York, 1967). Pluralism, I think, is the other side of anti-communist coin for American Catholicism in the 1950s. It opens up the possibility of being one of many in the American-Christian front against the communist threat. By then the collectivity principle embodied in the critique of capitalist individualism and materialism becomes transferred to the defense of a very safe American site: the family. Yet the conceptual problem remains. From a properly Catholic standpoint, there are inherent limits to the kind of nationalism one can promulgate. Ultimately the Papacy and the supranational community cannot be superseded.

growth; produced Bolshevism, the single most dangerous enemy the West had ever faced; created the conditions that would issue in World War II and so by, extension, the cold war. In a way, then, our present century is nothing but a long footnote to World War I, in itself the effect of pernicious nineteenth-century modernity, as condensed into nationalism.[12]

The biographical key here is to be found, not surprisingly, in the many years Kennan spent during the interwar period in countries such as Latvia, Germany, Austria, Czechoslovakia and the Soviet Union, witnessing at close range what he took to be (in many ways rightly) the sinister reverberations of the Great War. This was also the setting in which he articulated a politics of sorts, though typically never in the form of any stable attachments. Then, and later, he espoused support for some mainstream Western models—British parliamentarism and Norwegian social democracy—in line with his desire for governments that can be coherent, decisive, efficient and compact; but it is noteworthy that the two regimes he liked most in the 1930s and early '40s happened both to be authoritarian and strongly Catholic. Kennan already nourished a deep historical admiration for the Catholic Habsburg Empire and an obverse dislike for its dubiously national successor states. Yet it was the truly reactionary regimes of Kurt von Schuschnigg in Austria and António de Oliveira Salazar in Portugal that struck a particularly resonant chord in him. What distinguished these two from a whole host of other right-wing, corporatist dictatorships of the period was precisely their forthright allegiance to, and reliance on, Catholicism. Both typically also eschewed the fascist emphasis on the political party, favoring instead administrative programs imposed from above. Neither of them promoted any expansionist nationalism and both were radically antimodernist. When Schuschnigg promoted the medieval estates as a political ideal, his object was not so much national glory as the particularism of a traditional community combined with Catholic and necessarily transnational values.[13]

That Kennan should have found these two regimes not only palatable but praiseworthy had arguably to do with their antiliberal nature, not

---

12 His central statement in this vein is George F. Kennan, *Bismarck's European Order*. See also *Cragged Hill*, chap. 4.

13 See my *Kennan*, chaps. 1 and 2.

their Catholicism per se. Yet it was ultimately the specific character of their antiliberal system that appealed to him; and that character was, as mentioned, not divorced from their historical Catholicism. One should note that Kennan remained faithful to Salazar's legacy. As he wrote to me in 1995, the alternative to it, a policy of modernization, would very likely have transformed Portugal "into a single wretched industrial slum."[14]

I shall now shift to a potted history of the connection between nationalism, Catholicism and the particular ideology of the Abendland. The account lays no claim to any originality. It is merely a rudimentary genealogy for the purpose of argument.

A good starting point here is another proposition that Kennan sometimes mentioned in passing: nationalism was not only romantic but secular. In that word lies a history of its own.

The historical preconditions for nationalism, according to Benedict Anderson's influential view, were the coincidental advent of print capitalism and Protestantism in the sixteenth century, which made possible vernacular language identities within given territorial sovereignties. Not until the late eighteenth century, however, did this actually issue in what we now think of as nationalism. Nations in the sense of imagined communities existed before (as the primordialists insist) but not in a popular, political manner. It was chiefly (but unintentionally) through the French Revolution and its aftermath that nationalism assumed its modern form, proposing the universal right to territorial control based on cultural particularity as expressed in a unique language. This latter aspect was what Kennan liked to refer to as "romantic." Thus liberalism (at least on the continent) began to envision the future as a harmonious series of popular nationalities, each with its own unique properties, each contributing to the progressive evolution of rationality and peace among humankind. The archetype of this position is Guiseppe Mazzini, as he articulated it in his movement to unify the Italian peninsula against the strong opposition of the Papacy.[15]

---

14   George F. Kennan to the author, March 13, 1995.
15   Benedict Anderson, *Imagined Communities: Reflections on the Origin and Spread of Nationalism* (London, 1991). Against Eurocentric notions, Anderson emphasizes the role of New World creoles in the emergence of nationalism. For the best primordialist account, see Anthony Smith, *The Ethnic Origins of Nations* (Oxford, 1986).

A contributing factor to this liberal move away from eighteenth-century cosmopolitanism was that Metternich's restoration project after Napoleon was firmly antinational and antiliberal.[16] Over time, however, the contingent form of the European nation-state began to take on the air of universal history, the appearance of a natural terminus of civilization. But, contrary to liberal expectation, the nation also became available for openly reactionary purposes, as evidenced most clearly by the official nationalism of tsarist russification. After the failed revolutions of 1848, continental liberalism of Mazzini's type was in fact often subsumed by these more menacing forms of nationalism. As industrialization and the extension of political society increasingly came to take place within rigidly demarcated nation-states, politics and class practices turned national. Leaping advances in the technology of warfare abetted this development by wedding state, militarism and industry. Nationalism was an ideology that fit that common project. And thus, despite their overt attachment to rationalism, materialism and various forms of internationalism, socialists and liberals alike went to war in 1914 under national banners.[17]

The transformation within the French Revolution from the antinationalism of the Jacobin people's republic to a nationalist movement of sorts is more complex than commonly thought. Robespierre attacked any consecration of national sovereignty as egoistic and contrary to the appeal to humankind as such; patriotism was merely citizen solidarity with principles of self-government and was not exclusivist. He was also against revolutionary war. But the Revolution needed time and sovereignty was a handy device to preserve the gains. The defeat of the Revolution, after all, would be a defeat for humanity. To preserve it, indeed, one would have to suppress foreign influence and agents domestically along with the enemies of the people. Thus the discourse of raison d'état reappeared. In the end "the internationalist army defaulted into an army of republican patriotism, the brotherhood of nations gave way to a reenactment of the imperial conquests of the ancient Roman Republic" (Istvan Hont, "The Permanent Crisis of a Divided Mankind: 'Contemporary Crisis of the Nation State' in Historical Perspective," *Political Studies* XLII, 1994, 223). One recognizes the logic of the historical sequence.

16   Metternich, a Catholic Rhinelander by origin, told Wellington that "l'Europe a pris pour moi la valeur d'une patrie" (E. L. Woodward, *Three Studies in European Conservatism: Metternich: Guizot: The Catholic Church in the Nineteenth Century* [London, 1963], 18). In the Habsburg Empire he had reconstructed after Napoleon, he saw a confederational model for Europe as well as a vehicle to move civilizationally eastward, albeit in a prudent and nonmessianic way.

17   See, aside from Benedict Anderson, Michael Mann, *The Sources of Social Power: Volume II, The Rise of Classes and Nation-States, 1760–1914* (Cambridge, 1993). On czarist symbology, see Richard Wortman, *Scenarios of Power: Myth and Ceremony in Russian Monarchy, vol I: From Peter the Great to the death of Nicholas I* (Princeton, 1995).

This is a fairly conventional but important story; and it allows us to see the possibility of another opposition to nationalism. For if the French Revolution is the decisive national event that gives political content to ideas of cultural difference and popular self-determination, then we must look closer at the conservative reaction to it, indeed at the very invention of the reactionary itself. It is here that the Catholic counter-revolutionary tradition is of interest because in some ways it offered the most forceful opposition to popular nationalism in nineteenth-century Europe. The reason is not hard to see. The inescapable fact remained that it was the Protestant Reformation that had cut the *Respublica Christiana* asunder, finally shattering the Catholic medieval world that had combined a wide, normative community of Christian culture with an enormously variegated series of overlapping jurisdictions and local particularities. Thus, in early modern Europe, there had emerged a set of realms of inviolable borders controlled by secular rulers, in turn opening up the space for a moment when religion as such could be replaced by nationalism as the foundation of state and society. From a Catholic point of view, then, the target was not only the secular occupation (both conceptually and territorially) of a previously religious domain, but also the democratic pretensions of popular autonomy and self-determination: the twin ideas of the sovereignty of the individual over his own person (the individual was still a he) and the sovereignty of the nation-state that these sovereign individuals presumably produced in the aggregate through various contracts or constitutions, all spurious. Relatedly, the privilege accorded to reason had to be rejected because of the inherent potential for skepticism. Truth was a product, not of individual reason, but community tradition as interpreted, codified and institutionalized by the Church, the indispensable mediator between God and humankind. Thus religion could never be a private matter, one sphere among others in a secular and material society, for nothing was ontologically outside the supernatural.

Liberal Catholics in the nineteenth century were less inclined to wholesale condemnation of the French Revolution, and they wanted to make more room for accepting modern change. But even relatively open Catholics had difficulty escaping the notion that popular rule was inherently anti-Christian because it was inherently volatile: changing political authority was incompatible with constant religious control and integralist conceptions of society. The idea that atomized individuals, gathering together in some forum supposedly expressive of the national will and thus invested with supreme command over all affairs human— this notion of state *secularization* was for obvious reasons exceedingly difficult even for liberal Catholicism to accept. The French Revolution, after all, had annexed the papal domains in France on the authority of plebiscites (and Napoleon himself had gone on to annex the Papal States). On the whole, in fact, the Catholic outlook had nothing but scorn for modernizing, national identity making and the mechanical sovereignties of atomized individuals. Catholic reaction, in short, was counterrevolutionary, antiliberal and antinationalist.[18]

The moment of the French Revolution is also when the notion of a medieval Abendland gains political currency.[19] Throughout the nineteenth century, Germanic Catholics tended to prefer the term "Abendland" to "Europe"—for the latter denoted Protestantism, nationalities and individual sovereignty. Philologically, the term had first entered German as the semantic counterpoint to Luther's translation of "the Orient (Sunrise/East) as *Morgenland*. From the French Revolution onward, the Abendland was used against the pretensions of Enlightenment Europe, propagating the Middle Ages as the organic contrast to contemporary fragmentation. Novalis, in his famous prose poem of 1800, *Christendom or Europe*, evokes the Middle Ages as a

---

18 Reinhart Koselleck, *Critique and Crisis: Enlightenment and the Pathogenesis of Modern Society* (Cambridge, MA, 1979). See also Peter Steinfels's interesting article "The Failed Encounter: The Catholic Church and Liberalism in the Nineteenth Century," in Douglas and Hollenbach, eds., *Catholicism and Liberalism*, 19–44. On the vagaries of the Catholic reaction to reason, see Patrick W. Carey's excellent "American Catholicism and the Enlightenment Ethos," in William M. Shea and Peter A. Huff, eds., *Knowledge and Belief in America: Enlightenment Traditions and Modern Religious Thought* (Cambridge, 1995), 125–64.

19 Where not otherwise noted, the following account is based on Friedrich Heer's extensive article "Abendland," in *Meyers Enzyklopädisches Lexikon* I (Mannheim, 1971); Peter Bugge, "The Nation Supreme: The idea of Europe 1914–1945" in Kevin Wilson and Jan van der Dussen, eds. *The History of the Idea of Europe* (London, 1995); Heinz Gollwitzer, "Zur Wortgeschichte und Sinndeutung von 'Europa,'" *Saeculum* 2, 1951, 161–72; Gollwitzer, *Europabild und Europagedanke: Beiträge zur deutschen Geistesgeschichte des 18. und 19. Jahrhunderts* (Munich, 1951); Richard Wallach, *Das Abendländische Gemeinschaftsbewusstsein in Mittelalter* (Leipzig, 1928); Heinz Hürten, "Der Topos vom christlichen Abendland in Literatur und Publizistik nach den beiden Weltkriegen," in Albrecht Langner, *Katholizismus, nationaler Gedanke und Europa seit 1800* (Paderborn, 1985); Hans Hecker and Silke Spieler, eds., *Die historische Einheit Europas: Ideen—Konzepte—Selbstverständnis* (Bonn, 1994).

brilliant period of Christian-European unity under a single spiritual leader. But it was his contemporary Joseph de Maistre, counterrevolutionary intellectual par excellence, who shaped Abendland discourse more than anyone. Influenced by Edmund Burke's acid attack on the French Revolution and all rationalist projects of political engineering, de Maistre was a far more extreme figure than his Anglo-Irish source. Burke's foundation was after all "the ancient, civil, moral, and political order of Europe," as he put it, the order against which the French revolutionaries were presumably sinning egregiously by their mere existence.[20] For de Maistre, by contrast, it was the Papacy that formed the spiritual center. Moreover, beyond revolutionary France, he was also obsessed with neo-Byzantine Russia, which he saw as a new fanatical, despotic and mystical East. To this fear of rising Russia, de Maistre's political descendants in the nineteenth century would add another crucial ingredient, the fear of rising America and the image of a squeezed and tottering old Europe in need of spiritual rejuvenation.[21]

The Papacy, mired throughout in corruption and theological obscurantism, struggling to maintain its autonomy against nationalist forces on the Italian peninsula, allied consistently and crassly with reaction, even to the point of undermining the Polish Catholic independence struggle against Russia. Pius IX's Syllabus of Errors in 1864 was a good summary of all the modern ills to be condemned, liberal nationalism prominent among them. The principle of papal infallibility, then consecrated, was rightly read as partially directed against the spreading doctrines of national sovereignty and devolution of religious authority.[22]

---

20 For Novalis, I used the Swedish translation, *Kristenheten eller Europa* (Lund, 1992). See Franco Moretti, "Modern European Literature: A Geographical Sketch," *New Left Review* I, no. 206 (1994). On Burke in this context, see Fred Halliday, *Rethinking International Relations* (London, 1994), chap. 5, quotation on p. 112.

21 On de Maistre, see Henry H. Walsh, *The Concordat of 1801: A Study of the Problem of Nationalism in the relations of Church and State* (New York, 1933); and J. S. McClelland, ed. and introduced, *The French Right (from de Maistre to Maurras)* (New York, 1970).

22 Steinfels, "Failed Encounter"; Lawrence J. Taylor, "Peter's Pence: Official Discourse and Irish Nationalism in the Nineteenth Century," *History of European Ideas* 16: 1–3, 103–7; title notwithstanding, Hugh Trevor-Roper, "The Phenomenon of Fascism" in S.J. Woolf, ed., *Fascism in Europe* (London, 1968), contains interesting remarks on the Papacy.

But the Papacy was not identical with European Catholicism as a whole. Consider for example Lord Acton. The Anglo-Catholic scholar wrote incisively about nationalism in the 1860s while attempting to preserve his liberal credentials. The emergent identity of state and nation was fatal, he argued, because every state had to include many nationalities; and if one of them came to define the state, then the others would have to be repressed so as to maintain that constitutive national principle. Acton was thus fully aware of the power of nationalism, than which no politics was "more comprehensive, more subversive, or more arbitrary." He predicted it would destroy both absolute monarchy and socialism, its central enemies.[23]

Prescient words, no doubt, though their historical validation would have to await a later moment. Meanwhile, Acton had to be concerned with the effects of nationalism on causes closer to home. For the hardening realities of state power and international confrontation toward the end of the century undermined the antinational politics in practice. The continental right, Catholic or otherwise, was by then becoming fervently nationalist. In France, infamously, it signed up in compact lines to revile Dreyfus on precisely such grounds, though a good many centrist Catholics did so because the other side was so outspokenly anticlerical. In the Habsburg heartland, antisemitism and anti-Slavism were rampant amid ethnic strife and Germanic resurgence (very much so at the moment when the young Adolf Hitler arrived in Vienna). At the same time, a growing strand of right-wing irrationalism found political expression in heroic nationalism. Yet this moment also produced a range of what might be called ideologies of the third way, attempts to invent a politics that was neither capitalist (at least not the liberal, individualist, rationalist and materialist kind) nor socialist (in the sense of collectivism, class division, rationalism and materialism). And here Catholicism was perhaps the preeminent source of inspiration, propelled to no little degree by the relatively liberal reign of Pope Leo XIII. It was out of this raw material, in any event, that the trope of

---

23   Lord Acton, John E. E. Acton, *The History of Freedom and Other Essays* (London, 1907). The quotations are from the essay "Nationality," originally published in 1862 (299). On the peculiar history of Anglo-Catholicism, see Roger O'Toole, "Refugees from the National Myth: The English Catholic Odyssey" in R. O'Toole, ed. *Sociological Studies in Roman Catholicism: Historical and Contemporary Perspectives* (Lampeter, 1989).

the Abendland would be revived in the 1920s as a full-fledged ideology.[24]

I must now, however, break the chronology once again and bring in the competing concept of Europe. Where does it come from? We need another brief survey, this time of a few millennia.

Classical antiquity assumed that the world centered around the Mediterranean and had three parts, Asia, Europe, and Africa, or Libya, as it was also known. Herodotus rightly admitted 2,500 years ago that no one really knows where these names come from or for that matter why they are feminine ones. Europe, for him, began on the northern coast of the Aegean, but he was honest enough to admit ignorance of where it ended. In pitching his *History* around the distinction of Eastern despotism versus Western freedom, Herodotus can actually be said to have articulated the first known case of Abendland ideology. He also refers to the East as "the region of the sunrise," which points to the theory, appealing but probably inaccurate, that the Assyrian polarity between the land of the rising sun, "*asu*," and the dark counter-land of the angry gods, "*ereb*," eventually became Asia and Europe. The polarity would then have been transvalued by the Greeks: the rising sun becomes an Eastern negative, the evening land the Western positive.[25]

---

24 John Weiss, *Conservatism in Europe, 1770–1945: Traditionalism, Reaction and Counter-Revolution* (London, 1977); Woodward, *European Conservatism*; Paul M. Cohen, *Piety and Politics: Catholic Revival and the Generation of 1905–1914 in France* (New York, 1987); Trevor-Roper, "Fascism."

25 Herodotus, *The History* (Chicago, 1987), 259–60, 297–98. Unless otherwise noted, the sources for my survey are, first and foremost, Kevin Wilson and Jan van der Dussen, eds., *The History of the Idea of Europe* (London, 1995), from which I got a lot of the inspiration for this essay; Stein Rokkan, "Territories, Centres, and Peripheries: Toward a Geoethnic-Geoeconomic-Geopolitical Model of Differentiation within Western Europe," in J. Gottmann, ed. *Centre and Periphery: Spatial Variation in Politics* (Beverly Hills, CA, 1980); H. D. Schmidt, "The Establishment of 'Europe' as a Political Expression," *The Historical Journal* IX, 2 (1966), 172–8; Gollwitzer, *Europabild*; Jürgen Fischer, *Oriens-Occidens-Europa: Begriff und Gedanke "Europa" in der späten Antike und im frühen Mittelalter* (Wiesbaden, 1957); J. G. A. Pocock, "Deconstructing Europe," *London Review of Books*, December 19, 1991; Klavs Randsborg, "Barbarians, Classical Antiquity and the Rise of Western Europe: An Archaelogical Essay," *Past and Present* 137, 8–24; K. J. Leyser, "Concepts of Europe in the Early and High Middle Ages," *Past and Present* 137, 25–47; J. H. Elliot, "A Europe of Composite Monarchies," *Past and Present* 137, 48–71; Stuart Wolf, "The Construction of a European World-View in the Revolutionary-Napoleonic Years," *Past and Present* 92; Denys Hay, *Europe: the Emergence*

The division, in any case, ceased to have much meaning once classical antiquity became intercontinental through Alexandrian Hellenization and the Roman Empire. Cartographically, however, the ancient image survived more or less intact for almost two millennia. Indeed, the geography of the Middle Ages was in some ways inferior to its classical sources. Hence the great chronicler of universal history, Otto of Freising, could only repeat in the twelfth century the geographical account that Augustine's protégé Orosius had put forth in his famous *Apology* in the early fifth century; and Orosius himself was merely rehashing in attenuated form the vision of the ancients.[26]

Orosius's early Christian appropriation is nevertheless interesting because he pointed, as was customary, to the Don as the waterway separation between Europe and Asia; and therein would lie a source of great future difficulty. The very idea of continents presupposed water as the separating entity. One was compelled consequently (and aided by ignorance) to produce the image of a massive waterway, on the order of the Nile, cutting Asia and Europe apart as the continuation of an already exaggerated Sea of Azov. It would take another thousand years before geography began to realize that the future Russia was not a narrow isthmus, at which point one faced a conceptual problem.

After the fall of Rome and the disintegration of Mediterranean unity, it was the emergence of Muslim power in the south and the survival of the Byzantine Empire in the East that created the foundations for the real cultural invention of Europe. The first to appear under the proper name "Europeans" had been the Roman troops of the West around 200 CE. But Europe in our sense really begins, if only momentarily, when Charlemagne assumes the Roman imperial title in 800 as the putatively sixty-ninth emperor after Augustus. Muslim expansion had been stopped and Frankish power was in a position, therefore, to assume or translate the Roman heritage from Byzantium, the East. Accolades to Charlemagne speak of him as "rex, pater Europae." His Frankish Europe consisted roughly, as many have noted, of the same area as the future

---

of an Idea (Edinburgh, 1968); Christopher Dawson, *The Making of Europe* (New York, 1956). None of these authors is being invoked to validate the synthetic view I put forth here.

26 Otto of Freising, *The Two Cities: A Chronicle of Universal History to the Year 1145 AD* (New York, 1966, [repr. 1928 ed]); Orosius, *Seven Books of History Against the Pagans: The Apology of Paulus Orosius* (New York, 1936).

European Union, Britain not included. Yet this Carolingian idea of Europe was a fleeting geopolitical moment, replaced by the decentralized Christian community of the feudal period, bounded not by geography but by norms. For whatever its boundaries, Europe obviously contained a good number of heathens and hence could not be invested with any ideological surplus value.

The contours, meanwhile, of what will become our Abendland ideology emerged out of the Roman Papacy's struggle to establish doctrinal hegemony over Constantinople, the newer, Second Rome. Thus Gregor the Great in the late sixth century tried to mobilize the West in the name of something he called "societas reipublicae christianae." And throughout the Middle Ages the Pope would be the pre-eminent protector of the right-thinking peoples of the West, eventually also the organizer of the highest cultural and military expression of that orthodoxy, namely the crusades. For the targets of these forays were not only the Muslim world but also the mystical and heretical East of Byzantium.

A new concept of Europe, on the other hand, would not emerge until the decline of papal power and humanist and renaissance scholars began to invoke Europe as an essence of intelligence and light, in contrast to barbarian darkness on the outside and papal Rome's centralism on the inside. This trope would remain a constant, reinforced of course in the Reformation and lasting through the Enlightenment, when it became connected up with the discovery of civilization and culture. In the imperialist nineteenth century, *the* European century, civilization is understood for all intents and purposes as Europe and vice versa.[27]

A second, partly parallel and related notion of Europe was also articulated from the sixteenth century onward. Here the essence of Europe is its diversity, its pluralism, its very lack of a dominant center. This notion was used to combat all attempts at a Catholic universal monarchy, whether by the Habsburgs or subsequently by the Bourbons. The Treaty of Utrecht in 1713, putting an end to all such moves, recognized explicitly the principle of balance, the balance of power, as the right and fundamental way in which Europe does its business of war and peace. Edmund Burke and others would later attack both the Jacobins and Napoleon in the name of this basic European principle of plurality and equilibrium.

---

27 See Eric Hobsbawm, *The Age of Empire, 1875–1914* (New York, 1987), 18.

Neither of these concepts, light and balance, had anything much to do with the development of the geographical definition of Europe, which followed its own logic, more precisely that of Muscovy and Russia. The gradual realization, beginning in the fourteenth and fifteenth centuries, that this was a huge expanse of land and that the Don was not only nothing like the Nile in size but also did not flow to the extreme North—this realization occasioned a search for alternative waterways that could demarcate the continent. The search was ultimately unsuccessful. Few cared, however. The Russians themselves evinced little interest. The incentive for a real shift would have to await Peter's modernization project and his defeat of the Swedes in the early 1700s, which made Russia indisputably a Great Power in Europe (and eliminated Sweden from that select group). Peter's Europeanization had to include a properly European imperial status, and that necessitated in turn drawing a clear line somewhere internally between what was now supposedly a European metropole on one side and Asian colonies on the other. His chief geographer Tatischev, together with a Swedish officer, a prisoner of war who had drawn the first real map of Siberia, then came up with the Ural Mountains as the new "natural" border of Europe, thereby breaking the waterway paradigm that had reigned conceptually supreme for two millennia.[28]

Russian Pan-Slavists such as Nikolai Danilevsky in the 1860s would make fun of the arbitrariness of this allegedly natural border. Arguing that Europe was nothing but a peninsula of Asia and not a real continent, Danilevsky quite rightly went on to ask: "If the Urals separate two continents, then what do the Alps, the Caucasus, or the Himalayas separate?"[29] At the Ural Mountains, nevertheless, the border has

---

28 On Russia, Europe and geography, see the two excellent accounts by W. H. Parker, "Europe: How Far?," *The Geographical Journal* CXXVI, no. 3 (September 1960): 278–97, and by Mark Bassin, "Russia between Europe and Asia: The Ideological Construction of Geographical Space," *Slavic Review* 50, no. 1 (Spring 1991), 1–17. August Strindberg, in the late nineteenth century, was one of the first to pay proper attention to this remarkable prisoner of war. His admiring essay, "Philipp Joann von Strahlenberg, hans karta och beskrivning över Asien" (*Samlade Skrifter*, vol 4 [Stockholm, 1919]), is quite nationalistic, though Strahlenberg was actually born in Stralsund, then a possession within the Swedish Baltic Empire—hence his name. Strahlenberg spent thirteen years in Siberia, during which he produced the first decent map of the region, much to the subsequent interest of Tsar Peter.

29 Quoted in Bassin, "Russia," 10.

remained, geographically speaking, that is. The story of Russia and *political* Europe is more complicated. After Peter, Russia was understood for the next two hundred years as European, albeit odd and suspect. It was excommunicated because of the October Revolution of 1917. In the 1990s, it was thought to be once again becoming European—if not to undivided Western acclaim. And thus we may turn again to the Abendland.

The Bolshevik Revolution and the effects of the Great War served to crystallize the notion of the Abendland into a widely disseminated discourse in the 1920s. It became a catchword of the political vocabulary in 1919 through the publication of Oswald Spengler's *Der Untergang des Abendlandes*. Its English title, *The Decline of the West*, fails to convey the sense of imminent destruction in the German original, the "going under," rather like *Titanic*'s sliding into the dark and icy waters of the North Atlantic. Spengler, mostly concerned to articulate a cyclical theory of history and civilization in terms of biological morphology, never theorized his notion of the West, leaving it deliberately spiritual and vague—the suggestive wordplay on decline and the West/evening/setting sun is indicative. But he refused explicitly to identify the Abendland with Europe. Europe, to him, was a mere geographical expression of uncertain Eastern extension, artificial and mechanical, "an empty sound" as opposed to a spiritual essence. The real historical polarity was East and West. Russia, whose westernization Spengler considered unsound and ephemeral, was decidedly on the other side. Here he was of course reiterating Danilevsky's stance but inverting its Pan-Slavic value order.[30]

Though Spengler himself came from a Protestant background, his Abendland was picked up by Catholic thinkers as a way to rekindle images of an organic order in a European frame, whence could radiate a restored civilizational movement. When these thinkers founded a journal in 1925 devoted to European culture, politics and economics,

---

30 Oswald Spengler, *The Decline of the West: Form and Actuality* (New York, 1939), 16n. On Spengler, see Hans Erich Stier, "Zur geschichtlichen Wesensbestimmung Europas," in Anton Mirko Koktanek, *Spengler-Studien* (Munich, 1965); Heer, "Abendland"; Gollwitzer, *Europabild*; H. Stuart Hughes, *Spengler: A Critical Estimate* (Westport, CT, 1975 [1952]); Hürten, "Der Topos vom christlichen Abendland"; Herf, *Reactionary Modernism*, chap. 3.

they named it, symptomatically, Abendland. It was to be a West, then, that transcended the twin horrors of American and Soviet materialism, at the same time as it would not fall into simple nationalism and German revenge. The old Abendland opposition to Eastern Byzantium, to Eastern Islam, to Eastern Turks, could now be redeployed in opposition to Eastern Bolshevism and the spiritual emptiness of the materialist West. What these thinkers had in mind, more positively, was some form of neo-Carolingian reconstitution of Western Europe. At the heart, spiritually and geographically, of that project lay the Rhineland, the historic intersection between France and Germany, as well as the center of the Carolingian Empire, the space where Antiquity, Germanium and Christianity had met in the happiest of all syntheses. This modern simulacrum of the Holy Roman Empire would take the form of a new spiritual community, a *Geistesgemeinschaft*. One way or another, Abendland thought was in fact always an attempt to overcome the growing Western split between *Gesellschaft* and *Gemeinschaft*, society and community.

In the context of Kennan's politics, the conservative aspect of all this will have been attractive. For beyond Western revival, there were of course other aspects to this sort of politics: hierarchy and order, for example. Just as the idealized vision of the premodern Catholic West, the inheritor of all that was good in the pre-Christian classical world, made possible a kind of nonnationalist patriotism, so it permitted one to imagine a thoroughly integrated organic society run by the proper elites. The mass politics of fascism, loudly modern, was from this viewpoint an anathema. Not only did it deploy the new technological means of politics, it also centered strategically on mass mobilization, permanent political movement through a party. These features of fascism were utterly abhorrent, philosophically as well as personally, to Kennan. He always evinced a deep fear of—and revulsion for—anything that physically looked like collective movement: national flag-waving, working-class marches, disorderly students milling about in antiwar demonstrations, even Western victory celebrations. Anything amassed and aroused in the name of "abstractions," national or otherwise, was really "hysteria," bordering on fanaticism. His way of being toward the world, a sort of cult of existential solitude, was reflected in his consistent rejection of the general, the total, the abstract and the universal, his conservative insistence on the virtues of the particular.[31] Theological pretensions of the universal Church could however be overlooked in favor of its congenial catholicity, its local allowances for established ways of doing things. One is reminded in this context of Kennan's central reference text, Edward Gibbon's *Decline and Fall*. Gibbon was famously hostile to the fanaticism of early Christianity and its subsequent Byzantine strand (a view strongly echoed in Kennan's seminal analyses of the Soviet Union). But the historian of Roman decline took a fairly favorable view of the Papacy once it had become the institutional backbone of the cosmopolitan West. On some level, Gibbon's history was a reflection, like all Abendland projects, on the possibility of recasting cosmopolitan Rome in a Western European setting under novel conditions. What he had in mind was an enlightened community where Reason was a product of elite conversation and certainly not popular imposition of Right in the name of unequivocal Truth.[32]

Kennan's Abendland orientation, alas, is not directly provable. The argument remains a matter of symptomatic connections and elective affinities. Yet the case is not weak. He certainly read Spengler in Germany in the late 1920s. More saliently, the concept of the West in the sense of the Abendland and the concomitant theme of Western declinism would become lifelong concerns of his. So would the critique of materialism.

I want now, however, to relate the Abendland view to two more specific and diverging (Germanic) projects of European integration of the same period that can be summarized in the terms *Paneuropa* and *Mitteleuropa*. Seen in the context of the 1920s, they represented a response to the stark duality of nation-state and global universalism expressed in the Treaty of Versailles. Paneuropa and Mitteleuropa alike

---

31   Kennan, *Decline*, 418 ("hysteria"). See also Kennan, "Notes for international relations project," n.d. (1950?), GFKP, box 26. On Kennan's horror at mass politics, see Stephanson, *Kennan*, part III. I owe the pithy "existential" formulation to Perry Anderson. Another aspect of this solitary orientation is Kennan's characteristic reluctance to engage with, or rely on, anyone explicitly. Only when stung hard did he typically polemicize by name. His books of "opinion" are otherwise written as though outside any clearly demarcated debate, as though his thoughts issued from somewhere twice or thrice removed. His practice, when he ran the Policy Planning Staff in the late 1940s, of lugging off to the Library of Congress to write nearly all of the now legendary PPS studies himself, is part and parcel of the same disposition.

32   On Gibbon in this context, see J. G. A. Pocock, "Was He One of Them?," *London Review of Books*, February 23, 1995.

were supposed to be something more and something less than this, but above all something more organic, regional and functional.

Paneuropa was the invention of Richard Coudenhove (1896–1972), a striking aristocratic figure of Austrian Japanese parentage.[33] Initially impressed by the Pan-Islamic ideas of an Indian friend of his father and by the ancient example of the Pan-Hellenic league against Philip of Macedonia, Coudenhove came to interpret World War I as a conflict between Pan-Germanic and Pan-Slavic nationalism for the domination of Europe. Austro-German nationalism, the movement that produced Adolf Hitler, he found utterly odious; his own allegiance lay with the internationalism of the imperial-aristocratic elite and the cosmopolitan Jews. His underlying view of German history here was relentlessly dualistic: "the European and the anti-European, the southern and the northern, the Catholic and the Protestant, the Austrian and the Prussian." The demarcation of good and evil is clear enough. The dualism is not dissimilar from Kennan's, when he traced the German past after the war in terms of a polarity between the Roman Christian tradition (westward, aquatic, mercantile, moderate in orientation) and the Eastern, land-based, neurotic tradition, feudal in its roots (no reference, however, to the Protestant component).[34]

Having witnessed the failure of the Wilsonian model of the self-determining nation-state and the obverse rise of Bolshevism in the East, Coudenhove began to see a model instead in the Pan-American association and the regionalist aspect of the Monroe Doctrine (whose hegemonic aspect he rather failed to understand). When France occupied the Ruhr in 1923 and postwar disillusion was at a peak, he published a

---

33 On the biographical aspect, see Richard N. Coudenhove-Kalergi, *Crusade for Pan-Europe: Autobiography of a Man and a Movement* (New York, 1943). The name is often rendered Coudenhove. See also Peter Bugge, "The Nation Supreme: The Idea of Europe 1914–1945"; Reinhard Frommelt, *Paneuropa oder Mitteleuropa: Einigungsbestrebungen im Kalkül deutscher Wirtschaft und Politik 1925–1933*. Coudenhove's father married his mother, a Japanese woman, while serving as a diplomat in Tokyo in the 1890s (an unusual match for that period). Behind his Austrian nationality lay a long, aristocratic lineage of numerous European nationalities, ranging from Cretan to Norwegian.

34 Richard N. Coudenhove-Kalergi, *Europa ohne Elend* (Paris, Vienna, 1936), 59; see also Coudenhove-Kalergi, *Crusade*. The specter of Rapallo was of course another important part of the equation in 1923. For Kennan on Germany, see Kennan, "Draft Article on Germany for *Foreign Affairs*, not used," 1949, GFKP, box 25.

widely popular programmatic work calling for a supranational European federation as a way of escaping what he had earlier called the "Scylla of Russian military dictatorship and the Charybdis of American financial dictatorship." While the Eastern threat was political, the Western was economic. Association would rejuvenate the soul of Europe, which for him was always "the Christian cultural community of the Abendland." A political as opposed to geographic community, Europe was not to include Russia—for Russia was the present-day Macedonia. To avoid Russian conquest, Europe had to consolidate; and to consolidate, its central problem, French-German hostility, had to be resolved. These two nations could either pursue nationalist-chauvinist solutions and perish; or they could join in a democratic European spirit and become the center of a continental renaissance.[35]

Coudenhove, who combined pacifism with an admiration for Nietzsche, actually had peculiar ideas about democracy, tracing Europe's decline to the disappearance of the great deed and the feudal aristocracy, calling elsewhere for a new kind of aristocratic elite and a new heroic ethic, for a break with all materialism, Soviet and American, as well as with modern, massified democracy. Over the whole Pan-European project hovered a not so subtle medievalism. Coudenhove's concrete proposal, however, included the whole of non-Soviet and non-British Europe, as well as their colonial hinterland all the way down to Angola. He divided the world politically into five world-historical blocs (almost identical, in fact, to Kennan's strategic conception of the world in 1948).[36]

The affinities here with Abendland ideology are obvious, and indeed Paneuropa became a popular slogan among Catholics—as well as among a host of other European federationists. Mitteleuropa, by contrast, was an altogether more German and precise concept. Various ideas about a Germanic Mitteleuropa had existed from the early 1800s onward; but it

---

35 The quotation about "Scylla/Charybdis" (in Frommelt, *Paneuropa*, 13) is from an open letter to Mussolini when Coudenhove still thought the Italian could be a useful vehicle; Coudenhove-Kalergi, *Europa ohne Elend*, 71.

36 The European areas would exclude Britain and the Soviet Union. After World War II, Kennan delineated in his strategic assessment of the world five political areas capable of serious military-industrial power (the United States, Britain and the Commonwealth, Europe, the Soviet Union and Japan); this geopolitical vision corresponded almost exactly to Coudenhove's.

was the World War that gave it the form it would retain throughout the interwar period. Friedrich Naumann, a Protestant theologian and liberal-nationalist fellow of Max Weber, published its founding tract, *Mitteleuropa*, in 1915.[37] Naumann proposed Mitteleuropa as an economic bloc, a *Weltwirtschaftskörper*, centered on Germany and Austria-Hungary and with a periphery of auxiliary states in the south and east. Only such a constellation, secular, unified and economic, would allow German survival in the competition with the other *Weltwirtschaftskörper*, Britain, the United States, and Russia. In essence, Naumann's concept was merely an extension of German nationalism, but, as often in its liberal guises, there was an element of social compromise at the bottom of it.[38]

The emphasis on an economic *Grossraum* was, not surprisingly, to be typical for the German approach to Mitteleuropa. Thomas Masaryk and other non-Germanic Central Europeans responded by attempting their own Democratic Union of Mitteleuropa, envisioned as a federation of states in between Russia and Germany. Other schemes also existed along the Danubian basin. But in Germany, by 1930 the choice really had boiled down to the Pan-European scheme organized around Franco-German cooperation or the eastward expansionist solution, Mitteleuropa. The latter, of course, in the particularly malignant and extreme form of the Nazi *Lebensraum*, emerged victorious in this period. It would take another world war to defeat it. After 1945, consequently, the political space for Mitteleuropa had vanished. Europe was divided along a razor-sharp line into East and West. The whole concept of Mitteleuropa faded. When it finally reappeared in the 1980s, it was as a sort of utopian desire on the part of Eastern European intellectuals for the rearticulation of an older cultural unity, roughly that of the Austro-Hungarian sphere, a space designed to eliminate precisely their Eastern

---

37 Friedrich Naumann, *Central Europe* (New York, 1916). See also Hans Hecker, "Mitteleuropapläne als Versuche einer europäischen Friedensordnung" in Hecker and Spieler, *Die historische Einheit Europas*. The idea was not new; it had been peddled in various forms, on and off, since 1814; Henry Cord Meyer, "Mitteleuropa in German Political Geography," 1946 in his *Collected Works, Volume 1: Essays and Articles, 1937–1960* (Irvine, CA, 1986).

38 Naumann was confident (*Central Europe*, 76–7) that the antisemitism of the Austrian Germans would fade after the war since the Jewish soldiers had "ratified their citizenship by death" in the trenches. In such conditions, he thought, "mutual irritation" could not be sustained.

heritage and connect them up once again with the West. Ironically, when that reconnection did happen, wholly unexpectedly, in 1989, Mitteleuropa disappeared again, its space taken over by a culture of hamburger joints and shaky stock markets. (Though expansive German voices have since been heard to the effect that Mitteleuropa would be a viable alternative if the European Union fails to move in a suitable direction.)[39]

Paneuropa, meanwhile, in modern form, has been altogether more successful. The Abendland tradition not only survived the Nazi horror but could be revamped quite readily to fit the circumstances of the early cold war. It was in fact an excellent solution to the problem of European nationalism, especially its German form, in addition to which it permitted the reinvention of the Carolingian Empire as a bulwark against the old semioriental East, now appearing in the shape of an enormously extended state Bolshevism. It was based indeed on Coudenhove's essential Franco-German compromise. The fact that the actual borderline here was on the Elbe, the traditional thousand-year-old demarcation between West and East, between the area where the Romano-Germanic synthesis called feudalism took real hold and where it did not, was in a sense only appropriate. Three Catholics, Konrad Adenauer of West Germany, a former Rhineland separatist; Robert Schuman of France, who had grown up in Lorraine when it was Lothringen and had been educated in Bonn; and Alcide de Gasperi of Italy, who had been a representative in Vienna, gathered round, conversing in German, to outline the future Western European project of integration—counterrevolutionary but no longer antiliberal—that which would eventually become the EEC and thus Europe. Coudenhove, meanwhile, hailed the Schuman Plan as a move toward a modern re-creation of "the mighty realm" of Charlemagne, the collapse of which had been "the greatest disaster to Europe since the fall of the Roman Empire." By then, however, the rival version of the Abendland vision had been displaced, the older and more radical Catholicism that wanted to become a geopolitical third way, a bridgebuilder between the atomistic United States and the collectivist Soviet Union. That idea, declared Coudenhove in 1950, "is finally buried." There were now only two real world powers and the Atlantic

---

39 See references in note 37 of this chapter. See also Perry Anderson, "The Europe to Come," *London Review of Books*, January 25, 1996.

Ocean was now to be the new Mediterranean. Adenauer, who referred constantly to the Abendland in his speeches, by contrast always assumed that the condition of possibility for the post-national project was a security umbrella to be provided by the United States. This was understood by his two cohorts as well, facing as they did not a Soviet army on the border but powerful communist opposition at home.[40]

*

Kennan sympathized wholeheartedly with the integration of the Abendland but parted from the Catholic statesmen in their desire to have the United States become organically (that is, militarily) involved in it. Moreover, Germany according to his concept, would have been integrated as a set of independent regions after mutual Soviet-American withdrawal had taken place. He had little sympathy for the ideas of NATO and the Bundesrepublik. His own nation, in the end, always seemed too immature, too fickle, too unwieldy, too universalist, to be able to play the role of a world power. Put differently, the United States was very much an adolescent part of the West. "The older cultural centers of Europe," he professed, "are the meteorological centers in which much of the climate of international life is produced and from which it proceeds."[41] Hence they must reconstitute themselves in their own

---

[40] Wolfgang J. Mommsen, ed., *The Long Way to Europe: Historical Observations from a Contemporary view* (Chicago, 1994); Wilfried Loth, "The Germans and European Unification," in ibid.; Alan S. Milward, *The European Rescue of the Nation-State* (London, 1992), chap 6. Wilfried Loth, in his *Der Weg Nach Europa* (Göttingen, 1990), 42, cites Adenauer in March 1946: "Asia stands on the Elbe... Only an economically and spiritually sound Western Europe, to which the decisive part of Germany not occupied by Russia will belong, can stop further Asian advances in spirit and power."

[41] George F. Kennan, PPS 4, July 23, 1947, in the United States Department of State, Policy Planning Staff, *The State Department Policy Planning Staff Papers* (New York, 1983), I:67. For an interesting and different perspective on Kennan here, see John Lamberton Harper, *American Visions of Europe: Franklin D. Roosevelt, George F. Kennan, and Dean G. Acheson* (Cambridge, 1994). Perhaps this is the place to mention the example of Kennan's friend Helmuth James Graf von Moltke. Moltke, executed for his opposition to Hitler, was a Protestant for whom the Christian community of the Middle Ages was preferrable to the nationalist present. As a sort of communitarian Christian socialist, he envisaged for the postwar era a united Europe as far east as possible. See Ger van Roon, *German Resistance to Hitler: Count von Moltke and the Kreisau Circle* (London, 1971). Kennan, in his memoirs, calls Moltke "one of the few genuine Protestant-Christian martyrs of our time" and a man who had been, to him, "a pillar of moral conscience and an unfailing source of political and intellectual inspiration" (Kennan, *Memoirs I*, 122).

terms and perhaps resume their leading, moderating role. Here, crucially, he also differed from the three founders of the neo-Carolingian, catholic Europe of the west. For Kennan, their views on the variable boundaries of "the West" were altogether too restrictive. For Kennan, the Abendland always included the old Habsburg extensions into the East, everything indeed that was not entirely within the state boundaries of the oriental despot in the Kremlin. And perhaps, in the end, Kennan, like de Gaulle, always believed somewhere deep down, at least after Stalin died, that Europe actually stretched all the way to the Urals, that the Abendland after all was a "European Europe."[42]

One must say dialectically then that the very success of Europe is dissolving it, putting its eastern boundaries and cultural distinction in perpetual question. The condition of possibility for Europe— Mitteleuropa, Paneuropa and Abendland alike—is some kind of Eastern outside that can define it as a continent. Today we do not know where Europe is or what it might be. Some people, meanwhile, think they know where the Abendland and its competing civilizations are to be found. I do not.

---

42 On de Gaulle, see Hans-Dieter Lucas, *Europa vom Atlantik bis zum Ural? Europapolitik und Europadenken im Frankreich der Ära de Gaulle (1958–1969)* (Berlin, 1992).

11

Senator John F. Kennedy: Anti-imperialism and Utopian Deficit

Opinions of John F. Kennedy differ but it is commonly agreed that he was an impatient man and easily bored (though when he was laid up lengthily in a hospital bed, which happened not infrequently, his stoicism and patience were nothing short of astonishing). It stands to reason, then, that one of the things that bored him in the 1950s was the cold war, by then solidified into a dogmatic and rigid system. It is the ideological nature of that boredom, or discomfort, its dilemmas and limits, that interests me here. My double wager is that if one pursues Kennedy's idiosyncrasies on this score without reading him backward from the unflinching cold-war policies he actually launched, apparently, in his presidency, then one will learn something both about the cold war at the time and about Kennedy himself.

Idiosyncrasy, of course, never became apostasy. Kennedy would not have been elected president had that been the case.[1] Arguably, the surviving cold-war thematic within his posture—the militancy, if you will—became more pronounced as he got closer to the election. That option was always a possibility in his own system (or set of gestures) as it evolved in the mid-1950s. Nevertheless, his position featured throughout a studied

---

1   Thus he could never have gone as far as George F. Kennan, alleged architect of containment, who did in fact become an apostate in the 1950s, confronting directly the whole cold-war axiomatic. Kennedy read Kennan but prudently kept him at a distance, fobbing him off in 1961 with the ambassadorship to Tito's Yugoslavia.

ambiguity whereby vibrant calls for more and better efforts in the competition with the Soviet Union would typically be coupled with similarly strong appeals to keep that competition within a peaceful frame, at the same time as he would insist that the epochal antagonism should in no way be the sum total of what the United States ought to do in the world and certainly not what was necessarily decisive about any given event. This pragmatic critique of the cold war as totality, as closure, is worth consideration, if nothing else precisely because of its ultimate impossibility but also because what followed is not exactly what it seems. The degree to which the cold warrior of 1961 was an overdetermined figure is thus open to debate; he somehow seemed to sense in his more dialectical moments that one would have to go through rather than confront a certain present in order to displace and transcend it. One might, however, also argue that he never intended that invigorated cold-war struggle to be a cold war at all, at least not in the sense of orthodoxy.[2]

The substantial part of his critique had to do with imperialism—anticolonial liberation was the wave not only of the future but of the present, which would have happened with or without communism; and the United States should not subordinate its support for that wave to its cold-war concerns by supporting, in effect, the colonial powers of Western Europe just because they also happened to be allies in NATO.

---

2 Kennedy said little systemically about the cold war, in part because there was no gain in doing otherwise, partly because of the genuine difficulties, both conceptual and political. One intriguing dialectical remark he made is reported by Harris Wofford: "The key thing for the country is a new foreign policy that will break out of the confines of the cold war. Then we can build a decent relationship with the developing nations and begin to respond to their needs. We can stop the vicious circle of the arms race and promote diversity and peaceful change within the Soviet bloc" (Harris Wofford, *Of Kennedys and Kings: Making Sense of the Sixties* [New York, 1980], 36–7). Wofford was an adviser in the 1960 campaign, a specialist on civil rights and also a part of the organizing of the Peace Corps. The quotation is indirectly rendered but rings quite true. We need to end "the frozen, belligerent brink-of-war phase of the long Cold War" as he also said (speech at Rochester, October 1, 1959, reprinted in John F. Kennedy, *Strategy for Peace*, ed. Allan Nevins [New York, 1960], 37). "The phase but not the war?" one might ask. Around 1960, too, he would sometimes refer in an offhand manner to Arnold Toynbee's notion that the cold war might turn into the kind of long-term truce and acceptance that eventually came to mark the relationship between Islam and Christianity, two other all-or-nothing positions analogous to the contemporary East-West antagonism. See, for example his speech in South Eugene, Oregon, April 22, 1960, available at jfklibrary.org. A large number of his speeches from 1960 have been digitized by the John F. Kennedy Library (henceforth JFKL), far fewer for the preceding years.

Those allies turned out in practical terms to be only one ally, namely, France, whose imperial wars in Vietnam and then Algeria became salient targets for Kennedy in some of the most important acts he ever performed in his relatively short career as a senator. There was, however, also a procedural part to his dissatisfaction: orthodoxy, whatever its actual content as a set of propositions, constrained leadership and action, the ability to wield power for *whatever ends* in an intelligent way.

A symptomatic reading of this presupposes, then, some kind of concept of the cold war as US orthodoxy, against which Kennedy's alternative, deliberately inchoate and ambiguous as it ultimately proved, can be gauged. Before I offer such a sketch, however, two things should summarily be addressed: historiography and biography. First, there is a mountain of writing about Kennedy and the Kennedys, the mastering of which would require several scholarly lives. A good deal of it concerns in various ways the mythology that attaches to the subject matter, what with its abundant source materials of family, drama, legend, money, glamour, sex, crime, politics, charisma, disease, and, of course, unspeakable tragedy. A certain debunking is thus rightly part of that historiographical operation.[3] I keep this mythologizing/demythologizing in mind but my purposes here are only indirectly related to that polarity. Kennedy's anti-imperialism in the 1950s, meanwhile, has not been a central concern (or problem) in the standard biographies, but there have been some excellent accounts that do center on it. Mine will differ from them less on what actually happened than, as will be evident, on the framing and purpose of the argument.[4]

---

3   For reasons of space, references to the vast secondary literature will be kept to a minimum. Of the standard, sympathetic accounts, I have found especially useful Ted Sorensen, *Kennedy* (New York, 2009 [1965]); and Robert Dallek, *An Unfinished Life: John F. Kennedy, 1917–1963* (New York, 2004). The classic debunking text, centering on Vietnam, is of course David Halberstam, *The Best and the Brightest* (New York, 1972), a book that should be reread periodically by all; and similarly Seymour M. Hersh, *The Dark Side of Camelot* (New York, 1998). On the earlier period, see Nigel Hamilton's *JFK: Reckless Youth* (New York, 1993), excessive but fun to read. Stephen Rabe, *The Most Dangerous Area on Earth: John F. Kennedy Confronts Communist Revolution in Latin America* (Chapel Hill, NC, 1999) remains a devastating indictment. A recent, typically judicious synthesis is Alan Brinkley, *John F. Kennedy* (New York, 2012).

4   Thus Dallek in his authoritative and informative *Life* of 800 pages spends only a few paragraphs on the Algerian speech. Vietnam, because of what happened afterward, has been more widely explored but the Algerian intervention in 1957 was more

Second, historiography and myth aside, I do need to say something about the biographical context, not as truth but by way of indicating how I myself grasp Kennedy as a figure and in particular what I think is pertinent about his background. This brief account is not meant to explain his subsequent position but, more modestly, to suggest a range of conditions of possibility in which the social meets ideology. For the sake of concision, I will merely enumerate these aspects:

(i) Kennedy did not have to work for a living and never had a proper job except for some journalistic dabbling at the end of World War II. He did not even, perfunctorily, get the law degree requisite for the typical political career in the United States. His one sustained activity before Congress was his illustrious military service. The immensely wealthy, self-made Joseph Kennedy, Sr. (a more complex character than is generally understood) set his numerous progeny up to become relatively autonomous, not to be members of the idle rich, certainly, but able to devote themselves to something worthy beyond the drudgery of material worries. It was a clear concept of independence as absence of external determinants. JFK was always outside or at some remove from the social structure.[5]

---

controversial and strongly pitched. See, first, the pioneering effort by Ronald J. Nurse, "Critic of Colonialism: JFK and Algerian Independence," *The Historian* 39, no. 2 (1970), 307–26; later Jeffrey A. Lefebvre (1999), "Kennedy's Algerian Dilemma: Containment, Alliance Politics and the 'Rebel Dialogue,'" *Middle Eastern Studies*, 35, no. 2, 61–82; and Theresa Romahn, "Colonialism and the Campaign Trail: On Kennedy's Algerian Speech and His Bid for the 1960 Democratic Nomination," *Journal of Colonialism and Colonial History* 10, no. 2 (2009).

5 On Kennedy Sr., see David Nasaw, *The Patriarch: The Remarkable Life and Turbulent Times of Joseph. R. Kennedy* (New York, 2012). Empirically sound, Nasaw's book still has some difficulty with Kennedy as a character. Joseph, unlike his second son, was a materialist of reductionist persuasion: interests, mostly of a fairly crude kind, govern the world. Hence his oddly naive view that the Nazis could be bought off in 1938–39. After 1946, he kept a low political profile so as not to jeopardize John's career. His speech at Robert's law school (Virginia) in December 1950 was an exception—worth a read for its unflinching attack on cold-war policies in the name of a retooled notion of Fortress America. As he asked rhetorically, "What business is it of ours to support French colonial policy in Indo-China or to achieve Mr. Syngman Rhee's concepts of democracy in Korea?" See Joseph P. Kennedy, "Present Policy is Politically and Morally Bankrupt," *Vital Speeches of the Day* 17, no. 6 (1951) 170–3.

(ii) Kennedy was the second son. In the typically hierarchical and gendered process, Joseph Sr. centered his overpowering hopes (the presidency, no less, lurking somewhere on the horizon) on his eldest son, Joseph Jr., whom he adored. Until Joseph Jr.'s death in 1944 on a near-suicidal air mission, his brother JFK, sickly and a bit goofy, thus escaped the full intensity of paternal expectations. JFK was twenty-seven years old and still unclear about his career when the focus now shifted onto him. Two years later, in 1946, he was elected to the House of Representatives in a safe Boston seat engineered by his father. The upward trajectory from House to Senate and perhaps beyond was in the works from the beginning.

(iii) John F. Kennedy, at forty-three famously the youngest elected president ever, had a stellar war record and exuded youth, vigor, virility and masculinity; but he was the most physically challenged person to enter the White House in the twentieth century, the possible exception being (though I doubt it) wheelchair-user Franklin D. Roosevelt. With a multitude of chronic ills and illnesses, Kennedy was near death on several occasions and required an astonishing number of medications (liberally interpreted) to get through the day. It was, existentially, a life of being toward death.

(iv) Kennedy, as far as I can tell, was neither a particularly good Catholic nor a good Irish American, by which I mean that neither identity (or orientation) was constitutive. He fulfilled both roles without hypocrisy when he was called upon to do so and it fit his purposes; but neither function was anything but a tradition, a reference and a given toward which one had to position oneself, depending on the circumstances. He kept a clear distance from that familiar figure, the Irish American politician, as personified by his maternal grandfather, John Fitzgerald. Indeed, Kennedy was more at home (to the extent he ever was) in the salons of the English aristocracy than in the Irish wards of Boston.[6]

---

6   Kennedy, while hailing the Irish nation for obvious reasons, never romanticized (unduly) Irish resistance, even at "Irish" occasions. See for example his remarks at the Irish Institute, New York, January 12, 1957, JFKL. With clear reference to recent events in Hungary, he pointed out that in the seventeenth century "the Irish people were brutally slaughtered and enslaved by a ruthless and relentless Cromwell," following

(v) Kennedy was the most well read of the four brothers and the only one with intellectual interests, chiefly politics and history. He was not, however, an intellectual.[7] Philosophical inquiry as such did not excite him. Nevertheless, he was capable of what one might call second-order reflection, thinking above the action about the conditions of that action. From his contemporary analysis of the British unwillingness to challenge Nazi Germany in the 1930s to the ideal of Burkean individualism and transcendence on display in the *Profiles in Courage* of the mid-1950s, the problem of political will and historical limits is at the forefront.[8] This kind of informed intelligence (as I think one can call it) is not always typical of presidents.

(vi) Kennedy was also unusually well traveled. A good number of presidents in the twentieth century had experience abroad but few (possibly Teddy Roosevelt) had the sustained political travels and extended stays that Kennedy had from the mid-1930s onward. He traveled far beyond the Grand Tour of the typical upper-class, East Coast American. From early on, courtesy of his totally unabashed father, he would meet and converse with important people abroad. In mid-1939, for example, one finds the twenty-two-year-old Kennedy in Jerusalem and also in Moscow.

---

which the population declined by 50 percent. The punchline—that the Irish eventually gained freedom as the Hungarians no doubt would—did not disguise the Cromwellian lesson of his remark. In the Senate debate on Poland in August 1957, indeed, he said that it had taken the Irish seven hundred years of disastrous rebellions to get to their goal, which was not a good recipe for the Poles. See *Congressional Record*, Senate, 103:11 (August 21, 1957), 15540.

7 Couve de Murville, who knew Kennedy at the time in Washington before he returned to France to become de Gaulle's Foreign Minister, called him retroactively "an intellectual," by which he meant "a man who reads, who thinks, and who believes that life is more complicated than it generally appears." See Maurice Couve de Murville, Oral History Interview—5/20/1964, JFKL. Given that laconic but expansive notion (intriguing in itself), I would agree Kennedy was an intellectual; but he did not fit the mold in any stricter sense. He was not interested in intellectual inquiry for its own sake.

8 John F. Kennedy, *Profiles in Courage* (New York, 2004 [1956]). He says, disapprovingly, by way of preface that the cold war had generated "rigid ideological unity and orthodox patterns of thought" (17).

(vii) Congress bored him, the Senate less so than the House, no doubt because senators had more power and there was more about foreign relations, always his chief interest. Nonetheless, Kennedy took care of his political obligations and became, in time, an indefatigable, well-informed and powerful campaigner, aided by a first-rate staff (which he could afford); by his brother Robert, who turned out to be an equally first-rate campaign manager; and by his father's machinations with the media and important people. The political rise of JFK in the 1950s from inexperienced representative to successful presidential candidate was nonetheless astonishing. He was, one should recall, the first Catholic to be elected president. Given contingencies and (very) long odds, it is notable that he did not always play things in a politically safe way. The risks were certainly calculated to give the candidate-to-be deeper colors and sharper contours. The operation was nothing if not instrumental. Still, his anti-imperialism, however calculated, was not only risky but also expressive of a relatively coherent way of thinking about history and the world.

(viii) Kennedy's politics remained ambiguously related, no doubt intentionally, to the archetypal cold-war liberalism one might think at first sight he embodied. He was never a Stevenson liberal. Here, as elsewhere, he preserved a certain license, a capacity for potential reversal and fluidity of motion. Eleanor Roosevelt had had every right to suspect him. Kennedy was not interested in commitment to social blueprints or indeed *dogma*. He was interested in movement, energy, action and power, or, to put in another way, process as utopian transcendence.

From this arbitrary list, I take as salient the detachment, a distancing operation that translates not into spectatorial passivity (obviously) but a certain play and irony. It is analytical intelligence coupled with the will to win, where the very notion of the race is foundational.

Kennedy was assassinated at the very moment when the cold war, *stricto sensu*, was waning and arguably (at least I have so argued) turning into something else, thus raising the unanswerable question what he would have done in that novel conjuncture. I leave that problem aside, except to say, by way of negation, that he was not Lyndon B. Johnson.[9] The cold war, meanwhile, is still debated as a periodizing device, though the conventional view that, in any case, the whole thing came to a resounding end with the end of the Soviet Union around 1990–91 now reigns supreme from left to right. That problem, too, I will leave aside, except to point out that the focus on the existence of the Soviet Union for the concept of the end tends to produce a focus on the Soviet Union as the cause. My own view, for the record, is that the cold war was a US project: the weaker Soviets, with good reason, had no wish for it and tried clumsily to counteract its very structure. One might still argue that, whatever the intention, the ultimate cause of the cold war, what made the United States put it into effect, was the actions of the Soviet Union (or the character of Josef Stalin, and so on, and so on). About the orthodox US view as it had crystallized by the early 1950s, there is however less controversy since it was simple and liberally on exhibit.

The orthodox US view can be summarized briefly. The cold war is not only caused by the Soviet Union, it *is* the Soviet Union. Totalitarian Moscow, like its totalitarian Nazi relative, is inherently about world conquest. For the sake of necessity and convenience, the communist regime has chosen, unlike the Nazis, to accomplish its evil designs by means of cold rather than hot war. This, too, however, is a war to death that can end favorably only with the end of the Soviet regime itself. Real diplomacy in the traditional sense of deals is in such circumstances tantamount to appeasement, that is merely whetting the totalitarian appetite. Ultimately, the only legitimate deal one could make with the communists would concern the practicalities of their unconditional surrender. In the meantime, a vast preponderance of strength is necessary to keep Moscow expansionism at bay and the only power that can do that is of course the United

---

9   For better or worse: Johnson the bone-crushing dealmaker proved far bolder and more of an activist on domestic policy (witness the epochal reform years of 1964-65) than Kennedy, who was inclined to see limits and problems. Inversely, Johnson had none of Kennedy's confidence and knowledge about foreign policy. When push came to shove, Johnson was stuck in the shibboleths of the 1950s. On the specter of Vietnam, all I indicate in this chapter is that there is no set answer and we might as well give that game up; though if I were pressed up against the wall for an answer, I would have to say that the idea of Kennedy sending half a million troops to Vietnam seems really far-fetched.

States, leader of the Free World, a domain defined in turn as that which is not communist.[10]

This is condensed, of course, but not a caricature. One needs to add that the functional point of the edifice is less the actual policy (or non-policy) toward the Soviet Union than the massive, global imperative to order and control the Free World. The power of the cold war as a project, the *beauty* in all its crudity, if you will, is that it makes uncontroversial US globalism. Given the unlimited, existential threat, there could be no limit to the response. The story of the 1930s and World War II demonstrated this and the obverse errors of isolationism with the greatest clarity: never again and so forth. After 1948 and, say, the defeat of Henry Wallace, no one could gain any political traction, at least nationally, by challenging the basics of cold-war orthodoxy.

The trouble, alas, was that the threat may have been unlimited but the actual resources of the United States, however powerful, were not. And so, in 1949, Washington chose rightly not to intervene extensively in China to prevent the creation of the People's Republic. This and the ensuing, stalemated Korean War gave rise to a strategic and tactical controversy between Democrats and Republicans concerning containment and liberation which essentially turned on the efficacy and morality of just stopping the communists as opposed to actively destroying them areas beyond one's own control. What is important about that debate, firmly situated within orthodoxy, is that it illustrates what one might call the cold-war deficit, namely that the posited threat not only opened up for any action anywhere, on principle, but also made determinate action, also on principle, morally and politically imperative. All things being equal, in short, *one could never do enough*. Orthodoxy, accordingly, opened up for the opposition the ability to claim that the responsible people in power were coming up short because they were *by definition* coming up short. Hence the nasty Republican claims in the election campaign of 1952 that equated containment with appeasement. Hence the claims that Truman (or the spies in the State Department) had lost China. Hence also the claims that there was a sorry lack of will

---

10 No single document expresses this in full, but NSC 68 of April 1950 comes close. Written by a committee of the Policy Planning Staff (and not only, as is often said, by Paul Nitze, the PPS's presiding spirit), it remains the most ideologically charged condensation of the US position on the early cold war: true in its exaggeration.

to make use of nuclear superiority.[11] Against this, the practical counter-argument about essential/inessential came up distinctly short: If freedom is indivisible, what makes China any less important than Western Europe and possibly Japan? Why not indeed extend the Korean War into China, going nuclear if need be, and rid the world of the new communist regime?

As it turned out, once in power the Republicans also saw the logic of the ordering of essential free-world domains while avoiding any too offensive attacks on the evil empire, liberation (and massive retaliation) more or less ending up as a more rhetorical version of containment.[12] And so, having made the same Faustian deal as the Democrats, Republicans opened themselves up to the kind barrage of criticism for laxity of cold-war conduct that the young Senator John F. Kennedy would unleash on them toward the end of the 1950s and leading up to his election in 1960.

Impatience with the sterilities of the cold war, then, took the predictable form here of the given powers that be were "not doing enough" and "what was actually being done was wrong." Kennedy's alternative was more and better nuclear weapons, more and better ground troops, more and better everything, but also (in a simultaneous and typically contrary move) a demand for a serious approach to negotiations, especially on arms control. Kennedy, notably, rejected explicitly the notion that negotiations were appeasement, though he never pushed that point to challenge orthodoxy head on. Most of all, however, Kennedy wanted two things: energetic leadership coupled with specificity and flexibility in policy. For the key notion in Kennedy's emergent posture was precisely flexible particularity over rhetorical generality: intelligent mastery in addressing actually existing problems rather than striking (as he saw it) politically safe poses.

---

11   Kennedy, the young Democratic congressman, chimed in with some trite babble here in early 1949, blaming the State Department and the White House for the "disaster" in China and for relying on advice from "the Lattimores and the Fairbanks." *Congressional Record*, House, 95:1, (January 25, 1949), 532–3.

12   This is not to say that nothing was ever done by way of attacking the Soviet Union and auxiliary regimes: the extent of the psy-war—including all manner of actions far beyond the psychological—was both varied and sustained. It is merely to say that the *decisive* aspect was always the globalist agenda with regard to the Free World.

What was wrong with orthodoxy, then, was chiefly that it was a systemic constraint.[13]

Nevertheless, if the cold-war deficit opened up for a predictable cold-war response, there was also a kind of pragmatic break with orthodoxy on substantial grounds. First, as we shall see, he used the cold war quite cleverly as a way of questioning the strategic viability of both containment and liberation as applied to Eastern Europe, saying in effect that successful execution of the cold war required that the basic cold-war scenario of black and white had to be adjusted to allow for gray, as not all satellites were alike. This thesis appealed to cold-war efficacy while actually eliminating one of its very foundations. Second, and more important, Kennedy reduced explicitly the scope of the cold war. Rather than an all-encompassing system, it became an aspect of the more fundamental conflict in world history between imperialism and freedom. The most serious and challenging form of imperialism, to be sure, was the Soviet one; but, as he insisted in 1956, "the most powerful new force to shape the world since World War II" was "surging African-Asian nationalism," or, as he also called it, "the revolt against colonialism, the determination of people to control their national destinies"; and this development had nothing inherently to do with the cold war. The United States, because of misplaced abnegation before the narrow interests of European allies, had largely missed this revolutionary change. Home of the famous Declaration of Independence, the postcolonial United States had thus fallen into mealymouthed neutrality in the struggle between Western imperialism and anticolonial emancipation and so, disturbingly, also opened up for the now dangerously agile post-Stalinist Soviets to pose as the true friends of national liberation. Whereas neutrality between East and West was officially condemned as immoral, the United States itself, ironically, espoused the very same position in the struggles between North and South.[14]

---

13 He stated this to various degrees on many occasions. His speeches (and Senate interventions) are more incisive, not surprisingly, than his career-enhancing efforts in the mainstream media, which tend to the bland, predictable and overly calculated. For synthetic statements in 1957, see his "A Democrat Says the Party Must Lead—Or Get Left," *Life Magazine* (March 15, 1957), 164–77 (Kennedy was on the cover); and "A Democrat Looks at Foreign Policy," *Foreign Affairs* 36, no. 1 (October 1957), 44–59. Leadership was a tactically useful theme but also essential to Kennedy's outlook, the substance of process so to speak.

14 On Eastern Europe, see reference below, note 29. For the quotations on decolonization and nationalism, see his strong speech at the Los Angeles World Council,

Put differently, Kennedy was arguing that the United States had projected anti communism beyond its proper domain, extending, negatively, the countering communism promiscuously to conflicts and problems that had nothing as such to do with it. None of the four crises racking the Mediterranean at the time, for example, had in his view anything intrinsically to do with the struggle with communism or the Soviet Union: the Suez Canal, Cyprus, Israel and French North Africa. Still, he recognized the strategic difficulties:

> We want our Allies to be strong, and yet quite obviously a part of their strength comes from their overseas possessions. And thus our dilemma has become a paradox. We want to keep the world free from Communist imperialism—but in doing so we hamper our efforts, and bring suspicion upon our motives, by being closely linked with Western imperialism.[15]

He was referring to the kind of posture (and policy) that marked the Truman and Eisenhower administrations alike: yes, colonialism is no doubt on the way out, but, the cold war being absolutely decisive, it is essential that the process of decolonization be stable, gradual and above all orderly so as not to give the communists any openings, all of which makes it prudent for the United States, generally, to support properly supervised introduction, step-by-step, of Western-orientated reformist leaders who would find it natural then to integrate their new nations in the Free World struggle against the global threat of totalitarianism; *but*, should that happy solution be unavailable, one might have to give extensive support to existing Western imperialism, especially in cases where the anticolonial opposition shows any communist flavor.[16] Kennedy, by

---

September 21, 1956, JFKL. See also "A Democrat Looks at Foreign Policy" and his speech at the University of Pennsylvania, "The New Dimensions of American Foreign Policy," November 1, 1957, JFKL. On the irony of "neutrality," see his speech at Eastern Oregon University, November 9, 1959, in *Strategy for Peace*, 140.

15 Speech at Los Angeles, September 21, 1956; speech at Irish Fellowship Club, Chicago, March 17, 1956, JFKL.

16 I am simplifying, of course, and beneath the official surface, even John Foster Dulles had a fairly clear idea of where the colonial question was heading. Nonetheless, the logic of the cold war did determine in the last instance. See the nuanced discussion in Robert B. Rakove, "A Genuine Departure: Kennedy, Johnson and the Non-Aligned World" (PhD diss., University of Virginia, 2009), chap. 1. Typically, the Basic National

contrast, thought this would land the United States on the wrong side of history. The solution, dilemmas notwithstanding, was to take an unequivocal stand for the right to independence and let the proverbial chips fall where they may.

Exhibit A here, as it happened, was France. It was relatively easy to single out France, devoid of any constituency in the United States and saddled with extensive colonial wars in Vietnam and then Algeria. Kennedy knew a good deal about both wars and they formed the target of two of his most important sallies in the Senate. In the autumn of 1951, he had made an exhaustingly long trip, together with Robert and his sister Patricia, from Europe through the Middle East to South and Southeast Asia, ending up in Japan where, once again, he almost died from illness. His stay in Indo-China and Vietnam made a strong impression.[17] The futility of the enormous French endeavor to defeat the Viet Minh militarily was duly noted, as was the degree to which this effort was almost entirely underwritten by the United States. Once elected (in 1952) to the Senate, he made a serious attempt (in 1953) to stop US support for the

---

Security Policy statement of 1956 dictated support for "constructive" nationalist movements and "orderly evolution of political arrangements toward self-determination" (Rakove, 25); but the Eisenhower policy of pacts and alliances, in a larger sense anticommunism, gave priority to more important things than self-determination.

17 The notes I have seen specifically on Vietnam are not extensive but give an indication. There was a dinner (no notes) with Bao Dai, the would-be emperor, and a good deal of interaction with the French. Kennedy flew over the Hanoi Delta, fiercely fought over, with the French commander Marshal de Lattre, whom he greatly respected. Kennedy grasped that Ho Chi Minh controlled most of the countryside and he also believed, as did "many Americans" in the area, that the French could have avoided the overall problem by giving Indochina its independence after World War II. He also thought Asian "leadership" here would recast the conflict from one "between native communists and western imperialists, between the white and the yellow man" to "a struggle to preserve Asiatic democracy and the independence of native governments against the new imperialism of the communists." His conclusion was clear: "The support of the legitimate aspirations of the people of this area against all who seek to dominate them—from whatever quarter they may come." JFKL, Pre-Presidential Papers, Box 011, Boston Office Files, Speech Files 46–52, "Far Eastern Trip, 1951." Throughout this trip, he met important individuals (from Ben-Gurion to Nehru). Curiously, in view of the times, the Indian foreign minister told him that the Chinese, being independent-minded, would part ways with Moscow; but not if there was continued, compact resistance to them from everyone else. What prevented any opening (Kennedy reflected) was however the required Western concessions: recognition, of course, a series of other measures that were essentially a gamble and exceedingly difficult.

sham, French-sponsored Bao Dai regime in Vietnam. His basic argument (he was strongly supported, interestingly, by Barry Goldwater) was simple: without "a crusading and reliable army" of the Vietnamese, the struggle was hopeless; and there would be no such army without real independence, a real nation to defend. Hence the United States must tie any material support to the relinquishment of French sovereignty.[18]

A year later, when the epic disaster at Dien Bien Phu finally ended French rule, Kennedy wobbled a bit as the crisis narrowed the choice, apparently, either to the French or the Viet Minh: no viable third force could realistically be envisaged in May 1954. He was hazy on the solution but not on the egregious mistakes of the Eisenhower administration in its constant predictions of imminent victory and soon-to-be independence. "No amount of American military assistance in Indochina," he said, "can conquer an enemy which is everywhere and at the same time nowhere."[19]

So much better, in any case, that the eventual partition Kennedy had dreaded turned out, unexpectedly, to permit not only the formation of an independent republic (it was thought) south of the 17th parallel, but one led by a Catholic to boot, a regime thus deserving wholehearted US support. For the rest of the 1950s, Kennedy thus believed, or allowed himself to believe, in the properly nationalist and reformist credentials of the Diem regime; and he was indeed to play a role in "the Vietnam Lobby."[20] Nevertheless, he was fully aware of Ho Chi Minh's stature as a

---

18 Kennedy's chief statement on Indochina, June 30, 1953, is in the *Congressional Record*, Senate, 99:6 (1953), 7622–25. See also the debate July 1, 1953, ibid., 7780–84.

19 For Kennedy's varying statements on the emerging and intensifying crisis from March to May 1954, see *Congressional Record*, Senate, 100:3, (1954), 2904; ibid., 100:6, 4671–81 (quotation on p. 4673); speech at Cook County Democratic Dinner, April 20, 1954, JFKL; speech at Princeton University, May 11, 1954, JFKL; speech at St. Michael's College, Vermont, May 16, 1954, JFKL.

20 See his Panglossian address to the Friends of Vietnam, the organized lobby, on June 1, 1956, JFKL. Kennedy complained wrongly that Vietnam, after the dramatic turn for the better, had disappeared from US media—it was actually covered, if not extensively; the *New York Times* reported censorship and arrests at the same time as it editorially expressed support for the Diem regime and US aid (see February 15; March 11; April 11; and July 2, 1956). His speech on June 1 was a truly appalling ode to Diem and his regime: "Vietnam represents the cornerstone of the Free World in Southeast Asia, the keystone to the arch, the finger in the dyke . . . Where once a playboy emperor ruled from a distant shore, a constituent assembly has been elected. Social and economic reforms have likewise been remarkable. The living conditions of the peasants have been

national (if not necessarily nationalist) fighter against the Japanese and the French; and in 1954 he believed the Communist would win open elections. Indeed, in the wake of Dien Bien Phu, he expressed respect (in suitably guarded language) for the way the insurgents had "instilled into their people a philosophy that shows itself in the most extraordinary acts of dedication and self-sacrifice."[21]

"Dedication and self-sacrifice" were in fact precisely the kind of qualities Kennedy himself liked to invoke but found lacking both in the cynical West and the chillingly neutralist Asia. Individualized qualities of this type are often privileged in Kennedy's outlook. Yet, again, one must also recognize the structural element. The cold war was an integral part, but only a part, of the world-historical struggle for national independence. Hence (ran one unspoken corollary) the center of the universe was not the Atlantic or the transatlantic relationship. Moreover, democracy and national liberation as a project entailed no preordained, constitutive place for free enterprise, a Western or perhaps even American notion that was largely meaningless for the deprived and brutalized peasant masses of the colonial world. Western democracy and capitalism were, if you will, site-specific, the result of several centuries of development not easily reproduced or even possible elsewhere.[22]

If Vietnam was a tricky issue for Kennedy because of the communist leadership of the national liberation struggle, Algeria provided a much easier case. The Front de libération nationale (FLN) was demonstrably not communist, and Kennedy, from 1956 onward, learned about it

---

vastly improved, the wastelands have been cultivated, and a wider ownership of the land is gradually being encouraged. Farm cooperatives and farmer loans have modernized an outmoded agricultural economy; and a tremendous dam in the center of the country has made possible the irrigation of a vast area previously uncultivated. Legislation for better labor relations, health protection, working conditions and wages has been completed under the leadership of president Diem." He knew better. Ironically, he also noted that, historically, the Vietnamese had resisted and stopped Chinese expansion in the region; so, presumably, he would not have been surprised in 1979 when the two communist powers went to war.

21 Quotation from speech at St. Michael's College, May 16, 1954; also his Senate speech June 30, 1953; and his Senate speech on April 6, 1954, *Congressional Record*, Senate, 100:4 (1954), 4671–81.

22 On site specificity, see, among other statements, his speech at Rockhurst College, Kansas City, June 2, 1956, JFKL; and his speech at University of Florida, Gainesville, October 18, 1957, JFKL.

extensively through personal contacts, chiefly with central Tunisian figures in Washington.[23] The difficulty with Algeria (or at least with the three northernmost *départements*) was that, technically, it was part of metropolitan France and, again technically, the United States recognized this. Whenever the issue came up in the UN from 1955 onward, France would insist that it was an internal matter and not a UN concern. The United States supported this, despite some typical mumbles and misgivings. The United States also supported, de facto if not explicitly, the massive military operation comprising several hundred thousand troops that the French, now out of Indochina, launched in 1956. Above all, the United States provided its NATO ally with military materiel.[24] Kennedy, as in Indochina, wanted the US to insist on independence for the colony, indeed to quit accepting the French pretense that Algeria was not a colony in the first place.

The Suez crisis, however, complicated matters for him: Eisenhower's decisive action against the Anglo-French and Israeli operation in October 1956 seemed to fit well—too well—the spirit of his own concepts at the same time as, conversely, he was committed for political (and other) reasons to Israel. Furthermore, the United States and the Soviet Union found themselves, momentarily and awkwardly, rather on the same side in the UN. So Kennedy said relatively little about this and nothing at all about Israel's role.[25] Eisenhower then helped him out in

---

23 Two sources were Habib Bourguiba Jr. (very briefly) and above all Mongi Slim, who served as combined Tunisian ambassador to the United States, the UN and Canada. Yet I think Kennedy, helped out on French materials by Jacqueline, always kept an eye on the problem of French colonialism because of the fiasco in Indochina.

24 The specific references to Kennedy and Algeria in note 5 aside, see more generally (from a variety of perspectives) Egya N. Sangmuah, "The United States and the French Empire in North Africa, 1946–1956: Decolonization in the Age of Containment" (PhD diss., University of Toronto, 1989); Daniel Byrne, "Adrift in a Sea of Sand: The Search for United States Foreign Policy toward the Decolonization of Algeria, 1942–1962" (PhD diss., Georgetown University, 2003); Irwin Wall, "The United States, Algeria, and the Fall of the Fourth French Republic," *Diplomatic History* 18, no. 4, 489–511; Matthew Connolly, *A Diplomatic Revolution: Algeria's Fight for Independence and the Origins of the Post-Cold War Era*, (New York, 2002). Sangmuah's account is especially clear on the lackluster result of trying to maintain a favorable view of decolonization in principle while hanging on to a cold-war frame.

25 On the background for Kennedy's support for Israel, see Warren Bass, *Support Any Friend: Kennedy's Middle East and the Making of the U.S.-Israeli Alliance*, New York, 2003), chap. 1. In 1956, Kennedy gave a couple of pandering speeches, the second on account of Golda Meir's visit right after Suez, where he says blandly that "the

early 1957 by recharging cold-war orthodoxy in the region in announcing what became known as his Doctrine: anticommunist aid to regimes in the area and, implicitly, serving geopolitical notice that Arab nationalism, at least in its Nasserist form, was under suspicion. On July 2, in any case, Kennedy gave his Algerian speech in the Senate, probably the single most important one he ever gave in that congregation. He himself invested it with tremendous significance, printing and distributing thousands of copies beforehand. It was a long and didactic effort that outlined his general position on imperialism and his specific one on Algeria, namely that the United States had to stop being neutralist on colonialism and take a stand in favor of national independence, recognizing that Algeria was no internal French matter that Paris would somehow resolve in good faith. Nothing in recent imperial French history indicated so.[26]

One might wonder why, as an emerging candidate for the Democratic nomination in 1960, he chose to make Algeria such a prominent issue. The Algerian imbroglio was known and debated in informed circles, if nothing else for the good Eurocentric reason that it was destabilizing the Fourth Republic and distracting from the cold war; but it was scarcely in the thick of things. The answer, ultimately, is not known. Several instrumental reasons can be adduced. He happened to know the question and it offered a relatively risk-free way of making a splash, thus improving his stature in foreign relations. Having kept a low profile on the anything but risk-free struggle over civil rights at home, he used Algeria and his concern with Africa as a symbolic way of shoring up his standing among

---

complexities of the present turmoil" will not diminish consideration for Israel. When he did address those "complexities" they did not include any reflection on Israel's place in the Suez sequence. See his remarks at a dinner in Boston honoring Golda Meir, November 25, 1956, JFKL; and his earlier Yankee Stadium address, April 29, 1956, JFKL. It is noteworthy that, between these two speeches, he also observed the influence of national lobbies: "The conduct of our policies with respect to Israel, Ireland, Greece, Italy, Poland and others will be determined more by the political potency of nationality groups in this country than by the stricter requirements of our national interest as a whole." See his address to the Los Angeles World Council, September 21, 1956, JFKL.

26 The speech and the debate are in the *Congressional Record*, 103:8 (July 2, 1957), 10780–93. This is the best place to read the speech since it includes the surrounding remarks and the debate. The perky atmosphere, controversy notwithstanding, is striking. It is (by current standards) remarkable how chummy the senators are across the dividing lines. Kennedy restated his position succinctly in the Jesuit journal *America*, October 5, 1957, 15–17.

African Americans. Abundantly aware of the potency of Richard M. Nixon as a coming rival, Kennedy was peremptorily staking a certain claim: in early 1957, Nixon had gone on a wide tour of Africa, occasioned by the celebration of Ghana's independence, and Kennedy knew well that Nixon was one of the few major figures who actually shared his interest in Africa and indeed was not so far from his own position.[27] The speech, as it turned out, earned him no great gains at home. He was roundly castigated by the Establishment (for example, the *New York Times*, *Time* magazine, Dean Acheson and, in remarkably unequivocal words, Adlai Stevenson). French authorities expressed extreme displeasure; the FLN and sympathetic forces, strong support.[28]

The speech may well have been calculated for expedient reasons (how could it not have been?) and probably all the ones given above. However, a more interesting instrumental question in the present context is the degree to which it was meant, if at all, to be a more efficient way to fight the cold war. There was certainly an alert in that sense to the functional danger of continuing existing policy. In a dissolving Algeria, "moderate

---

27 See references above in note 5 for various versions of the instrumental reasons. Clearly, it was meant to gain attention and reinforce his stature as a potential candidate but that is hardly surprising. On Nixon, see Byrne, chap. 5; and Thomas D. Matijasic, "It's Personal: Nixon, Liberia and the Development of US African Policy," *White House Studies* 11, no. 1 (2011), 39–55.

28 Dean Acheson rapped him across the knuckles, more or less intimating that he was an immature twit; and so Acheson went on to support Lyndon Johnson in the early campaign of 1960. "Nothing can be more injudicious than this proposal except making it" was his characteristic verdict on Kennan's speech (*New York Times*, October 26, 1957). *The Times* (July 3, 1957), in more polite language, took pretty much the same view. *Time* magazine (July 15, 1957) ridiculed him in a cartoon as a boy in shorts setting off a firecracker under the properly attired and diplomatic John Foster Dulles. More surprising was Adlai Stevenson's view. Coming back from a trip to Africa, Stevenson praised France, Britain and even the Belgians (!) for their "great advances in education, industrial and economic developments" (*New York Times*, July 9, 1957). A little later he excluded North Africa from the frame (*New York Times*, July 17, 1957), though he also said independence would mean chaos (*New York Times*, July 30, 1957). The speech generated a very large response in correspondence, many exceedingly critical, the FLN jubilant. See John F. Kennedy, Pre-Presidential Papers, JFKL, Senate Files, "Algerian Speech Files," box 919. Kennedy defended himself forcefully. In one interesting passage, he denied that he harbored any "dogmatic faith that nationalism merely by its proclamation, deserves American support" as there were indeed "retrogressive, reactionary forms of nationalism." This, then, was a reason to support Algerian independence before it was taken over by either Communist or "reactionary Islamic forces." Kennedy to John Harriman of the *Boston Globe*, n.d. (but probably August 1957).

people become extremists, extremists become revolutionaries, and revolutionaries become Communists." The argument then seems to turn on an empirical disagreement within the mainstream frame, namely:

> Contrary to Establishment views, the revolutionary movement in Algeria is precisely the kind of moderate nationalist government in the making that we say we want and consider future members of the Free World proper, and this, relatively speaking, is more important than the problem of metropolitan France and the French settlers. In fact, this will help France in the long run and so help us to fight the cold war in Europe.

Kennedy said as much and it would have been silly not to. However, he retained his partial concept of the cold war and the separate, autonomous process of decolonization and national liberation. Fundamentally, he insisted that these events were external to the cold war as such and should not primarily be evaluated in cold-war terms. In short, he did not derive the logic of support from the logic of the cold war.

The distinction becomes clearer when one considers that the month following Kennedy's Algeria speech there was his intentionally symmetrical Polish speech. This did pertain to the anti-imperialist struggle of the cold war, the struggle that *was*, in a way, the cold war. Kennedy was asking how the bankrupt strategies vis-à-vis the subjugated sphere of Eastern Europe might be changed. Liberation, the Republican and supposedly activist alternative to Democratic containment, had achieved nothing, its emptiness amply and painfully demonstrated the previous year during the Soviet suppression of the Hungarian revolt when the United States issued rhetorical support and rhetorical support only. Intriguingly, as already indicated, Kennedy's cold-war alternative was, in effect, less by way of cold war. He wanted to change the indiscriminate trading laws regarding Eastern Europe to allow for de facto openings to nationalist (or national-leaning) communist regimes such as Wladyslaw Gomulka's in Poland. Success in encouraging, within the Soviet sphere, a measure of national independence could only be achieved by forgetting (so to speak) the rigidities of anti-communism and by concentrating on nonideological practices of trade and exchange. The map of Eastern Europe was not uniform and it was myopic, consequently, to treat all satellites identically. "There can be shades of gray between these blacks and white," he said, "a limbo or twilight zone between complete Soviet domination ... and a free, friendly government—a nationalist Communist government such as is evolving in the case of Poland." A predictable debate about the morality of aiding and abetting the enemy ensued but the speech proved not nearly as controversial as the Algerian predecessor. In both cases, however, Kennedy's organizing principle was "national independence" versus imperialism or empire.[29]

Meanwhile, alas, the bracketed Soviet Union refused to play the role of inanimate object. The post-Stalinist regime in Moscow was leaving behind Stalin's continental isolationism for a variegated, erratic activism, not least in the emergent third world. More pressingly, on October 4, 1957, six weeks after Kennedy's Polish speech, the Soviets stunned the world and the United States in particular by propelling into orbit an actual satellite, the first in history. The *Sputnik* was tiny but the rocket that put it up there was not. The cold war would turn into a "race" and not only in terms of arms.

From the autumn of 1957 to the advent of his presidency, John F. Kennedy, always ready to race, became increasingly fixated on competing with the Soviet Union. This required an account not only of the competitor but also of the competitiveness of the United States itself. This became a problem, then, that spanned the domestic and the foreign. More fundamentally, it also put into question the nature of the race. This is hard to sort out, but competing with the Soviet Union was not necessarily the same as fighting the cold war more intensively and effectively, though this is the way, inevitably, it was received and understood.

It is difficult for us today to imagine the Soviet Union as a promising and even attractive model of modernity. In the late 1950s it was not very difficult at all. Kennedy was impressed and worried about its growth rates; he was impressed and worried about its technological achievements, its educational and scientific focus; and he was impressed and worried about its capacity to mobilize its collective resources and intelligence for instrumental purposes, the very toughness of the system. While the United States made Edsels, the Soviets made Sputniks; while

---

29 See the *Congressional Record*, 103–11, (August 21, 1957), 15446–54. The rubric was in fact "The Anti-Imperialist Struggle, Part II."

the United States was wallowing in consumer goods, comforts and luxury, the Soviets were concentrating on the real stuff. And he worried a great deal that the Soviet Union would be a logical and inviting model for the emergent nations in the third world, as it seemed to offer "the glamour of novelty, a disciplined, coherent, and irresistible answer to the overwhelming problems of economic management and progress." Translating this competition onto two analogues, he also worried, extensively, that the People's Republic of China was edging ahead of India. As if this were not enough, he found himself thinking that Nikita Khrushchev appeared to be more flexible and agile in his outlook than John Foster Dulles.[30]

How indeed all this could be done by a system he also described, in more baffled moments, as akin to that of ancient Egypt, Kennedy could not explain or chose prudently not to ponder. Nor did he explore how one kind of imperialism, the Western one, could be doomed to the world-historical dustbin while the other might very well be on the historical rise. What was clear, however, was that the United States would have to "prove that we can devote as much energy, intelligence, idealism and sacrifice" to the open society "as the Russian despots can extort by compulsion."[31]

---

30 The quotation is from a speech at B'Nai Zion, New York, February 9, 1958, in *Strategy for Peace,* 156. These concerns come to the fore on numerous occasions, not least in the election campaign speeches of 1960. Here is a representative sample (all available at JFKL): Speech at University of Pennsylvania, November 1, 1957; Speech at National Conference of Jews and Christians, Chicago, December 3, 1957; speech at Knights of Columbus, South Boston, January 12, 1958; speech at University of New Hampshire, Durham, March 7, 1960. Finally, see his speech in the Senate, *Congressional Record*, 106:10, (June 14, 1960), 12523–9. His "A Democrat Looks at Foreign Policy," *Foreign Affairs*, October 1957, describes the inflexibility of John Foster Dulles; his speech at Rochester, October 1, 1959, says that Nikita Khrushchev "is shrewd, he is tough, he is vigorous, well informed, and confident," and, moreover, "not the prisoner of any ancient dogma or limited vision" (*Strategy for Peace*, 34).

31 Speech at University of New Hampshire, Durham, March 7, 1960, JFKL. This is perhaps the place to say a word about modernization. In a larger sense, that was what Kennedy had in mind and he was, by late 1957, certainly influenced by Max Milliken and Walt Rostow's powerful account of it. Nevertheless, one should be wary of any simple equation here. Kennedy thought the model too economistic (as it were). My own view, slightly discordant, is that he saw fairly clearly that this kind of approach might rather easily become a new dogma, a new ideology of closure. On this generally see Michael Latham's now classic *Modernization as Ideology: American Social Science and Nation-Building in the Kennedy Era* (Durham, NC, 2000).

Toughness, efficiency and technological prowess, reflecting assumed Soviet virtues, could easily be integrated mirrorlike into the cold-war axiomatic, the proverbial cold-war deficit, the alarm bells ringing to the effect that we are not doing enough to meet the threat, we are falling behind in missiles, bombers, education, engineering, and so on and so forth. Indeed, the complex of ills fit exactly, and so, irresistibly, Kennedy now found himself reinforcing orthodoxy. The constitutive gap, he intimated, was in fact widening: a new, much more flexible and vigorous regime in Moscow corresponded inversely to the platitudinous, predictable and stolid Eisenhower administration, whose stiff anti-communism and commitment to massive retaliation seemed to translate, oddly, into a mixture of timidity and laxity, generating (as Kennedy's election rhetoric of 1960 would have it) nothing but "dust, dullness, languor and decay."[32] A political terrain was opening up, then, that was ideally suited to the appearance of bouncy, young activist Kennedy in contrast to the decrepit, old and passive Eisenhower. The polarity, at once political and iconographic, became the center of Kennedy's persona, its condition of possibility. The operation was exceedingly successful. Nixon, only four years older and very young by presidential standards (forty-seven), appeared unfairly, even in sympathetic coverage, to belong to a stale and stodgy world of yesteryear, an awkwardly suburban and solitary figure against the famously rich, glamourous and (presumably) athletic Kennedy, centering his perpetually grinning clan.

All of which is well known and endlessly pursued. Kennedy even scored easy points on Nixon's putatively frivolous Kitchen Debate with Khrushchev, ridiculing his rival for privileging color televisions over success in space.[33] What interests me, however, is again how the polarity served to push Kennedy in the direction of orthodoxy. Notably (and characteristically), he extended the thematic of intelligent, flexible activism to the domain of arms control, criticizing, rightly, the Eisenhower administration for its lack of any realistic program in that regard; and his campaign book in 1960 was, after all, entitled *Strategy for Peace*. Still, his peaceful move was subordinate to the overarching line that only by

---

32 Introduction to *Strategy for Peace*, 28.
33 Speech at High School Stadium, Alexandra Virginia, August 24, 1960, JFKL. Kennedy brought up the Kitchen Debate on several occasions in a derisory sense—to which one must add that the view imputed to Nixon about consumerism seems to give him the final laugh here.

redressing the balance elsewhere into that safe and more comfortable preponderance of power that was essentially US hegemony, or even supremacy, could real progress be made.[34]

To this one can then add that the shifting terrain in the third world, indeed the very transformation of the colonial world into the third world, was also conducive to cold-war activism. Contrary to what any informed observer in the West might have said in 1945, colonialism in world-historical terms as well as actual politics was dead as a doornail already by 1960, when seventeen new states came into being in Africa alone. The war in Algeria, to be sure, was still grinding on; but with the advent of the Fifth Republic and Charles de Gaulle's assumption of power in May 1958, Kennedy chose to acquiesce in the official US hope, a pleasing one, that in due course the general would resolve the problem by granting independence.[35] The question of the third world, in any case, was now less about support for national liberation than about how one might compete with the Soviets geostrategically on this new terrain. While the European theater (Berlin always excepted) had settled into a war of position, borders and zones more or less set by tacit agreement, the third world opened up, in orthodox terms, for a war of movement.

And there the argument might then conveniently stop. Emerging as a viable presidential candidate in a political conjuncture conducive to dynamic prosecution of the cold war, Kennedy fulfilled that historic role with gusto. We know the rest.

A more satisfactory or at least open-ended end will require some additional reflection on the utopian deficit (as I like to think of it), and on what it is to "race." Kennedy's impatience with cold-war orthodoxy featured constantly the problem of leadership, both presidential and US leadership in the world. Evidently, this was largely about being intelligently active in contrast to the torpor, real and imagined, of the

---

34 His Senate speech on June 14, 1960, is a good summary. It is also notable for its heavily disguised trial balloon on doing something new with regard to the People's Republic of China. Overall, he seems to have thought about the difference between the Soviet Union and the PRC as a matter of stages: the former had come out of its Stalinist one while the latter was going through it. He also seems to have imagined, but not in any sustained way, an emerging, multipolar world of diversity and heterogeneity.

35 See Irwin Wall's acerbic "De Gaulle, the 'Anglo-Saxons,' and the Algerian War," *Journal of Strategic Studies* 25, no. 2, 118–37, for an excellent corrective which reveals de Gaulle's highly malleable position.

Eisenhower administration, movement as opposed to stagnation. The positive notion that the United States inherently must be the leader (to be the United States is to be the leader) was negatively dramatized by the now apparent threat of losing that preeminence in a variety of ways to the Soviet counterpoint. At a deeper level, that dark scenario was about a certain loss of transcendence. Kennedy was irritated by the fact that third world leaders read and were inspired by Marx rather than Thomas Jefferson, author of the Declaration of Independence.[36] (The Virginian, of course, was also a large-scale owner of African American slaves, which may have impeded African enthusiasm for him; but this aspect did not enter Kennedy's vision.) An element of resentment, even envy, is in any case discernible in his account of the new communist support for third world anti-imperialism and national liberation.

If the Eisenhower administration thus lacked inspirational overcoming of the real, coming up with nothing better than Nixon's dishwashers, Kennedy's desire had to do with militance (not the same as militarism), sacrifice, collective mobilization as well as individual bravado, breaking new ground, a certain heroism if you will: the famous burdens and the crossing of new frontiers. The injunction to lead was accordingly more than a competitive necessity, it was a regenerative process that would restore to the United States its rightful identity as the home of the future, its aura of utopian transcendence, as in, say, putting a man on the moon within ten years. It helped, of course, that the mythological Kennedy himself in every way personified this utopian transcendence.

It will be remarked at once, and correctly, that this desire, or fantasy, was masculinist to the core, Teddy Roosevelt redux, nothing but an updated version of Progressivism circa 1900. The focus on process and

---

36   See for example speech at State Capitol at Albany, September 29, 1960, JFKL. Or in the same spirit: "There is not a present American statesman who is quoted by any African leaders today" (speech at Government Square, Cincinnati, October 6, 1960, JFKL). On occasion, he would refer to Franklin D. Roosevelt and Woodrow Wilson by way of contrast. By "utopian," in any case, I mean something along the lines of Fredric Jameson's theorization, not the notion of a ready-made plan for an alternative future society but an intrinsic part of the ideological operation. From that starting point, one might indeed go on in Jameson's spirit to map Kennedy's dilemmas and closure by means of the semiotic square that Jameson, in turn relying on Algirdas Greimas, tended to favor: more work to be done, I think. One place to start would be Fredric Jameson, *Archaeologies of the Future: The Desire Called Utopia and Other Science Fictions* (London, 2005).

conduct, the Weberian adequation of means and ends, the importance of study and particularity, the nonideological commitment to state action and improvement, the deep belief in regenerative deeds and selfless sacrifice, the emphasis on masculine physicality and fitness: it is all there. Historical antecedents aside, however, the question remains how this played out in the specific conjuncture of the late 1950s and cold-war orthodoxy.[37]

The obvious answer has already been given: more and better efforts to meet the threat.

This argument, generally, was still in 1960 indisputable and so a winner. Nonetheless, this was not, say, 1948: the threat was different. On the one hand, it was more dangerous on more levels (missiles, developmental model); on the other, it was also precisely about being a model in a competition rather than one of two forces in a posited (mutually lethal) confrontation, however abstract. The assumption of war in the cold-war matrix was, one must recall, no mere metaphor: the Soviet Union and its auxiliary communist states were by definition a condition of war, a force bent on world conquest. To oppose the Soviet Union was therefore, conceptually speaking, to engage in combat, and to win that combat, that war, was ultimately to destroy the threat. The threat of the Soviet Union was axiomatic, the derived need for global US action likewise so. The space for dissent and debate, to reiterate, was thus restricted to the appropriateness of the US counterstrategy, archetypally containment versus liberation, but in fact amounting in both cases to putting the Soviet Union in brackets while organizing the noncommunist universe known as the Free World.

This was ideology as closure. Decolonization and the emerging third world threatened to crack that closure, rendering simple anticommunism difficult if not unworkable. Kennedy's solution was to restrict the cold war and invent a positive American concept for this new site: postcolonial (US) support for decolonization and national liberation. Ingeniously, he also revised the cold-war matrix itself by turning the Soviet Empire into a series of varied regimes on a scale from

---

37 The central article on the gender aspect is Robert D. Dean's great "Masculinity as Ideology: John F. Kennedy and the Domestic Politics of Foreign Policy," *Diplomatic History* 22, no. 1 (1998): 29–62. The emphasis on the Progressive analogue is more my own.

black to gray. By raising, too, the more fundamental utopian deficit, however, he was putting into question (evidently) the character of the United States itself, its very fitness as it were. In the Soviet Union, no longer bracketed, he recognized a competitor in a race, a world-historical race, to be sure, but a race nonetheless. Such an event required the United States to live up to its billing, to prove its mettle. Hence his litany of ills after 1957 went far beyond the standard formula of not doing enough to cover the cold-war deficit—he asked, directly, why Eisenhower's United States was falling short of being the United States, which is to say its utopian credentials.

It would be wrong to think this just a reinforced and invigorated version of the orthodox matrix. For the world-historical racecourse is not a fight to the death or unconditional surrender except in the sense that the Soviets imagined their system to be superior and would win out in the long run. Such a competitive setting involved, ironically, greater intensity by way of real action in the imaginary race to the finishing line: the third world as a site stimulated greater real competition.[38] This is why Kennedy launched into his several third-world initiatives with such enthusiasm: Alliance for Progress, Peace Corps, aid to advertise that the United States was indeed a progressive model; but also counterinsurgency, Green Berets, fierce and abiding support for sundry repressive regimes and other relentlessly pursued, supposedly intelligent strategies of specificity, including the preposterous obsession with the figure of Fidel Castro.

That the race took this form and in this space was of course not unrelated to the advent of mutually assured destruction, the identity and recognition encapsulated in the devastating fact of nuclear terror. As far as the direct relationship was concerned, the obviousness of the mutual interest in stability and predictability would have to await the hair-raising experience of the Cuban Missile Crisis, an existential moment of truth if there ever was one. There followed the Test Ban Treaty and the beginning of a managed relationship. That none of this, cold-war orthodoxy or not, made any difference in real life to the Vietnamese peasant south of the 17th parallel is another story.

---

38 This is where Odd Arne Westad's notion of the cold war in a global context as residing, in intensive form, in the third world comes into new light and perhaps our disagreement could turn more interesting.

Still, here as elsewhere, one should never forget Kennedy's detachment, his fluidity and (let us say) his sense of dialectical movement in history. Beyond the greatness of deeds, he was not locked into any ideology, "ideology" conventionally understood as a coherent, explicit, normative position. His discomfort and irritation with cold-war orthodoxy were precisely that it was orthodoxy: correct opinion and received wisdom, closure, that stifled bold and new action. What that action might be was subject to change, sudden possibilities requiring unorthodox ways of thinking and, of course, vigorous leadership with the ability to master the particular and the contingent. Kennedy, in his better moments, was willing to contemplate doing otherwise, if not actually doing it in the end.

12
Law and Messianic Counterwar from FDR to George W. Bush

Law and normativity returned in the 1990s as central problems of international relations for the first time since the end of the Second World War. A good deal of the phenomenon took the form of proliferating talk by self-promoting interests; but a real historical shift of some magnitude was plainly opening up the possibility for that movement in the first place. Thus there was extensive expansion of law or lawlike procedure across the whole social and political register, a process one might refer to as juridification. Law, in short, became a master signifier. As this coincided with the waning of geopolitical rivalries in the aftermath of the Soviet collapse, it is tempting, hypothetically, to see a connection between the two developments, juridification corresponding in some manner to the erosion of the geopolitical. One might then also ask what it was, historically, that had made the earlier moment of international normativity possible and why it came to a close. And, finally, one might ask what the present assertion of US rule might mean for the status of law as a foundational value, the name in which matters international are necessarily supposed to be carried out.

In the wake of September 11, 2001, these questions indeed became urgent, as the United States arrogated to itself radically expanded rights and privileges in its open-ended "war on terrorism" (or "war on terror," in the now preferred term). This is conducted under the ostensible sign of law: the war is in fact said to be its very fulfillment. Yet it actually undermines international law in its traditional political form, as the

United States is in effect laying claim to global sovereignty, the power to decide what is legitimate anywhere and everywhere without consideration of the sovereign and presumably inviolate borders that have hitherto formed the central ground of international law. Much of the rest of the world, meanwhile, promotes quite a different idea of international right, a view centered (by necessity) on the authority of the United Nations and some modified version of sovereignty. Thus the struggle over the direction of world politics has come to pivot around issues of law and normativity, or, put differently, who has the ultimate right to decide what is legitimate. This is more than a philosophical and political matter. The staggering military superiority of the United States infuses any divergencies on international legality with the greatest lethal potential.

The matter is considerably complicated by the deeply rooted and partly contradictory US conception of war itself, which has served to make the "war against terror/ism" at once metaphorical and real. First, actual war has been seen, not as a legitimate policy of state, but as an act inflicted on the inherently peaceful by criminal outsiders. The United States, on this view, never engages in war wantonly, only defensively in response to intolerable provocation or unjustified attacks by others. Symptomatically, since 1941 the United States has not declared a single one of its many wars: such a declaration implies, in the traditions of international relations, recognition of the enemy as a legitimate equal. Combatting militarily the criminal assault may then be grasped either as a policing operation to restore law and order, or, more ambitiously, as a war against war itself. Second, there is at the same time an ingrained practice of using war favorably as a metaphor for domestic mobilization of the body politic for grander, collective purposes, for massive exertion of effort in the name of some worthy purpose (war on poverty, drugs and so forth).[1] Arguably, there is a common element in the two

---

1 It was William James, ironically for pacific and anti-imperialist reasons, who originated the political use of this bellicist metaphor in 1910. With his "moral equivalent of war," he wanted to redirect the mobilizing potential of the martial spirit toward useful purposes, to find a warlike way to mobilize the utopian, disciplinary and indeed military spirit of society for constructive projects. The formula became, in a way, the very conceptual center of the New Deal and has since of course been deployed extensively. See William E. Leuchtenberg, "The New Deal and the Analogue of War," in *The FDR Years: On Roosevelt and His Legacy* (New York, 1995) and William James, "The Moral Equivalent of War," in *Writings, 1902–1910* (New York, 1987): "The martial type of character can be bred without war. Strenuous honor and disinterestedness abound elsewhere" (1292).

conceptions in that both assume some alien attack or abnormality to be combatted regeneratively, if not by an outright crusade, then at least by total, all-out commitment. The war on terror, in any case, conjures up domestic exertion while simultaneously encompassing actual counterwar in the sense of policing. To complicate things even further, the counterwar in Iraq was also a grand attempt to attain geopolitical paramountcy.

All of which may finally be related to a peculiar pattern that has persisted since the early cold war but gained salience only in the halcyon days of the Reagan administration, namely, that the United States seems unwilling to ratify international treaties even though the often harmlessly idealistic and universalist content of these treaties on such matters as human rights looks like nothing so much as a manifestation of archetypally American values in the first place. Opposition to international criminal procedure is the most revealing case: utter abhorrence of the idea that any outsider should have the right to judge members of the US armed forces for alleged war crimes, an abhorrence coupled with plenty of browbeating to coerce other states into offering blanket immunity from such international jurisdiction.

On immediate reflection, the explanatory problem when it comes to international treaties may not involve much of a conundrum. The United States, sometimes in the guise of powerful groups in the Senate and elsewhere, sometimes in the guise of an abrasively nationalistic administration, understands such agreements as base infringements on US sovereignty by the lesser lights of this world, and thus, somehow, a grave threat to what is viscerally felt to be the American Way.[2] The US rejection of what would seem to be the expansion of its own universal values, in this case the universal value of law itself, can then be explained by reference to a range of historical and cultural features, usually to be found somewhere under that hoary old umbrella term American exceptionalism.

Such an explanatory scheme is not without value but it easily takes on the form a culturalist account of everything and nothing, at once endlessly expansive and flatly reductionist. My wager here, by contrast, is that a single aspect of the latently limitless structure of exceptionalism

---

2 This view is not exclusively right wing. There is a left-of-center critique of supranational jurisdiction as well. Dennis J. Kucinich's opposition to the World Trade Organization is grounded in a similar spirit.

may serve to illuminate the various related problems I have set out above. I am referring to the pervasive sense of messianic chosenness. This idea of a redemptive mission posits a constitutive difference between inside and outside, in which the former assumes absolute, world-historical priority and so is inherently beyond external judgment. As a true sovereign, the agent is subject only to a higher law. Whenever this posture becomes dominant, then, it disturbs in interesting ways the whole field of international law and sovereignty, war and peace.

The epithet "messianic" is, however, often used diffusely to indicate nothing more than a certain salvational attitude in foreign policy or an inclination to self-righteous moralizing in the name of a special dispensation. There have, in fact, been several messianic tropes, figures and currents. One must be precise. For one thing, it is more than simply a calling by a higher authority to carry out decisive things. The traditional Judaic sense of chosenness, for instance, is a highly particularized projection in which the transcendence of the whole is far from clear.[3] The messianic self-conception must also be distinguished from the weaker or less ambitious understanding of national identity in terms of mission. Mission indicates an ordinary sense of particularity (such as the national) according to which the given entity is uniquely fitted, or perhaps even chosen, to do something specific amid a potentially open-ended mass of other entities similarly eligible to be called upon to do something specific and unique. This is nationality as the analogue of the liberal idea of individuality. There might even be an explicit hierarchy among missions; but if the head (to invoke one such notion) is more important in the body politic of the world than the feet, the latter have their indispensable and legitimate role to play. The structure is a continuous oneness. By contrast, the separation between the messianic force and the rest is necessarily dramatic and absolute. Whether it forms the actual salvational power or only that which lays the groundwork for the coming of the messiah, the agent is elected on supra-historical authority to perform crucial, world-historical deeds in the interest of humankind as a whole.[4] Because the given nation is thus pivotal for the future of

---

[3] On the Judaic issue, see Gershom Scholem, *The Messianic Idea in Judaism and Other Essays on Jewish Spirituality* (New York, 1971).

[4] This distinction is elaborated by Peter Duncan, *Russian Messianism: Third Rome, Holy Revolution, Communism and After* (New York, 2000). The messianic idea of Moscow as the Third Rome was far less prominent than is commonly thought.

world history, indeed the *only* possible project of such significance, one is always acting under the sign of the universal. What the elect do determines the fate of the whole, but at the same time they remain absolutely apart from that whole. As everything is invested with monumental significance, one must have an account, moreover, of what is to be done. One is always inherently obliged to choose. This necessitates interpretation, in turn giving rise to quarrels among the elect. These quarrels, however, must result in a decision as to what is *absolutely right*. Like Leninism, messianism is nothing if not decisionism. Indeed, the posture is not always explicitly religious at all: history or eternal principles may well fill in for God.[5]

How this entity (and process) should relate concretely to the outside is open to question. More often than not, the posture has been one of isolation: to play out the universal model in one's own time and space, a withdrawal on the part of the sacred (and perhaps suffering) remnant, a refusal to be contaminated by the soiled outside so as to be able to preserve the model for purposes of future redemption. Sometimes, certainly after 1941, the posture has been one of interventionism, movement into the degraded outside to redo it in the image of the model Self or at least control its trajectory. If there can be disagreement, accordingly, as to what ought to be done about the outside, there can be no disagreement on the proposition that the outside should never be allowed to infringe on the fundamentals of the inside. Whether in pristine Protestant or secularized form, redemptive chosenness renders the domestic space and order sacred, above and beyond external judgment precisely because they represent the very highest achievements of humankind and so are impossible to improve upon. The United States is the particular condensation of the eternal universal, or, if you prefer, the end of history.

An asymmetry, a sort of synecdochical inversion, is thus at work that opens up an unbridgeable gap. The United States is the world but the world is not the United States. Though there is an outside, it cannot count as properly realized. The rest of the world is either a not-yet or an evil nothingness. Toward that outside, from the most developed and culturally proximate to the most alien and unrecognizably different,

---

[5] I draw here on my *Manifest Destiny: American Expansionism and the Empire of Right* (New York, 1995).

there is always an irreducible, constitutive distance and difference. Like ancient Rome, then, the United States is a political entity that can have no equal: a world empire in Otto Hintze's terms.[6]

Though messianism has never been far from the surface in the political identity of the United States, its eminence, role and effects have varied: overdeterminant in some sense but not always dominant. In the Second World War, my historical starting point, the sanctity of international law was very much on the agenda at the same time as it was unusually hard to see the relationship between the United States and the outside in messianic terms. The leading figure here, and the leading figure of this chapter, is the ambiguous and endlessly slippery Franklin D. Roosevelt. It was Roosevelt, above all, who criminalized war and promoted the concept and practice of policing in world politics. It was he, too, who established in a Wilsonian vein that security for the United States could only be achieved when the world accepted its progressive values. Yet it was he as well who put the United States in a line of continuity with the world, who avoided the messianic route and advocated cooperation among Great Powers, in which regard he differed radically from his postwar successors. For in the period 1947–63, the period of cold war proper, the United States became the messianic leader of the free world and international law, not coincidentally, turned into something tainted: the normative disappeared in the name of the normative as it were. In other respects, however, the cold war was in fact a selective reworking of Roosevelt's terms.

After tracing this transition, I move on to some reflections on the 1990s, when the world really did seem to have become the one, single universe of Roosevelt's wartime projection: juridification gathered momentum along with neoliberalism, while the United States exerted effortless domination, without messianism but also increasingly under the sign of international normativity. The abrupt coda on September 11, 2001, then opened the way for a massive return of the messianic, not in the cold-war version of hegemonic domination but as pure supremacy, the right to act in accordance with world-historical election and to reject

---

6 Otto Hintze, *The Historical Essays of Otto Hintze* (New York, 1975): world empires are "those states of ancient times and of non-European civilization which established a universal authority in an area they regarded as the known and inhabited world, and which recognized no other states as equal" (468n).

forthrightly any encroachments, real or imagined, on the sacrosanct sovereign of sovereigns.

My considerations do not aspire to explanation as straight causality. Messianism is neither a variable, nor some idealist construction. It is, rather, an ideological act that produces certain political possibilities and closures, all of which are historically contingent (and so subject to other and more specific kinds of historical analysis). Because the United States is a world empire with no possible equal, its relation to the putative international community of which it is said to be a member will always be problematic. The constellation of war, sovereignty, law and messianism may tell us something about that contradiction.

Roosevelt's manner of preparing and executing the US entry into the Second World War, putting the country once and for all into the world and ending the possibility of any separation from the game of geopolitics, created a formidable legacy for his followers, even when they thought they were partly or wholly rejecting it. As I see it, his understanding of the war and its aims can be distilled into two conflicting thematics, both of them grounded in the idea of security.

The first is the proposition that security for the United States and the world after the war would be a matter of maintaining law and order among states. This seems bland and uncontroversial enough, but the notion was derived from a diagnosis of the enemy that was unorthodox and significant. For Roosevelt, the enemy was first and foremost the Nazis and only secondarily the Japanese militarists—Mussolini counting, if at all, as a very distant and essentially trivial third. The Nazi regime appeared to him literally as lunatic gangsters, Al Capones with a twist so to speak. What made Hitler lethally dangerous, then, was that he had shown himself an irrational but powerful criminal, intent on the greatest possible crime of all, the conquest of the world. With such a "rattlesnake" (in Roosevelt's vivid language) there could be no agreements or real peacemaking, only unconditional surrender, total liquidation, the slate wiped clean once and for all, the beginning of something new, a new world order.[7]

---

7 For the remark about the rattlesnake, see Franklin D. Roosevelt, *The Public Papers and Addresses of Franklin D. Roosevelt. 1940: War—and Aid to Democracies* (New York, 1941), 10:390.

While FDR had become convinced by the end of the 1930s that internal Nazi criminality corresponded to external aggression, it is important to note that the primary criterion of lawlessness was the conduct of the regime abroad. German (and Japanese) behavior indicated complete contempt for the rules of normal interstate relations. Roosevelt's criterion, in short, was ultimately measured by the standards of international law. Thus he was able take a relatively relaxed view of dictatorship or authoritarianism as general phenomena. Lawlessness necessarily supposed dictatorship, but dictatorship did not necessarily suppose lawlessness. Certain dictators, while not properly attired for civilized salons, favored the status quo and could be included and influenced, the assumption being that time and circumstances would serve to refine their comportment. FDR was disinclined, in the end, to divide the world into dictatorships and democracies, preferring instead to draw the line between lawless and lawful, aggressive and quiescent. Hence his fairly unruffled manner of handling Josef Stalin. The deal with Nazi Germany and war against Finland notwithstanding, the Soviet Union seemed essentially interested in maintaining the international system and so might eventually develop into something better and more agreeable.[8]

Once the wartime alliance had been formed, Roosevelt took this a big step further. He began to envision Moscow as a central member of the policing outfit he had in mind for the postwar world, a world to be subjected, literally, to extensive regional patrolling to quell any criminal aggression against the international order. Policing assumed the sanctity of sovereignty as the foundation of international law at the same time as it allowed, implicitly and contradictorily, for the right of the responsible powers to contravene that very sovereignty in practice. Roosevelt's model was the interstate relationships in the Western hemisphere, now supposedly equalized in the spirit of the Good Neighbor Policy but in fact determined by the authority of the United States to decide when and where transgression had occurred.

Though anticolonialist in orientation, FDR's position had a strong flavor of nineteenth-century imperial rule, metropolitan forces pacifying and suppressing sundry colonial disturbances. For the standards Roosevelt evoked were doubtless conceived of in terms of

---

8 Here I follow Warren Kimball, *The Juggler: Franklin Roosevelt as Wartime Statesman* (Princeton, 1991).

civilization, as that concept had emerged in the preceding century. This (European) model conventionally imagined the world as a tripartite and progressive division of space and time: savagery, barbarism and civilization. Because progress from one stage to the next required pacification, eradication of lawless elements and thorough supervision, it was incumbent on the civilized to impose and maintain order everywhere. Dealing with barbarians, however, involved an element of consent along with coercion: one could work on and to some extent with them, lifting *very* gradually into a higher state. Savages, by contrast, could be handled with brute force alone. (More recent analogues of this scheme can be found in John Rawls's distinction between liberal, illiberal and lawless states.)[9]

Policing, then, would entail surveillance and disciplining of deviance, chiefly of states *qua* international actors. If the criterion was ultimately civilizational, it was also negative in the sense that it required, in effect, only the absence of outwardly aggressive behavior. Though globalist in scope, moreover, the United States was not to be the sole world policeman but one of four (or so).

Roosevelt's second thematic was also civilizational and globalist, but far more intrusive. By extension, it was also unilateralist in spirit. One might call it, infelicitously, "security as the implementation of freedom everywhere." Here, Hitler was not only a criminal; he was also a massive threat to universal values, standing as he did for everything the United States did not. Beyond obliteration of the physical threat, final security would require the subsequent presence of a series of features that Roosevelt outlined programmatically in the Four Freedoms and the Atlantic Charter. This maximalistic concept of liberal, positive values paid no respect to classical sovereignty or state borders. It made domestic structure and behavior the central criterion of legitimacy. What any given regime was actually doing by way of foreign policy was not decisive: legitimacy was a matter of domestic adherence to the timeless values of humankind. Transgressions would not only disqualify the state in question from membership in the international order: they would make it, ipso facto, a security threat, an object to be dealt with.

Roosevelt sometimes referred to the values of "God-fearing democracies"; but overall he pitched his message from the standpoint of the

---

[9] On Rawls and on civilizational standards, see Gerry Simpson, "Two Liberalisms," *European Journal of International Law* 12, no. 3 (2001): 537–71.

United States alone, its security in the world.[10] The implications were staggering. From now on, there could be no theoretical limit as to what might count as a US security problem. The whole notion of a security boundary or perimeter had been eliminated. Any event anywhere was now in principle to be subjected to scrutiny by the president of the United States from the viewpoint of absolute security, to be measured in terms of freedom. It was an astonishing change. How the United States would actually operate after the war to secure itself by means of freedom on a global scale was not clear. Any principled posture along these lines would sharply put into question the relationship with the Soviet Union. Stalin's regime, whatever it may have been, was not a God-fearing democracy. Yet the implications largely disappeared from view. Once Roosevelt had established his master signifier, he refused to deal with concrete political arrangements, concentrating instead on liquidation of the enemy, on winning the war. Very much in character, he saw no reason to reconcile these contradictory approaches, if indeed he saw any contradiction.

His political target at home was, of course, the isolationists, and his obvious aim to prevent any postwar repetition of the Wilsonian debacle. Doubtless, there was thus an element of expediency in his limitless concept of security. Nothing in the outside world, he was arguing, can really be ignored: isolationism is over and done with. Doubtless, too, Roosevelt, much in the manner of imperial policymakers in the nineteenth century, thought that initial pacification and subsequent patrolling would lay the foundation for historical development in the interest of everyone and eventual achievement of freedom everywhere. His actual account, however, indicated no such temporal sequence of development. The suggestion remained that he had invested, in the name of security, the US president with the obligation of addressing unfree areas of the world as security risks. It deserves mention that some of the much maligned isolationists grasped the globalist consequences and inherent dangers to any democratically conducted foreign policy, as well to traditional precepts of international law. Pearl Harbor, however, had reduced them to political rubble.

Roosevelt, remarkably enough, avoided the temptation to fit his globalism into the messianic matrix of chosenness and redemption.

---

10   Quoted in Fritz Grob, *The Relativity of War and Peace: A Study in Law, History, and Politics* (New Haven, CT, 1949), 19.

Three factors may explain this. First, his relentless (and in many ways unfair) attack on the isolationists emphasized the relatedness and imbrication of the United States in the world; and to that extent it was also by connotation an attack on exceptionalism, any notion of the United States as absolutely separate and apart. Second, the nature of the war itself was not conducive to messianism. For three full years, it was above all the Red Army that battled the Nazi Wehrmacht. The Japanese attack on Pearl Harbor occurred almost six months after the German onslaught against the Soviet Union had initiated that epic confrontation, which was to overshadow almost everything in the Pacific theater. If Woodrow Wilson had been able to imagine in 1917 that he was entering the bloody stalemate of the First World War as a savior, Roosevelt had no such option. This was a military coalition, a genuine alliance in which the United States was one of the three central members. Roosevelt himself took this position early on, eschewing the Wilsonian precedent of distinct and separate status as an associated as opposed to allied power. Meanwhile, the other side was not singular either: two main enemies in two wholly separate areas of the world, in effect fighting two different wars. Hence, while the basic division was obviously a binary one between good and evil, the actual configuration of forces did not lend itself easily to heroism of the messianic kind. The character of the war, in fact, implied that the postwar world, too, had to be imagined as one of cooperation rather than US singularity.

The third factor had to do with the president himself. Exceptionally, FDR was no American exceptionalist. His formative period had been the so-called Progressive Era of the early 1900s, the one moment in which the political culture featured a strong US sense of connection to, and inclusion within, a larger Western civilizational movement, in no small measure because of the common imperialist project. Not accidentally, it was also a period when, for once, there was a certain political space to question systematically the whole orthodoxy of government and to do so in a comparative frame. In short, while Progressive uplifters would certainly see the United States as the cutting edge of the civilized world (usually slightly ahead of Britain), they would also understand that world as one of temporal and spatial continuity rather than qualitative separation. The prototypical figure here was of course Teddy Roosevelt, FDR's distant relative, predecessor and source of inspiration. Wilson, FDR's other exemplar, had spent much of his academic life admiring the British system of parliamentary government and did not fully embrace the messianic role until 1917. Roosevelt was in any case far from a proper Wilsonian: he did not believe in the formal equality of self-determining states across the board, nor for that matter in any transparency and publicity of diplomatic procedure.

The potential conflict between Roosevelt's two thematics was clearly reflected in US framing of the Nuremberg trials. Nowadays it is often forgotten that the central charge against the Nazis was that they had, as FDR had always argued, undertaken a war of aggression. Robert Jackson, the chief prosecutor, reiterated this authoritatively in his opening speech at the trials: "Resort to war—to any kind of war—is a resort to means that are inherently criminal."[11] Understanding war as a crime in this vein presupposes the concept of sovereignty, an inviolate attribute that is violated by the transgressive act of war. Jackson's affirmation of the sanctity of sovereignty could not have been more explicit. By implication, Nuremberg seemed not to prohibit a regime with outwardly peaceful relations conducting mass murder at home within its borders; any ensuing outside action to avert it would arguably be illegal according to this foundational principle. Likewise, however, the Nuremberg Charter also held sovereigns legally responsible for domestic atrocities by instituting (ex post facto) the category of crimes against humanity, consequently calling upon the forces of rightness to engage in policing across the very sovereign borders that it guaranteed. The same contradiction marked, as mentioned, FDR's position. Indeed, it is still very much with us—witness the formally illegal bombardment of Yugoslavia.

The framing of Nuremberg entailed another notable element peculiar to the United States. Much as the German government was commonly referred to as the "Hitler Gang" during the war, it was defined in the trials as a criminal conspiracy: presumably the Nazi regime was criminal to the core while the state of Germany was not. This was not mere rhetoric. Conspiracy was a time-honored legal formula in the United States, used by capital in the late nineteenth century to crush labor unions and later deployed by the FBI in fighting organized crime. The

---

11 Quoted in David Lubin, *Legal Modernism* (Ann Arbor, MI, 1994), 351. My discussion of Nuremberg draws on Lubin. He points out that aggression was actually not defined until 1974.

charge was juridically useful because it made mere membership in the gang a criminal act, so that individuals became responsible for the whole.[12] The procedure would be repeated with the greatest clarity in the postwar trials against members of another criminal conspiracy, namely, the Communist Party. Current reverberations of the formula are much in evidence.

In the early cold war, the messianic disposition turned into necessity. Roosevelt's premise, that victory would give birth to an *unus mundus*, a single normative universe devoid of profound or qualitative divisions, was gradually destroyed in the two years after 1945. Harry S. Truman, faithful to the president but not privy to his intimate thinking—nor, had he been so, really capable of coming to grips with it—was soon convinced that the world was still very much divided, as the alliance for freedom had concealed (it was now becoming horribly clear) a Hitler-like member in its very midst. The solidifying Soviet position in Eastern Europe was thus recast from liberation to totalitarian conquest achieved in a war against another totalitarian power. So the essential wartime division of the globe remained intact, albeit in novel guise.[13]

The new configuration was tailor-made for messianic exceptionalism: a polarized world, featuring two superpowers, sharply defined ideologically and increasingly entrenched geopolitically, totalitarian intrusion seemingly threatening the remaining Western parts of Europe. In this crucial hour of history, only the United States, victorious and unblemished, had the wherewithal to save the Free World. But did it have the will to fulfill the role history had so plainly intended? Indeed it did. And so onward, redemptively, to the Marshall Plan, NATO, Korea, interventionism, atomic armament and a global string of military installations.

Roosevelt's wartime frame(s), accordingly, had to be modified. Clearly, there was no room in a divided world for his concept of Great Power policing coupled with wheeling and dealing. Security was now exclusively about the global implementation of freedom, in fact first and foremost about saving the remaining sphere of freedom from continued totalitarian subversion. That struggle required the United States to perform the exclusive role of redemptive force. The Soviet form of

---

12 Ibid., 3.
13 See chap. 3.

totalitarianism, however, introduced a range of new problems. To confirm the initial identity between Nazi Germany and the USSR seemed easy enough: criminal conspiracy, aggression, disregard for traditional distinctions between war and peace, world conquest, all projected onto a historical background of aggression and disastrous appeasement in the 1930s. With this sort of power, in itself a form of quasi-war, there could be no recognition and certainly no appeasement, only liquidation. Hence the binary division was no more symmetrical than its wartime predecessor had been. The Free World was the real world. The other side, the totalitarian side, was a netherworld of slaves and enslaving agents, parasitical on that real world. As a binary, this was a straightforward gloss on Christian orthodoxy. Yet the Soviet enemy was clearly different, too, from the Hitler Gang of blustering bullies engaged in undisguised aggression. For Moscow, and the international conspiracies it was allegedly promulgating, constituted a creeping, ultimately far more insidious and dangerous kind of lawlessness. Had they not patiently been playing democrats during the war? This was a far more conspiratorial conspiracy, as it were. Working undercover, typically deploying Trojan horse tactics, the Soviets even appeared to prefer carrying out conquest amid conditions of ostensible peace.

How to combat this sort of crime (what the United States posited as the Soviet launching of the cold war) was consequently much more problematic than Roosevelt's massive but forthright mobilization to win on the global battlefield, where victory was clear and decisive. Though there were serious people in the United States who advocated preventive war against the Soviet Union, such an attack in the end could only be prepared, never launched. Where Moscow held overt territorial sway on the Eurasian landmass, it could not be eliminated for the foreseeable future, only frozen out (or in). Military attempts at covert subversion were real enough, but war here became largely symbolic, pure ideology, coupled with mobilization for outright war. Elsewhere, however, even the remotest semblance of communism was peremptorily to be crushed by all means necessary. In a turn that I am tempted to call peculiarly dialectical, Roosevelt's policing authority came to be an exclusive prerogative of the United States and applied only in the realm of the free, or more precisely the realm that was not communist. Policing presupposed a single world, as policing, having no other value than order itself, would make no sense unless it was grounded in normative unity. Because the Free World now fulfilled that role, it thereby became the space for open-ended interventionism or counterwar.

Other ironies ensued. Roosevelt's operative position on the wartime coalition had actually been closer to the Soviet notion of an antifascist alliance than to his own, officially stated, front for global security as global freedom. Now Truman, having become leader of the Free World and so the redemptive force in its expansion, reinvented FDR's proto-Soviet version of antifascism in the form of anti-communism, that is, as a post-Leninist strategy of forming the broadest possible coalition for the prevention of unfreedom, the object being to allow history to run its spuriously natural course toward actual and final freedom. Truman, Eisenhower and Kennedy, on this logic, all came to support the most reprehensible dictatorships because these regimes, however far from actual freedom, were deemed a precondition for progressive history: right-wing dictators suppressed conspiracy and prevented the kind of disorder that provided grounds for communist exploitation (and so on). Here, then, in a reworking of Roosevelt's formula, emerged the magnificently self-serving distinction between authoritarian and totalitarian dictatorships, the one subject to favorable historical change, the other perpetually doomed to stasis or collapse.[14]

The thorny issue of international law and sovereignty, meanwhile, could be nullified by means of a bit of conceptual magic: any movement or phenomenon identified by the US president as a totalitarian threat was by definition a plot to violate the sovereign independence of non-communist states, and hence a legitimate target for policing in the name of collective security and freedom across otherwise sacrosanct borders. Actions technically illegal consequently became morally and politically legitimate. NSC 68, the foundational cold-war document of the United States, is quite eloquent on this: in the war against conspiratorial slave-masters, the choice of means was to be limited only by instrumental efficacy.[15] Moreover, undemocratic actions against forces defined as

---

14 On this distinction, which goes back far beyond Jeane Kirkpatrick's notorious formulation in 1979 to the Truman administration, see David F. Schmitz, *Thank God They're on Our Side: The United States and Right-Wing Dictatorships, 1921–1965* (Chapel Hill, NC, 1999), chap. 4.

15 United States Department of State, *Foreign Relations of the United States* [*FRUS*], 1950, 1:237–92. Here is the relevant passage: "The integrity of our system will not be jeopardized by any measures, covert or overt, violent or nonviolent, which serve the

undemocratic were also legitimate. An example of how this worked, powerfully laid bare in the work of Mario Del Pero, can be found in the energetic attempts by the United States in the early 1950s to get the Christian Democrats in Italy to outlaw the Italian Communist Party (PCI), which represented a good quarter of the population.[16] It is easy to associate that policy by analogy with the geopolitical moves of Henry Kissinger against Salvador Allende and Eurocommunism in the 1970s. Kissinger, however, grasped these actions as eradication of anomalous spots on an otherwise coherent and clean map of superpower control, while the only anomalous aspect of the PCI for Truman and Eisenhower was its size. Its appearance, by contrast, as a Trojan horse under conditions of ostensible peace, was precisely what one would expect. To eliminate a party that was inherently hostile to democracy was not a normative issue but an operational problem, the chief aspect of which was really only the appallingly wobbly character (as some US observers came to see it) of its executors, the corrupt Christian Democrats.

The constitutive relation of the United States to the world, in short, no longer corresponded to Roosevelt's view. The self-proclaimed leader of the Free World became thoroughly messianic: a massive global struggle against evil featuring the United States as the all-important central actor of goodness and redemption. While the relation to evil was of course absolutely antagonistic, the relation to the rest of the free world became conceptually, if not organizationally, different as well. The United States was not alone but it was qualitatively separate. Ultimately, the burden of leadership authorized the White House to decide where and when a breach of order had occurred or for that matter where and when the mere threat of a breach might occur.

As the world so became sharply dualistic after 1947, the space for universal or indeed any other legalism shrank commensurately. The posited

---

purposes of frustrating the Kremlin design, nor does the necessity for conducting ourselves so as to affirm our values in actions as well as words forbid such measures, provided only they are appropriately calculated to that end and are not so excessive or misdirected as to make us enemies of the people instead of the evil men who have enslaved them" (244).

16 See Del Pero's excellent "American Pressures and Their Containment in Italy during the Ambassadorship of Clare Boothe Luce, 1953–1956," *Diplomatic History* 28, no. 3 (June 2004): 407–39.

existence of an unrecognized evil outside wiped out all official desire for general agreement in the pseudo-universal frame and opened up, as mentioned, the prospect of unlimited interventionism. The very idea of the international was stained. Witness, indicatively, the wide rhetorical use of references to international communism. Actually existing internationalism, meanwhile, included institutionally a Trojan horse, the very force that had made (it was now becoming apparent) the gullible Roosevelt believe his alliance had been fighting for democracy and then infamously tricked him into the Yalta agreements. Given that the Nuremberg trials had included the Soviet Union as a judging power, they too were now under suspicion. The dénouement of many Nuremberg convictions in the 1950s was odious and tragic but not surprising. As Peter Maguire has shown with disturbing clarity, the freeing (and in some cases ensuing intelligence employment) of war criminals in the Bundesrepublik took place in not very subtle exchange for political alignment with the United States.[17] "International," in the 1950s, came to imply sanctification of bad sovereignty, the sort of sovereignty that provided cover for totalitarian subversion. For the same reason the United Nations, too, was contaminated, except for those instances such as the Korean War where it happened to follow entirely the US position.

Reneging on the Nuremberg judgments and similar matters necessitated no extensive internal argument and certainly none in public. A very public debate, by contrast, did ensue about the sputtering remainders of international legalism, such as the UN Genocide Convention of 1948. That debate produced in the United States a coherent right-wing critique of international treaties that was wider in scope than the seminal opposition to the Versailles Treaty in 1919 but less politically diverse, for the arguments of 1920s and '30s were never quite as simple as they were made out to be in the 1950s, when liberal internationalism became conventional wisdom. Cold-war internationalists of the 1950s, though abstractly in favor, were not interested in international legalism or any other bothersome treaties in the name of universal norms. The political problem here was compounded by the embarrassing issue of civil rights, something in which the cold-war internationalists did have a strong and genuine interest, but in part because racial conflict and repression were

---

17 Peter Maguire, *Laws of War: An American Story* (New York, 2001).

having deleterious effects in the ideological struggle against the Soviet Union. Proposed legislation to rectify the most glaring aspects, such as lynchings and segregation, could thus be justified in instrumental ways by reference to the geopolitical exigencies of anti-communism. No one across the political spectrum, of course, could oppose that. The right was thus obliged to accept a strong federal state, abhorrent in principle, as regards defense and vigorous action abroad. What it was not obliged to accept was federal action on domestic issues such as race relations. UN treaties of the late 1940s, the Genocide Convention along with the Covenant on Human Rights, were understood and situated politically in that potentially explosive context.[18]

Opposition forces may have been right wing but they were by no means marginal. Thus the American Bar Association, though divided, was prominent in the attack on the treaties, its president perhaps their most vociferous and articulate critic in the land. Moreover, this critique proved effective. The argument was threefold. First and most important, such compacts were said to diminish US rights by supposedly overriding the Constitution and thereby eroding sovereignty. Though exaggerated, the point was not trivial. The Constitution is ambiguously worded on the status of foreign treaties, and it is not clear that domestic constitutional provisions would take precedence. Hence the proposed Bricker Amendment in the early 1950s, which was explicitly occasioned by, and directed against, the Covenant on Human Rights. To the extent, then, that the legal status of treaties was in doubt it was a priori legitimate to ask if such commitments would (i) infringe on constitutional sovereignty, and (ii) in fact weaken existing US jurisprudence. The answer in both instances was no, but the questions were not wholly implausible. It is another matter that the ABA couched the contention in terms highly derogatory of the foreign, indicating that US freedom would come to be judged by outsiders insufficiently schooled in native virtues. The second criticism was an extension of this jaundiced view: subjection to the UN and other international organs would allegedly expose the United States to communist and socialist influence and infiltration. Finally and relatedly, supranational government by treaty would undermine and

---

[18] The ensuing discussion of law in the 1950s follows Natalie Hevener Kaufman, *Human Rights Treaties and the Senate: A History of Opposition* (Chapel Hill, NC, 1990).

eventually destroy the federal system and its constitutive feature of states' rights. This last tenet was an ill-disguised attack on all manner of civil rights legislation, being then and now a code word for racist obstructionism.

The constitutional controversy went beyond mere worries about infringed sovereignty. For any legislation or binding agreement originating outside the sacred space, itself inherently expansive and eternal, was by nature an attack on the natural order of things, historically regressive. Along the lines of Truman, one might well refer to endemic racism as a passing shortcoming in the existing democratic system; but one could not suggest that anything was truly wrong with the system as such. Truman, however, made his claims in the wake of an enormously successful war effort; Roosevelt, by contrast, was operating in the wake of a catastrophic Depression in which the United States seemed exceptional chiefly because of the depth and longevity of its economic crisis. Whereas both believed that the essentials of the final, unsurpassable stage in the history of humankind had come into being with the founding of the United States, Roosevelt maintained, as mentioned, some plural notion of "God-fearing democracies" rather than a single, shining example. Coupled with the anticommunist matrix, at any rate, the notion of a historical end served to severely diminish any institutional universalism or legal commitments in that spirit.

Cold war proper was followed by a period of attempted Great Power management—détente—the basics of which certainly did not include emphasis on international law or for that matter any norms other than those emanating from the mutual interest in avoiding nuclear catastrophe and maintaining respective spheres of domination while jockeying for relative advances. Foreign relations conducted as traditional geopolitics did not necessitate glory for the United States; but it did necessitate the avoidance of general debacle. By 1980, gloomy and galling developments seemed to be adding up to precisely such a debacle. Messianic election thus returned with a vengeance in the Reagan administration, cold-war mentality replayed as postmodern pastiche, replete with the requisite Armageddons and Evil Empires. I leave aside the dynamics of that process, which deserve another essay. I note in passing, however, that venomous messianism generated similarly venomous denunciations of internationalism. Reagan's dismissal of international law in the

Nicaraguan case was eloquent in its unapologetic contempt.[19] The moment ended, of course, in what appeared to be a total victory, triumphant success in the messianic struggle. The world at long last had become one, an *unus mundus*, after the implosion of the Soviet Union and the termination of its historical principle. From now on, history could only be about the quantitative extension of the American principle.

But if Roosevelt's single normative frame looked to be at hand, the question still remained of what a specifically American foreign policy might entail after the end of the long postwar epoch, in which leadership had always been predicated on the existence of a clearly present and powerful adversary. The messianic itself had presupposed not only an identifiable layout of the strategic terrain, but the very presence of such a terrain. In the 1990s, it was no longer clear where that was situated, much less what its topography might be. The large strategic community suffered a commensurate loss of confidence and direction.

Until September 2001, Washington would make two attempts to resolve the question of world power, one by design and the other mostly by default. The initial pitch was the ill-fated attempt, in the context of the first Gulf War, to institute a New World Order. Its conventional tone was largely a product of the previous Iraqi aggression against Kuwait. For the first time since the Second World War, a member of the United Nations had invaded another for the purpose of annexing it, liquidating it as a state.[20] Hence the senseless Iraqi gamble attacked the one sovereign prerogative that had remained intact during the tumultuous half-century of superpower conflict. Inscribed in the very foundation of the United Nations, itself a direct organizational outgrowth of the wartime coalition against "illegal aggression," the rules absolutely forbade any such initiatives. The Gulf coalition, formally grounded in the UN, therefore assembled in the name of sovereignty to punish criminal aggression. The larger goal, beyond restoration of Kuwait, was thus the reaffirmation of international law. If, in effect, the New World Order was

---

19 On Reagan and Nicaragua, see David P. Forsythe, *The Politics of International Law: US Foreign Policy Reconsidered* (Boulder, CO, 1990).

20 There had been, to be sure, many aggressive wars and some outright annexations, but, crucially, no war for the annexation and elimination of a full, recognized member of the United Nations. The first Gulf War was thus quite different, legally speaking, from the second.

ultimately to be backed by US hegemony and military power, the normative content of that system was at this stage conceived of in a thoroughly traditional manner.

For a set of related reasons, the project evaporated almost immediately. The first Gulf War ended in a question mark. The US-led coalition stopped short of liquidating the liquidator, partly because of residual attachment in Washington to the idea of retaining Iraq as a buffer against Iran, the cynical policy that had generated the egregious support for Saddam's savage war in the 1980s, when his "Hitlerian" criminality was evidently not an issue. Proper Iraqi sovereignty was now suspended and the regime essentially reduced to the status of a domestic criminal on probation. Still, the principle itself was maintained and thus too the veneer of international law and order. Horrendous and lethal events elsewhere, however, made the very notion of a global order nothing less than a sick joke. The world, it turned out, did not extend to Africa. Only after much hypocrisy and hesitation did it come to include the Balkans. What these events had in common aside from monstrous violence against innocent civilians was that they severely put into question the principle of state sovereignty. Inaction amid graphic displays of mass murder inside states destroyed the image of any irenic Pax Americana. From the perspective of the US public, the clarity of the Gulf War was thus rapidly replaced by incomprehensible messiness, exemplified by the galling televisual documentation of US ineptitude in Somalia. At home, by contrast, important and quite comprehensible developments were clouding over the international horizon altogether, namely, the Bush recession and the ensuing Clinton boom.

The contingent, haphazard nature of George H. W. Bush's world order and its tenuous material underpinnings were revealed by the rapidity with which that order faded away. It had come up, in effect, against another decisive asymmetry in the relation between the United States and the outside. If the United States is the world, but the world is not the United States, it is also true that the United States is far more important to the world than the world is to the United States. The US ruling class has never, as a whole, been anchored in geopolitical (or international) space in the manner of, say, nineteenth-century Britain. A trivial survey of foreign travel experience among congressional politicians would be enough to illustrate the point. Given the purposely divided political system and overrepresentation of rural states, the result is not conducive to continuity and coherence in foreign relations, unless there is a clearly identifiable threat. This condition did not obtain between the Gulf War and September 11, 2001. US politics in the 1990s, not surprisingly, was wholly dominated by domestic concerns.

And, indeed, why worry? The period was driven by the massive and astonishing expansion of the US economy, while the international realm, distant catastrophes aside, seemed to be moving along soothingly, if unevenly, toward a semblance of the domestic norm. Thus the new world actually required little policing: a huge expansion of US power was taking place without any extensive reordering of "inferior" states. Redemptive chosenness could be performed as model laissez-faire while dominance took care of itself in a hyper-Gramscian movement of consent on the part of the governed (or, to put it differently, by surface acquiescence amid the postmodern jumble). The autonomous workings of the market appeared to work brilliantly at home and abroad. Seen within our Rooseveltian frame, then, the project of security as freedom looked as though it was being implemented without much state action at all, beyond forceful insistence on the globalization of markets. The one consistent foreign policy of the Clinton administration was in fact market liberalization, ordering states in accordance with the precepts of free trade and exchange, as exemplified by NAFTA. Disciplining of deviance took place mainly through the IMF and the World Bank, organs dominated by the United States and its Treasury. The rest of foreign policy, from a political standpoint, was essentially fluff, expendable surplus value.

Clinton's security as market freedom was enshrined in two symbolic trinities: liberalization, deregulation, and privatization in the economic domain, and democracy, law and human rights in the political.[21] The two corresponded but were not in fact equivalent. For the principle of capitalism, summarized as the free market, was said to predicate and indeed generate the rest. Democracy would follow the free market. Without the free market there could be no democracy; and if there happened to be markets but no democracy, the latter would inevitably follow. This was the basis for the otherwise curiously benevolent view of

---

21 See Peter Fitzpatrick, *Modernism and the Grounds of Law,* (Cambridge, 2001), 213–16.

the marketizing dictatorship of the proletariat in the People's Republic of China, an approach in many ways similar to the benevolence once displayed toward the Pinochet regime in Chile. The problem with European democracy, meanwhile, could be diagnosed as various degrees of deficiency in the realm of capitalist freedom.

Becoming the standard of civilization, then, brought no real impositions or onerous duties on the universal nation in the 1990s: its model was successful not only in economic terms but also as a political norm. Less visible, however, and certainly not felt in the heartland of strategic comfort and economic dominance, was the exponential growth in relative military power, as the huge US defense apparatus rolled along largely on its own in the post-Soviet era.[22] As it happened, neither market liberalism nor massive military power was to offer much protection against the kind of threat posed by Osama bin Laden.

In the wake of September 11, FDR's maximalistic vision of security reappeared in strongly messianic form, overflowing with the salvationist language of radical Protestantism. Ingeniously evoking Roosevelt and Reagan in a single expression, "the Axis of Evil," George W. Bush thus gave unequivocal expression to the limitless scope of the quasi-war against terrorism and the appointed function of the United States to carry it out. There would be no security for the United States until evil everywhere had been rooted out and the president reserved the right to act accordingly where and when the situation so might require.[23] In an atmosphere heavily charged with desire for drastic action, the war on terrorism was hazily defined and deterritorialized. Terrorism—or the threat of terrorism—was everywhere, certainly anywhere one might choose to find it; and so it was a perfect justification for US globalism. As evidenced by the attack on Iraq, there was not even a need for any actual connection with terrorism: declaring the future possibility of

---

22   On military developments, see Andrew J. Bacevich, *American Empire: The Realities and Consequences of U.S. Diplomacy* (Cambridge, 2002).

23   This was a persistent theme. Thus George W. Bush on the eve of the Iraqi war: "Once again this nation and all our friends are all that stand between a world of peace and a world of chaos and constant alarm. Once again we are called to defend the safety of our people and the hopes of all mankind. And we accept this responsibility ... Whatever action is required, whenever action is necessary, I will defend the freedom and security of the American people." State of the Union address, *New York Times*, January 28, 2003, A12.

such a connection was enough. Once subdued, indeed, Saddam Hussein's Iraq turned out to possess neither weapons of mass destruction nor anything much by way of terrorist connections. By then, however, the war on terrorism had become the war on terror, an even more nebulous target that had the virtue of allowing for the retroactive inclusion of Saddam, whose undeniable capacity to terrify was far more tangible than his terrorist credentials.[24]

For terrorism, as the administration soon discovered, is not a real enemy: it is not a concrete political adversary. It is not an -ism, for one thing. No one stands for terrorism as though it were an ideology, a normative view of change. It is, rather, a range of violent actions, undertaken illegally for political and ulterior reasons. Governments have engaged in it. Chiefly, however, it is a strategy of the weak and the ruthless. The object is a massive surplus effect, in which respect it resembles a warped kind of economy. More to the point, because it is not an -ism, a positive claim in itself, terrorism as such can only be fought negatively and preventively. It can never, any more than crime, be eradicated as such. One can only narrow its openings. In fighting a technology of political violence, one can be more or less technically effective. Because terrorism is not a singular political enemy, it is not an entity on which one can wage war. The Taliban regime was a political adversary, as was Saddam. Specific terrorists might be adversaries. Terrorism in general is not. A war on terrorism, consequently, implies perpetual mobilization in constant search of concrete enemies.[25]

Yet the global interventionism that September 11 opened up for the Republican administration was anything but arbitrarily general: it was in fact framed within a massively ambitious attempt to remake the world

---

24 The significance of the rhetorical shift from "terrorism" to "terror" has not been sufficiently noticed. Initially, the move was probably made in order to focus on Iraq's putative WMDs, connecting their potential to induce terror with the terror of terrorism. In due course, however, it became a way of connecting September 11 with almost anything the administration wished to bring into focus. I owe the image of the "terrifying" Saddam Hussein to Mischa Byruck.

25 Specific terrorist movements must of course be countered with properly political solutions to the problems of which they are a symptom; but to terrorism as a strategy in general there is by the same token no blanket response beyond policing. Choosing to pitch the battle as a war, the Bush administration unwittingly served the interests of the perpetrators in that they would now be categorized, understood, and, in a way, dignified precisely as they themselves wanted, namely, as warriors.

systemically and unequivocally to the strategic advantage of the United States, all meant to be in the sharpest possible contrast to the fuzzy Clinton years (as well as to the failures of the elder Bush). The strategic scenario was quite precise. It centered on the notion of regime change. Initial success in Iraq would thus set into motion a vast wave of upheaval throughout the region, turning Syria and the proto-nuclear Iran into congenial, Westernized regimes. Disagreeable powers everywhere would be suitably intimidated and pressured into similar adaptation. The supreme goal lay in the East: regime change in the People's Republic of China, singled out at the one potential competitor and threat to the United States in the coming decades. This vision, breathtakingly grandiose, had already been articulated by dissident insiders at the end of the first Bush administration. These neoconservatives spent the 1990s in profound alienation from the reigning vision of finance capital, complaining that the United States was squandering its virtual supremacy instead of using power to remake the world in its own interest, which is also that of the universe. September 11 crystalized this messianic project, at once religious and secular, into a formidable gambit for global power.[26]

The strategic shortcomings (and parochialism) of that gambit are now evident, as indeed they always were. The kind of military superiority the United States achieved in the 1990s, push-button warfare designed to overwhelm the enemy and minimize casualties, was never appropriate for the task of maintaining peace on the ground amid a less than welcoming population. Here, however, I am more concerned with the political and normative contradictions. For in the 1990s, another development was taking place that would put a damper on this zealous attempt to reconfigure the world.

Freeing up fields of action for capitalist rule by eliminating jurisdiction in the form of state regulation also made possible, conversely, the decentered, independent expansion of law as an autonomous international system—a process peculiarly analogous to the domestic growth and

---

26 On the 1992 plan and the ensuing history of the 1990s, see David Armstrong, "Dick Cheney's Song of America: Drafting a Plan for Global Dominance," *Harper's*, October 2002.

function of law in the nineteenth-century United States.[27] This may in turn be seen as part of the wider development I have referred to as juridification: the application of law or lawlike procedure across the whole social register. That there has indeed been a proliferation of law or legalism is not an uncontroversial proposition; nor, if true, is it clear what that means. However, it seems that the conduct of institutions and individuals has increasingly fallen under the purview of rules that, though neither legislated nor proclaimed by the state, are encoded in legal terms. Sectors previously governed by administrative rule have become subject to private law or drifted into some novel kind of gray zone between the public and the private. On another level, transnational claims in the name of human rights, claims that are essentially political, are being made on legal grounds. NGOs and other entities have also assumed quasi-legal status outside of the jurisdictional boundaries and classical precepts of international law. Finally, there has been a remarkable spread of *lex mercatoria*, law governing commercial transactions, contractual obligations across state borders without any conventional means of coercive sanction, yet apparently functional and enforceable by internal mechanisms, such as arbitration through privately appointed quasi-courts. This process, already gaining pace in the 1980s, was immeasurably accelerated by the destruction of the Soviet Union and the concomitant fading of geopolitical inscriptions of the world.[28]

Though there are easily identifiable instances of contractual domination in the case, for instance, of the IMF and the World Bank, the process, taken as a whole, has no clear origin, certainly not in any legislative or elected body. It has been described in the manner of Niklas Luhmann as an example of autopoiesis, a self-reproducing, self-validating system. Another word for it might be "globalization," less a global phenomenon than relentless penetration of capitalist market conditions in quite select places, but certainly lacking the old form of monopolistic, territorialized rulemaking. Alternatively, one might see the process in Foucauldian terms of normalization, the sweeping expansion of regulatory norms for the conduct of conduct, norms being a standard and a

---

[27] On the nineteenth century and US law, see Morton Horwitz, *The Transformation of American Law, 1780–1860* (Cambridge, MA, 1977).

[28] I am drawing here on, among others, Fitzpatrick, *Modernism*; Gunther Teubner, ed., *Autopoietic Law: A New Approach to Law and Society* (Berlin: Walter de Gruyter, 1988); Teubner, ed., *Global Law Without a State* (Aldershot, UK, 1997).

procedure by which a given population (or institution) can judge itself internally and relationally. In wider terms of normativity, the development can then be related to the accelerating growth in communications, digital and physical, in the globalizing parts of the globe. Juridification, in any case, takes place when these expansive norms are encoded in specifically legal terms.[29] However one theorizes the process, it has very little to do, generally, with the traditional concept of international law as an interstate operation between sovereignties. It has no visible identity or origin. Thus, notably, it does not permit any separation between sacred messianism and a degraded outside. Not being from anywhere, it cannot be understood as infringement by anything external. If specified as a principle, on the contrary, it must be understood as the generalization of the internal.

Normalizing proceduralism in international politics proper, however, came to be centered symbolically and institutionally in the United Nations. To no little degree this occurred because the United States declared itself the sole and ultimate author of the norms and procedures it might need, which made others begin to see and use the UN as the only possible counterpoint and to do so explicitly in the name of the normal and the legal. On the face of it, this is a strategy of depoliticization, the promotion of an image of the world as essentially devoid of fundamental antagonism and contradiction, subject to supposedly neutral legal norms and arbitration. The dialectical effect, however, was the opposite: the reinvention of international politics. For the movement of legalism and normativity is at odds with the imperial and messianic status of the United States, whose decisionistic authority is always in the last instance overdetermined by the absolute distinction between itself and the outside.

---

29 On Luhmann, see Teubner's two collections *Autopoietic Law* and *Global Law without a State*. On Foucault, see Mitchell Dean, *Governmentality: Power and Rule in Modern Society* (London, 1999); and Alan Hunt and Gary Wickham, *Foucault and Law: Towards a Sociology of Law as Governance* (London, 1994). Another version of this, highly expressive of its moment before September 11, is Michael Hardt and Antonio Negri, *Empire* (Cambridge, MA, 2001). But if the 1990s signified the emergence of a decentered empire without imperialism, it is not clear how we should understand the current US position.

Index

A
Abendland, 3–4, 277–305
abolitionism, 68, 91, 95
academia, 198
Acheson, Dean, 5–6, 51–3, 54, 70, 81, 111, 119n23, 124, 324n28
Acton, Lord, 292
Adams, John Quincy, 41, 230n13
Adenauer, Konrad, 303–4
Adler, Les, 179
advent of theory, 191
agency, 196
Algeria, 309n4, 321–5
Allende, Salvador, 124, 273, 350
Almond, Gabriel, 194
Alperovitz, Gar, *Atomic Diplomacy*, 156–7
Althusser, Louis, 196
American exceptionalism, 198–9, 257
American globalism, 179
American imperialism, mobilization against, 84
Americanization, 90, 204

American policymaking, 162–3, 180
American Revolution, 33, 59, 70–1
American universalism, 164
America's Half-Century (McCormick), 172
Amerindians, 239–40, 241, 261
Anderson, Benedict, 202, 287
Anderson, Perry, 132, 132n35, 183n81, 204–5, 299n31
Anglo-Saxon England, 61n16
Anglo-Saxon liberties, 60
anthropology, 193
anti-colonialism, Roosevelt on, 342–3
anti-communism, Kennedy on, 318
antifascist legitimacy, 38–9
anti-imperialism, Kennedy on, 307–33
anti-Nazism, abolitionism with, 68
Apology (Orosius), 294
a priori, 57
Aquinas, Thomas, on war and peace, 28–9

Architects of Illusion (Gardner), 151–2
Aristotle, 63, 264
Aron, Raymond, 46, 113, 113n19
Around the Cragged Hill (Kennan), 279n3, 280, 283–4
Ashley, Richard, 200
Asiatic despotism, 63
Atlantic Charter, 42, 80–1, 144, 343
Atomic Diplomacy (Alperovitz), 156–7
Augustine
 on war and peace, 28–9
 solution to problem of evil amid omnipotence of God, 114n20
Austro-German nationalism, 300
Axis of Evil, 357

B
Bailey, Thomas, 212
 A Diplomatic History of the American People, 208
Balance of Power, 31, 162–4
Bartlett, Robert, 259n12
Baruch, Bernard, on the cold war, 23–4
Beaufre, André, on the cold war, 23–4
bellicism, 33, 39
Bemis, Samuel Flagg, 266
 A Diplomatic History of the United States, 208
Benjamin, Walter, 19, 147
Bentham, Jeremy, 33
Bernstein, Barton, 157
bin Laden, Osama, 357
bipolarity, 35, 99, 100, 124–5, 126, 129, 131, 182

Blitzkrieg, 24
Bohlen, Charles, 66, 66n26
Bolshevik Revolution (1917), 131, 152, 154, 184, 297
Bolshevism, 278, 285–6, 298, 300, 303
Bonaparte, Napoleon, 290, 295
Bond, James, 22–3
Brandt, Willy, 125, 128
Braudel, Fernand, 172, 205n3
Brezhnev, Leonid, 12
British parliamentarism, 286
Bulgaria, 159, 173
Bundesrepublik, 304, 351
Burke, Edmund, 109–10, 291, 295
Burkharin, Nikolai, 5
Burnham, James, 24–6, 267–9, 271, 272, 274
 The Managerial Revolution, 25
Bush, George H. W., 98n1, 274, 355
Bush, George W., 108n12, 133, 225–6, 251, 273, 357, 359
Byzantine Empire, 294

C
Calvin, John, 58
capitalism, 36–7, 107n11, 132n35, 162
Captive Nations, 68
Carter, Jimmy, 11
Castro, Fidel, 10, 23, 263, 332
Catholic Counter-Reformation, 67
Catholicism, 67, 278–9, 279n3, 284–7, 289, 290, 291, 292, 295, 303, 304–5
causal reasoning, 163
Celestial Mandate, 274
Centre for Cultural Studies, 196
Chace, James, 53n4

Index

Channing, William Henry, 68
Charlemagne, 294–5, 303
Chile, 124, 126, 357
China, 100, 123, 124, 125, 129, 142, 159, 180, 250, 274, 315–16, 327, 356–7, 359
Chou En-Lai, 125
Christendom, 109–10
Christendom or Europe (poem), 290–1
Christian Democrats, 350
Christianity. *See also* Manifest Destiny
   attitudes toward Islam, 27–8, 131n33, 231–2, 308n2
   Christian life, 58
   disputes over, 212
   O'Sullivan on, 229
Churchill, Winston, 7, 41, 105
Cicero, 30–1, 40, 63, 272
Civil War, 55–60, 67, 68–9, 70–71
Clash of Modernizations, 130
class conflict, 36
classical antiquity, 63, 293–4
classical realism, 111–12
classical republican tradition, 58–9
class war, 36–7
Clausewitz, Carl von, 33–6, 44, 46–7, 215
Clinton, Bill, 273, 274, 356, 359
Cohen, Stephen F., 5, 179
cold peace, 5, 124
The Cold War and Its Origins (Fleming), 155
cold war. *See also specific topics*
   about, 1–15
   concept of, 19–47
   considered as a US project, 75–95
   development of, 97–133

fighting on a global scale, 8
   how it was coined, 103
   Kennedy on, 308n2
   as a metaphor, 27
   mobilization during, 97
   pause in, 23
   as US ideology, 51–73
   writings of the, 137–88
colonialism, 281, 317, 318–19, 329
communism
   conflation of, 7
   evil, 90
   fascism and, 84
   international, 121, 128
   totalitarian, 7
   totalitarianism and, 7, 99
Communist Party, during 1920s, 14
competing concepts, 10
conflict, American way of, 68–73
consensus school, 148
Constantinople, 295
containment, 72, 89, 91, 93, 108n12, 113, 115–16n21, 315–16
continuity thesis, 98, 102–7
contradiction, 38
Co-Prosperity Sphere, 181
corporatism, 167–74
Coudenhove, Richard, 300–1, 303–4
Council of Foreign Ministers, 145
court-packing scheme (1937), 80
Covenant on Human Rights, 352
Cromwell, Oliver, 30
crucial rejectionist component, 85
Cuba, 11, 128, 244–5, 253, 263, 266
Cuban Missile Crisis, 10, 13, 21, 47, 55, 78, 121, 122, 142, 332
cultural history, 191–3, 203

culturalism, 88
cultural studies, 190, 192n10, 195-6
Culture and Imperialism (Said), 192
Culture and Society (Williams), 196
culture and theory, considerations on, 189-206
Cumings, Bruce, 182
Curti, Merle, 148-9, 198-9
Czechoslovak Spring, 125

D
Danilevsky, Nikolai, 296-7
decentering, 130
Declaration of Independence, 70n34
Declaration of Liberated Europe, 144
declassification, 183
Decline and Fall (Gibbon), 299
The Decline of the West (Spengler), 297
decolonization, 331
de Gasperi, Alcide, 303
de Gaulle, Charles, 125, 329
Del Pero, Mario, 125, 350
Delta Council, 51-2, 54
de Maistre, Joseph, 291
de Man, Hendrik, 279-80
democracy
 about, 240-1
 Coudenhove on, 301
 identification, 73n40
 O'Sullivan on, 229
Democracy in America (Tocqueville), 240
Democratic Review, 228, 241n31
de Murville, Couve, 312n7
Denning, Michael, 198-9
denouement, 120-6
Depression, 14, 207, 210, 353

design, 66-7
despotism, fragile structure of, 64
destinarianism, 230, 240
détente, 226
dictatorship, 342
Diebold, William, 171
Dien Bien Phu, 320-1
Dilthey, Wilhelm, 151
A Diplomatic History of the American People (Bailey), 208
A Diplomatic History of the United States (Bemis), 208
diplomatic history
 about, 137-8, 202
 war and, 207-20
Diplomatic History, 191
diplomatic rejectionism, 78
displacement, 241
domination, 195
drôle de guerre, 24
Duhamel Georges, 112n17
Dulles, John Foster, 94, 121, 318-19n16, 324, 327

E
Eagleton, Terry, *Literary Theory: An Introduction*, 191n6
Economic Security and the Origins of the Cold War (Pollard), 165-6
Eisenhower, Dwight D., 93, 94, 121, 322-3, 328, 330, 332, 349, 350
Elementary Aspects of Peasant Insurgency in Colonial India (Guha), 201
emergence and periodization, 108-20
empire, US as an, 253-75
Empire of and for Liberty, 95, 239, 247-8, 258, 260, 262-3, 265, 273

Empire of Civilization, 265, 267
Empire of Slavery, 271
Engels, Friedrich, 36–7
Enlightenment, 32, 72, 295
Episcopalianism, 279n3
escapism, 91
ethics, exit of, 64n22
Europe. *See also specific countries in Europe*
  extramural relationship between Islam and, 79
  Kennan on, 277–305
European imperialism, 244
Europeanization, 296
European Other, 265
evil, as a challenge sent by God, 62
evil communism, 90
exceptionalism, 198–9, 228n8, 257
executive power, 225n6
existential presence, of Vietnam, 140n3
expansionism, Soviet, 43, 144, 162
extramural relationship, between Europe and Islam, 79

F
Fanon, Frantz, 44–5
fascism
  about, 80
  communism and, 84
  conflation of, 7
  growth of, 285–6
  nature of, 86
  protofascism, 118
  totalitarian, 7
fascist aggressions, 112
fascist Spain, 92–3

Feis, Herbert, 156–7
Ferdinand III, Castilian king, 26
Fifteen Weeks (Jones), 51–2
Fifth Republic, 329
First World War, 212, 218
Fleming, D. F., *The Cold War and Its Origins*, 155
Fleming, Ian, 22
Foucault, Michel, 205
Four Freedoms, the, 42, 80–1
France, 109–10, 319–20
Franco, General, 92–3
freedom
  in American image, 57–61
  appropriation of, 81–2
  as natural condition of humankind, 90
  under siege, 60, 70–1
  slavery and, 270–1
"freedom from want," 43, 70
free enterprise, 73n40
Free World, 6, 9, 15, 113–14, 116, 234n20, 250, 318, 348–9
French Revolution, 33, 287–8n15, 289–91
Front de libération nationale (FLN), 321–2
Fukuyama, Francis, 131–2, 132n34, 183n81
functionalism, 162

G
Gaddis, John Lewis, 98, 139–40n2, 158, 159, 161, 162, 163, 164, 165, 171, 175, 176, 177, 178
  Strategies of Containment, 163
  The United States and the Origins of the Cold War, 160

Gadsden Purchase (1853), 243–4n33
gangsterism, 41, 79–80
García-Arias, Luis, *Libro de Los Estados*, 26–7
Gardner, Lloyd, 149
   Architects of Illusion, 151–2
Gaullism, 179
Geertz, Clifford, 193, 201
geopolitics, 9, 182–8, 187n87, 234, 240, 254n3
George III, King, 54, 61, 64
German idealism, 151, 283
Gettysburg Address, 70n34
Gibbon, Edward, *Decline and Fall*, 299
Gingrich, Newt, 225n5
Ginzburg, Carlo, 193–4n14
global interventionism, 358–9
globalism, American, 179
The Global Cold War: Third World Interventions and the Making of Our Times (Westad), 107, 127
Goldwater, Barry, 320
Gomulka, Wladyslaw, 325
Good Neighbor Policy, 342
Gorbachev, Mikhail, 98n1
Gorodetsky, Gabriel, *Grand Delusion: Stalin and the German Invasion of Russia*, 86–7n5
Gramsci, Antonio, 196, 197, 199
Grand Alliance, 209
Grand American Narrative, 133
Grand Delusion: Stalin and the German Invasion of Russia (Gorodetsky), 86–7n5
Grant, Ulysses S., 82

Great Power, 5, 8, 24, 75, 77, 102, 124, 144, 153, 211, 215, 245, 247, 273, 296, 340, 353
Gregor the Great, 295
Grotius, Hugo, 29–31, 40
Guam, 248
Guha, Ranajit, *Elementary Aspects of Peasant Insurgency in Colonial India*, 201
Gulf coalition, 354
Gulf War, 354–5

H
Haas, Michael, 202
Hague Convention (1907), 40
Halle, Louis, 146, 186
Halliday, Fred, 26, 186n84
Hamilton, Alexander, 257
Harbutt, Fraser, 182n80
Harriman, Averell, 117
Harrington, Fred Harvey, 148–9
Harrington, James, 272
Hayes, Carlton J. H., 284–5
Hegel, G. W. F., 19, 33–6, 44, 46, 47, 132, 143, 191
hegemony, 272n25
Henry, Patrick, 55n7, 56
Henry, William Wirt, *Patrick Henry: Life, Correspondence and Speeches*, 56n7
Herder, Johann Gottfried, 189–90, 191–2, 203, 260
Herodotus, 293
Hintze, Otto, 95, 257, 273, 340, 340n6
Hitler, Adolf, 40, 41, 109–10n14, 113–14, 292, 300, 343
Hitler Gang, 346, 348

Index

Hitler–Stalin Pact, 71
Hobbes, Thomas, 29–31
Hobsbawm, Eric, 223n2
Ho Chi Minh, 319–20, 319n17
Hogan, Michael, *The Marshall Plan*, 170
Hoggart, Richard, *The Uses of Literacy*, 196
Hoover, Herbert, 168
hostility, forms of, 31
hot war, 7, 27
"House Divided," 69–70n33
Huizinga, Johan, 203
humankind, philosophical history of, 189
Hussein, Saddam, 358
hyperdiplomacy, 126
hyperrealism, 86–7n5

I
idealism
  German, 151
  philosophical compared with political, 199–200
ideology/morality
  dominance of, 187
  of exceptionalism, 210
  role of, 146
  Soviet, 188
  theories of, 195
imperialism
  about, 254n3
  advent of, 245
  American, 84
  European, 244
Indochina, US presence in, 14
Insular Cases (1901), 264
insurgency, 11

intellectual history, 201
international communism, 9, 121, 128
international gangsterism, 41
internationalism, 37, 179
international law, 349, 353–4, 361
international relations, history of, 139–40n2, 140
interventionism
  about, 130
  global, 358–9
  third world, 127
interwar period, 103
intra-Christian conflicts, 30
Iraqi sovereignty, 355
Irish nation, 311–12n6
Iriye, Akira, 195
iron curtain, 7, 105
Islam
  Christian attitudes toward, 27–8
  extramural relationship between Europe and, 79
isolationism, 82, 252, 344
Italian Communist Party (PCI), 350
Italian democracy, 125–6

J
Jackson, Andrew, 241–2, 241n31, 346
James, William, 336n1
Jameson, Fredric, 1, 106n9, 203n32, 330n36
Japan, 181, 244
Japanese Kwantung Army, 112
Jefferson, Thomas, 61n16, 225, 236, 257, 258–9, 261, 261n14, 273
Johnson, Lyndon B., 122, 313–14, 314n9

Jones, Joseph M., *Fifteen Weeks*, 51
Judaism, 28
Judeo-Christian component, 57

K
Kant, Emmanuel, 31–3, 34
Kennan, George F.
  Abendland, 3–4, 277–305
  alternative of, 115
  on American universalism, 164
  on Aron, 113n19
  Around the Cragged Hill, 280, 283–4
  on Christian themes, 62
  on the cold war, 26, 30, 44–5, 72n38
  compared with Truman, 87
  on containment, 72, 89, 307n1
  contrary position of, 115–16n21
  on Empire, 269
  on escapism, 91
  on Europe, 277–305
  on mass politics, 299n31
  Memoirs, 14–15
  morphological image of object-parasite, 88–9
  on nationalism, 277–305
  on Orientalist themes, 65
  on periodization, 163
  on realism, 109
  rejectionism, 78
  on the Soviet Union, 85, 92
  on totalitarianism, 84
  on the United States, 86, 223
  on universalist discourse, 146
  on ways of being toward the world, 88
  on the West, 277–305
  Western culturalism, 88
  X article, 3, 77, 108
Kennedy, John F.
  on Acheson, 324n28
  on anti-communism, 318
  on anti-imperialism, 307–33
  on cold war, 308n2
  on colonialism, 318–19, 329
  de Murville on, 312n7
  on foreign relations, 55n7
  on imperialism, 4
  relationship with Fleming, 23
  on Test Ban Treaty, 75
  on Utopian deficit, 307–33
Kennedy, Joseph, Jr., 311
Kennedy, Joseph, Sr., 310–11
Khrushchev, Nikita, 327, 328
Kimball, Warren, 156, 213
Kissinger, Henry, 10, 12, 125, 126, 226, 250, 350
Kitchen Debate, 328
Kolko, Gabriel, 77, 127, 152, 153, 154, 215n5
  The Politics of War, 154–5
Kolko, Joyce, 127, 154, 155
Korea, 180–1, 219
Korean War, 120, 124, 181, 208, 315–16, 351
Kotkin, Stephen, 5
Kremlin design, 66
Kubrick, Stanley, 120
Kucinich, Dennis J., 337n2
Ku Klux Klan, 285
Kuniholm, Bruce, 176

L
LaFeber, Walter, 149

law
  governing commercial transactions, 360–1
  messianic counterwar and, 335–61
Lears, T. J. Jackson, 198–9
Le Carré, John, 104–5, 105n7
  The Spy Who Came in from the Cold, 13, 22
Leffler, Melvyn, 98n1, 174, 175, 177
  The Preponderance of Power, 176–8, 182–3
Lenin, Vladimir, 36–7, 39–40
Leninism, 86, 339
Leo XIII, Pope, 285, 292
Liberal World Order, 6, 142
Libro de Los Estados (García-Arias), 26–7
Lichtheim, George, 147n10
limited competition, structure of, 100
Lincoln, Abraham, 69–70n33
Lippmann, Walter
  on Burke, 110–11
  on the cold war, 23–4, 44–5, 78, 112n17
  on containment, 113
  critique of Kennan's X, 3, 77–8
  on differences between Soviet Union and West, 78
  on diplomacy, 108–9
  on incommensurability, 109
  on Kennan's X article, 108
  semantic field and contextual politics, 112
  on Soviet policy, 86
  use of term cold war by, 7, 55
Literary Theory: An Introduction (Eagleton), 191n6

Live and Let Die (film), 22
"long crisis," 190
Long Telegram, 85
The Long Revolution (Williams), 196
"Lublin" regime, 144
Lukacs, Georg, 151
Lundestad, Geir, 158–9, 158n37, 160
Luther, Martin, 32–3

M
Machiavelli, Niccolò, 63
Maguire, Peter, 351
Maier, Charles, 138n1, 169
The Making of the English Working Class (Thompson), 196
The Managerial Revolution (Burnham), 25
Manchuria, 112
Manifest Destiny, 2, 223–52
Mann, Michael, 220, 271n24
Mannheim, Karl, 151
Manuel, Don Juan, 24, 26–8, 131n33
market, identification of the, 73n40
Marshall Plan, 53, 73, 145, 154, 159, 171, 173, 175, 177
The Marshall Plan (Hogan), 170
Marx, Karl, 36–7, 186
Marxism, 184, 196
Marxist Enlightenment critique, 36
Marxist-Hegelian notion of contradiction, 116–17
Masaryk, Thomas, 302
mass culture, 198–9
"Massification," 280
Mastny, Vojtech, *Russia's Road to the Cold War*, 161
Matthiessen, F. O., 198–9

Mazzini, Guiseppe, 237, 260, 287, 288
McCormick, Thomas, 149, 172–74
 America's Half-Century, 172
McMahon, Robert, 180
McNeill, William, 220
Meinig, D. W., 95
Memoirs (Kennan), 14–15
messianic counterwar, law and, 335–61
metric of imperialism/anti-imperialism, 10–11
Metternich, Klemens von, 288
military history, diplomatic history as counterpoint to, 212
Milward, Alan S., 170–1
Mitteleuropa, 280, 299–300, 301–3
Moltke, Helmuth James Graf von, 304n41
Monroe Doctrine, 235–6, 247, 261, 272, 300
Montesquieu, on contrast between East and West, 63–4
Mr. X. *See* Kennan, George F.
Mukden incident (1931), 112
multilateralism, 166, 267, 273
multipolarity, 34
Muslims, 26–8, 294
Muslim Saracens of Spain, 27

N
nationalism
 Austro-German, 300
 historical preconditions for, 287
 Kennan on, 277–305
 third world, 282n7
national security, 6
National Security Council, 94

National sovereignty, 282–3
NATO, 125, 145, 173, 182, 304
Naumann, Friedrich, 302, 302n38
negative agent, 61–6
negativity, 72n39
neoorthodoxy, 100
neorealism, 99, 100
neutrality, 115
New Deal, 43, 60, 81, 84, 170, 172
New Left, 148
New World Order, 67, 273, 354–5
Niethammer, Lutz, 279
Nietzsche, Friedrich, 214
Nitze, Paul, 59, 66, 72n38, 90, 92
Nixon, Richard M., 10, 12, 19, 55n7, 102, 121, 125, 250, 324
nondialectical component, 85
Non-Proliferation (1968) Treaties, 10
Northwest Ordinance (1787), 236, 259
Norwegian social democracy, 286
"not-warmaking," 40
NSC 68, 46, 54, 55, 56, 57, 59, 62, 65, 66, 66n26, 71–2, 90, 91, 92, 93, 94, 115, 268, 269–70, 315n10, 349
NSC 162/2, 94
nuclear strategy, development of in US, 120
nuclear weapons, 9–10, 120, 142
Nuremberg trials, 346, 351

O
Obama, Barack, 11, 98n3
October Revolution (1917), 297
One World, 118
Open Door thesis, 149–51, 152, 159
Orientalist themes, 65

Index

"Origins of the Cold War" (Schlesinger, Jr.), 147
Orosius, *Apology*, 294
orthodoxy, 316–17, 328, 329, 348
Orwell, George
   on the cold war, 24–6
   "tacit agreement," 46
   "You and the Atom Bomb," 24
Ostpolitik, 125
O'Sullivan, John, 228–31, 228n9, 234–5, 238, 240–1, 243, 251
Ottoman Empire, 63
Otto of Freising, 294

P

Paine, Thomas, 31–3
paix-guerre, 23
Paneuropa, 280, 299–301, 303
Papacy. *See* Catholicism
Parker, Theodore, 68
parliamentarism, British, 286
Parsons, Talcott, 194
Paterson, Thomas, 179
Patrick Henry: Life, Correspondence and Speeches (Henry), 56n8
Pax Americana, 355
pax vera, 29, 42–3
Peace of Utrecht (1713), 31
"peace-war," 40
periodization, 2, 12–13, 20–1, 100, 102, 106–7, 108–20, 163, 216
Philippine Reservation, 246
Phony War, 23, 78
Pietz, William, 65n23
Pius IX, Pope, 291
Pius XI, Pope, 284
Poland, 159, 166, 173, 325–6
polarity, politics, space, and, 45–7

Policy Planning Staff (PPS), 15, 90
political controversy, as a driver of diplomatic history, 210–11
political embodiment of Progress, 38
political realism, 86–7n5
political science, 212n2
politics, polarity, space, and, 45–7
The Politics of War (Kolko), 154–5
Polk, James, 243
Pollard, Robert, 167n51
   Economic Security and the Origins of the Cold War, 165–6
post-revisionism, 158–67
poststructuralist theory, 203–4
The Preponderance of Power (Leffler), 176–8, 182–3
principle of nonidentity, 115
proceduralism, in international politics, 361
productionism, 169
Progressive Era, 81, 123, 245–6, 247, 248, 249, 330–1
Protestantism, 56
Protestant Reformation, 289
protofascism, 118
Putin, Vladimir, 165n48

Q

Quarantine Speech, 41
quasi-anthropological culturalism, 202–3
quasi-Mosaic trek, 233n17
Quasi-War, 40–1, 46

R

radical Protestantism, 56
Ranke, Leopold von, 191
Rawls, John, 343

Reagan, Ronald, 14, 97, 98, 98n1, 100, 102, 121, 126, 273, 353–4
realism, classical, 111–12
realist narrative, 146–7
Realpolitik, 184
Red Army, 109, 166, 345
Red China, 71n37
Red October, 147n10
rejectionism, 78
Respublica Christiana, 278–79, 289
revisionism, 147–57, 179–80
revolutionary France, 109–10
Revolutionary War, 209
rigid state theory, 72–3
Romania, 159, 173
Roosevelt, Franklin D.
  on anticolonialism, 342–3
  on the Civil War, 68–70, 82–3, 214
  on the cold war, 39–43
  on colonialism, 342–3
  conception of Hitler's Germany, 109–10n14
  on containment, 161
  cooperative policies of, 155, 156, 157
  on destiny, 249
  Four Freedoms speech, 42
  on freedom, 60
  on globalism, 344–5
  on God-fearing democracies, 353
  health of, 311
  on isolationism, 344
  on mortal threats, 86
  on the New Deal, 171
  on notion of "unconditional surrender," 21
  personal way of being toward the world, 185
  Progressive Era and, 123n24
  on Second World War, 341–2
  on self-determination, 346
  specific conceptualization of World War II, 79
  studies of, 213
  on unconditional surrender, 55
  on war, 209, 215, 216–18, 219, 340
  wartime frame(s), 347–8
  wartime matrix, 92
  on World War II, 267
Roosevelt, Theodore, 247, 247n38, 330–1, 345–6
Roosevelt Corollary (1904), 272
Rosenberg, Emily, 204
Rossi, John, 172
Rousseau, Jean-Jacques, 31–3
Royal Proclamation (1763), 242
Russian syndrome, 5
Russia's Road to the Cold War (Mastny), 161

S

Sahlins, Marshall, 193
Said, Edward, 191
  Culture and Imperialism, 192
Salazar, António de Oliveira, 286–7
Schlesinger, Arthur, Jr., 68
  "Origins of the Cold War," 147
Schuman, Robert, 303
Schurz, Carl, 68
Schuschnigg, Kurt von, 286
Second World War, 207, 208–9, 210, 211, 212–13, 215, 216–17, 218, 220, 252, 267, 270, 341–2
secularization, 290
security, reaching for, 174–8
self-determination

about, 267, 281–2
empire and, 259–60
Roosevelt on, 346
semantic field, 190
September 11, 225–6, 274, 335,
    340–1, 354, 357–9, 358n24,
    358n25
Seward, William, 243–4n33
Shattered Peace (Yergin), 155–6,
    156n31
Shulman, Marshall, 179–80
Sino-Soviet conflict, 8, 10, 55, 122
Sklar, Martin, 168
slavery
  about, 115
  in American image, 57–61
  as an attempt to destroy freedom, 90
  freedom and, 270–71
  Southern slavocracy (1850s), 90
  to totalitarianism, 54–6
Slotkin, Richard, 202
Smith, Adam, 33
social order, 186
social theory, 168, 183–4
sovereignty, 349
Soviet despotism, 65
Soviet expansionism, 43, 162
Soviet ideology, 188
Sovietology, 179
Soviet totalitarianism aggression, 111
Soviet Union, end of, 76
space, politics, polarity, and, 45–7
Spain, 92–3
Spanish-American War, 253n2
Spanish-Catholic legacy, 240
Spanish Civil War, 40
spatial and temporal parochialism,
    139–40n2

Spengler, Oswald, 299
  The Decline of the West, 297
Spenglerian culturalism, 87
Sputnik, 326
The Spy Who Came in from the Cold
    (Le Carré), 13, 22
Stalin, Joseph, 5, 37–9, 73, 86–7n5,
    86–8, 109, 113–14, 118, 120,
    160, 165, 176, 184, 186, 314,
    342
Stalinism, 72
Steel, Ronald, 179
Stimson, Henry, 69, 82, 214
St. Louis Louisiana Exposition
    (1904), 247
Strategies of Containment (Gaddis),
    99n5, 163
Strindberg, August, 296n28
Suez crisis, 322–3
Susman, Warren, 102n12, 198–9
Sweden, 211
Swope, Herbert Bayard, 23–4
Syllabus of Errors, 291
systemic model, 186–7, 186n84

T
Taliban regime, 358
territorialization, 117
terrorism, 357–8
Test Ban (1963), 10
Test Ban Treaty, 13, 23, 47, 75, 78,
    142, 332
theories of ideology, 195
Theory of International Politics
    (Waltz), 99n5
Third World, 126–33
third world interventionism, 127
third world nationalism, 282n7

Thompson, E. P., 148, 188n88
The Making of the English Working Class, 196
Thorne, Christopher, 138n1
Tilly, Charles, 220
to-camp delineation, 116
Tocqueville, Alexis de, *Democracy in America*, 240
totalitarian communism, 7, 85
totalitarian fascism, 7, 85
totalitarianism, 43, 53, 54–6, 99, 347–8
totalitarian Moscow, 314
totalitarian thematic, Americanization of, 90
Trachtenberg, Marc, 139–40n2
traditionalism, 144–7, 180
traditional war, 36
Tragedy of American Diplomacy (Williams), 150–1
traveling theory, 191
Treaty of Utrecht (1713), 295
Treaty of Versailles, 299, 351
triptych, 143
triumphalism, 73
Trojan horse tactics, 348
Trotsky, Leon, 37
Truman, Harry S., 42–3, 51, 53–4, 86–7, 115–16n21, 119, 155–7, 161, 251, 269, 315, 347, 349–50, 353
Truman Doctrine, 61, 77–78, 87, 88, 89, 108, 112n17, 145, 166, 173, 176, 177
tyrants, 83

U

Ulam, Adam, 180
unconditional surrender, 21, 69

UN Genocide Convention, 351–2
unilateralism, 161–2
United States (US)
    as epitome of free world, 70n34
    globalism, 83, 315
    hegemony, 21, 125
    interventionism, 128
    matrix, 113, 120, 123
The United States and the Origins of the Cold War (Gaddis), 160
universalism, American, 164
universalist view, 269–70
The Uses of Literacy (Hoggart), 196
Utopian deficit, Kennedy on, 307–33

V

Verba, Sydney, 194
Vietnam, 10, 13, 21, 77, 122, 140, 140n3, 148, 179, 180–1, 210, 219, 224, 224n4, 226, 271, 273, 319–20, 319n17, 320–1n20
Vietnam Lobby, 320
Voltaire, 63

W

Walker, J. Samuel, 157
Wallace, Henry, 82
Wallerstein, Immanuel, 172
Waltz, Kenneth, *Theory of International Politics*, 99n5
war on terror, 226, 250–1
war on terror/terrorism, 133, 207–20, 336
Warsaw Pact, 46
wartime matrix, 92
Watt, D. C., 167n51
Waugh, Evelyn, 190
Weber, Max, 220, 302

Weltanschauung, 150–1, 166–7, 192
West, Cornel, 199–200n22
West, Kennan on the, 277–305
Westad, Odd Arne, 127n30, 129–30, 131, 183, 183n81, 332n38
   The Global Cold War: Third World Interventions and the Making of Our Times, 107, 127
White, Justice, 264
Williams, Raymond, 197
   Culture and Society, 196
   The Long Revolution, 196
Williams, William Appleman, 3, 77, 148, 192
   Tragedy of American Diplomacy, 150–1
Wilson, Woodrow, 39–42, 71, 207, 218, 232, 233, 249, 251, 267, 345
Wilsonian Progressivism, 168
Winter War, 71

Wisconsin School, 152, 172
world empire, 217, 257, 257n7
World War I, 212, 218
World War II, 207, 208–9, 210, 211, 212–13, 215, 216–17, 218, 220, 252, 267, 270, 341–2

X
X article (Kennan), 3, 62, 77, 87, 108

Y
Yergin, Daniel, *Shattered Peace,* 155–6, 156n31
"You and the Atom Bomb" (Orwell), 24
Yugoslavia, 219–20n7

Z
Zhdanov, Andrei, 116